Chile: The Making of a Republic, 1830–1865

Chile enjoyed unique prestige among the Spanish American republics of the nineteenth century for its stable and increasingly liberal political tradition. How did this unusual story unfold? The tradition was forged in serious and occasionally violent conflicts between the dominant Conservative Party, which governed in a sometimes authoritarian manner from 1830 to 1858, and the growing forces of political Liberalism. A major political realignment in 1857–8 paved the way for comprehensive liberalization. This book examines the formative period of the republic's history and combines an analysis of the ideas and assumptions of the Chilean political class with a narrative of the political process from the consolidation of the Conservative regime in the 1830s to the beginnings of liberalization in the early 1860s. The book is based on a comprehensive survey of the writings and speeches of politicians and the often rumbustious Chilean press of the period.

The late Simon Collier was Professor of History at Vanderbilt University. From 1965 to 1991 he was on the faculty at the University of Essex, England. His previous books include *Ideas and Politics of Chilean Independence, 1808–1833* (Cambridge, 1967); *A History of Chile, 1808–1994* (Cambridge, 1996), coauthored with William F. Sater; and *The Cambridge Encyclopedia of Latin America and the Caribbean* (Cambridge, 1992), coedited and coauthored with Thomas E. Skidmore and Harold Blakemore.

CAMBRIDGE LATIN AMERICAN STUDIES

General Editor
Alan Knight, Oxford University

Advisory Committee
Malcolm Deas, Stuart Schwartz

89
Chile: The Making of a Republic, 1830–1865
Politics and Ideas

Chile: The Making of a Republic, 1830–1865

Politics and Ideas

SIMON COLLIER

CAMBRIDGE UNIVERSITY PRESS
Cambridge, New York, Melbourne, Madrid, Cape Town, Singapore, São Paulo

Cambridge University Press
The Edinburgh Building, Cambridge CB2 2RU, UK

Published in the United States of America by Cambridge University Press, New York

www.cambridge.org
Information on this title: www.cambridge.org/9780521826105

First published 2003
This digitally printed first paperback version 2006

A catalogue record for this publication is available from the British Library

Library of Congress Cataloguing in Publication data

Collier, Simon.
Chile, the making of a republic, 1830–1865: politics and ideas / Simon Collier.
p. cm. – (Cambridge Latin American studies ; 89)
Includes bibliographical references and index.
ISBN 0-521-82610-1
1. Chile – Politics and government – 1824–1920. I. Title. II. Series.
F3095 .C67 2003
983′.05–dc21 2002034803

ISBN-13 978-0-521-82610-5 hardback
ISBN-10 0-521-82610-1 hardback

ISBN-13 978-0-521-03312-1 paperback
ISBN-10 0-521-03312-8 paperback

Publisher's Note

Simon Collier died in February 2003,
shortly after he reviewed the proofs of this book.

Contents

Acknowledgments

I owe a special debt to the Directors of Libraries, Archives, and Museums of the Republic of Chile and to the *Conservadores* (Keepers) of the National Archive over the past quarter century, especially Enrique Campos Menéndez and Sergio Villalobos R. (Chile's greatest living historian) among the directors, and Javier González Echenique among the keepers, as well as to the friendly staffs of the National Library and the National Archive. Nearer home, my path was greatly smoothed by the Vanderbilt University Library and its Latin American Bibliographer, Paula Covington. It would take too long to list the many Chilean scholars and friends (some, alas, now dead) from whom, over the years, I have learned so much about the history of their country, my *segunda patria*, not forgetting a handful of historians in Europe and North America, but I hope that each and every one of them knows how greatly I have relished the experience. My warm thanks go to the Institute of History, Catholic University of Valparaiso, which named me *profesor visitante* in 1994, extended generous hospitality, loaned me an office in its delightful Italian-style hillside villa in Viña del Mar, and allowed me to ransack its library and lecture to its amazingly tolerant students. It has always been a distinct pleasure to work with Frank Smith at Cambridge University Press in New York. I am grateful to the Press's three anonymous readers for some stimulating comments on my original manuscript, and I particularly appreciate the willingness of Professors J. León Helguera, Iván Jaksić (then busy with his superb book on the great Andrés Bello), William F. Sater, and Sol Serrano to read and comment insightfully on an early draft. Its mistakes (and opinions) are mine alone. One final acknowledgment: I have been lucky enough to have spent nearly all my academic career in two very friendly History departments, one on each side of the Atlantic. For that, my thanks go to my Vanderbilt colleagues and my earlier colleagues at the University of Essex.

S.C.
Nashville, Tennessee
April 2002

Abbreviations Used in the Notes

ACT	*La Actualidad.*
AI(A)	Intendancy Archives, Atacama Province (Archivo Nacional, Chile).
AI(V)	Intendancy Archives, Valparaiso Province (Archivo Nacional, Chile).
AMI	Ministry of the Interior archives (Archivo Nacional, Chile).
AR	*El Araucano.*
AUCH	*Anales de la Universidad de Chile.*
BACH	*Boletín de la Academia Chilena de la Historia.*
CHAM	[Diego Barros Arana, Marcial González, José Victorino Lastarria, Domingo Santa María]. *Cuadro histórico de la administración Montt* (Valparaiso, 1861).
CN/D	Congressional record, Chamber of Deputies.
CN/S	Congressional record, Senate.
DIS	*La Discusión.*
DP	*Documentos parlamentarios.* 9 vols. (1858–61).
EDP	Ernesto de la Cruz and Guillermo Feliú Cruz, eds., *Epistolario de don Diego Portales*, 3 vols. (1937).
FE	*El Ferrocarril.*
MV	*El Mercurio*, Valparaiso.
M(S)	*El Mercurio*, Valparaiso (edition for Santiago).
M(V)	*El Mercurio del Vapor*, Valparaiso (steamship edition of MV).
PR	*El Progreso.*
RCAT	*La Revista Católica.*
RCHG	*Revista Chilena de Historia y Geografía.*
SCL	Valentín Letelier, ed., *Sesiones de los cuerpos legislativos de la República de Chile*, 1811–1845. 37 vols. (1887–1908).
TRI	*La Tribuna.*

A limited number of works consulted are identified in full in the notes, but most books and articles are cited by the name(s) of the author(s), sometimes with an identifying initial, and, with the author(s) of several works, by a shortened title of the publication. (In newspaper and magazine titles, the definite article is omitted.) Full details can be found in Sources.

Introduction

It is a textbook commonplace that the Republic of Chile was a byword for political stability in nineteenth-century Latin America. Commonplaces are usually at least half true, and often more than half. Chile *was* the only Spanish American republic to win this reputation in the eyes of the outside world. The only other Latin American country to enjoy similar esteem was the Empire of Brazil, which almost until the end was a slaveholding society. (Slavery in Chile was abolished five years after independence.) Chile's transition to stability, however, was more eventful than the textbook commonplace assumes, with political life in what we may call "the early republic" marked by serious conflict as well as a promising degree of institutional continuity. The Chilean political tradition was forged in sharp and occasionally bloody struggles between government and its Liberal (and later Liberal-Conservative) adversaries. Not until the early 1860s were order (the key ideal of the Conservative governments) and greater political liberty (the principal demand of successive oppositions) reconciled to the satisfaction of most politicians. The ideas and politics of this formative period are the subject of this book.

The most perceptive review of my earlier book on the ideas and politics of Chile's independence period,[1] by French historian Jean Meyer, hinted that my approach to the history of ideas rested on *"une conception 'hégélienne de droite.'"*[2] The label is not congenial, but he had a point. Ideas should not seem to float in the air (*"dans un vide sidéral,"* as Meyer put it), as perhaps they sometimes did in that book. I remain convinced, however, of their intrinsic importance. At the very least, it is vital to draw an accurate picture of what they *were*, and this is the main task undertaken in this long-intended and late-flowering sequel to that earlier work. But although it is important to present political ideas against the background of the society and culture in which they were expressed, it also is very necessary to relate them to the political *events* of their time. Politics is, of all human

---

1 *Ideas and Politics of Chilean Independence, 1808–1833* (Cambridge, 1967).
2 *Revue Historique*, No. 499 (July–September 1971), pp. 231–34.

activities, perhaps the most rapidly shifting, and political ideas are often altered by circumstances. My emphasis in this book is still certainly on what people *thought* or *said* was happening, but I attempt, by the inclusion of four narrative chapters, to explore the connection between what people thought and said and the political *flow* of the period in which they were doing the thinking and saying. Only the reader can decide whether this is a risky strategy. These chapters are not a comprehensive narrative of the period, something that can be found in several classic works.[3] Their aim is to tease out the political implications of the most salient events, sometimes in ways the classic works did not attempt, while also adding fresh (and hopefully useful) detail. My prime interest in politics and ideas means that the narrative chapters pay particular attention to partisan maneuvering (at which Chilean politicians quickly became adept) and partisan propaganda. The propaganda, in particular, illustrates the terms of debate among Chilean politicians at certain critical junctures, the most serious being the dramatic confrontations of 1849–51 and 1857–9.

To describe the stage on which these dramas were enacted (and to set up a defense, though hardly a Maginot Line, against further suspicions of right-wing Hegelianism), Part I of the book (Chapters 1–2) offers a brief socioeconomic sketch of the new Chilean republic and examines the political system imposed by the ruling Conservative party, some knowledge of which is indispensable if the political tussles of the time and the making of the republican tradition are to be understood at all. My description of the political system is not conceived as a study of (although it would be foolish to deny that it has an unavoidable connection with) nineteenth-century Chilean state formation, a topic that would take me into a number of fields that are not germane to my main theme. It is a topic that has certainly attracted interesting scholarly work in recent times in the case of other Latin American countries.[4] Political ideas and attitudes in the

---

3 For the 1830s, Barros Arana, *Historia*, vol. 16, and Sotomayor Valdés, *Historia*; for the 1840s, Barros Arana, *Decenio*; for the 1850s, Alb. Edwards, *Gobierno*. For the 1860s there is no narrative as good as these, though Ag. Edwards, *Cuatro presidentes*, which covers the years 1841 to 1876, is passable, if patchy. For 1846–51, Vicuña Mackenna's *Jornada* and *Historia* are immensely readable, as is, for 1851–61, CHAM, pp. 30–242 (written by Barros Arana). For the years to 1850, I. Errázuriz, *Historia*, is a narrative still worth close attention. Encina, *Historia* (X, 443–XIV, 313) covers the whole period, although his "psychoethnic" judgments need to be taken with a large grain of salt, and, ideally, his text should be checked against Ricardo Donoso, *Francisco A. Encina, simulador*, 2 vols. (1969–70), II, 186–268.

4 Examples for other countries (mostly covering longer periods) include Charles F. Walker, *Smoldering Ashes. Cuzco and the Creation of Republican Peru, 1740–1840* (Durham, N.C., 1999) [pp. 84–230]; Mark Thurner, *From Two Republics to One Divided. Contradictions of Postcolonial Nationmaking in Andean Peru* (Durham, N.C., 1997); Peter Guardino, *Peasants, Politics and the Foundations of Mexico's National State* (Stanford, Calif., 1996); Florencia Mallon, *Peasant and Nation. The Making of Postcolonial Mexico and Peru* (Berkeley, Calif., 1995). It should be noted that all of these are based on studies of specific

early postcolonial decades, by contrast, have not aroused quite the same attention,[5] and there is still plenty of work to be done here, too.

Part II of the book (Chapters 3–4) starts the political narrative and takes the story from the mid-1830s, and the first, distinctly muted division among the ruling Conservatives to the bloodily opposed election in 1851 of the third Conservative president, Manuel Montt, the key political figure of the mid-century years. Part III (Chapters 5–8) is in some ways the core of the book. It is an attempt to portray (across the whole period) educated Chileans' political attitudes and their general view of Chile and the outside world, their *cosmovisión* or *imaginario*, as it is nowadays sometimes termed in Spanish. Here I make a fairly liberal use of representative short quotations, representative in that they reflect a point of view or a train of thought which could easily (to a point well beyond tedium) be illustrated by numerous similar examples. This is the best (indeed the only) way I know of conveying something of the argumentative and linguistic *flavor* of the time. The narrative resumes in Part IV (Chapters 9–10), and follows the story through Montt's presidency and into the first years of that of his successor, José Joaquín Pérez, years that brought the first stage of political liberalization and completed the foundations on which Chile's essential political tradition was built.

In the past thirty years or so, scholars have gone a long way toward rectifying our previous substantial ignorance of the economic, social, and cultural history of Chile's postindependence decades,[6] and a number of valuable studies have touched on aspects of political life.[7] There is no "traditional" overall political interpretation of the early republic in serious Chilean (still less, non-Chilean) historiography. Chile's classic nineteenth-century Liberal historians Diego Barros Arana, Miguel Luis Amunátegui,

---

regions rather than nations as a whole, an approach that may be less applicable to the Chilean case. Other promising approaches may be found in Paul Gootenberg, *Between Silver and Guano. Commercial Policy in Postindependence Peru* (Princeton, N.J., 1989) and Jeremy Adelman, *Republic of Capital. Buenos Aires and the Legal Transformation of the Atlantic World* (Stanford, Calif., 1999).

5 For Chile, the classic work by Ricardo Donoso, *Las ideas políticas en Chile*, 3rd ed. (Buenos Aires, 1975), covers the entire nineteenth century on an issue-by-issue basis. For Mexico, see Charles A. Hale, *Mexican Liberalism in the Age of Mora, 1821–1853* (New Haven, Conn., 1968), and for Colombia (with wide coverage of ideas), Jaime Jaramillo Uribe, *El pensamiento colombiano en el siglo XIX* (Bogotá, 1964). José Carlos Chiaramonte, *Ciudades, provincias, Estados: Orígenes de la Nación Argentina, 1800–1846* (Buenos Aires, 1997) is a notable contribution for Argentina. Carmen McEvoy, *La utopía republicana. Ideales y realidades en la formación de la cultura política peruana, 1871–1919* (Lima, 1997), deals with a later period in Peru, but see also her valuable critical introduction to Juan Espinosa's *Diccionario para el pueblo* (Lima, 2001), pp. 11–100.

6 For example, works by Bauer, Bengoa, Cavieres, del Pozo, Grez Toso, Jaksić, Romero, Salazar, Serrano, Villalobos, and Woll, listed in Sources.

7 For example, works by Brahm García, Bravo Lira, Gazmuri, Kinsbruner, Loveman and Lira, and Stuven, listed in Sources.

and Benjamín Vicuña Mackenna, and their Conservative colleague Ramón Sotomayor Valdés, wrote about segments of the period, but did not cover it as a whole. Their various partial narratives never quite coalesced, at the hands of the next generation (as they could easily have done), into a Chilean equivalent of the "Whig interpretation" of English history.[8] We owe perhaps the most seductive of later "revisionist" interpretations to the lively mind of Alberto Edwards (1874–1932). In a classic book of 1928, he presents the politics of the period (and beyond, to his own time) in terms of what he calls an "aristocratic *fronde*," comparable to the mid-seventeenth-century efforts of the French nobility (and Paris *Parlement*) to rein in the Bourbon monarchy.[9] Edwards's reading fits the facts to the extent that the political agitation of 1849–51 and 1857–9 resembled the French *frondes* in their attempts to curb a powerful regime, and that one of the standard Liberal demands throughout the early republic (and well beyond) was the reduction of executive power. My sense is that there is a case here for Ockham's razor. The pressure for greater elite control over government, if that is what it was, was not expressed in those terms, but simply as a liberal demand, and historians are generally chary of identifying underlying motivations in the absence of hard evidence. Like Queen Elizabeth I of England, we have no way of opening "windows into men's souls."

A more recent interpretation, lucidly presented by Bernardino Bravo Lira, views the early republican governments (especially those of Diego Portales in the 1830s and of Manuel Montt in the 1850s) as prolongations of the enlightened despotism that had striven to overhaul and remodel the Spanish Empire in the later colonial period.[10] This is persuasive as a description of how the governments of the early republic actually *behaved*, and even, maybe, as a picture of their style. The first two or three generations of Chilean politicians were still close to the colonial era and its authoritarian framework. "The monarchical state," as Mario Góngora once put it, "may have disappeared in 1810, but not the notion of ... an active and decisive state."[11] Portales and Montt combined a genuine (in Montt's case a zealous) interest in practical reform with a distinct reluctance to liberalize the political system. At a subconscious level the model of enlightened despotism may possibly have exercised its pull in the early republic. Once again, however, it is not a point that can easily be established from what politicians *said* or *wrote*. For all their constantly reiterated emphasis on order, Chilean Conservatives did not espouse despotism (enlightened or otherwise) as a

8 I explored this point (briefly) in "The Historiography of Chile's 'Portalian' Period," *Hispanic American Historical Review,* 57:4 (1977), pp. 666–69.
9 Alb. Edwards, *Fronda*, pp. 46–119.
10 Bravo Lira, *Absolutismo*, pp. 183–430.
11 Interview in *Hispanic American Historical Review*, 63:4 (1983), p. 668.

political ideal, and certainly did not affectionately look back to the colonial era, however often their Liberal adversaries may have depicted their regime as a "colonial reaction."

Rather in the spirit of the old Liberals, Julio Heise González once described the early republic as "the last and most beautiful chapter of Spanish colonial history."[12] It was not. It was the first (and by no means the least interesting) chapter of Chile's political life as a free republic. My own view, hopefully insinuated in the pages that follow, is inclined to attribute the political change of the early republic to the impressive thrust of nineteenth-century liberalism, to which educated upper-class Chileans (whatever their party label) became increasingly susceptible as their wealth expanded and their society became more sophisticated, as it did between the 1830s and the 1860s. By the end of the 1850s, the majority of the Chilean political class clearly wished to embrace the nineteenth-century modernity of which liberalism was the supreme emblem. A glance at the terms of debate at certain points (the elections of 1851 and 1858, for instance) shows, very revealingly, that in appealing to public opinion government and opposition alike used more or less the same language. Despite certain differences of emphasis, it was a fundamentally liberal, even liberal-democratic language. It may seem trite to argue that the eventual liberalization of the Chilean political system was the result of liberalism, but why should this surprise us? The same pressures were felt virtually everywhere in the Western world of which Chile was (and is) a part in that "century of hope," as the British Socialist politician John Strachey once memorably defined the nineteenth century.[13]

European and American scholars have sometimes been patronizing in their interpretation of the liberal tradition in Spanish America, failing to understand the seriousness of the liberal thrust in the region, and conveniently overlooking its vicissitudes in mainland Europe for much of the nineteenth and twentieth centuries, not to mention the persistence of slavery in the United States and its disgraceful sequel, the long reign of Jim Crow in the South. What can be detected beneath all such patronizing (and surely unhistorical) attitudes is the assumption that there was somehow a "lack of fit" between liberalism and some of the hierarchical, conservative societies in which it took root. Chile would definitely be a case in point. In the most controversial chapter of his great masterpiece, Edward Gibbon (tongue in cheek) contrasts "Religion as she descended from Heaven, arrayed in her native purity" with the "inevitable mixture of error and corruption which she contracted ... among a weak and degenerate race of beings."[14] Something

---

12 *150 años de evolución institucional* (1960), p. 45.

13 *The Menace of Fascism* (New York, 1933), title of chapter 2.

14 *The History of the Decline and Fall of the Roman Empire*, ed. David Womersley, 3 vols. (London, 1994), I, 446.

similar could be said of liberalism. None of the societies (in either hemisphere) where it appeared, at the time it appeared, remotely measured up to its long-term democratic implications. Do any of them, even today?

The materials on which this study is based are drawn mostly from an exhaustive survey of what literate and articulate Chileans wrote or said – in their newspapers, books, pamphlets, and broadsides, in their parliamentary debates, and sometimes in their private correspondence, although too much of this is still hidden away in inaccessible family archives. (I have made only light forays into archival sources.) Foreign comments on Chilean affairs (easy enough to find) are kept to a minimum. My interest is in how *Chileans* saw their own affairs. Not all of them. Not even very many of them. When I use the phrase "educated Chileans," as I do (deliberately often), it serves as a reminder of the fact that educated, upper-class Chileans were a very small minority in the early republic, and articulate, educated upper-class Chileans an even smaller one. They were, however, for better and worse, the Chileans who *mattered* in political life, and who had an overwhelmingly greater influence than anyone else on the making of the republic.

This book deals with their "public" face. It does not go into their private *mores*, their deepest personal thoughts, or their intimate culture as a class – a fascinating topic in its own right and one that could do with a full-scale study. It also must be admitted that their thoughts and opinions are easier to reach and reassemble than those of, say, the vast mass of the laboring poor, the numerical majority of Chileans at this period, whose story needs to be approached by more indirect means. Here there have been some valiant efforts in recent years, and it must be hoped that such efforts will continue. Until we have further studies of social history, our picture of the early republic will remain incomplete. Yet, while we can all surely rejoice that history is nowadays less than ever "the propaganda of the victors," in the poet Ernst Toller's phrase, it remains important not to lose sight of what the "victors" (in this case, at least in a vague sense, the upper levels of Chilean society) were up to, or what they thought they were up to. I share Eric Hobsbawm's wish to rescue not only "the stockinger and the peasant, but also the nobleman and the king"[15] from what another fine English historian, Edward Thompson, once called the enormous condescension of posterity.

Posterity should feel no condescension, enormous or otherwise, toward the upper-class Chilean writers and politicians of the early republic. They were engaged, in their own eyes at least, in finding a decent political framework for themselves and ultimately their country. The Conservatives can hardly be faulted for their belief in order, without which no society can easily make progress, and their opponents cannot be faulted for their faith in liberty, our prime political value in the era since the eighteenth-century

15 Eric Hobsbawm, *On History* (New York, 1997), pp. 184–85.

Enlightenment. The ferocious storms through which the Chilean republic had to pass in my own time (which marked everyone who lived through them) are a sufficient reminder of the permanent importance of the quest for a proper balance between order and freedom, in Chile – and everywhere else. If we ever abandon that quest, we are lost, perhaps irretrievably, in Dante's dark wood, and in the inferno lying beyond.

A note on language. The terms "Liberal" and "Liberalism" in this book are applied to the Liberal *party* of the period, while "liberal" and "liberalism" refer to the broad nineteenth-century liberal political *philosophy*, which was by no means confined to partisan Liberals. The same goes for "Conservative," "conservative," and so on. It also should be remembered that the seasons of the year, when mentioned, are those of the Southern hemisphere.

PART I

The New Republic, 1830–1865

I

The Early Republic: A Sketch

On Saturday, April 17, 1830, a three-hour battle was fought near the confluence of the Claro and Lircay rivers, just outside the town of Talca in the
Central Valley of Chile. The smaller of the two armies was led by General
Ramón Freire, the liberal-minded hero of the wars of independence who had
been Chile's president a few years earlier. His adversary, General Joaquín
Prieto, another veteran of independence, was the champion of the Conservatives who had recently seized power in Santiago, the capital, bringing
to an end the series of false starts that had marked Chilean politics since
1823, mostly under the leadership of politicians calling themselves Liberals. With reinforcements brought by Colonel José María de la Cruz from
Chillán, Prieto had assembled a force of around twenty-two hundred. It
quickly overwhelmed Freire's seventeen hundred soldiers, many of whom
fled for their lives across the little Lircay river, leaving behind them around
two hundred dead.[1]

General Prieto's victory at the Battle of Lircay (as it became known)
assured the triumph of the new Conservative regime. Eleven days earlier, the
Valparaiso trader Diego Portales had taken over two of the three portfolios in
the Chilean cabinet, thus becoming the most powerful figure in the country.
At Portales's behest, General Prieto would soon be elected president of the
republic. His victory at Lircay and Portales's rise to power ushered in more
than a quarter century of Conservative rule in Chile. During these years
and the few years that followed, the Chilean republican tradition was made.
The way it was made, and the contest between order and liberty that lay
at the heart of the politics of the period, would affect Chilean history from
that day to this.

Agriculture, Mining, Trade

The Chile of 1830 was a poor country on one of the remotest peripheries
of the Western world. Separated from the rich plains of Argentina by the

---

1 Barros Arana, *Historia*, XV, 564–71.

Cordillera of the Andes, and from Bolivia and Peru by a vast swathe of un-friendly desert, the fledgling republic was still very isolated from the rest of the world, an isolation only partly tempered by the widening of trade that had followed independence (1818), when foreign merchantmen began calling regularly at Valparaiso and other ports – about 200 each year in the late 1820s, well over 2000 by the 1850s. In the 1830s Chile was still usually more than three months by sailing ship from Europe or the eastern United States. In June 1843 the *Swallow* (famous for her fast passages)[2] furled her sails in Valparaiso bay, having done the trip from Liverpool in 107 days. Soon enough, however, sail began to give way to steam (for trav-elers at least), as nineteenth-century technology made its inevitable mark. In 1840 the British-financed Pacific Steam Navigation Company (P.S.N.C.) began a regular service between Chile and Peru. The arrival on Thursday, October 15, 1840 of its first two 700-ton paddle-steamers caused great excitement in Valparaiso and along ("down," as sailors in those days said) the coast to the north. The next day, for the first time, the Valparaiso news-paper *El Mercurio* proudly printed "Steamship *Peru* . . . Steamship *Chile*" at the head of its front-page shipping column. A one-way passage to Peru in the early years was advertised at 70 pesos;[3] passengers were asked not to wear shoes in bed.[4] A few years later, when the P.S.N.C. extended its route to Panama, it became possible (given a quick trans-isthmus connection) to reach Europe or the eastern United States in about forty days. *El Mercurio*, commenting on the completion of the first (unsuccessful) transatlantic cable in 1858, estimated that it normally took about thirty-six days for European news to reach Chile.[5]

Chile's effective national territory in the 1830s was the 700-mile strip between the Atacama Desert in the north and the so-called "Frontier" along the Bío Bío river in the south, beyond which the Mapuche (as they had called themselves since the eighteenth century) or Araucanians (as the Spaniards had called them since the sixteenth) still retained their stubborn inde-pendence, while also taking part in a thriving cross-frontier trade. Com-munications within the national territory were poor. Highways worthy of the name scarcely existed, apart from the well-used route between Santiago and Valparaiso, much traveled by *birlochos* (two-wheeled carriages) and a few larger coaches. When a local famine occurred in 1838–9 in the south, relief could not be shifted to the area in time to help. Though a certain amount of road construction (and improvement) took place with the creation of a

2 MV, No. 4459, June 7, 1843.
3 Throughout the period, the Chilean peso was worth about 45*d* (£0.3.9) sterling (18½*p*, post-1971) or about US$0.90, with only very minor fluctuations.
4 MV, No. 4071, April 26, 1842.
5 MV, No. 9373, September 25, 1858.

small Corps of Engineers in the 1840s, overland journeys remained laborious until the Central Valley railroad began inching its way southward from Santiago after 1857, reaching Curicó (120 miles away) by 1866. Trains began running between Santiago and Valparaiso in September 1863. In many ways the easiest way of traveling up and down the country was by ship. By the 1850s and 1860s, the main ports were reasonably well connected by steamer. An electric telegraph linked Santiago and Valparaiso from June 1852 onward, installed by the American entrepreneur William Wheelwright, the creator of the P.S.N.C. A national telegraph network was gradually put together; by 1867 it reached both Concepción in the south and the mining town of Copiapó in the north. A reorganized post office introduced postage stamps in 1856. All of these things played their part in the consolidation of the republic.

The early Chilean censuses were only roughly accurate. The first (1835) gives a figure of just over one million. It was reported as a "common opinion" in 1850 that the population was in decline,[6] but it rose to about 1.8 million by 1865. These figures do not include the several hundred thousand Mapuche south of the Bío Bío. Beyond the Indian homeland (two hundred miles long, north to south), there were three small, miserably poor appendages of the new republic, around Valdivia and Osorno and on the island of Chiloé. A fourth appendage, a penal settlement, was added after the Chilean flag was raised on the Magellan Strait in September 1843. The bulk of the population was concentrated (as it always had been and still is) in the Central Valley between Santiago and the Bío Bío. The overwhelming majority of Chileans were both poor and illiterate. It is a fair assumption that illiteracy was still well over 90 percent in 1830. The 1854 census (accurate to within eight per cent according to its supervisor)[7] gives a literacy figure of 13.5 percent (17.3 percent for men, 9.7 percent for women). By the time of the 1865 census one fifth of the male (and one seventh of the female) population could officially read and write. (Such figures were not drastically different from those for southern Europe at the same period.) Not all of the supposedly literate could spell properly. A Santiago newspaper of 1856 reported a shop sign that read: "*Ay para senar asao ensalá i pescao frito*" ("*Hay para cenar asado, ensalada y pescado frito*") – or as it might be rendered in similarly misspelled English, "Fore dynning there is roste, sallad and fried fish."[8]

At least four fifths of all Chileans from the 1830s to the 1860s worked in the countryside, as *inquilinos* ("tenant-laborers" or "tied peasants") and casual laborers (called by a variety of names) on the haciendas, or scratching a

6 *Comercio de Valparaíso*, No. 741, April 9, 1850.
7 *Censo general . . . 1854*, p. 8.
8 FE, No. 63, March 5, 1856.

living as best they could at subsistence level, sometimes falling into banditry or cattle rustling, a concern to the authorities throughout the nineteenth century. The ownership of a hacienda (or *fundo*, as it was also termed) was the clearest badge of membership of the new republic's governing class. There were perhaps about a thousand haciendas in the 1850s, with two hundred or so prime properties, and together they occupied at least three quarters of all agricultural land. Most were self-contained communities; there were no Mexican- or Peruvian-style villages in the Chilean countryside. In the 1830s and early 1840s, many haciendas were rather unprofitable, with only restricted markets for their produce. Smaller farms, *chacras* (sometimes called *quintas*), often owned by the hacendados, supplied the towns with fruit and vegetables, and often did better. Landowners' prospects improved notably in the later 1840s and in the 1850s. With the gold rushes in California (which attracted thousands of Chileans northward) and Australia, hacendados were able to capitalize on Chile's position as the only serious wheat-growing country on the west coast of the Americas. This surge of prosperity for the landowners was extended, after the inevitable end of the gold-rush booms, by the export of wheat and barley to England, at least until the mid-1870s.

Chile's rural economy was stimulated by these mid-century export booms, with the digging of irrigation canals and reservoirs, the domestication of new crops such as rice, and the arrival of Merino sheep. Poplar trees, introduced at the time of independence, spread fast through the mountain-framed Central Valley, giving a gracious appearance to its countryside. Starting in the 1850s, a number of landowners planted French vines, laying the foundations of a great viticultural tradition that would later produce some of the Western hemisphere's most respectable wines. A newspaper of 1858 optimistically suggested that Chile was destined to become "the Champagne of South America," outstripping Southern Europe with its "tired old lands."[9] The cultivated land area in the Central Valley may have tripled (possibly even quadrupled) during the export booms, and the number of haciendas increased. Yet none of these developments implied deep change in rural society. Hacendados seem to have expanded *inquilinaje*, tightening up the conditions on which peasants were allowed to settle on haciendas. The peasants themselves lived much as they had always done, barely touched by education or even the ministrations of the clergy. Farming methods remained highly traditional. Rural laborers, thought an American visitor in the 1850s, had "an unconquerable aversion to innovations."[10] But what incentive had they? "We have the Middle Ages enthroned in the nineteenth century," declared a Concepción newspaper in 1859, "and

9 FE, No. 929, December 21, 1858.
10 Smith, p. 102.

feudalism at its apogee amongst us." The sharp-eyed Vicente Pérez Rosales described the inquilino as "a true serf from the times of feudalism," and was doubtless correct in assuming that his precarious situation, subject to the hacendado's whim, meant that he "neither increases his comfort nor uses his labor except very superficially."[11] The landowners, according to Benjamín Vicuña Mackenna, were no better, working with *"une pénible langueur"* (as he wrote in an 1855 pamphlet for French readers), and with no real interest in improving their estates. A progovernment newspaper denounced them in 1854 for their "habits of idleness and unthinking routine," and two years later Manuel Miquel urged (to no avail) "the education of hacendados" as a national priority.[12] The slow-moving, patriarchal society of the countryside, the world of master and man, remained the deep background to the somewhat livelier culture of the cities, changing only slowly until the rural upheavals of our own time swept it away for ever.

Yet the Central Valley was by no means the only face of Chile. The much more thinly populated northern provinces of Coquimbo and (after 1843) Atacama had been developing since colonial times as a mining area, whose fortunes were greatly boosted after independence by significant strikes and new international markets for Chilean silver and copper. Mining became the real pacesetter of the economy. In June 1832, a La Serena newspaper reported "an amazing discovery of silver mines"[13] at Chañarcillo, in the arid hills to the southeast of Copiapó. In 1846, it was reported that there were 110 mines in operation there (with thirty-nine starting up), worked by thirteen hundred laborers.[14] Numerous fortunes were made at Chañarcillo, one of them by Miguel Gallo (d. 1842), Chile's first millionaire. Other, smaller silver strikes were made in later years, most importantly at Tres Puntas, to the north of Copiapó (1848). Copper over the years was even more profitable, and made the fortune of entrepreneurs such as José Tomás Urmeneta (who made his big strike in 1852) and José Ramón Ovalle. The largest fortunes of the time all came from the mining zone. Chile's first railroad (1851), locally financed and linking Copiapó to its port, Caldera (fifty-one miles away), was an eloquent symbol of the new wealth of the north, and another achievement of the enterprising William Wheelwright.

Mining operations changed only slowly. Most mines were small and shallow. They also were numerous – more than a thousand in Atacama and

11 *El Correo del Sur*, February 19, 1859, reprinted in Grez Toso, "Cuestión Social," p. 160. Pérez Rosales, *Memoria*, p. 135.

12 Vicuña Mackenna, *Le Chili*, p. 53; *Mensajero*, No. 193, January 10, 1854; Miquel, p. 32.

13 *Bandera Tricolor*, No. 40, June 8, 1832.

14 Intendant of Atacama to Interior minister, May 16, 1846 AMI, Vol. 211.

Coquimbo Provinces in the early 1860s.[15] The high-grade ores were not too difficult to mine, and it was in the processing of ores that the most important technical changes occurred. In copper smelting, for instance, the remarkable Franco-British entrepreneur Charles Lambert introduced (just before 1830) the reverberatory furnace long used in South Wales. From the 1840s onward, several large smelters were established both in the mining zone and in the south near Concepción, where coal mining began to develop in that decade. These plants were Chile's first "industrial" enterprises, along with the technically up-to-date flour mills on Talcahuano Bay and the Maule river, established at the time of the wheat booms. There was little or no manufacturing industry as such before the later 1860s. Interior minister Antonio Varas told the British *chargé d'affaires* that he doubted if Chile had anything to send to the Great Exhibition of 1851, and in fact Chile sent nothing.[16] Apart from a few reaping and threshing machines, Chile's own small National Exhibition (1854) displayed nothing in the way of industrial manufactures. By 1861, however, there were at least 132 steam engines in use in the country, only thirty-eight of these on the railroads.[17]

Mining and agriculture were the foundation of Chile's foreign trade, on which the Conservative regime after 1830 pinned its main hopes for prosperity. While protectionist impulses never disappeared from the official mind (or public opinion), government policies were tailored to increase the flow of trade. Successive customs ordinances (1834, 1842, 1851, 1864) lowered the level of the basic external tariff (25 percent in 1864), with a range of items (often machinery) taxed at lower levels or not at all. In order to boost Valparaiso's growth as an *entrepôt* for the eastern Pacific, Manuel Rengifo, the Conservative regime's first serious Finance minister, regularized the system (introduced earlier) of bonded public warehouses (*almacenes fiscales*) where goods could be stored at low cost for (after 1833) up to six years before being imported into Chile or dispatched to other countries. Valparaiso became the nexus of a large regional market, its commercial tentacles reaching up the South American coast and out across the Pacific to Tahiti and beyond. This Pacific market shrank somewhat after the 1850s, with the development of Callao in Peru and San Francisco in California. Valparaiso's traders were vaguely aware that the building of a Panama Canal might some day undermine their prosperity. Such a canal, reasoned the newspaper *El Progreso*, might consign the port to the diminished status of the Mediterranean cities after the Portuguese discovery of the sea route to Asia. To fend off this challenge, an intermittent dream of the period (never realized) was for a fleet of steam tugs to tow sailing ships through the Magellan Strait, thus enabling

15 *Anuario estadístico*, entrega cuarta (1862), pp. 449–51.
16 TRI, No. 304, May 10, 1850. See also Mayo, p. 68.
17 *Anuario estadístico*, entrega cuarta (1862), p. 457.

them to avoid the stormy Cape Horn passage. Others were more sanguine about a possible Panama Canal. "Fortunately for us," as Valparaiso's great organ *El Mercurio* explained in 1858, it would almost certainly never be built, owing to "the unhealthy climate of the isthmus."[18]

Chile's external trade grew in value from an annual average of 18.6 million pesos (£8.3 million or $20.6 million) in 1844–50 to 42 million (£19 million or $46.6 million) in 1861–5. From the mid-1840s to the late-1850s, the country experienced boom conditions. At the end of the 1850s, there was a serious recession, caused by two bad harvests, the fading of the Australian market for wheat, and a downturn in silver production, all of which was made worse by the international recession of 1857. The recession led to numerous bankruptcies and flattened the trade figures for three or four years, but high growth resumed by the mid-1860s and ended only with the more devastating economic crisis of ten years later. Government revenues, about two thirds of which came from commercial imposts, rose from around 3 million pesos in the early 1840s to more than 6 million in the early 1860s. In conventional economic terms, the record of the early republic was an impressive one. With banks and joint-stock companies appearing in the 1850s and 1860s, as well as railroads and telegraphs, with a new Commercial Code (1865) smoothing the path for entrepreneurs and traders,[19] it seemed obvious that Chile was acquiring many of the outward and visible signs of nineteenth-century modernity. Commercial expansion was probably a significant factor in the consolidation of the republic. Positive business prospects could sometimes distract the upper class from politics. Had Chile experienced the stagnation common in so many of the other Spanish American countries in the half century after independence, the story might possibly have been different.

Urban Life and Civilization

In many ways, Valparaiso, the focus of the expanding export economy, was the republic's liveliest city. Ever since independence it had been a fast-growing port, visited by the sailors of half the world, flocked to by the foreign (not least British) traders whose several dozen import-export houses (along with a dozen or so Chilean firms) held the commanding heights of the export economy and an important position, too, in the mining

---

18 "Revolución obrada por el vapor," PR, No. 3, November 12, 1842, and the series "Navegación y colonización del Estrecho de Magallanes," PR, Nos. 6, 7, 9, 11 and 16, November 16, 17, 19, 22, and 28, 1842; MV, February 1852; José Casimiro Mena, CN/D, July 1858; see also Véliz, pp. 74–75. For the canal prediction, see English Part, M(V), No. 101, July 15, 1858.

19 For an excellent analysis of the *Código del Comercio*, see Cavieres, "Anverso," pp. 47–56, and for a succinct overview of economic history, Ortega.

industry through the *habilitación* business, the extension of credit to mine owners. Valparaiso was sometimes the springboard for mighty non-Chilean enterprises: the Frenchman Antoine-Dominique Bordes, who arrived there in 1835 and ran an import-export house, would later build one of Europe's largest fleets of sailing ships.[20] Valparaiso was not an ideal port. Until the building of wharves (1870s–1880s), ships could not tie up. Before breakwaters jutted out into the bay (1910s–1920s), there was no protection against northerly winds, which could wreak havoc among the ships at anchor and dash them on to the beach. Heavy rains could bring mudslides from the encircling hills behind the foreshore. An English visitor in 1845 was "much disappointed both with the town and people," and found the port "a disagreeable place."[21] It was ahead of Santiago, however, in its municipal improvements – daily newspapers, bookstores, a fire brigade, a proper theater (1844), gas lighting, and water supply; the last two of these were further ventures by the amazing Wheelwright, who thoroughly deserved his statue in the port (1877). By the mid-1850s, a poet could write:

> . . . *es bello . . . mirar tus naves,*
> *Tus aguas cristalinas, tus banderas,*
> *Tus calles populosas, tus vergeles,*
> *Tus paseos, tus teatros, tus hoteles.*

> . . . it is beautiful . . . to see your ships,
> Your crystalline waters, your flags,
> Your crowded streets, your orchards,
> Your walks, your theaters, your hotels.[22]

Another English visitor around this time admired the "stately houses" and "other buildings of even more imposing aspect" that lined the main street, but did not fail to note "sailors' boarding houses and gambling hells of the dirtiest and most pernicious description."[23] Brothels (licensed by the municipality) could be found downtown easily enough. *El Mercurio* in 1860 thought this a disgrace to "the Pearl of the Pacific," and recommended that they should be relegated to the hillsides.[24]

Valparaiso's population rose to about seventy thousand in 1865. Its cosmopolitan nature set up some interesting contrasts. A trader visiting in

20 For *habilitación*, see Cavieres, *Comercio*, ch. 4; for Bordes, Barbance, chs. iv–vi.
21 *Recollections of a Ramble*, pp. 12, 18.
22 Francisco Palma, "A Valparaíso," *Mensajero*, No. 739, November 12, 1855. For interesting photographs of Valparaiso in 1860–1, see Alvaro Jara, *Chile en 1860. William L. Oliver. Un precursor de la fotografía* (1973), pp. 70–78.
23 Cornwallis, II, 17–18.
24 MV, No. 9805, May 12, 1860.

1828 thought of it as more "a foreign factory than a Chilean city." Fourteen years later, *El Mercurio* described it as more "a Hanseatic city" than part of Chile. Another of the port's newspapers found Valparaiso society "English, almost."[25] This was never really true, although English was the foreign language most often heard in the streets. In fact, while the commercial quarter closest to the Customs House came to remind travelers (it still does) of a small corner of London, the teeming Almendral district to the north was never less than completely Chilean in character.

By mid-century Valparaiso had long since supplanted once-proud Concepción as Chile's second city. Relatively isolated from Santiago, and the focus of the southern economy in later colonial times, Concepción remained an important military center, with its garrison watching over the Frontier, something that gave its inhabitants, the *penquistas*, illusions of power. Twice in the 1820s, Concepción's military muscle had overthrown governments, with General Ramón Freire's revolt against the liberator-dictator Bernardo O'Higgins in 1823, and again with General Joaquín Prieto's Conservative pronunciamiento of 1829. Concepción's third attempt, in 1851, was a failure. An earthquake in February 1835 completely devastated the city: "a state of complete ruin, not a single building standing," observed some British sailors passing through.[26] Ten years later, the main plaza was still full of "piles of stones and bricks."[27] Concepción revived fairly notably with the coming of the wheat booms and the milling industry, but even in 1865 its population was still no more than fourteen thousand, much the same as that of flourishing Copiapó in the north or the sleepy Central Valley towns of Talca and Chillán.

Nobody remembering the colonial era would have found the republic's capital dramatically changed in the 1830s and 1840s, although its view of the glittering snows of the Cordillera invariably provoked gasps of admiration from foreign visitors. Nearly all its houses were still one story, of adobe construction, with barred windows and secluded patios, sometimes incorporating rented shops facing the street. Santiago's population rose from about seventy thousand in the mid-1830s to nearly 120,000 in 1865. Its main avenue, the Alameda, planned by the liberator O'Higgins, developed into a handsome, poplar-shaded boulevard in the decades after independence. An 1847 guidebook praised its benches (some stone, others brick) and its two parallel streams of running water, whose murmur made it "doubly agreeable . . . , particularly on summer nights."[28] The historian Father José

---

25 Moerenhout, p. 24; MV, No. 4206, September 13, 1842; *Gaceta del Comercio*, No. 1072, July 22, 1845.
26 *Diary of the Wreck*, p. 76.
27 Domeyko, *Mis viajes*, II, 631.
28 *Guía general 1847*, p. 293.

Javier Guzmán claimed in the mid-1830s that a visitor to Santiago would note "more police, more cleanliness in the streets, more lighting . . . , more squares and markets" than at the time of independence.[29] In the 1840s, the authorities cleared a space southwest of downtown for military maneuvers and parades. Known at first as the Campo de Marte, or more colloquially as La Pampilla, it later (1873) became the city's main park.

Very little in the way of new public architecture appeared in Santiago before the 1850s, when the commercial boom had a tonic effect on the capital. Splendid new mansions were then constructed by the boom's beneficiaries. Gas lighting and horse-drawn streetcars were introduced in 1857. In March that year, the fine Municipal Theater was opened, to cater to the upper class's strong taste for drama (mostly Spanish or French) and opera (mostly Italian). "The progress of the last five years can be called fabulous," wrote (also in 1857) a resident not normally given to hyperbole. "Magnificent buildings are rising everywhere . . . ; the number of coaches for hire . . . is more than 300; the carriages belonging to individuals are numerous and splendid. To see the Alameda on certain days of the year makes one imagine oneself to be in one of the great European cities."[30] In one respect, however, the capital long remained without a vital service. On December 8, 1863, at an evening ceremony concluding a month of devotions to the Virgin Mary, a fire broke out in the crowded church of La Compañía. Some two thousand worshipers, most of them women wearing highly inflammable crinolines, were burned to death or asphyxiated – the most dreadful holocaust in Santiago's history. It was a high price to pay for the creation of the city's first fire companies, soon afterward.

The cities, inevitably, were the focus of most of the limited educational and cultural advance that occurred in the postindependence decades. According to Eduardo Hamuy's calculations, approximately 10 percent of the appropriate age group in Chile was receiving some kind of primary education in 1865.[31] *Escuelas normales* (teacher training colleges) were established in 1842 for men and in 1854 for women. During President Manuel Montt's active government (1851–61), the number of primary schools rose from 571 to 911, 648 of which were public schools. Public secondary education (regulated by the not well-enforced decree of February 1843) expanded more slowly, with (by 1865) eighteen high schools (styled *liceos* or *institutos*) operating from Copiapó in the north to Valdivia in the south – all for boys, none yet for girls. Private education (some of it for girls) also developed fairly strongly, some schools established by the religious orders, others, such as Valparaiso's Mackay School (1857), nourished by the foreign

29 Guzmán, II, 487.
30 Andrés Bello to Miguel Rodríguez, May 30, 1857. BACH, No. 51 (1930), p. 303.
31 Hamuy, p. 8.

trading communities. The key secondary institution of the early republic, the Instituto Nacional in Santiago, also provided the only secular higher education in the country, under the control of the University of Chile.

The University, one of the early republic's great achievements, was solemnly inaugurated in September 1843. Its first Rector, the Venezuelan polymath Andrés Bello, by then Latin America's most distinguished living intellectual, had settled in Chile in 1829. A tireless and conscientious (though never uncritical) servant of the Conservative regime, he was the obvious man for the job. His enormous contribution to the making of the republic included his single-handed compilation of its Civil Code (1855). His intellectual influence on educated Chileans for the rest of the nineteenth century was incalculable. The University, modeled to some extent on the Institut de France, was initially a deliberative body, charged with overseeing the entire educational system. Only after Bello's death (1865) did it begin to teach its students in a building of its own, still the University's headquarters today. Its work reflected the rather limited educational priorities of the upper class. Nearly two thirds of the 859 degrees it awarded between 1843 and 1857 were in law.[32] There were many in Chile, wrote Manuel Miquel in 1860, who believed that "you can't *be* anything, be *worth* anything, or *think* anything without being a lawyer."[33]

With a gradually growing readership available, the press – "a thermometer, marking the degrees of a people's civilization," according to an 1849 magazine[34] – played its part in the pattern of urban life. Dámaso Encina, the fictional mid-century magnate of Alberto Blest Gana's novel *Martín Rivas* (1862), seems to have taken all his distinctly variable opinions from the daily press. The great pioneer newspaper, Valparaiso's *El Mercurio*, had been founded in 1827 and appeared daily from 1829. The paper always had a high opinion of itself – as "the liveliest representative of the country," as "the patriarch of the Chilean press."[35] It still does, having long since become the Spanish-speaking world's oldest newspaper. By the end of 1860 it had produced ten thousand issues, and by then was publishing both a special edition for Santiago and (from 1848 to 1882) a *Mercurio del Vapor* ("Steamship *Mercurio*"), partly in English, which sold up the west coast as far as Panama. Bought in 1842 by an enterprising thirty-four-year-old Spanish immigrant, Santos Tornero (who had earlier opened Chile's

32 *Memoria* [annual report to Congress] of Justice minister (1858). DP, VI, 326. For Bello's work, see the excellent biography, Jaksić, *Bello: Scholarship*; its Spanish translation, *Bello: pasión*, includes a few previously unpublished letters.
33 *Semana*, No. 46, May 19, 1860.
34 *Picaflor*, No. 1, May 1, 1849.
35 MV, No. 4314, January 1, 1843; No. 4541, August 29, 1843.

first real bookstore), it remained his property until 1865, when it passed to his sons.

El Mercurio was the only daily newspaper in Chile until joined by Valparaiso's *La Gaceta del Comercio* in February 1842. Santiago did not get its first, *El Progreso*, until November that year, and in the mid-1850s once again briefly lacked one. The gap was filled in 1855 with *El Ferrocarril*, a distinguished newspaper that ran until 1911. *El Progreso*, we might note, was the first daily to print *folletines* (serials) of novels, a practice rapidly taken up by other papers. French novels (especially those of Alexandre Dumas *père* and Eugène Sue) and historical works enjoyed a particular vogue in the 1840s and 1850s. Spanish romantic novelists and the entirely inescapable Sir Walter Scott also were popular.[36] Such writings had definite effects on both taste and politics.

Apart from the house journal of the Catholic Church, *La Revista Católica* (whose first series lasted from 1843 to 1874), the magazines of the early republic tended to be ephemeral. Not much is known about the circulations of either magazines or newspapers. In the 1840s, *El Mercurio* sold around one thousand copies each day. *El Ferrocarril* claimed nineteen hundred by the end of its first year.[37] The government actually subsidized a number of newspapers in the 1840s and 1850s. Short-term, ad hoc newspapers often appeared at election time or at other moments of political tension. They will be described here as "news-sheets," even though they mostly contained views (usually very partisan) rather than news. Such news-sheets had proliferated in the 1820s. Their number fell sharply in the 1830s, but rose again in the 1840s. *El Mercurio* suggested in 1841 that such publications were a sign that "people are beginning to read and to interest themselves in public affairs, and that means a lot for the future of the Republic."[38] Maybe it did, but the Conservative governments of the early republic did not always see it that way.

"People," "The People," and the "Working Class"

In any account of politics and ideas, we obviously need to know the nature of the political actors and thinkers, and who made up the "political class," or "politically relevant population," or what French scholars sometimes call the "political nation." In Chile's early republic, we do not need to look much beyond the upper class. The new Chilean nation was riddled with

---

36 See Barros Arana, *Decenio*, II, 48–49, and Zamudio, pp. 29–40. The first French novel to be translated *in* Chile was *The Three Musketeers* (1845).

37 FE, No. 309, December 22, 1856.

38 MV, No. 3769, June 21, 1841.

class distinctions, although money could usually soften them. The French savant Claude Gay described the upper class of the time as a "moneyed aristocracy, whether by hereditary right, or by having made a fortune in trade, or having acquired an even greater fortune in the exploitation of mines," and it is hard to better this description, although, since titles of nobility had been abolished at the time of independence, Ambrosio Montt was correct in saying (in 1859) that there was no "true nobility, no aristocracy in Chile."[39] Older upper-class families with colonial lineages had aristocratic pretensions and often saw themselves (some still do) as a superior caste, but it was never difficult for successful traders or miners to be accepted socially. Many of them originated in the upper class anyway, and even when they did not they invariably became landowners. The mining magnates of the north who sunk some of their money into vineyards would form a salient group, at least in retrospect, though they were by no means the only vineyard owners.[40] During the early republic, "new money" certainly began to modify the character of the upper class, although this was perhaps even more noticeable in the decades that followed.[41]

Whether they were traders, miners, or landowners (or all three at once, as sometimes happened), upper-class Chileans all had a direct or indirect stake in the export economy, and it is difficult to find economic cleavages (minor regional ones apart) within the national elite. Contemporaries could not detect any such cleavages. "How many traders are there who are not also landowners?" asked a progovernment news-sheet in 1835.[42] "Among the material interests of the country," commented an opposition newspaper of 1858, "there is no antagonism whatever."[43] All the evidence suggests that Chile possessed that "sense of common identity in those who wielded economic, social, and political power" which the late J. H. Plumb identified as one of the three fundamental factors in the attainment of political stability in eighteenth-century England, the other factors being "single-party government" and "the legislature firmly under executive control,"[44] – both of which, rather strikingly, also applied in the case of nineteenth-century Chile, as we shall see in Chapter 2. What tied the upper class together, its material interests apart, was landownership and family connections. Hacienda ownership, as already mentioned, was the clearest sign of upper-class status. Family connections crisscrossed the commercial

---

39 Gay, I, 102; A. Montt, *Gobierno*, p. 61.
40 See del Pozo, pp. 77–90.
41 See Villalobos R., *Orígen*.
42 *Farol*, No. 2, September 7, 1835.
43 ACT, No. 93, May 20, 1858.
44 *The Growth of Political Stability in England* (Harmondsworth, 1969), p. 14.

and political life of the time in an endless though not quite a seamless web. President Manuel Bulnes (1841–51) was the nephew of his predecessor, the son-in-law of a Liberal president of the 1820s, the brother-in-law of a future president, a cousin of one of his Interior ministers, and a cousin of the general he fought on the battlefield in the civil war of 1851.

With the mid-century commercial boom, upper-class incomes rose appreciably, enabling more of the upper class to live in Santiago for much of the year – the great dream, according to *El Mercurio*, of "the southern landowner . . . , the northern miner," and even "the village idiot."[45] Mrs. Loretta Merwin, an American who spent three years in Chile in the mid-1850s, thought that "the great object of life" was "to accumulate wealth and remove to the capital, to lavish it in costly furniture, equipage and splendid living."[46] The coming of the steamship made overseas travel much easier all round. The generation of Chileans born around 1830 (a notable one) was the first to make a habit of visiting Europe. "The desire all the inhabitants of the republic have to go to Europe," commented a deputy in 1852, "is so extraordinary that if someone paid their passage they would all go."[47] Political exile, not uncommon during Manuel Montt's tough presidency in the 1850s, could sometimes be combined with a suitably educational Grand Tour in Europe or (less often) the United States. Such contacts with the outside world had their effect on upper-class tastes and fashions – the "European model" of society detected by another American visitor of the 1850s: "in Valparaiso the standard is rather English," he added, "in Santiago it is decidedly French."[48] England set the tone in masculine attire, the *frac* or frock-coat now becoming universal among upper-class men, and in the increasing popularity of tea drinking. (In 1844, the equipment of the Chamber of Deputies included two teapots and two milk jugs.)[49] If anything, however, France radiated a wider cultural influence – in styles of female dress, furniture, literary fashion, Catholic practice, even political rhetoric. In 1857, the young Vicente Reyes humorously noted the existence of a "special circle" of "Chilean dandies" who had visited Paris. These *Europistas* ("Europists"), as he dubbed them, liked to give the impression that nobody who had been in Paris could possibly enjoy Chile. Another social set, the *Europistas copias* ("copy-Europists"), who had never been abroad, did their best to ape those who had.[50]

45 MV, No. 4048, April 3, 1842.
46 Merwin, p. 95.
47 Máximo Mujica, CN/D, June 25, 1852.
48 Smith, p. 116.
49 Inventory of furniture, SCL, XXXIV, 666–67.
50 FE, No. 490, July 20, 1857.

In all these ways the Anglo-French impact was a notable one, and it had effects on many levels. The rising novelist Alberto Blest Gana tried to put it in context in an article written in 1861:

Contact with European people, the study of their literature, the influence of their trade, the ease of journeys to the old world and our constant communications with it – these things have worked a radical revolution in our habits, while at the same time various spheres of society still maintain notable vestiges of the customs of the colonial era.[51]

Blest Gana was especially interested in the challenge that this changing social scene posed to novelists like himself, in search of suitable subject matter. In a more significant way, however, his "radical revolution" can be regarded as one of the keys to the political sea change that occurred at the end of the 1850s and beginning of the 1860s.

Any definition of the "politically active" upper class would have to include some of its more impoverished members, and also men who were making their way into it by successfully practicing law or (less certainly after the 1830s) by winning military renown. By no means the whole of the upper class was seriously involved in political life. The effective "political class" was a smaller group consisting of its more articulate members, lawyers (as in so many political cultures) forming a strong component. It also must be noted that politics (until well into the twentieth century) was almost entirely a masculine affair. Society matrons such as Mercedes Marín del Solar (who acquired renown as a poetess) or Enriqueta Bulnes (first lady in the 1840s) sometimes hosted political and literary salons, and presumably joined in political conversations, but that was the extent of their influence.

At times, the boundaries of the "politically relevant population" (though not the political class as such) expanded to include other small sections of society. Between the *gente* (sometimes *gente decente*), as they called themselves ("people" or "decent people," the upper class) and *el pueblo* ("the people," the laboring poor), a number of intermediate social groups were (or at least became) visible in the decades after independence. We can hardly talk of a middle class as such, but there was at least a small "middle band" of society that grew more conspicuous with the mid-century's commercial expansion. The owners of small businesses and farms, the clerical staff of government offices and trading houses, foreign engineers, schoolteachers, lower-ranking army officers – all of these, and others, were snobbishly dismissed by the upper class as *medio pelo*, a term that was still familiar to twentieth-century Chileans. The better-off fringe of the "middle band" certainly included its share of social climbers, eager to imitate and if possible

---

51 "Literatura chilena," AUCH (1861), p. 90.

join the upper class. By the 1850s, these were a recognizable type, and were beginning to be described as *siúticos*, a word whose etymology is mysterious but whose introduction into common speech has traditionally been ascribed to the great Liberal publicist José Victorino Lastarria. In 1858 one of President Montt's ministers, Waldo Silva, was described as a *siútico* in print.[52]

Although *el pueblo*, "the people," was constantly evoked as a positive symbol in political rhetoric, this never meant that the laboring poor – the inquilinos and casual workers of the countryside, the mine workers of the north, the *rotos* (the generic Chilean term for urban laborers) – were included in the political system. Educated Chileans coexisted with them, but were not (with a few honorable exceptions) much interested in them. "The fate of the underprivileged classes barely attracts the attention of our society," suggested *El Ferrocarril* in 1859. "Since nobody dies of hunger, it considers its duty fulfilled.... [In] our society, love of the people is generally lacking."[53] There is no reason to contest the consensus among Chilean scholars that "the social question" (as it later became known) was largely absent before the 1870s, with only a scattering of writings devoted to the country's large-scale poverty.[54]

To what extent was "the people" feared? The authorities saw it (at least intermittently) as a potential threat, although only when stirred up by unscrupulous politicians opposed to the regime. The urban crowd in Santiago and Valparaiso had sometimes been stridently vocal during the 1820s. A serious disturbance had occurred in Santiago at one of the more uncertain moments (December 1829) during the Conservative takeover. The Conservative regime after 1830, no doubt aware of these precedents, attempted systematically (though not always successfully) to discipline the laboring poor wherever it could. Flogging remained a common penalty in town and country alike. Suppressed by large majorities in both houses of Congress in 1850, it was restored two years later. A fairly strict regime (one against which they occasionally revolted) was imposed on workers in the mining zone, who among other things had to carry identity papers.[55] Starting in 1837, Valparaiso's stevedores and boatmen (the latter indispensable in a port where ships could not tie up) were organized in a strictly supervised official *gremio* or guild.[56] The government also tried (to no great effect) to control the *fondas* and *chinganas*, the ramshackle taverns that proliferated in

52 *Copiapino*, No. 3123, November 20, 1858.
53 FE, No. 1138, August 24, 1859.
54 For a collection of writings on the "social question" in this period, see Grez Toso, *"Cuestión Social,"* pp. 57–162.
55 See Illanes.
56 See Grez Toso, *De la "Regeneración,"* pp. 248–56.

and on the outskirts of the towns. Their music and dancing was appreciated by the better-off as well as the poor. They were sometimes fulminated against by the Church, and Andrés Bello once denounced them as little better than "authorized brothels."[57] It was rumored in the 1830s that Diego Portales encouraged the *chinganas* as a means of distracting his adversaries from politics,[58] but in general the authorities made efforts to regulate them.

When educated Chileans used the term *clase obrera*, "working class," they were not thinking of the laboring poor so much as the artisans and craftsmen of the towns, especially those of Santiago and Valparaiso. Cristián Gazmuri's educated guess, extrapolated from the 1854 census, gives us a figure of about six thousand artisans and craftsmen in the Santiago of 1850,[59] with masons, carpenters, blacksmiths, and tailors in the largest categories. Immigrant foreign craftsmen took a place among them, catering especially to the tastes of the rich – to the extent that in 1854 a deputy complained that there were no truly Chilean workshops any more, that they all belonged to "a *Monsieur* This or a *Mister* That."[60] This was a gross exaggeration. In Santiago, according to the 1854 census, only one person in seventy was foreign, although in Valparaiso (where foreign shopkeepers were common) it was one in fourteen. A register of *patentes* (business licenses) for 1849 shows around seventy foreign artisans in Santiago, the majority of them French.[61] The artisanate as a whole shared, albeit modestly, in the rising prosperity of the period, and did its best, in public at least, to imitate fashionable styles of dress. Artisans themselves, as we know from some of the propaganda directed at them, were not eager to be confused with the laboring poor. Some of them certainly earned as much as minor government officials.

The *gremios* (guilds) into which artisans had been grouped in colonial times had either lapsed or were languishing. There were, however, some fitful attempts by artisans to organize themselves along more modern lines, in what would later be termed "mutualist" associations, to provide insurance and burial benefits for their members. Typographers, carpenters, and shipwrights in Valparaiso formed two ephemeral societies of this kind in 1850, and typographers in Santiago did likewise in 1853, their counterparts in Valparaiso following suit (their second attempt) soon afterward. A more general artisans' association was formed in Valparaiso in

57 For example, "Chinganas," RCAT, Nos. 115, 116, and 118, February 10 and 20, and March 12, 1847. Bello in AR, No. 69, January 7, 1832.
58 Zapiola, *Recuerdos*, p. 33.
59 Gazmuri, *El "48" chileno*, p. 51.
60 Alejandro Reyes, CN/D, August 8, 1854.
61 Grez Toso, *De la "Regeneración,"* p. 87.

1858 and not only solicited official approval from the municipality but actually got it. It was the only such organization to survive the political upheavals of 1858–9.[62] From the early 1860s, however, as we shall see, conditions became much more favorable for the organizing efforts of artisans.

Up to that point, the Conservative governments were suspicious of such efforts, in the belief that they were less genuinely "organizational" than disguised subversive movements. Such suspicions were not totally unreasonable. Artisans and craftsmen, although probably only a minority, certainly became implicated in episodes of political agitation like those of 1845–6, 1850–1, and 1858–9. They often bore the brunt of the repression that followed, treated more harshly than upper-class agitators. They need, therefore, to be included in any definition of the "politically relevant population," although not in any real sense as members of the political class, and we need to understand their precise role. Artisans tended to be drawn into political agitation for a particular reason. Many served in the Civic (or National) Guard, the national militia, and were therefore (as will be seen in Chapter 2) of vital electoral importance to the government. Both government and opposition had a clear incentive to control or capture their votes. The playing field was scarcely level. Governments always had an overwhelming advantage in this particular competition. The artisans' role in these political episodes was usually less spontaneous than ancillary, as electoral cannon fodder for the upper-class politicians. This is certainly not to say that artisans (the most articulate of the subordinate social groups and the most likely to be literate) did not have their own independent aspirations, or that they did not try to press their own agenda when they saw opportunities to do so.[63] When they did so, it was in the language of liberalism, sometimes intensified. But their ability to develop an independent political "space" for themselves was severely constricted by both the social hierarchy and the political system – more so, it might be suggested, than was true in, say, Mexico, a more complex society, where traditions of "popular liberalism" became deeply rooted and eventually fed through into the 1910 Revolution.[64] In Chile's early republic, when all is said, it was the upper class that led all serious political action, and it was the differences within that same class that created the dramatic political conflicts of the period. We now need to look at the stage on which these dramas were enacted.

---

62 For these attempts, see Grez Toso, *De la "Regeneración,"* pp. 385–87.

63 For an interesting examination of this theme, see Wood.

64 See Guy P.C. Thomson (with David G. LaFrance), *Patriotism, Politics and Popular Liberalism in Nineteenth-Century Mexico: Juan Francisco Lucas and the Puebla Sierra* (Wilmington, Del., 1999), and Alan Knight, *The Mexican Revolution*, 2 vols. (Cambridge, 1986), I, 68–69.

BOLIVIA
border undefined

Mid-19th Century
CHILE
Political

N

Atacama Desert

Caldera • Copiapó

ATACAMA

• Huasco

PROVINCES
Cities

30°S

La Serena • COQUIMBO

ACONCAGUA

Valparaiso • San Felipe

VALPARAISO • Santiago

SANTIAGO

• Rancagua

ARGENTINA

Curicó • COLCHAGUA

• Talca

TALCA

Cauquenes • MAULE

Chillán • ÑUBLE

Concepcion •

CONCEPCIÓN

• Los Angeles

ARAUCO

300 miles / 480 km.

MAPUCHE (Araucanian)
territory to 1860s

Valdivia • VALDIVIA

40°S

Lake Llanquihue LLANQUIHUE

Magellan Strait
700 miles

CHILOÉ

PACIFIC OCEAN

2

The Conservative System

The Liberals defeated in 1830 sometimes accused the Conservatives of having mounted a "colonial reaction." The content of this rhetorical flourish was thin. It is more sensible to see the Conservative settlement as a fusion of the authoritarian legacy of the Spanish Empire with the outward forms, and increasingly much of the substance, of liberal, republican constitutionalism. Yet it is certainly true that political processes in Chile's early republic not only took place within but were partly dictated by the shape and form of the political system imposed by the Conservatives after 1830. The creation of a particularly strong presidency and the government's systematic manipulation of elections required justifications from the Conservatives (who obviously felt them to be necessary) and sharpened the determination of oppositions to reduce overwhelming executive power. It can be argued, in fact, that the nature of the political system helped in many ways to determine the main lines of political debate throughout the period, focusing Conservative minds on the issue of order and Liberal minds on the issue of liberty. In terms of political behavior, the defense of order sometimes led the government to act in a distinctly authoritarian manner, while the opposition (the Liberals, and after 1857–8, the Liberal-Conservative Fusion) was twice tempted into serious armed rebellion. None of this can easily be understood without knowledge of the political system – its constitutional basis, its institutional and administrative structure, and the techniques that successive governments used to keep the ship of state on the course fixed by the Conservatives after 1830.

The 1833 Constitution

Diego Portales, the moving spirit of the new Conservative regime, was never much interested in constitutional theory. He scorned the legalistically minded. His own simple political ideals were embodied in catchphrases that have been quoted endlessly ever since – "A strong centralizing government whose men are true models of virtue and patriotism," "Social order in Chile is maintained *by the weight of the night*," "The stick and the cake, justly

22

and opportunely administered, are the specifics with which any people can be cured,"[1] and so on. But whatever his indifference to detail, Portales certainly favored a new constitution. The discussions (1831–2) through which the former Liberal constitution of 1828 was replaced by its successor of 1833 have been well described, and need not detain us. The document gave the Conservatives what they wanted. The ideas of Mariano Egaña, one of its most influential drafters, included both the indefinite reeligibility of the president and a hereditary senate. Both proposals were found far too reactionary by the constituent convention. Andrés Bello was evidently consulted about the final text, to what extent we do not know. During his early years in Chile, his intellectual authority was usually exercised reticently. His defense of the constitution was one of the first in print.[2]

The most striking feature of the 1833 Constitution was a strong presidency. The president, elected by "electors" in the departments (the main provincial subdivisions), was allowed two consecutive five-year terms, and a third after an intervening term. (None of the four "decennial" presidents of the early republic had a third term.) Only in 1871 was the president limited to one term in the first instance. He could not be impeached while president, only in the year after he had left office. He was given absolute power to name and dismiss cabinet ministers, provincial Intendants and departmental governors, ambassadors, and consuls. He was empowered to appoint a wide range of other public officials (judges, army and navy officers) in consultation with the Senate, or the Council of State (appointed by himself), which consisted of judicial, ecclesiastical, and military and naval dignitaries as well as the cabinet. The cabinet in the early republic was tiny by later standards. At the outset there were only three ministers: Interior and External Relations, Finance, and War and Navy. A new portfolio of Justice, Education, and Religion was added in 1837. The War-Navy portfolio was generally held by a distinguished Army officer. The Interior minister was, as a newspaper put it in 1849, "the prime minister . . . , the natural head of the cabinet."[3]

The executive had extensive emergency powers at its disposal. Congress could vote the president "extraordinary faculties," and when Congress was in recess he and the Council of State could decree "states of siege" in specific provinces, subject to later congressional approval, never denied. In both cases, all civil liberties were suspended. The government's power was

---

1 To J. M. Cea, March 1822, J. Tocornal, July 16, 1832, F. Urízar Garfias, April 1, 1837. EDP I, 177; II, 228; III, 486.
2 For the deliberations of the constituent convention, see Kinsbruner, pp. 43–79; Barros Arana, *Historia*, XVI, 301–32; Sotomayor Valdés, *Historia*, I, 209–20. Bello's defense is in AR, Nos. 307, 311, and 312, May 17 and 25, and June 1, 1833, reprinted in his *Obras completas*, XVIII, 85–92.
3 PR, No. 2054, June 18, 1849.

technically limited to arrest and detention within the national territory. Governments often went beyond the limit by imposing banishments. The emergency powers were used with regularity over the next thirty years – almost one third of the entire period from 1833 to 1861, according to the famous calculation by the historian (and so much else) Benjamín Vicuña Mackenna.[4]

Although the president's powers were substantial, those of Congress were by no means negligible, at least on paper. A two-thirds majority in both the Senate and the Chamber of Deputies could override a presidential veto, although only in the sittings of the year following the veto. Constitutional amendment was made deliberately cumbersome: if one congress found specific articles "reformable," only the next congress could vote on the amendments. Congress was also given the power to vote the so-called periodic laws: the budget, which had to be approved every year, and taxation and the military establishment, both of which needed a vote every eighteen months. In practice, the taxation and military laws were often voted annually. In January 1850, the Liberal deputy José Victorino Lastarria objected to this on impeccably constitutional grounds,[5] but he was overruled. In theory, a hostile majority in Congress could deny funds to the government. For reasons we shall come to, a hostile majority was not usually a likely prospect.

Congressional life was not very sparkling in the early republic. In the 1846 sessions, the young deputy Manuel Antonio Tocornal introduced the *interpelación* (parliamentary questioning of ministers) into the standard procedures of the Chamber of Deputies, but it was not much used before the 1860s. There were times of political excitement, it is true, when congressional sittings became very animated and genuine parliamentary tussles occurred. For the rest of the time, the annual sessions (usually June–July for "ordinary" sessions, and "extraordinary sessions" toward the end of the year) were lackluster and occasionally inquorate. In 1847, a fairly typical "quiet" year selected at random, there were fifty-three sessions of the Chamber of Deputies with duration and attendance recorded. The sessions lasted for an average of one hour, forty minutes, with an average attendance of thirty-two from a membership of fifty-three. The sixteen (out of eighteen) recorded Senate sessions of 1847 lasted an average of two hours, thirty minutes.[6] This was not an intensive schedule.

The 1833 Constitution was also highly centralist. Administration was based on a strict chain of command. Each province[7] was governed by an

---

4 *Introduccion*, p. 98. He omits two short states of siege.
5 CN/D, January 2, 1850.
6 CN/D, CN/S, 1847.
7 There were eight provinces in 1830: Santiago and Concepción (the colonial intendancies), Coquimbo (1811), and Aconcagua, Colchagua, Maule, Valdivia, and Chiloé (1826). New provinces created

Intendant, each department by a *gobernador* (governor), and each *subdelegación* (the smallest effective subdivision) by a *subdelegado*: the titles were inherited from the colonial era. An Intendant was also *gobernador* of the department where the provincial capital was located. The Intendant was defined as the "natural and immediate agent" of the president, a phrase repeated word for word in Chile's two later constitutions. Although provision was made for elected municipalities in the capital of each department, their authority was negligible. Intendants and *gobernadores* had absolute veto powers over them. Any serious local bylaws had to be submitted to the president and Council of State.

The Intendancy was in many ways the real nexus of local administration during the early republic. An Intendant served a three-year term, but was indefinitely reappointable – a privilege not enjoyed by his colonial predecessors, as a newspaper noted in 1843.[8] His powers remained roughly the same throughout the early republic (and beyond), but his status was somewhat enhanced by the comprehensive *Ley de Régimen Interior* (Internal Government Law) finally enacted (after many delays) in 1844, which gave Intendants the same honors as a brigadier-general, a special uniform and the title of *Su Señoría*, "Your Lordship."[9] Even the most cursory glance at the copious Intendancy archives shows that the Intendants were concerned with a wide range of business, and that they constantly reported to the Interior ministry. If we take a month at random (January 1846) in Valparaiso, whose Intendant was also Commandant of the Port, we find the Intendant forwarding the resignations of cavalry officers to the Inspectors General of the Army and Civic Guard, enlightening the Customs administration on points of law, thanking the British consul for news of an epidemic in Ecuador, contacting the governors of Constitución and Talcahuano about prisoners being sent to them, reporting on a prison visitation carried out the previous month, notifying the local criminal judge of a Customs fraud involving four boxes of cigars, advising the French consul about the will of a deceased Frenchman, announcing the dispatch of two or three prisoners to a criminal judge in Santiago, and requesting the Intendant of Santiago Province to hunt for a murderer.[10]

In communications with their opposite numbers in other provinces, Intendants often acted as *de facto* police chiefs, as (in British terms) chief constables or (in American terms) county sheriffs. As a sample of this side

---

between 1830 and 1865 were Talca (1833), Valparaiso (1842), Atacama (1843), Ñuble (1848), Arauco (1853), and Llanquihue (1861).

8 *Telégrafo de Concepción*, No. 17, February 18, 1843.

9 SCL, XXXII, 47.

10 AI(V), Vol. 42.

of their work, we might look at a message from the Intendant of Valparaiso to his colleague in Aconcagua, sent in July 1846.

We have news that in the Casuto mining district there is a certain Miguel Herrera, known by the nickname "stranger," who is known personally to José Espiñero who in the said place keeps a billiards establishment and a bowling alley. Espiñero is generally known in that Province of Aconcagua, he is a native of Colombia, tall of stature and thin, ordinary color, aged about 42. Herrera is a native of Aconcagua who also goes under the name of Ibacacheo Callado. Since these two individuals are companions of the two famous bandits José María Gomes and José León Mancilla who have recently been executed here, it is very important that they be apprehended and sent under full guard to this city to be placed at the disposition of this Intendancy. It is possible that the aforementioned Herrera and Espiñero are going around together, or that their whereabouts are known to a certain Valentín, surname unknown, and also Manuel Villagrán and Santiago Juares, who are of the same gang and who it also interests us to have sent, well-guarded, to this city. Juares is tall, large, pot-bellied, white and normally dressed.[11]

The Intendants themselves sometimes had local connections, as was the case with General José María de la Cruz in Concepción from 1846 to 1851. He was a southern landowner as well as a hero of the wars of independence. It was undoubtedly his local connections that impelled him into the leadership of the rebellion of 1851. In general, however, Intendants were recruited from a variety of backgrounds. Among those in office in the middle and later 1840s, for instance, we find prominent military figures (Cruz in Concepción, Admiral Manuel Blanco Encalada, another hero of independence, in Valparaiso), bright young men such as the poet Salvador Sanfuentes in Valdivia, and promising young political figures such as Domingo Santa María in Colchagua. A prosopographical study of the early republic's Intendants would be of the highest interest. It would probably be more difficult to do such a survey for the lower-level officials, the *gobernadores* and *subdelegados*, more of whom seem to have been recruited locally from the ranks of landowners, or occasionally from those who volunteered for such jobs, as was the case in 1856–7 with Robert Souper in the *subdelegación* of Pelarco (Talca Province). He was eager to serve in order to help suppress an outbreak of banditry in his district. Souper, an Englishman, was not even a naturalized Chilean.

The centralization implicit in the political system was often criticized by opponents of the Conservative regime. "There are no public powers apart from the Executive and his immediate agents," claimed a news-sheet of 1858.[12] But the system also had its defenders. *El Mercurio* in 1843, taking

11 Intendant of Valparaiso to Intendant of Aconcagua, July 8, 1846. AI(V), Vol. 42.
12 *Norte*, No. 1, February 18, 1858.

issue with some vaguely "federalist" arguments in a Concepción news-paper, suggested that the "unitary system" accorded with "the race, the customs and the traditions" of Spanish Americans in general, and that the concentration of forces provided by centralization meant that "the people . . . becomes superior to itself," able to achieve "greatness in every sense," and *El Ferrocarril*, fifteen years later, claimed that centralization gave the government "energy, dispatch and firmness."[13] Archbishop Valdivieso of Santiago, writing in 1860, thought that in the absence of firm demo-cratic roots, it was necessary "that everything should be done in an artificial way. For that reason, Governments normally . . . convert into political instruments anything that exercises influence in society."[14]

The negative side of centralization, as was sometimes recognized, was that it stifled local initiative. It was more than adequate to restrain the limited regionalist aspirations of the outlying northern and southern provinces, which, whatever their resentments, had no way of counteracting the deep-rooted hegemony of the capital and its hinterland: Santiago and the three adjacent provinces of Colchagua, Aconcagua, and Valparaiso accounted for nearly half the country's population. Centralization also discouraged independent enterprise. Lamenting the lapse into inertia (in 1849), after an encouraging start, of the Sociedad de Agricultura (set up to encourage agricultural improvement), Manuel Miquel noted: "We are obliged – sad confession! – to resort to the authorities on such occasions, and let them do everything, since on our own we are not capable of carrying forward a task of general interest which is not ordained by a *law*." There was a general belief, Miquel asserted, that "the State is a real being, with life and wealth of its own, independent of the lives and wealth of the other citizens."[15] There is no doubt that the establishment of a (by nineteenth-century standards) strong Chilean state played a (perhaps *the*) key part in the consolidation of a stable republic, but there was a price to be paid. Was the price too high? Who can say?

Mainstays of the System

Political systems are not maintained by constitutions alone. Their substan-tial constitutional powers enabled Chilean presidents to govern effectively (for the most part) within well-established rules, albeit rules that were some-times honored more in the breach than the observance. But what Portales called "the mainspring of the machine"[16] – obedience to the government

13 "Capitalismo, Provincialismo, Unidad, Federación," MV, No. 4618, November 15, 1843 (continued in Nos. 4619, 4622, and 4623, November 16, 19, and 20, 1843); FE, No. 662, February 8, 1858.
14 Valdivieso to Fray José Martínez, November 16, 1860. Valdivieso, *Obras*, II, 293.
15 Miquel, pp. 5, 156.
16 To Antonio Garfias, May 14, 1832. EDP II, 203.

and laws – could only be ensured by serious, determined, constantly replicated techniques of government, and by relying on certain mainstays that held the system together.

The most obvious mainstay was repression. It was a recurrent theme until 1861, after which it disappeared altogether for thirty years. Compared with the twentieth century's dismal record of repression (in Chile as elsewhere) it was not monstrously bloody, although it certainly had its rough edges. Nor was it comprehensive. Governments usually targeted only the ringleaders of opposition movements or revolts. Consulted by the Intendant of Atacama on how to proceed after the Copiapó revolt of December 1851, "as the number of those implicated is excessively high," Interior minister Antonio Varas told him to punish those who had "assumed the main responsibility" as "leaders or instigators," rather than those who had followed them "out of ignorance or as mere soldiers." Widespread repression, he implied, could perturb "the tranquillity of the province."[17]

The penalties meted out to those repressed were not especially savage. Capital punishment (by firing squad) was used as a civil sanction for murderers: executions were well attended, mostly by the poor. As a political sanction, the death penalty was normally only imposed after military mutinies or conspiracies resulting in violence, and not on a large scale. Following the serious military mutiny of June 1837, eight of the mutineers were shot almost immediately (and three more when captured soon afterward), sixteen others exiled to the Juan Fernández islands, others banished, still others simply reduced to the ranks. It is true that during the mutiny the high-handed Intendant of Aconcagua, Fernando Urízar Garfias ("one of the falcons Portales kept on his arm," as he was once described) had eleven militiamen shot for displaying lack of zeal, but this incident was aberrant: "that sterile pile of corpses" was still held against him thirty years later, by which time Urízar Garfias had become a benevolent prison governor.[18] The repression that followed the two armed rebellions of the 1850s also involved shootings: according to opposition figures, twenty-four after 1851 and thirty-one after 1859. No complete count seems possible, but it is likely that the number of political executions in Conservative Chile did not exceed double figures, whereas in the Argentina of the dictator Juan Manuel de Rosas the figure was at least two thousand.[19] Upper-class Chileans, it should be noted, although sometimes *sentenced* to death, were almost never

17 Interior minister to Intendant of Atacama, January 24, 1852. AMI, Vol. 263.
18 *Verdadero Chileno*, No. 13, June 4, 1850; Arteaga Alemparte, *Constituyentes*, p. 325.
19 Opposition estimates in *Ciudadano*, No. 27, March 27, 1858; CHAM, p. 194. For Argentina, see John Lynch, *Argentine Dictator, Juan Manuel de Rosas* (Oxford, 1981), pp. 242–46. It perhaps needs to be noted here that around four thousand Chileans were killed in the civil wars of 1851 and 1859. The figure for the (more numerous) Argentine civil wars is likely to have been at least three or four times larger.

shot. Only in the Curicó shootings of 1837 (to be mentioned in Chapter 3) was the rule broken. Upper-class politicians, however, were not exempt from less severe penalties – incarceration, internal exile ("relegation" as it came to be known), or banishment abroad for a set period. A fairly standard practice was for opponents of the Conservative regime (when they failed to evade capture) to go into exile voluntarily, depositing a financial bond with the government as surety. Even when political conflict degenerated into civil war, certain "gentlemen's agreements" were generally honored.

The Conservative political system also rested on a successful cultivation of the Catholic Church. Although somewhat weakened (owing to its generally royalist sympathies) during the wars of independence, the church remained the biggest single influence on the Chilean culture. Its holidays were profusely scattered across the calendar. The ceremonies and processions of Holy Week brought commercial life to a standstill. Holy men such as the Franciscan lay brother Fray Andrés Filomeno García ("Fray Andresito"), widely regarded by the faithful as a saint, were known to everyone in mid-nineteenth century Santiago. The Liberals of the 1820s had been mildly anticlerical. The Conservatives were not. Properties belonging to the religious orders that had been expropriated (1824) were returned to them, or compensation paid. "You believe in God," Diego Portales is said to have told Mariano (in some versions, Mariano's father Juan) Egaña, "I believe in priests." He certainly understood their uses in securing political and social stability. With General Prieto's elevation to the presidency in September 1831, the ties between state and church were tightened. The president and cabinet began attending important religious ceremonies, and on certain holidays the civic guard spread the national flag in the dust as a carpet for the priest bearing the sacred host. President Prieto, a pious man, took these things seriously. Many such practices were abandoned in the 1840s under Prieto's less pious successor. Portales also instituted censorship of the theater and of imported books, among which an early victim was a novel by Madame de Staël. This form of censorship was criticized by Andrés Bello (in the pages of *El Araucano*, the government's official newspaper, which he edited) and it did not add up to much in practice.

The Conservatives also strove hard to regularize Chile's anomalous ecclesiastical status. The two old colonial dioceses (Santiago and Concepción) were still nominally subject to the archbishop of Lima in Peru. In order to reorganize the church on national lines, Portales proposed to the Papacy the establishment of a new archdiocese of Santiago along with two new sees (Coquimbo and Chiloé), although he did not live to see the installation of Santiago's first archbishop, Manuel Vicuña, in 1841. The government never succeeded, however, in securing Rome's recognition of its right to the so-called *patronato*, the substantial control of the Church enjoyed by the Spanish crown in colonial times, which Chile, like the other Spanish American republics, had hoped to inherit as a successor-state of Spain's empire. The ultraconservative Pope Gregory XVI dashed all such hopes. In practice, however, procedural formulas were found that enabled the government to nominate (in effect, appoint) ecclesiastical dignitaries. In general, the Conservative regime treated the Church with great deference. For its part, the Church seems to have accepted the government's "regalist" position without too many reservations – for the time being.

The victorious Conservatives of 1830 were particularly aware of the military restiveness and propensity to mutiny that occasionally welled up in the 1820s. One of Portales's first actions was to cashier 136 army officers who had backed General Freire in the civil war of 1829–30. This stern treatment of officers had never been meted out before. Portales also put in hand a serious reorganization of the country's militias, the Civic (or National) Guard. By mid-1831 the Civic Guard numbered twenty-five thousand, and it more than doubled in size by 1850. Officered by upper-class supporters of the regime, its rank and file consisted of artisans, small-time traders and others of similar background. Portales himself was an efficient battalion commander both in Santiago and Valparaiso. He saw the guardsmen's regular drills (usually on Sundays) as "moralizing" measures. It was typical of him that he paid close attention to such details as the organization of morale-boosting musical bands, entrusting the task to a remarkable musician of modest origin, José Zapiola, who idolized Portales for the rest of his long life.[20]

In the Chile of 1849, the Argentine Domingo Faustino Sarmiento was convinced that the Civic Guard had "powerfully" helped create a genuine sense of "Chilean nationality."[21] It was the kind of bold assertion Sarmiento loved to make, and it needs to be qualified. The militia may have gone some way to "moralizing" its members. A Concepción newspaper claimed in 1843 that "the Sunday exercises of the militias" had done much to moderate alcoholism locally.[22] The government, certainly, was proud of its civic guards, seeing them "models of civic patriotism in the eyes of the foreigners who admire our morality, organization and discipline as unusual in America."[23] The reality was more complex. The officers were not always as attentive to their duties as they might have been. In 1858, the inspector of the Santiago Civic Guard drew attention to officers who derided their

20 Zapiola (1802–85) received a musical training in the patriot army during the wars of independence. He had been a fervent *pipiolo* in the 1820s, and would take part in radical politics again in 1850, but his admiration for Portales never dimmed.
21 "De las instituciones militares en Chile," *Crónica*, No. 38, October 14, 1849.
22 *Telégrafo de Concepción*, No. 13, February 4, 1843.
23 *Artesano*, No. 1, June 17, 1841.

orders (and even "the supreme authority of the State") and who skulked at home, rarely turning up at drills.[24] No latitude, however, was given to the rank and file. Service in the Civic Guard was often resented. It also imposed an economic burden, as militiamen were required to provide their own uniforms. As time passed, the demand for reform (or even the abolition) of the Civic Guard became a standard plank in opposition platforms.[25] Whatever its defects, however, the Civic Guard was (as it was intended to be) a credible counterweight to the Army, which rarely numbered more than three thousand except in time of war or civil war. (Finance minister Rengifo's ideal, never realized, was an Army of one thousand.) It would be no exaggeration to say that the Civic Guards twice saved the Conservative regime – in the mutiny of 1837 and the Santiago insurrection at Easter 1851.

Electoral Intervention

The militiamen also had an openly political role. They were a (usually) captive voting bloc for the government. Electoral "intervention," the systematic manipulation of elections by the executive, was undoubtedly one of the secrets of Chilean stability in the early republic. Not that it was ever a secret. Opposition parties it disadvantaged were prone to denounce it vehemently, with a wealth of detail about particularly flagrant incidents.[26] For most of the nineteenth century, well beyond the early republic, Congress was mostly chosen by the president or his ministers. It was the agents of the state itself, rather than, as in some other Latin American countries, a network of local political bosses *(caciques* or Brazilian-style *coronéis)* in a comfortable, symbiotic relationship with the state, that masterminded the state's electoral supremacy. The contrast with other political systems should probably not be pressed too far. Although the chain of command was clear, the relationship of the Intendants with their subordinates, the governors and *subdelegados*, involved no deep conflict of interest, given that landowners formed the governing class. Votes were not hard to accumulate in the countryside. In the towns, a greater effort sometimes had to be made.[27]

The "electorate" was tiny – barely more than 2 percent of the population in 1846, when twenty-four thousand votes were cast in the congressional

24 Juan Vidaurre Leal to Intendant of Santiago, August 14, 1858, printed in *Ciudadano*, No. 59, August 25, 1858.

25 See Grez Toso, *De la "Regeneración,"* pp. 269–281.

26 See, for example, *Manifiesto del partido de oposición, Manifiesto de la oposición.* For 1851, see the reports in PR, Nos. 2590, 2593, 2594, 2595, and 2596, June 28 and July 2–5, 1851.

27 The Chilean system bears some resemblance to that of the late nineteenth-century regime of Antonio Cánovas del Castillo in Spain, where the government masterminded elections in the cities, although also relying on a network of *caciques* in the countryside.

elections (twenty-one thousand for the government). In 1864, the total was actually two thousand lower. Such figures no doubt roughly reflect the number of votes cast, but they also are absolutely meaningless. It is impossible to say how many votes were genuine and how many simply fraudulent. The elaborate theories of "voting behavior" so cherished by modern political scientists are totally inapplicable to nineteenth-century Chile.[28] The 1833 Constitution limited the vote to "active citizens," literate males over twenty-one (twenty-five if bachelors) with fixed property, trading capital, or an income from a craft or trade. For reasons that are not hard to fathom, the literacy rule was not to be enforced until 1840. In 1842, for exactly the same reasons, Congress allowed all illiterates registered before 1840 to go on voting until they died.[29] A separate electoral law in 1833 spelled out the precise property or financial qualifications for voting, on a province-by-province scale. The highest were for Santiago (a fixed property of 1,000 pesos, a trading capital of 2,000 pesos, or an annual craft or trade income of 200 pesos). The lowest were for impoverished Valdivia and Chiloé (where the figures were 300, 500, and 60 pesos respectively). These scales cunningly spread the net wide enough to include most of those who were liable for service in the rank and file of the Civic Guard.

The voting system under the 1833 law offered scope for manipulation at every stage. The entire Chamber of Deputies and one third of the Senate were renewed every three years. Voters registered toward the end of the year preceding an election. At tables set up in each parish, they were issued with *boletas de calificación*, popularly known as *calificaciones* – certificates that had to be presented at election time to the *mesas receptoras* (voting tables) before a citizen could cast his vote. The government distributed *calificaciones* in bulk quantities to each Intendant. Unused certificates were returned to Santiago, sometimes in large numbers. Governors and *subdelegados* were always able to exercise rough control over the issue of *calificaciones*. In November 1839, for instance, the Intendant of Talca prevented muncipal councilmen from presiding over registration tables, as they were theoretically required to do, insisting that his subaltern officials did so instead. They conveniently exhausted their supply of *calificaciones* before the opposition could register.[30] Such tactics could sometimes lead to undignified tussles with the opposition, as happened in the *subdelegación* of Pelarco in 1850.[31] In 1857, the Interior minister asked the Intendant of Valparaiso

---

28 Voting figures (incomplete) in national elections for 1830–64, are presented in Urzúa Valenzuela, pp. 89–169 and 190–200.
29 Barros Arana, *Decenio*, I, 265–67.
30 *Alcance al No. 3 del Liberal*, February 11, 1840.
31 See Donoso Vergara, "Revolución," RCHG, No. 145 (1977), pp. 31–32.

for a report on alleged irregularities in the locality of Putaendo, a small place near San Felipe whose sole claim to fame was (and is) that the Liberator San Martín had tethered his horse there in 1817. The Intendant expressed astonishment over the accusation that the tables had been manned by individuals with "close relationships with the Governor's family," since this "normally happens everywhere in the republic in townships or departments like Putaendo."[32]

There were, in fact, any number of ways in which suspect voters could be removed from the scene at registration time. In the case of Talca Province in 1839, a rural priest with opposition sympathies (and doubtless with influence over his flock) was summoned to the provincial capital for "consultations," and a Liberal councilman was sent off to Santiago to discuss the accounts of the local high school. By the same token, Conservative (and Liberal) hacendados often equipped their inquilinos with spurious qualifications to enable them to register. In the small town of Ovalle in 1841, according to one source, the registered electorate consisted exclusively of "a few landowners and . . . an endless number of inquilinos."[33] In the case of Putaendo in 1857, according to the report already quoted, numerous inquilinos "did not present themselves to register voluntarily, and . . . were forced to do so by their respective landlords."[34] In 1859, the progovernment *El Ferrocarril*, with unusual frankness, condemned the "shameful farces" of rural elections, where "an hacendado drives his *huasos*[35] to the urns, in the same way he drives his livestock to the corral."[36] This particular habit was not uprooted until well into the twentieth century.

Given their voting potential, particular care was taken with the *calificaciones* of the civic guardsmen. "A battalion is formed," as a newspaper of 1858 put it, "and the voice of command tells it: 'Hand over your *calificaciones*!' "[37] The Intendant of Valparaiso claimed in 1857 (with a straight face?) that the guardsmen did so "spontaneously." Once handed over, the certificates were held by the officers until election day, when the *cívicos* marched to the voting tables as a "regimented, disciplined phalanx, voting tactically," in Diego José Benavente's words[38] – although hardly in the modern sense of "tactical voting." In 1855, Luis Waddington, working for the government in Copiapó, rather too openly boasted that he held all the *calificaciones* of his Civic Guard battalion. On this occasion, the local newspaper, *El Copiapino*, printed a list of those who had registered, and urged

32 Intendant of Valparaiso to Interior minister, December 31, 1857. AI(V), Vol. 101.
33 *Estrella del Norte*, No. 7, July 13, 1841.
34 Intendant of Valparaiso to Interior minister, December 31, 1857. AI(V), Vol. 101.
35 Peasants, inquilinos or otherwise, with horses.
36 FE, No. 1138, August 24, 1859.
37 ACT, No. 147, July 23, 1858.
38 *Cartas Patriotas*, No. 5 (Letter 9), n.d. [1839/1840], pp. 54–55.

the opposition to "exhort" them appropriately.[39] The tactic must have been effective, since the opposition won.

Prior to election time itself (March for congressional, April for municipal, June for presidential elections) "the government or cabinet makes lists," according to a description from 1845, "to nominate deputies, senators, and electors for president, and sends it to the Intendants so that he gets them elected. [The Intendants] send them on to the governors and . . . , where it concerns them, to the *subdelegados.*"[40] All Intendants could regularly expect to receive letters of the kind Interior minister Manuel Montt sent to the Intendant of Valdivia in February 1846:

I hasten to communicate to you the persons who in our judgement should be elected as deputies to Congress for your province. You will find their names at the foot of this letter. . . . I leave all this business of elections in that province in your care, and all I will permit myself to add is that if it proves necessary to make some expenses, have the goodness to do so, and advise me confidentially so that, of course, they can be covered.[41]

One of the names Montt sent was his own.

The government also took reasonable pains to ascertain the state of opinion in the provinces. The reports that flowed back to Santiago sometimes included the actual state of play with *calificaciones*. In March 1851 (three months before the presidential election of that year), the Intendant of Aconcagua told the Interior minister: "In Putaendo the election is going badly at the moment; we only have 144 certain votes and we need 28 more to win . . . , and with the measures that are being taken we are gaining ground every day, or so the Governor tells me." In the department of San Felipe, meanwhile, the Intendant had only managed to collect 125 of the 857 *calificaciones* issued, but was confident that he could increase the total as soon as the harvest was over.[42] In the event, he did.

Delivery of the vote, as we can see from this, was an important aspect of an Intendant's work. Failure to deliver meant dismissal at worst, official disfavor at best, as even that hero of independence Admiral Manuel Blanco Encalada discovered in 1849, while Intendant of Valparaiso. It was, however, possible for Intendants to go too far. When, in 1849, the Intendant of Colchagua, the young Domingo Santa María, followed the president's instructions to win the elections *a todo trance* ("whatever it takes") a bit too zealously, his behavior won him dismissal when the cabinet fell into the hands of his enemies soon afterward. (As a Liberal president more than

39 *Copiapino*, Nos. 2142–2144, March 12–14, 1855.
40 *Penquisto*, No. 17, November 22, 1845.
41 Montt to Salvador Sanfuentes, February 12, 1846. Amunátegui Reyes, *García Reyes*, II, 279–80.
42 Juan Francisco Fuenzalida to Antonio Varas, March 7, 1851. Varas, *Correspondencia*, IV, 19.

thirty years later, Santa María would show even greater interventionist expertise.) Disputed elections were sometimes discussed (and very occasionally disallowed) in Congress. But elections were by no means always contested. Given the government's immense electoral advantage, it is hardly surprising that most seats were not fought in most elections. In seven of the eleven congressional elections held between 1833 and 1864 the opposition scarcely bothered to run candidates at all.

When it did, the competition could be fierce. Voting took place over two days, allowing both government and opposition to adjust their tactics while the election proceeded. Money came into play here, for "the scandalous traffic in *calificaciones*" noted by the opposition in 1858[43] was in evidence at all contested elections. The opposition, according to one source, spent the nontrivial sum of 8,000 pesos in Copiapó during the presidential election of 1841.[44] The detailed description of the presidential election of 1851 in Santiago by an American naval officer, Lieutenant Archibald MacRae[45] shows both government and opposition vote buyers operating near the *mesas*, and the price of votes fluctuating in accordance with apparent voting trends. Information was passed from parish to parish by messengers nicknamed *vapores* ("steamships"). An exchange in the Chamber of Deputies soon after the election underlined the importance of vote buying.

MARCIAL GONZÁLEZ [*Liberal*-San Fernando]: This victory was won by means of bribery, corruption and the most scandalous violence.
MIGUEL GALLO [*Conservative*-Copiapó]: False! False!
MARCIAL GONZÁLEZ: No, true! True! It is a fact as clear as day.
MIGUEL GALLO: Everybody bought votes, sir, everybody!
MARCIAL GONZÁLEZ: The Cabinet, yes. The opposition did not have the money to buy them . . .
MIGUEL GALLO: The opposition bought as many as it could.[46]

Lieutenant MacRae's account suggests that the Liberal opposition simply ran out of money on the second day.

Bribery scarcely exhausted the government's manipulative techniques. If necessary, impersonation was used. It was alleged in 1858, for instance, that the government had brought in one hundred workers from the Southern Railroad, disguised them as policemen, and sent them off to vote.[47] If the opposition seemed to be winning, voting could be suspended (as also happened in 1858) so that the government could recoup its position. Physical

43 ACT, No. 132, July 6, 1858.
44 *Estrella del Norte*, No. 7, July 13, 1841.
45 Gilliss, pp. 305–07.
46 CN/D, July 18, 1851.
47 *Manifiesto de la oposición*, pp. 29–49.

intimidation was also often used to prevent opposition voters from reaching the voting tables at all. In 1851, Lieutenant MacRae noticed groups of *apretadores* ("tighteners") near the tables, jostling and shoving opposition voters out of the way, and in one parish (La Catedral) two lines of soldiers barred the way forward, only clearing a way to the tables when the voter seemed reliable. (The president of the *mesa*, thought MacRae, "became both short-sighted and deaf whenever the applicant belonged to the liberal party.") Physical intimidation of this kind was complemented by every kind of moral suasion. Public officials were expected to vote the proper way, and were often threatened with dismissal if they showed any inclination to do otherwise. Refractory civic guardsmen (there were always some) could if necessary be confined to barracks.

The sketch written by José Joaquín Vallejo ("Jotabeche") of the election of 1846 in Copiapó gives us a classic account of how the government machinery operated when seats were uncontested. It is too well known as an essay to warrant extended quotation, but it shows the entire pattern: the Intendant's marshaling of his forces ("mining managers from Chañarcillo, militiamen from Tierra Amarilla, Nantoco and Potrero Grande, more militiamen from Ramadilla, and the public officials from the Port"), and the marked ballots distributed to the militiamen with the warning that if the proper vote did not appear in the urns "we shall know that you . . . are an enemy of the government."[48] Although strongly devoted to the Conservative regime, Vallejo was not alone in finding such spectacles demeaning and pointless. From the government viewpoint, however, electoral intervention may have been demeaning, but it was certainly not pointless.

An opposition party stood no chance of beating the well-coordinated government machine on a nationwide scale. In practice it needed to focus its efforts on particular districts, where it could sometimes mobilize sufficient local influence (through sympathetic hacendados) to win seats in the Chamber. And there were always parts of Chile that were friendly to oppositions, for example, Valparaiso – "revolutionary *par excellence*," as a magazine of 1849 somewhat exaggeratedly described it.[49] Aconcagua Province, where the distribution of land was somewhat less skewed than in the Central Valley, had something of a tradition of political nonconformity. The mining provinces of the north, likewise, with their fluid and volatile society, tended to be congenial territory for opposition candidates. José Joaquín Vallejo's election in the Huasco valley in 1849, marvelously described by himself, was a classic case where an appeal to public opinion defeated the efforts of the local Intendant.[50] But such cases were rather rare.

48 "Las elecciones en Copiapó," Vallejo, *Obras*, p. 348.
49 *Picaflor*, No. 3, May 15, 1840.
50 "Elecciones del Huasco," Vallejo, *Obras*, pp. 359–66.

The government sometimes tried to pretend that intervention did not happen, but it also had to answer opposition charges, and one of the commonest answers was that such things were normal in elections everywhere. The argument was eloquently made in a government manifesto after the 1851 elections:

> Will there have been abuses in the elections . . . ? We . . . swear . . . that there must have been many, very many. . . . Popular elections, the basis of our institutions, give scope in every country in the world for the most serious abuses. Every day we receive newspapers from Europe denouncing the abuses that occur in France, England and Spain . . . ; even in the oldest and most cultured states there are abuses in the elections, bribery, disorders, frauds, and wickedness. . . . Only time and education can partially cure this; it will never extirpate it completely, for [if it did] men would cease to be men and become angels, in which case there would be no need for elections, as the Catechism does not teach us that angels elect their archangels and seraphim.[51]

Political Parties

Politicians had shown their capacity for partisanship in the 1820s, and the existence of political parties was taken for granted in the early republic. "Owing to a misfortune inherent in the human species," a newspaper observed in 1842, "the citizens must divide for elections . . . God has told us, *tot capita, tot sententiae.*"[52] *El Progreso* in 1844 suggested that since the "national will" was "unfathomable," parties were the "only manifestation of public opinion," and that a government was "more truly a national expression when it represents a more numerous or perhaps more intelligent party."[53] Because politicians and writers used the word constantly, and often claimed a party affiliation, it is important to understand what they meant. What they did not mean was an organized and structured political following with rules governing leadership and membership. Only the slightest traces of modern party organization are to be found in Chile much before the 1870s and 1880s. "Parties" at this earlier period essentially consisted of groups of like-minded politicians, most of them living in Santiago, with smaller such groups in provincial towns, and, with few spaces available for public gatherings, at least before the 1850s, mostly meeting in each other's houses. Parties (in this sense) often formed ad hoc directing committees, usually before elections, and such committees sometimes organized correspondence with provincial sympathizers.

51 *"Manifiesto del partido de oposición . . . ,"* p. 12.
52 *Telégrafo de Concepción,* No. 1, December 15, 1842.
53 PR, No. 525, July 20, 1844.

For much of the period covered by this book, the only party in Chile with serious continuity was the ruling Conservative party – "the great Conservative party," as eulogized by a progovernment newspaper of 1852, "which in all difficult circumstances has saved the country . . . , the Conservative party composed of the most intelligent, honorable and wealthy part of the nation."[54] The Conservatives had been insultingly nicknamed *pelucones* ("big wigs") as early as the 1810s. Like the term "Tory" in England, the insult was adopted as a badge of honor by its recipients. Until the great realignment of 1857–8, the *pelucones* were the politicians whose support for the government was strongest and from whose ranks the government recruited most of its public officials and congressmen. The Liberal party, forcibly excluded from power in 1829–30, was exposed to repression in the 1830s, and its *raison d'être* was undermined in the tolerant 1840s. The Liberals' old nickname, *pipiolos* ("greenhorns"), came to be applied mostly to the older, "unreconstructed" Liberals whose main motive was revenge for the defeat of 1830. The Liberal revival of the late 1840s only rather tenuously reflected real continuity from the *pipiolismo* of the 1820s; as we shall see, it came about as the result of an excision from the *pelucón* ranks.

Whether Conservative or Liberal, party politicians used much the same techniques in attempting to influence public opinion. Because public opinion was effectively confined to the ranks of the literate, the press was seen as a particularly valuable political weapon. It was sometimes possible, as with the Vial family in the 1840s, to establish more or less long-running daily newspapers such as *El Progreso*. *El Ferrocarril* after 1855 tended to reflect the political line of the then Interior minister Antonio Varas. The "dean" of the Chilean press, *El Mercurio*, was largely middle-of-the-road in politics, usually (but never uncritically) supportive of the government, except on the rare occasions when it was drawn into opposition. But long-running dailies were expensive, and it was easier to launch shorter-term news-sheets, which vanished as soon as the particular pretext for their existence had passed. These were supplemented at election time with hastily printed broadsides designed to catch the attention of voters.

Political banqueting was a further technique that found its place in the political culture of the times. The government sometimes splashed out on celebratory dinners to mark notable events or the national holidays. When did opposition parties adopt the tactic? *El Progreso*, reporting a banquet held at the Quinta Zañartu in November 1850, attended by "almost all the notabilities of the [Liberal] party," somewhat implied that this kind of gathering was new, or newish, in Chile.[55] The previous year the opposition in Aconcagua had launched a local election committee with "a

54 *Civilización*, No. 160, March 26, 1852.
55 PR, No. 2476, November 5, 1859.

splendid banquet."[56] By the time of the political agitation of 1858, the tradition was well established. The famous "protest banquet" of October 1858 was, as we shall see in Chapter 9, a political event in its own right. Anticipating it, *El Mercurio* noted that "the table will be sumptuous, with 400 places set." The newspaper fully approved: "the public spirit is enlivened this way," it suggested, for "those banquets are the cradles of the great ideas."[57] Alcohol clearly played its part in the formation of Chilean political ideas in the early republic. By the end of the period it was possible for the rising novelist Alberto Blest Gana to poke fun at the banquet tradition.

Just a few glasses instil such noble inspiration in the most indifferent and apathetic souls! Our banquet is proof. . . . Here is someone who deals with the inquilinos of his hacienda with a whip in his hand, and he talks of fraternity among men . . . ; here is another who pays the workers on his estate in tokens only redeemable in his mayordomo's store . . . , and he orates in favor of freedom of trade . . . ; over there is someone who regards all foreigners as accursed heretics, and who is wildly advocating freedom of worship, and someone else over there who packages up his inquilinos' *calificaciones* to make them vote for him, and who is raising the roof with his demand for freedom of elections.

At government banquets, Blest Gana observed, the speeches were very similar, "minus the toasts against tyranny, which are replaced with congratulations on the prosperity of the country; but the results are the same . . . , which only goes to prove that we are all good Chileans."[58]

"All Good Chileans"

To what extent did the Conservative scheme of things appeal to, or even rely on, the sentiment expressed by Blest Gana – "we are all good Chileans"? To what extent did the early republican governments actively foster a national culture? The revolution for independence had presented itself as a national struggle. Its leaders had taken the framework of the nation-state for granted. The immediate postrevolutionary governments were certainly aware of the need to promote an appropriate national spirit. Supreme Director Ramón Freire, in 1824, noting the "importance of making the feelings of Chileans as *national* as possible," decreed that the name "Chile" should be used in all appropriate contexts instead of the vaguer word *patria*, "homeland." The governments of the early republic did not make superhuman efforts to sponsor the "invention" of a national tradition, but neither were they

56 *Aconcagüino*, No. 9, October 4, 1849.
57 M(S), No. 9388, October 13, 1858.
58 "Los banquetes patrióticos," *Semana*, No. 12, August 6, 1859.

completely idle. If the writers of the political class, more spontaneously, developed the idea of Chile as an "imagined community," and from what they wrote it seems clear that they did (see Chapter 7), the ways in which the idea was diffused and the speed at which it was diffused are less easily identifiable.

Indeed, it is almost impossible to assess how far a genuine feeling of nationality or *chilenidad* ("Chilean-ness)" spread through the population in the decades after independence. A far too often quoted article on hacienda life in 1861 asserted that an inquilino, for instance, had little or no awareness that he was Chilean, that "If he hears tell of Spaniards or Indians, he does not even imagine that he has a contact with those races, that it is their blood that circulates in his veins."[59] It is not altogether easy to believe that inquilinos were so completely insulated from the rest of society. Did they never see the national flag? Did they never get drunk on the national holidays? We must not assume too readily that peasant awareness of national affiliation was nonexistent, however vague it may have been.

It is no doubt true that national consciousness came in what might be called "strong" and "weak" forms. The "strong" form was most likely to have been felt by the educated and literate, for whom it became available with the gradual spread of the "print-capitalism" vital (as Benedict Anderson suggests) to the diffusion of modern nationalism.[60] Print-capitalism in Anderson's sense, however, had only a limited range in Chile before the 1860s and 1870s. There is no doubt that the press encouraged patriotic sentiment with enthusiasm, but newspapers and magazines reached a relatively small segment of the population. Nor, given its limited scope, can education be seen as a serious instrument for the transmission of patriotic values. (Suitably patriotic history textbooks for schools by Chilean authors did not become available much before the 1860s.) For the upper class, the theater might have become a vehicle for patriotism, but of the roughly eleven hundred productions on the Chilean stage between 1830 and 1850, no more than two or three were devoted to national themes. The titles of the musical compositions of the period (including the polkas and waltzes so popular at balls) somewhat more often reflected national topics, yet it is unlikely that (apart from marches played by the Civic Guard bands) they were much heard outside the salons and theaters of the towns.[61] Music is an ambiguous medium at best. "Popular poetry" was not printed until later in the nineteenth century, by which time it was strongly patriotic,

59 Atropos, "El inquilino," *Revista del Pacífico*, Tomo V (1861), pp. 101–02.

60 Benedict Anderson, *Imagined Communities*, revised ed. (London–New York, 1991), pp. 37–46.

61 For a list of plays, see Pereira Salas, *Teatro*, pp. 386–99. For a list (doubtless incomplete) of musical compositions (to 1886) see Pereira Salas, *Biobibliografía*, pp. 15–132. Of the 221 dance pieces identified by Pereira Salas, 32 percent were polkas and 26 percent waltzes.

often combining intense patriotism with disdain for the rich. However widespread it may have become during the early republic, national feeling seems to have grown spontaneously, building on the rough sense of community already created by Chile's long colonial isolation, and reinforced, perhaps, by the country's victory in the 1836–9 war (see Chapter 3) and its growing stability. It was surely also reinforced by annual patriotic rituals, by such things as the patriotic imagery on the country's coins (standardized after 1834) handled every day, and by the visible or audible signs of nationality – the flag, the coat of arms, the anthem.

Like other Spanish American republics, Chile adopted these outward symbols of nationhood at an early date. The national flag in the form we know today first appeared at the independence ceremonies in 1818. In 1832, President Prieto instituted a competition for a new national coat of arms, the old one being thought inferior, and both government and Congress showed intense interest in the details of the design presented by the winner, the soldier-artist Carlos Wood. Prieto and Interior minister Joaquín Tocornal, in presenting the new design to the legislature, were already invoking a certain distinctive conception of Chilean symbolism.

Congress will observe a field of two colors, whose well known attributes fit perfectly with the nature of the country and the character of its inhabitants. . . . The supports represent a huemul and a condor, the latter being the strongest, most spirited and most substantial bird that populates our skies, the former being the rarest and most singular quadruped of our mountains, from whose skin, noted for its strength and elasticity, our valiant natives make their corslets and boots for warfare. Finally, the naval crown that surmounts both animals' heads will be the monument that will forever recall the glorious triumph of our maritime forces against those of Spain in various Pacific waters.

Some members of Congress objected to the crowns as symbols of monarchy, but it was explained that there were good precedents in classical antiquity. Others questioned the appropriateness of the huemul. Most Chileans never set eyes on this particular species of Andean deer. But the coat of arms was accepted, and since then has only been altered by the addition in 1910 of the national motto (*Por la razón o la fuerza*, "By right or might"),[62] which had appeared on silver coins since 1834.

The story of the national anthem is more ambiguous, and shows that the "invention of tradition" by the new republic could be positively haphazard at times. The music of the earliest version (1819) was changed in the mid-1820s, the new score commissioned from a distinguished Catalan musician, Ramón Carnicer (1789–1855), then director of the Barcelona opera. In the mid-1840s, following the peace treaty between Chile and Spain

62 Valencia Avaria, *Símbolos*, pp. 36–39.

(April 1844), Spanish residents in Chile (and Spain's popular new *chargé d'affaires* in Santiago) suggested that the vividly anticolonial words (by the patriot Bernardo de Vera y Pintado) be replaced. The press was divided about the proposal. One news-sheet thought that it appealed to "the noble feelings worthy of gentlemen,"[63] although others did not see this as sufficient reason to change the anthem.[64] Interior minister Manuel Camilo Vial asked one of his subaltern officials, the young poet Eusebio Lillo, for a new, more conciliatory version. "There was never a decree to order the change," Lillo himself would remember. "I carried out what I thought was an order from my boss." He showed his text to the republic's supreme literary arbiter, Andrés Bello, who approved it, though he did not like Lillo's decision to retain Vera y Pintado's original refrain – "*Dulce Patria, recibe los votos . . .*" ("Dear homeland, receive the vows . . .") – which offended his strict views on prosody. Otherwise, Lillo radically altered the underlying sentiments. The Spaniard was no longer the bloody monster of Vera y Pintado's version: "*ya es hermano el que ayer invasor,*" "yesterday's invader is now our brother."[65] A thousand copies of the new text were printed immediately, an interesting indication of the government's determination to impose the new version.[66] Why it was so determined, and why its procedures were so casual (Congress was not consulted and there was never a specific law), is hard to interpret in the absence of further evidence. It could simply have been a fancy in Vial's imperious mind. It is also conceivable that he was sufficiently confident of the solidity of national feeling (at least in the political class) to risk a change that in other circumstances might have proved controversial. There was certainly intermittent resistance to the new "invented tradition" from the public, at least for a while, but nothing resembling a storm of protest. The tune always remained popular. *El Ferrocarril* complained in 1860 that organ-grinders were playing it far too often, and urged that this be stopped lest familiarity breed contempt.[67]

The celebration of September 18, the *dieciocho*, as Chile's principal national holiday had begun in 1811. By the 1840s, the annual festivities extended across three days – "NATIONAL FIESTA," as one of the numerous almanacs of the period advertised them, "Flags and illuminations on the 17th, 18th, and 19th. Commercial establishments closed."[68] Drinking and dancing often continued for several days afterward. For the *Revista Católica*,

---

63 *Orden*, No. 23, January 4, 1846.
64 E.g., *Gaceta del Comercio*, No. 1426, September 23, 1846.
65 In 1909 Lillo himself (in extreme old age) changed "*invasor*," "invader," to " *opresor*," "oppressor."
66 Details of the story of the anthem are from Silva Castro, *Eusebio Lillo*, pp. 28–46. The new words and the music were not printed together until 1859. Pereira Salas, *Biobibliografía*, pp. 46–47.
67 FE, No. 1362, May 16, 1860. José Zapiola thought the music too complicated for most vocal registers: *Recuerdos*, pp. 69–73.
68 *Almanaque chileno para . . . 1849*, p. 11.

looking back on the *dieciocho* of 1860, it was all a happy blur of "patriotic hymns, the thump of the cannon, the national flag, the harmonious military music."[69] The atmosphere of the annual festivities is beautifully evoked in Blest Gana's novel *Martín Rivas*, an incomparable portrait of the Santiago of 1850, and there are numerous other descriptions of ways in which the holidays were celebrated in the mid-nineteenth century, including a distinctly lighthearted account by the historian Diego Barros Arana, not normally noted for lightheartedness. [70] Mrs. Loretta Merwin's American eye was dazzled by the celebrations in Valparaiso in 1854, especially by the military parade.

It was a beautiful spectacle, presented in full view of the great Pacific – thousands of military marching and countermarching, with music and streaming flags and flashing arms – men and women on horseback and in birlochos, and a joyous rout on foot, hurrying hither and thither with the restlessness of crowds, and entering and emerging from the innumerable gay refreshment-booths that dotted the plaza.[71]

The Conservatives reinforced the tradition in certain ways. It was no accident that Joaquín Prieto, the first elected Conservative president, was inaugurated on a September 18 (as were all presidents, bar one, until 1906). The ceremonial surrounding the holiday that year (1831) set the pattern for all *dieciochos* from then until now, with a solemn Te Deum on September 18, and a military parade the next day. In provincial towns, horse racing sometimes replaced the parade. Throughout the 1830s, a lavish presidential ball marked the holidays, a tradition abandoned after 1841 because of its cost. There were similar official rituals throughout the country. For the *dieciocho* of 1838, for instance, the Municipality of Valparaiso hosted a large banquet for 150 guests – public officials, the foreign consuls, traders, both Chilean and foreign. "There reigned a happiness," reported *El Mercurio*, "that could only be compared to the abundance of food on the table and the choice wines that flowed profusely. The toasts were endless."[72] In the provinces, the Intendants usually hosted *soirées* for local society. The recently arrived Polish scientist Ignacio Domeyko, attending one in La Serena in 1838, was pleased to note that the leading local members of the opposition Liberal party were invited.[73] The press occasionally claimed that the *dieciocho* was no more than a pretext for eating and drinking, and chided the populace on its failure to remember the high significance of the holiday. In 1844, *El Mercurio* editorialized on "the filthiest licence" observable in the Valparaiso festivities

69 RCAT, No. 653, September 29, 1860.
70 "Revista Semanal," *Museo*, No. 16, September 25, 1853.
71 Merwin, pp. 68–69.
72 MV, No. 2931, September 21, 1838.
73 *Mis viajes*, I, 366.

of that year.[74] In encouraging the popular festivities, however, the government seems to have had a deliberately relaxed approach. "The Police tirelessly pursue the idle and the drunken, but during the Dieciocho holidays it conducts itself with great indulgence," reported the Intendant of Atacama around 1850.[75] The *subdelegado* of Chañarcillo, writing to the same Intendant in September 1851, noted that during the *dieciocho* "the masses are conceded a certain license which would not be appropriate on ordinary days."[76]

The government's evidently indulgent attitude to the *dieciocho* can surely be interpreted as the reinforcement of an invented tradition. And whatever its alcoholic excesses, the holiday was the focus, each year, for patriotic rhetoric. Newspapers rarely failed to commemorate the anniversary with suitable editorials or even special issues. Just two examples will suffice. In 1854, the *dieciocho* issue of the progovernment *El Mensajero* includes no less than ten patriotic poems (none of them much good), a short story set in the independence period, recollections of the wars of independence, and reprints of the *Acta* of September 18, 1810, the Proclamation of Independence, the preamble to the 1833 Constitution and President Prieto's accompanying proclamation, and, somewhat incongruously, a report on the first anniversary of the creation of the typographers' society in Santiago.[77] In 1843, *El Mercurio*'s elaborately designed front page shows four highly ornamented classical columns. The space between the two middle columns is occupied by a patriotic "hymn" of no great literary merit, while the names of the major battles of the wars of independence (with brief descriptions) appear between the two outer columns. Interestingly, the paper's editorial that day gives an approving account of Robespierre's Festival of the Supreme Being in 1794, noting admiringly that "The French Republic knew how to impress the masses, and to excite in them a feeling for great and good things." When the entire earth is covered by free nations, suggests *El Mercurio*, the "festivals" of the French Republic will be the model for a "regenerated world," a world in which Chile will certainly have her place.[78]

74 MV, No. 4925, September 20, 1844. See also MV, No. 4563, September 21, 1843.
75 Quoted in Hernández, *Juan Godoy*, I, 161.
76 *Subdelegado* to Intendant, September 22, 1851. AI(A), Vol. 86.
77 *Mensajero*, No. 399, September 18, 1854. The poets included Guillermo Matta, Eusebio Lillo, and Jacinto Chacón.
78 MV, No. 4561, September 18, 1843.

PART II

From Portales to Montt, 1835–1851

3
Authoritarians and Moderates, 1835–1846

The Return of Portales

During Diego Portales's first ministry (1830–1), the Conservative regime had consolidated its grip on the new republic. Portales's seventeen months as Interior minister put the stamp of firm government on the country, with Portales assuming an astonishing personal command over his collaborators and the regime itself. How he achieved this will always have an element of the mysterious. Few characters have so fascinated Chilean historians, who have written about him time and time again. Those who have tried to debunk him have usually fallen short of their aim. He obviously had an extraordinary personality – full of nervous energy, in private fun-loving and in public austere, by turns vehement and charming, supremely clear-headed yet also self-deluding: his belief that his true vocation was trade was never borne out by conspicuous business success. He was both loved by his friends and feared by his opponents. Many of his own supporters were jittery about him.

Politically, the record is clear. Portales brooked no opposition from the defeated Liberals, persecuted them, and largely reduced them to silence. He both purged and imposed new standards of order and regularity on the public administration, insisting on such important details as the regular cleaning of government offices, and he successfully beat off all challenges, most of them conspiracies by army officers on the losing side at the Battle of Lircay. By the mid-1830s, the Conservative government had lasted longer than any other since independence, leaving aside the liberator O'Higgins's six-year dictatorship (1817–23). We know in hindsight that the Conservative regime was to prove durable. Portales himself, as we can tell from his candid and gossipy correspondence, seems to have been seized by doubts about its staying power, sometimes complaining that its officials were insufficiently firm. His occasional caustic mockery of them was an open secret. Having established his credentials as the "omnipotent minister" of legend, he had quit the Interior ministry in September 1831. His aversion to office was genuine, but aversion to office was not aversion to power, or at least influence. He watched the political scene closely from Valparaiso, where he was governor for a while, and later from his farm in the Ligua Valley.

What prompted him back into office in September 1835 was the first sign of serious division within the Conservative fold. This is where the history of political argument under the Conservative regime begins. It is important not to overstress the coherence of the "Conservative" identity in the early 1830s. The three factions that joined hands to destroy the Liberal government in 1829–30 (the genuinely conservative *pelucones*, the O'Higginists who dreamed of a restoration of the exiled liberator, and Portales's own following, the so-called *estanqueros*) took time to coalesce into a common "Conservative party," an expression that nowhere appears in Portales's surviving correspondence. It could be argued that the process was only complete at the end of the 1830s, although the mildly divergent agendas of the three groups of 1829–30 ceased to have much relevance as the regime took shape. The O'Higginists, who had the most serious alternative agenda, were swiftly neutralized by Portales by the simple expedient of awarding the presidency to the somewhat colorless but conscientious General Prieto, their most prominent figure (and the country's most powerful soldier).

Yet from the outset of the new regime, there was a division in the victors' camp between those who supported Portales's hard line, and others who hankered after a more emollient approach. No consistent labels were used for the two tendencies at the time. Can we be more consistent in hindsight? The second tendency is accurately describable as "moderate." It would be caricaturing the less moderate Conservatives to call them (as was sometimes done) "extreme" or "ultra," terms that imply they were a minority; they were not. The term "authoritarian," which will be used here, can only be accepted if it is remembered that moderate Conservatives, too, sometimes felt obliged to accept authoritarian measures. The Interior minister in 1835, Joaquín Tocornal, was devoted to Portales and an authoritarian. The talented Finance minister, Manuel Rengifo, who had begun to distance himself from Portales, was by this stage a definite moderate. Another notable moderate was a former Interior minister, Ramón Errázuriz, whose removal from office (in favor of Tocornal) Portales had engineered in April 1832. Errázuriz was a prominent member of a very extensive family, a natural focus around which a moderate *pelucón* movement could form. It was joined by several of the disillusioned Liberals who had earlier become close allies of Portales, notably Manuel Antonio Gandarillas and Diego José Benavente. Gandarillas objected to Portales's harshness. Benavente, always something of a maverick, had fallen out with him over a personal incident in 1831.[1]

---

1 Sotomayor Valdés, *Historia*, I, 386–88.

As allowed by the new Constitution, President Joaquín Prieto intended to run for reelection in 1836. It was part of the Conservative scheme that he should. As a successful Finance minister (and a cousin-in-law of Prieto), Manuel Rengifo cherished presidential illusions of his own. His moderate Conservative supporters became known as the *filopolitas*, from the news-sheet, *El Philopolita*, they created to advance their cause. A modern reader is likely to be struck by its extreme cautiousness. It hardly laid down a severe challenge to the regime. Yet its language, heavily coded, was sufficient to bring an immediate reaction from the authoritarian Conservative camp, to the extent that *El Philopolita* felt itself obliged to deny that it was promoting Rengifo's presidential candidacy, despite which it printed a glowing eulogy of Rengifo in a later issue.[2] Portales's closest and most trusted personal collaborators, the Spaniard Victorino Garrido and Fernando Urízar Garfias, men who were both as active and determined as he was, entered the fray with an anti-*filopolita* news-sheet, *El Farol*, whose language was much less restrained (and far more personal) than that of *El Philopolita*, which it described in its first issue (August 13, 1835) as printing "logico-political gibberish" designed to "undermine social order." The *filopolitas*, it declared, in language that would become wearisomely familiar over the years, were no better than "sansculottes."[3]

It would be tedious to follow the war of words between *El Farol* and *El Philopolita* in detail. There were two short-term issues that provoked dissension between the Portales-Tocornal camp and the *filopolitas*. One was a proposal to reinstate some (or even all) of the Liberal army officers unceremoniously cashiered by Portales in April 1830. However justified the measure had been at the time, suggested *El Philopolita*, magnanimity was now in order.[4] A second and noisier matter was the government's proposal (July 1835), strongly opposed by the *filopolitas*, to send a legation to Spain in hopes of securing Spanish recognition of Chile's independence. Congress ratified the proposal, with the *filopolita* Diego José Benavente giving it vehement support, apparently in the belief that Portales could be persuaded to head the mission to Spain (which in fact never left) and thus be got out of the way.[5]

The arguments over the Liberal officers and the Spanish mission alarmed Portales, who also was obdurately determined to stop Rengifo's presidential bid – "No, No, No," as he told his Santiago business agent.[6] President

2 No. 11, October 14, 1835.
3 No. 2, September 7, 1835.
4 No. 6, September 9, 1835.
5 Sotomayor Valdés, *Historia*, I, 413–14n.
6 To Antonio Garfias, August 24, 1834. EDP, III, 301.

Prieto was also alarmed. Deeply pious, he was offended by some of the obvious anticlerical attitudes of the *filópolita* group – among other things *El Philopolita* had criticized the influence of "the ferocious Hydra of fanaticism" in education.[7] Tocornal, if anything even more devout than Prieto, worked on the president through his confessor. Prieto soon acted. On September 21, 1835, Portales arrived at the office of the War and Navy ministry even before news of his reappointment as minister reached the public. *El Mercurio*, whose political comments in these years were sparse, hailed his return as "a praiseworthy event," claiming that it would strengthen public order and energize the public administration.[8] Rengifo's presidential dreams melted away. Tocornal succeeded him as Finance minister, and Portales took over as Interior minister (November 9, 1835).

Portales's return meant the defeat of the rather half-hearted challenge of the moderates. It flickered for a while, then faded. With *El Philopolita* soon vanishing, another pro-*filopolita* news-sheet, *El Voto Público*, continued to criticize Tocornal (though not Portales) for a few weeks, and then closed down, regretting that the country had reverted to a "time of servility."[9] There was only the faintest opposition to the reelection of President Prieto, expressed in ephemeral Liberal news-sheets, one of which, *El Barómetro de Chile* (edited by Nicolás Pradel, an unreconstructed *pipiolo*), put forward the name of General José María de la Cruz, a hero of the wars of independence, who was noted, according to Pradel, for "a rational tolerance for all bands and parties."[10] Cruz had briefly been War and Navy minister in 1831, but Portales had forced him out, partly because of his undisguised O'Higginism. Cruz also had made known his dislike of the regime's harsher measures. Another unreconstructed *pipiolo*, Pedro Félix Vicuña, put out two news-sheets in favor of Cruz, *El Republicano*, and the longer-running *Paz Perpetua a los Chilenos,* which coupled its support for Cruz with a general condemnation of the Conservative regime. Vicuña, one of the founders of *El Mercurio*, was the son of Francisco Ramón Vicuña, the last of the Liberal presidents of the 1820s, and had fled with him from Santiago during the Conservative seizure of power, the presidential sash concealed in a hat. In old age, it would be said of Vicuña that, like the Bourbons, he had forgotten nothing and learned nothing.[11] For the next fifteen years, he would be a thorn (mostly a minor one) in the government's side. But none of the mild, barely observable agitation of 1836 had the slightest effect. In July 1836 the electoral colleges gave 143 of their 158 votes to Prieto.

---

7 No. 3, August 19, 1835.
8 MV, No. 2053, September 22, 1835.
9 No. 8, December 5, 1835.
10 *Barómetro de Chile*, No. 24, May 4, 1836.
11 Arteaga Alemparte, *Constituyentes*, p. 285.

Tragedy and Triumph

Three months into President Prieto's second term, Chile went to war. There had been strained relations with Peru for several years: Peru had failed to repay a Chilean loan made at the time of independence, and there had recently been a short tariff war, with Peru imposing a duty on Chilean wheat, Chile retaliating with a double tariff on Peruvian sugar, and Peru penalizing merchandise imported from Valparaiso's bonded warehouses. These irritants were swept aside by an altogether more ominous development. A powerful Bolivian caudillo, General Andrés Santa Cruz, forcibly merged Peru and Bolivia in a new Confederation (October 1836), with himself as Protector. We may doubt whether the Confederation, riven with internal tensions, would have lasted very long. Portales quickly came to see it as a menace to Chile's commercial and political position on the Pacific coast. How far his opinion was shared is impossible to say, but in the Chile of 1836 it was his opinion that counted. At the time of the tariff war, he had speculated whether it might be necessary at some point to take military action against Peru.[12] His determination to act was reinforced by an expedition mounted (July 1836) by the exiled General Ramón Freire, then living in Lima, in hopes of overthrowing the Conservative regime. Freire managed to establish a foothold on the island of Chiloé, but was soon captured.[13] Santa Cruz's apparent complicity in Freire's venture gave Portales the pretext he needed. An attempt by his close collaborator Victorino Garrido to capture Peruvian ships from Callao was checkmated by the Protector's arrest of the Chilean *chargé d'affaires* in Lima. Portales next sent Mariano Egaña to Peru as a plenipotentiary, with a peremptory demand for the immediate dissolution of the Confederation, an ultimatum that Santa Cruz naturally rejected. Egaña issued an immediate declaration of war, duly ratified by Congress (December 24, 1836), and in January 1837 Congress approved a nationwide state of siege for the duration of the war.

Portales's aims were devastatingly simple. In a famous letter to Admiral Manuel Blanco Encalada, he portrayed the war as a stark struggle for power. "The Confederation must disappear for ever from the American stage . . . ,"

---

12 To Antonio Garfias, August 30, 1832. EDP, II. 272.

13 Much to Portales's fury, the death sentence Freire received a few months later was commuted on appeal to banishment. After a few months on Juan Fernández, Freire was taken to Sydney, Australia, arriving there in June 1837. He moved to Tahiti before the end of the year, partly to live more cheaply, partly to be in touch with Chile from the ships that called there. His circumstances were modest. In 1839, he returned to South America, taking up residence in the Bolivian port of Cobija. Fearing complications with Chile, in 1840 the Bolivian government ordered him inland, to Sucre. At the end of 1841, he moved back to Chile under the general amnesty of October that year, and lived quietly in Santiago, playing no part in politics, for the ten years that remained to him.

he wrote. "We must dominate for ever in the Pacific."[14] He also believed that a Chilean victory might well be "an example that would make us stronger in the eyes of the European nations."[15] Politically, however, his war brought great risks to the Conservative regime. "Those who want war are demons," Nicolás Pradel's news-sheet had asserted in August 1836, "and those who want peace are angels."[16] (Portales had Pradel's printing press destroyed and "relegated" him to Juan Fernández.) How many Chileans were demons and how many were angels we cannot say. What is certain is that the unpopularity of the emergency powers and the forcible enlistment of soldiers gave ample opportunity for renewed conspiracies. A serious plot to subvert the Maipó Battalion and to assassinate Portales was uncovered in November 1836; the would-be assassin was shot. The vehement side of Portales's character was now fully on display. In January 1837, he pushed through a drastic measure by which all exiles returning to the country without permission were to be shot within twenty-four hours. Another new law (February 2, 1837) set up "permanent courts-martial" in every province, charged with judging all cases of subversion, with no possibility of appeal. The law was not much used, but its first application claimed one set of victims, in Colchagua Province, whose recently named Intendant was the restless and active Antonio José de Irisarri. Guatemalan by birth, he had played several noteworthy roles in Chile's struggle for independence. A pathetic attempt at organizing armed revolt in Colchagua led to the execution of three Liberals, two of them well-known local hacendados.

There is little doubt that the key figure of the web of conspiracy that now developed was Colonel José Antonio Vidaurre. A known troublemaker in the 1820s, he had fought for the Conservatives at Lircay. His Maipó Battalion was well trained and disciplined. His network of contacts in the Army was extensive. Portales summoned Vidaurre to Santiago in February 1837 to question him personally about rumors that he was conspiring. Vidaurre's elliptical reply is legendary: "Minister, when I make a revolution against you, you will be the first to know."[17] He was true to his word. What followed is one of the classic tragedies of Chilean history, a story often vividly retold.[18] With the projected expeditionary force for Peru assembling around Valparaiso, Portales decided to inspect the Maipó Regiment (as it now was) at its encampment in Quillota. Once there, he was taken prisoner, thrown into irons, and compelled by Vidaurre to accompany the

14 To Blanco Encalada, September 10, 1836. EDP, III, 453–54.
15 To Ventura Lavalle, May 20, 1837. EDP, III, 503–04.
16 *Barómetro de Chile*, No. 41, August 27, 1836.
17 Sotomayor Valdés, *Historia*, II, 370.
18 See Sotomayor Valdés, *Historia*, II, 377–438; Vicuña Mackenna, *Introducción*, pp. 379–451; Hernández P., *Portales*, pp. 126–30.

now mutinous regiment as it advanced on Valparaiso. The port was well defended by soldiers and civic guardsmen led by Vidaurre's own cousin Juan Vidaurre,[19] and the rebels were easily repulsed, but too late to save Portales. In the early hours of June 6, on the Cerro Barón high above Valparaiso, the "omnipotent minister" was taken from his *birlocho* and killed. His lacerated corpse was found by soldiers chasing the fleeing mutineers.

The political impact of the murder seems to have been immense. At sundown on June 6, a somber and silent crowd collected outside the government palace in Santiago's Plaza de Armas, and heard the news from the president's military aide.[20] On June 7 *El Mercurio* printed an "extraordinary" issue that described the event as "a public calamity for Chile," and the newspaper (black-bordered from June 10 to July 4) recorded the "profound sensation" as the news spread throughout the country.[21] Short-lived news-sheets mourned "**DON DIEGO PORTALES**" (printed in very dark type) as "the strongest support of the tranquillity of Chile," as someone who would be remembered as long as there *was* a Chile.[22] General Manuel Bulnes, the army commander at Concepción, who personally disliked Portales, was convinced that the feeling of grief would be universal, and reported that his officers and men had asked his permission to wear mourning.[23]

The impressive ceremonial that surrounded Portales's state funeral was clearly designed to reinforce the legitimacy of the Conservative regime. The elaborate stage-management was tailored for maximum effect.[24] The funeral carriage, accompanied by the irons and the *birlocho* of the minister's final agony, made a slow nine-day journey to Santiago, where the embalmed remains (minus the heart, claimed by Valparaiso) lay in solemn state in the church of La Compañía. Before the body was interred in the Cathedral (to the sound of a requiem mass composed by Portales's musician-protegé José Zapiola) there was an outpouring of eloquence by the young priest Rafael Valentín Valdivieso. Taking his text from the First Book of Maccabees,[25] the future archbishop of Santiago exalted the "inexhaustible resources" of

---

19 Later permitted to add Leal ("Loyal") to his surname.
20 José Victorino Lastarria's essay on Portales (1861) alleged that, on hearing the news, the crowd gave vent to a quiet *"viva!"* of delight and relief. Lastarria implies that he was there, which he could have been. He was stiffly reproved for the assertion at the time the essay appeared. One wonders. The sudden removal of a strong ruler can produce very mixed reactions.
21 MV, No. 2561, June 10, 1837.
22 *Boletín Oficial*, No. 2, June 7, 1837; *Perrero*, No. 1 (black-edged), July 19, 1837. No. 4, September 1, 1837, has a twenty-one-line Latin poem in Portales's honor.
23 Note to War ministry, June 12, 1837: Sotomayor Valdés, *Historia*, II, 436n.
24 For a full account: AR, No. 361, July 21, 1837. See also *Perrero*, No. 1, July 19, 1837.
25 1 Maccabees, 14:35–6: "The people . . . made him their governor and high priest . . . for the justice and faith which he kept to his nation. . . . For in his time things prospered in his hands, so that the heathen were taken out of their country."

Portales's "creative genius," which had given "nerve and respectability to the Government, credit to its promises, morality to the masses, economy and cleanness in the administration of the public finances." He also praised Portales's piety,[26] which must have surprised the dead man's closest friends. Joaquín Tocornal (Interior minister once again) was equally eloquent. Receiving the funeral procession at the western end of the Alameda, and speaking as "the interpreter of an entire nation's feelings," he noted that the "dragon of anarchy" had raised its "insolent head" at Quillota, but "Chilean order" had triumphed "on the Barón heights even as the religion of Jesus Christ triumphed at Golgotha."[27]

The rising poetess Mercedes Marín del Solar asked:

> *Justicia eterna . . .*
>
> *. . . ¿así tornas ilusoria*
> *la esperanza halagueña*
> *que un porvenir a Chile prometía*
> *de poderío, grandeza y gloria?*

> Eternal Justice . . .
>
> . . . Thus do you render illusory
> the rosy hope,
> the future promised to Chile,
> of power, greatness and glory?[28]

Her despair was unjustified. Tocornal was right. The Conservative regime *was* somehow strengthened by the tragedy, almost as if Portales had been its necessary blood-sacrifice. The trauma of June 1837 stiffened the determination of Portales's political heirs (especially perhaps Tocornal) to maintain a stable course. They were given a free hand by Congress, which suspended its sittings soon afterward and did not resume them for nearly two years. Only in June 1839 could President Prieto praise Portales to Congress as "an illustrious minister, a model of fervent patriotism."[29]

The assassination had a second significant effect. As *El Mercurio* pointed out six months later, "the horrendous crime . . . increased the popularity of the war."[30] There was a widespread belief (never substantiated) that Vidaurre's mutiny had been aided and abetted by agents of Santa Cruz.[31]

---

26 Valdivieso, *Oración*, pp. 8, 13.
27 Tocornal, pp. 4–5.
28 "Canto fúnebre a la muerte de don Diego Portales," AR, No. 361, July 28, 1837, often anthologized. Marín del Solar (1804–66) was the first writer of the "national" period whose poems rise (just) above the pedestrian.
29 AR, No. 457, June 3, 1839. Andrés Bello wrote all the annual presidential messages until 1860.
30 MV, No. 2727, January 2, 1838.
31 See MV, No. 2561, June 10, 1837.

The government, for its part, was determined to prosecute Portales's war with due vigor. The first expedition to Peru, an army of twenty-eight hundred under Admiral Manuel Blanco Encalada, was rapidly outmaneuvered by Santa Cruz. In November 1837, he forced Blanco Encalada to sign a pact (the Treaty of Paucarpata) guaranteeing Chilean recognition of the Confederation. The pact was immediately repudiated by the Chilean government. To judge from the sudden flurry of news-sheets and pamphlets that appeared, the Paucarpata treaty aroused rather mixed responses, although with indignation well to the fore. One such publication, *Balas a los traidores* ("Bullets for Traitors"), pinned the blame on Antonio José de Irisarri, who had accompanied the expedition as political adviser. He never returned to Chile. Another publication evoked the ancient Roman practice of exonerating generals who had suffered "involuntary reverses" in appealing for clemency for Blanco Encalada,[32] who was being court-martialed. (He was acquitted by one vote). Other periodicals demanded a speedy resumption of the war, if only as a way of avenging the death of Portales, "the *Chilean Canning*, that great and exalted soul"[33] – not a description Portales himself would have liked; he thought Canning too liberal. But the bellicose spirit was not universal. There were a few dissenting voices. Some proposed the renegotiation of the Paucarpata treaty, warned against military ambition, and scoffed at the idea that Santa Cruz was a threat to Chile.[34]

The government had no intention of temporizing with Santa Cruz. A second, much larger invasion force (fifty-four hundred men) sailed from Valparaiso in July 1838, under the command of General Manuel Bulnes, with General José María de la Cruz as his chief of staff. A small naval squadron took the offensive at sea, winning the only naval battle of the war (Casma, January 12, 1839). Landing in Peru, Bulnes found that the president of the North-Peruvian State (one of the Confederation's three components) had broken with Santa Cruz; to assert his independence, he demanded a Chilean withdrawal. Bulnes ignored the demand and occupied Lima at the cost of some sharp fighting. But with the Peruvian capital's unhealthy climate sapping Chilean strength, he soon undertook a tactical withdrawal to the north, a move interpreted by Chileans back home as meaning imminent victory for Santa Cruz,[35] who, indeed, set out in hot pursuit of the Chilean army. His men attacked it as it crossed

32 *Eco de la Verdad* (1838), reprinted in SCL; XXIV, 491–96.

33 *Eclipse en Paucarpata*, No. 10, June 11, 1838.

34 *Recuerdos de Colocolo*, Nos. 1–2, January 5 and 20, 1838; *Juicio sobre los tratados y opinión sobre la Guerra con el Perú* (December 24, 1837), reprinted in SCL, XXIV, 486–89, and *Ilustración del papel publicado por unos chilenos sobre tratados y guerra con el Perú* (December 30, 1837), reprinted in SCL, XXIV, 489–91.

35 MV, No. 3014, December 31, 1838.

the Buin river (January 6, 1839), but they were beaten off. With the odds turning against him, Bulnes chose to stand his ground. The battle of Yungay (January 20, 1839) was a devastating Chilean victory. Of the nine thousand soldiers on the battlefield, about two thousand were killed. A fatally wounded officer, Captain Justo Urra of the Valparaiso Battalion, had just enough time to write to his wife that "this glory obtained for our Chile" was balsam enough for "a wound that appears to be mortal."[36]

When the news of the victory reached Santiago one month later, President Prieto threw the government palace open for a public celebration. Hilarión Moreno, the Argentine actor-manager running Santiago's main theater company, improvised a suitable triumphal chorus (with music by José Zapiola) that insisted only a Virgil could do justice to Chile's feats of arms.[37] A few weeks later President Prieto presided over further celebrations in Valparaiso, culminating in an all-night *soirée*. In Copiapó the festivities went on from 8:30 P.M. to sunrise, and were enhanced by a patriotic march composed by a certain Dr. Rafael Valdez. Less exalted towns also celebrated. Quillota's jamboree lasted for ten days and included fireworks and a grand public banquet-ball.[38]

The rejoicing was justified. With Santa Cruz's defeat, the Peru-Bolivian Confederation disintegrated. As Portales had wished, Chile's international prestige was also enhanced. The European powers had not viewed Chile's attack on the Confederation with sympathy, and their representatives were obstructive to Bulnes while he was in Lima. The conflicting views of the British envoys in Chile (strongly pro-Chilean) and Peru (strongly pro-Santa Cruz) caused British foreign secretary Lord Palmerston to comment wryly that the Pacific did not really deserve its name. The British certainly contemplated some kind of intervention.[39] Joaquín Tocornal, annoyed by British (and French) partiality for the Confederation, even urged the United States to "take the head of an American league" against European pretensions.[40] All European criticism of Chile ceased after Yungay. In Paris, King Louis-Philippe personally congratulated the Chilean *chargé d'affaires*.

Did victory in this war help to boost the growing sense of Chilean nationhood? This is often alleged, even in school textbooks, but not quite as easy to document as we might wish. If it did, the process was a mixture of

---

36 Letter printed in MV, No. 3077, March 15, 1839.
37 Pereira Salas, *Teatro*, p. 197. Poem printed in MV, No. 3090, April 3, 1839.
38 MV, No. 3114, May 2, 1839; No. 3089, April 2, 1839; No. 3095, April 9, 1839.
39 See Ramírez Necochea, "El gobierno."
40 Richard Pollard (U.S. Minister to Chile) to John Forsyth (Secretary of State), April 10, 1839. Manning, p. 169.

the official and the spontaneous. The government subsidized a twenty-page epic poem by a provincial judge, pedestrian and uninspiring.

> *¡¡¡Victoria una y mil veces*
> *A los héroes chilenos,*
> *Que impertérritos, firmes y serenos,*
> *Han destruido el tirano en pocos meses!!!*

> Victory a thousand and one times
> To the Chilean heroes,
> Who, dauntless, firm, serene,
> Have destroyed the tyrant in a few months![41]

The poem sank without trace. By contrast, one of the most enduringly popular of Chilean songs was written to honor Bulnes's victory, and with no official encouragement.

> *Cantemos la gloria*
> *del triunfo marcial*
> *que el pueblo chileno*
> *obtuvo en Yungay.*

> Let us sing of the glory
> of the martial triumph
> the Chilean people
> obtained at Yungay.

The words were by Ramón Rengifo (brother of Manuel), the music once again supplied by José Zapiola. The song was an instant hit. It had to be repeated constantly at President Prieto's celebrations both in Santiago and Valparaiso. (It was the first music ever to be printed in Chile.)[42] Two of the "popular" heroes of the war – Ensign Juan Felipe Colipí (the hero of the battle of Buin and the son of one of the friendly caciques of Araucania) and the diminutive Candelaria Pérez, "Sergeant Candelaria," who fought bravely at Yungay – seem to have remained alive for a while in the folk memory, through ballads and puppet shows.[43] The great victory parade held in Santiago (December 1839), like Portales's funeral, was stage-managed to secure maximum public impact, with Santiago bedecked in flags, military bands playing all day (with interminable repetitions of the Zapiola-Rengifo song), triumphal arches on the Alameda showering flowers on Bulnes. It was easily the most spectacular celebration of its kind since independence. As an American eyewitness

41 Torres, *Canto*, p. 18. Andrés Bello also honored Bulnes with a (rather lackluster) poem.
42 MV, No. 3114, May 2, 1839; Pereira Salas, *Biobibliografía*, pp. 9–10.
43 Barros Arana, *Decenio*, I, 55.

reported, "The uncovered heads, the handkerchiefs in the air, the unanimous exclamations, the general hubbub – all this left no doubt that
the triumphs won by the hero of Yungay had profoundly impressed the
country."[44]

Both the government (in a further contribution to the "invention of
tradition") and the press made some effort to incorporate the 1836–9 war
into the general pattern of patriotic sentiment. The name Yungay was given
to a new district then being developed to the west of downtown Santiago,
although a monument to the battle decreed at the same time never got
built. *El Mercurio* hoped that the anniversary of Yungay would become one
of "the national festivities of Chile," and for many years it did. In 1840,
the newspaper called the battle "one of the greatest events in the history of
South America," and deplored the relative lack of celebration the following
year. Another newspaper, eleven years later, insisted that the anniversary was
one of the "days that do not die, that must never die for a nation."[45] Miguel
de la Barra's short historical essay on the 1836–9 war (1851) included a
hymn in honor of Yungay.

> *Cantemos al Señor de las alturas,*
> *Ensalzemos su gloria;*
> *Porque somos su Pueblo y sus criaturas;*
> *Porque nos dió este día la victoria*
> *Y la paz bienhechora.*

> Let us sing to God in the highest,
> Let us extol his glory;
> Because we are his People and his creatures,
> Because he gave us glory on this day,
> And beneficent peace.[46]

De la Barra mentions neither Ensign Colipí nor Sergeant Candelaria. Colipí
had died before the victory parade, but Candelaria Pérez (on horseback,
near Bulnes) won much acclaim there. She soon lapsed into obscurity
and poverty. In 1849, attending a lavishly produced play about Yungay,
she received frantic applause from a Santiago theater audience. In 1857,
the young Vicente Reyes tracked her down and wrote an article about
her, proposing she should be given a special life pension by the government. She never was; and the government seems not to have included

---

44 Causten, pp. 47–48. The parade is beautifully evoked in the opening section of Alberto Blest Gana's
   novel *El loco estero* (1909).
45 MV, No. 3113, April 30, 1839; No. 3328, January 28, 1840; No. 3682, March 18, 1841. *Civilización*,
   No. 105, January 20, 1852.
46 De la Barra, *Reseña*, p. 25.

her in a gratification awarded in 1861 to survivors of the Peru-Bolivian campaign.[47]

Commemoration of the war was never unanimously supported. During the 1847 congressional sessions, the Chamber of Deputies drafted a comment on a government proposal to mediate in a dispute between Bolivia and Peru. It included the phrase: "Ours were the actions that pulverized the Peru-Bolivian colossus." Deputy Antonio Varas found the words offensive to Chile's neighbors. Deputy Pedro Francisco Lira thought it perfectly appropriate to "remember the country's glorious events." But the Chamber agreed with Varas and suppressed the phrase by a vote of 30 to 5.[48] Doubts were sometimes expressed about the annual Yungay commemoration, which, according to a magazine of 1851, simply aroused hatred against Peruvians and Bolivians[49] – although it had become an undeniably popular celebration, to the point that in 1847 the *Revista Católica* felt obliged to denounce the drunkenness and prostitution that surrounded it.[50] In February 1851, an article in *El Progreso* (then antigovernment) suggested that it would be far better to commemorate the battle of Chacabuco on February 12 (the celebration of the anniversary had lapsed in the late 1830s), since Yungay "was a victory won over brothers, and which served to enthrone *peluconismo* with its caudillo Bulnes."[51]

Political Relaxation and the Presidential Succession

El Progreso's retrospective comment was accurate. The battle of Yungay gave Bulnes the presidency. The victory induced a mood of relaxation all round. The emergency powers of 1837 and the "law of permanent courts-martial" were soon rescinded. Between October 1838 and February 1840, Tocornal having fallen sick, the Interior ministry was occupied by the young Ramón Luis Irarrázaval, a personable lawyer of the moderate *pelucón* tendency, which seems to have encouraged the general tranquillity. The only threat to public order during these months was a strictly nonpolitical riot in Santiago in September 1839, sparked by popular indignation when a visiting balloonist failed to make his advertised ascent.[52]

47 "La Sarjenta Candelaria," *Semana*, No. 4, June 11, 1859; M(S), No. 10,148, June 22, 1861. President Prieto promoted her to second lieutenant in 1840, and she received a military pension, though when she put in for an increase, she had to wait four years for an answer. She died in March 1870. See L. Ignacio Silva A., *La Sargento Candelaria Pérez* (1904).
48 CN/D, June 21, 25, and 30, 1847.
49 *Album*, No. 4, January 25, 1851.
50 RCAT, No. 112, January 13, 1847.
51 PR, No. 2517, February 12, 1851.
52 *El Mercurio* in 1842 reported the balloonist as French: MV, No. 4044, March 30, 1842; Diego Barros Arana, sixty years later, remembered him as American: *Decenio*, I, 82–83n.

Meanwhile, in the freer atmosphere that followed the war, and with congressional elections due in March 1840, the diminutive Liberal opposition began to stir. Its propaganda tended at first to be oblique or satirical. Juan Nicolás Álvarez's caustic news-sheet *El Diablo Político* (1839–40), for instance, purported to convey the Devil's "advice" to the government – its title, riposted a Conservative publication, "suits perfectly the doctrines it pours out,"[53] and even the usually temperate *El Mercurio* denounced the *"revolutionary opinions"* put out by such publications.[54] The former *filopolita* Diego José Benavente, whose feelings were badly ruffled by the fact that he had been arrested in July 1837 for alleged complicity in the Vidaurre mutiny, published a series of *Cartas Patriotas* (1839–40), with more open attacks on the government. Both Álvarez and Benavente took potshots at Portales's memory, though not usually naming him, and blamed him for the recent war – a dangerous tactic, in view of the war's popularity.

In February 1840, a handful of Liberals formed a Patriotic Society to work for opposition candidates in the upcoming elections, and issued a four-page pamphlet rehearsing many of the standard Liberal grievances – the illegality of the regime, the "null, abject and servile character" of Congress, the farce of elections, and so on – while expressing the hope that the new Society would "raise the public spirit from the prostration in which it finds itself" by electing a few Liberal deputies.[55] These statements were sufficient to bring swift condemnation from a Conservative news-sheet, *La Antorcha*, which described the Liberals' confabulations as "an anarchic meeting of revolutionaries who ... propose to take advantage of ... the elections to produce an upheaval in the nation."[56] Similar criticisms were voiced by another news-sheet, *El Conservador*, and were fiercely rebutted by a Liberal periodical, which denied strongly that the Patriotic Society was in any way subversive.[57] Meanwhile, the government's patience with Álvarez and *El Diablo Político* finally wore out, and it prosecuted him under the press law. He was fined a modest 200 pesos (both *La Antorcha* and *El Conservador* criticized the mildness of the sentence),[58] and an excited crowd staged a demonstration in the streets, complete with stone-throwing. Later that day a former army officer appeared, half drunk, in General Bulnes's house and claimed that a number of well-known politicians had paid him to assassinate the general. The plot was a fiction dreamed up in a tavern, but

53 *Época*, No. 5, October 5, 1839.
54 MV, No. 3252, October 17, 1839.
55 *Noticia de una reunión*.
56 No. 8, January 29, 1840.
57 *Día y el Golpe*, No. 34, March 10, 1840.
58 *Antorcha*, No. 11, March 5, 1840; *Conservador*, No. 4, February 25, 1840.

it was sufficient, on top of the day's near-riot, for the government to decree a state of siege for Santiago Province. The conspiracy was soon shown up for what it was, and the supposed conspirators were eventually absolved, though not before Diego José Benavente, wildly accused of complicity, had spent two more months in jail.[59]

The congressional elections of March 1840 were the first since the start of the Conservative regime to be contested even feebly by the Liberals. They elected nine deputies. Not surprisingly, Liberal ideas of reform were ventilated in the ensuing congressional sittings. Liberal deputy Melchor de Santiago Concha (a survivor from the 1820s) proposed limitations on the emergency powers and, supported by Joaquín Campino (another *pipiolo* of 1820s vintage) strongly opposed the greater restrictions on the press then being advocated by Mariano Egaña, Justice minister since 1837. Liberal opposition to Egaña's proposed new press law was sufficiently fierce for the government to keep the existing Liberal law (1828) on the statute book. Heartened by this, the opposition stepped up its minor propaganda offensive. The Liberal Bernardo José de Toro (one of the sponsors of the Patriotic Society), writing ostensibly as a recently arrived "Pole," denounced the "farce" of the February assassination plot.[60] Another ephemeral news-sheet openly lamented the "fatal period of don Joaquín Prieto, the Egañas and Tocornals" (but, interestingly, not Portales) and described the president as "unqualified to govern the most miserable village," also claiming that Egaña's proposed press law was symptomatic of "the hatred the Government professes for the free circulation of thought."[61] The mediocre poet whose epic on the 1836–9 war had been subsidized by the government repaid this generosity with a personal attack on Mariano Egaña, once again in deplorable verse, alluding directly to his "enormous PAUNCH,"[62] which was real enough. There was even a parody of the popular Hymn of Yungay.

> *Lloremos los males*
> *Del triunfo fatal*
> *Que con mil desgracias*
> *Se adquirió en Yungay.*

> Let us weep for the ills
> Of the fatal triumph
> Which with a thousand misfortunes
> Was gained at Yungay.[63]

59 Barros Arana, *Decenio*, I, 91–98.
60 *Cartas de un Polaco*, No. 2, August 24, 1840.
61 *Censor Imparcial*, No. 1, July 10, 1840; No. 4, August 19, 1840.
62 *Nuevo Maquiavelo*, No. 3, June 30, 1840.
63 *Moción*, No. 3, August 13, 1840.

By now, however, all eyes were turning toward the presidential election. Joaquín Tocornal's yeoman service to the Conservative regime gave him a strong claim on the presidency, and he wanted it. But President Prieto had decided that his nephew, General Bulnes, the "invincible hero" of Rengifo's song-lyric, would be a better choice, that an aura of military glory would strengthen the Conservative system. Bulnes's laurels at Yungay merely added to those he had won in the wars of independence, and in his successful defeat (1832) of Chile's most notorious bandit chiefs, José Antonio and Pablo Pincheira. In July 1840, to undercut the groundswell of support for Tocornal among Conservatives, the president named the thirty-one-year-old Manuel Montt, former Rector of the Instituto Nacional, as Interior minister. He was strongly supported by *El Mercurio*, but the Tocornal camp soon ungraciously described him as "conceited by his pride in so rapid a promotion."[64] Another news-sheet, Liberal in tone, declared that, unlike Tocornal, Montt was at least a man of the nineteenth century, and that it was odd, therefore, that he did not seem to believe in electoral freedom.[65] But Montt knew the job he had to do, and did it.

The Liberals' ideal candidate would have been General Ramón Freire, whose government (1823–7) they remembered affectionately, but Freire was still in exile. After the usual discussions common among Liberals, with Pedro Félix Vicuña in good voice, their choice settled on Francisco Antonio Pinto, the Liberal president between 1827 and 1829, although some held it against him that he had withdrawn too quickly from politics when realizing the inevitability of the Conservative takeover. Neither Tocornal nor Pinto could expect to win against the government machine, but for the government the situation was altogether more fluid than was desirable. With Tocornal standing in as Vice-President (i.e., acting president), Prieto took leave from the presidency for five months (February–July 1840), ostensibly on the grounds of poor health, but in reality to foster support for Bulnes, who was not popular among Liberals, nor (obviously) among Tocornal's substantial *pelucón* following. The pious Tocornal also enjoyed fervent support from the clergy. Interior minister Manuel Montt worked hard to ensure the loyalty of the public administration. In December 1840, he took on the additional War and Navy portfolio. By coincidence, the government revealed the discovery of a couple of subversive plots, neither of which amounted to anything. Montt's use of the scare tactics that were one of his later trademarks thus began with a whimper, not a bang.

Despite Montt's efforts, there was no question of Bulnes's candidacy being unopposed. The most ferocious opposition came less from the Liberals than from the *tocornalistas*, in a new and aggressive news-sheet, *La Guerra*

64 *Porvenir*, No. 2, May 14, 1841.
65 *Tribuno*, No. 1, March 5, 1841.

a la Tiranía, partly written by a stubborn *pipiolo*, Colonel Pedro Godoy, who had returned from exile in Argentina to serve in the 1836–9 war, and partly by José Joaquín Vallejo, making his first (but by no means last) appearance in print. Godoy was well known in Santiago for his pungent sarcasms. Godoy and Vallejo spared nobody in their satirical attacks, some of which were ostensibly reports from "Turkey." The corpulent (and anglophile) Mariano Egaña was memorably dubbed "Lord Callampa" ("Lord Mushroom"). Both Prieto and Bulnes were given offensive nicknames implying that they were idiotic or drunk or both. In one issue, "Abraham Asnul" ("Abraham Donkeyoh"), that is, Prieto, signs a treaty leaving his empire to "Bulke Borrachei" ("Bulky Drunky"), that is, Bulnes. Article 13 promises Bulnes "the right to eat ham and drink wine every day of the year" – except on the Islamic holiday, which the authors apparently believed was Saturday.[66] Bulnes was furious, and confronted Tocornal in his office. Tocornal brushed off his accusations. Colonel Godoy, refusing a trumped-up order to go to Valdivia, was retired from the Army. A 600-peso fine failed to deter *La Guerra a la Tiranía*. Interior minister Montt decided to respond in kind, sponsoring a news-sheet, *El Nacional*, to promote Bulnes's cause, and enlisting some talented collaborators, one of them a recently arrived Argentine exile, Domingo Faustino Sarmiento.

At the end of March 1841, Tocornal (still Finance minister) and Justice minister Mariano Egaña both left the cabinet. Montt moved to Justice; and a new minister of the Interior, José Miguel Irarrázaval, took over, though he was replaced two months later by his amiable brother Ramón Luis. The main danger the new cabinet perceived was a possible alliance between the *tocornalistas* and the Liberals. Such an alliance was certainly talked about. Whether serious negotiations took place is not clear. The cabinet asked ex–Finance minister Manuel Rengifo to make overtures to the Liberal leadership, such as it was. On May 21, 1840, at a meeting attended by sixty people (including Montt and Irarrázaval on the government side), the Liberals accepted a deal. Both sides agreed to support either Bulnes or Pinto, whoever won. The government promised an orderly election and, should Bulnes win, a general amnesty.[67] "What a triumph, what glory have we gathered today!" remarked Admiral Blanco Encalada to Pedro Félix Vicuña as they left the meeting. Vicuña did not share the sentiment,[68] but he was in a minority. A happy coincidence – Bulnes's betrothal to Pinto's elder daughter, Enriqueta – set the seal on this gentlemanly agreement. Vicuña assumed that this was part of the deal,[69] but in fact it was

66 *Guerra a la Tiranía*, No. 27, April 6, 1841.
67 Barros Arana, *Decenio*, I, 177–80.
68 Vicuña, *Vindicación*, pp. 8–9.
69 Vicuña, *Vindicación*, p. 5.

a love-match. Andrés Bello was commissioned to make the proposal on Bulnes's behalf.[70]

All three groups – pro-Bulnes Conservatives, pro-Tocornal Conservatives, and pro-Pinto Liberals – did what they could to mobilize public opinion. This is the first opportunity we have had in the Conservative period to examine a reasonable spread of competitive electoral propaganda. A scrutiny of this propaganda, perhaps disappointingly, shows that it is based much less on broad philosophical principles than on simple tactical arguments, perhaps because the three-cornered contest (with two *de facto* oppositions) somewhat obfuscated the issues. *El Nacional*, among a dozen or so news-sheets, continued to press Bulnes's claim. *El Mercurio* lent strong support to Bulnes, publishing numerous editorials in his favor in April–May 1841. Several news-sheets were aimed (in a way that would be familiar from now on) at the artisan audience. "The loyal heart of the poor man and the artisan," declared one of them, knew that Bulnes was "the ONLY PERSON" for the presidency.[71] *La Justicia*, another such news-sheet, adopted a rather strikingly egalitarian language, favoring Bulnes on the grounds that, as a military man, "he frequently eats and sleeps with his soldiers . . . [and] this rubbing alongside his inferiors makes him frank, liberal and inclined to embrace the dogma of equality."[72] Bulnes, it hardly needs pointing out, was no more ready to embrace the dogma of equality than, say, King Louis XVIII of France. A Liberal broadside called Pinto a "philosopher-candidate,"[73] which to some extent he was, and a news-sheet, *El Miliciano*, expressed its support for him in verse: *"Pinto ilustre, el destino te llama / A salvar nuestra esclava nación."* ("Illustrious Pinto, destiny calls you / To save our enslaved nation.")[74] *El Miliciano* also instructed civic guardsmen in the exercise of their constitutional rights, which provoked *El Mercurio* to exclaim in horror: "We could almost believe that there are Chartists here, as in England, who ask, with arms in their hands, for *freedom in elections*, universal suffrage."[75] As for Tocornal, the Liberals accused him of "all the old colonial ideas,"[76] and reminded the civic guardsmen that "in his administration everything was disastrous for the Nation."[77] Tocornal's propaganda, not surprisingly, attributed all of Chile's recent progress to

70 Alb. Edwards, *Páginas*, p. 147. For the circumstances of their first meeting, as recounted by Bulnes, see Domeyko, *Mis viajes*, I, 511–12.

71 *Artesano*, No. 2, June 19, 1841.

72 *Justicia*, No. 2, February 27, 1841.

73 *Verdadero miliciano*, June 25, 1841.

74 *Miliciano*, No. 17, June 25, 1841.

75 MV, No. 3767, June 19, 1841. The Chartists were unarmed, except at the Newport demonstration of November 1839.

76 *Voto Liberal*, No. 1, May 20, 1841.

77 *A los cívicos de Santiago* (handbill), June 25, 1851.

himself, never mentioning Portales.[78] Both Liberals and *tocornalistas* turned their fire on Bulnes, questioning whether Chile should become "the patrimony of a single family," snidely suggesting that his victories were due to luck, and insinuating that the "despotism of a military caudillo" lay ahead.[79] There was nothing much more profound than this in the electoral propaganda of 1841.

The elections for the electoral colleges (June 1841) took place in a generally calm atmosphere. The Conservative machinery of intervention was by now getting well into its stride. Nicolás Pradel reported to a kinsman that the government spent around 20,000 pesos for vote buying in Santiago alone, and that he had heard of voting tables where

A *tocornalista* or a Liberal approached the table with his *calificación*, and the president of the table rejected him, saying: "You have voted already." At this point all sorts of disputes and inquiries began, and the president ended [them] by saying: "I am not under any obligation to inquire which person has voted by usurping your name."[80]

In two or three districts, notably Purutún (near Quillota), where the strongly Liberal Vicuña family had its estates and was defeated (despite mobilizing its inquilinos), there were minor disturbances. In La Serena, the pro-Bulnes intendant, Juan Melgarejo, prevented the Liberals in charge of the voting tables from depositing the urns at municipal headquarters at the end of the first day's voting, and stopped the second day's voting altogether. The matter was eventually resolved, tactfully, by the supreme court.[81] None of this made any difference to the result. Bulnes won 154 electoral votes, Pinto nine and Tocornal none. Of the votes cast for the electors in Santiago, Bulnes took nearly two thirds, and Pinto got more than Tocornal.[82]

Immediately after the vote, the Santiago Liberals sent a delegation to congratulate Bulnes, and Bulnes led a group of Conservatives to pay a courtesy call on Pinto. This harmonious atmosphere was mildly disturbed when news of the goings-on at Quillota and La Serena reached Santiago. Some Liberals and *tocornalistas* hoped that a movement of public opinion might compel the electoral colleges to select someone else as president.[83] This was a pipe dream. Four days before the newly married Bulnes's inauguration, Manuel Rengifo, who had been invited to rejoin the cabinet, expressed the hope that the new government would "attract those who were enemies

78 See *Infante de la Patria*, No. 3, June 24, 1841.
79 *Infante de la Patria*, No. 3, June 24, 1841; *Porvenir, passim*.
80 Nicolás Pradel to Bernardino Pradel, July 7, 1841. RCHG, No. 12 (1913), pp. 196–97.
81 Barros Arana, *Decenio*, I, 190–92.
82 Bulnes, 2349; Pinto, 886; Tocornal, 614. *Artesano*, No. 6, June 28, 1841.
83 Nicolás Pradel to Bernardino Pradel, July 7, 1841. RCHG, No. 12 (1913), pp. 198–200.

of the administration now expiring." This "conciliatory system" might be interpreted, thought Rengifo, as a "tacit condemnation" of the Conservative regime, but there was an essential difference between 1830 and 1841. In 1830, "there still remained a multitude of adventurers who belonged to the revolutionary generation." The new government would be ruling "a country which has now acquired habits of order."[84] Rengifo spoke too soon, but in September 1841 he certainly spoke for many.

The Irarrázaval Cabinet

Bulnes's inauguration on September 18, 1841 (marked by one of the great Andrés Bello's better poems), was swiftly followed by the promised general amnesty. As he told Congress, he saw it as his "special mission to wipe out the last traces of our past dissensions."[85] The moderate *pelucón* Ramón Luis Irarrázaval stayed on as Interior minister in Bulnes's first cabinet, with the equally moderate Manuel Rengifo back at Finance, and Manuel Montt, the solitary authoritarian, who continued at Justice (as a very active minister). The new president himself was bluff but always courteous. A man of imposing presence, he was known for a healthy appetite. Santos Tornero, the owner of *El Mercurio*, watched him dine one evening at the inn at Curacaví, the halfway point on the Santiago–Valparaiso road, and saw him gobble down nine or ten bread rolls along with his chicken stew (*cazuela*), which he also wolfed down.[86] His occasional nickname, "*panzón*" ("big paunch"), was accurate. Politically, he was sometimes indecisive, but he could be stubborn when he felt he needed to be. His deliberately conciliatory approach and the relaxed, tolerant attitudes of the Irarrázaval cabinet yielded very good political results. Over the next few years, Liberalism as a political force came within measurable distance of being killed by kindness. Unreconstructed *pipiolos* such as Pedro Félix Vicuña and Colonel Pedro Godoy may have remained obdurately hostile to Bulnes, but many Liberals, including Bulnes's new father-in-law, ex-president Pinto, were fully reconciled to the regime. Juan Nicolás Álvarez, the former editor of *El Diablo Político*, did his best to keep old passions alive with a news-sheet, *El Demócrata*, in which he retrospectively excoriated the Prieto government. He also took on *El Mercurio*, which mildly reproached him: "it is honorable to be called champions of tyranny when the tyranny is a government like the one Chile has today."[87] The government

---

84 Manuel Rengifo to Bulnes, September 14, 1841. RCHG, No. 12 (1913), pp. 201–05.
85 Message to Congress, October 13, 1841. SCL, XXIX, 373. For the amnesty and subsequent additional conciliatory legislation, see Loveman and Lira, pp. 150–53.
86 Tornero, p. 192.
87 MV, No. 4367, February 24, 1842.

did not even bother to prosecute Álvarez. *El Demócrata* disappeared after nine issues.

The Chile of the early 1840s seemed to breathe an atmosphere of expansiveness and optimism, and to be entering what *El Mercurio* called "a new and essentially liberal era of circumspect progress and beneficent civilization."[88] In November 1842, Santiago at last got its first daily newspaper, *El Progreso*, heavily subsidized by the government. The planting of a settlement on the Magellan Strait (September 1843), hailed by an ephemeral English-language newspaper as another sign of "the forward march of civilization,"[89] enthused many educated Chileans, as did the ceremonious inauguration (that same month) of the new University of Chile. The congressional elections of 1843 (with very few districts contested) reflected the new mood of calm. The French minister in Santiago, reprimanded by his superiors in Paris for not sending sufficient political reports, riposted that there was nothing to report; and Interior minister Irarrázaval, summing up Bulnes's first two years, complimented his fellow citizens on "the evidence given every day of our love of institutions and profound respect for public morality."[90]

Yet, below the calm surface of political life, other kinds of life were stirring. In the settled conditions now apparently prevailing, there was space for new cultural pursuits. These were partly stimulated by the arrival of Argentine intellectuals fleeing from the ruthless "federalist" dictatorship of Juan Manuel de Rosas. Among them were Sarmiento (as already mentioned) and Vicente Fidel López. Sarmiento's vigorous journalism quickly won attention. Both López and a peripatetic Colombian man of letters, Juan García del Río, published ephemeral literary magazines in 1842. Coinciding with these efforts was the formation of a Literary Society by students at the Instituto Nacional.[91] One of the Instituto's professors, José Victorino Lastarria, was invited (or invited himself?) to direct the new society, and opened it with a long address that advocated French romanticism as the best model for would-be Chilean writers. The establishment (July 1842) of a Chilean literary magazine, *El Semanario de Santiago*, gave them an outlet. Enjoying the support of Andrés Bello, its moving spirits included Lastarria and the moderate *pelucones* Manuel Antonio Tocornal (Joaquín's son) and Antonio García Reyes, as well as Salvador Sanfuentes, a man of increasingly Liberal sympathies and the best poet of his generation. All four men were exact contemporaries, born in 1817. The slightly older José Joaquín Vallejo (veteran of *La Guerra a la Tiranía*), who had recently begun publishing his charming sketches of Chilean life in *El Mercurio*, was another collaborator.

88 MV, No. 3957, January 1, 1842.
89 *Valparaiso English Mercury*, No. 3, December 30, 1843.
90 J. Edwards, "Decenio," p. 10; *Memoria* of Interior minister (1843). DP, II, 112.
91 For its eighty-odd sessions, see "Sociedad Literaria."

The strictly literary implications of the so-called Movement of 1842 do not concern us here, although the atmosphere of the minor cultural revival was, if not Liberal, certainly liberal. Neither *El Semanario* nor its successor-magazine *El Crepúsculo* (1843–4) had a definite political agenda. *El Crepúsculo* nonetheless played its part in the first minor tempest of Bulnes's presidency, by publishing (June 1844) "Sociabilidad chilena," a long essay by Francisco Bilbao, a popular young law student at the Instituto Nacional. Bilbao had made himself conspicuous a month earlier, at the funeral of the veteran patriot José Miguel Infante – the keynote speaker at the historic *cabildo abierto* of September 18, 1810; the prime mover of the abolition of slavery (1823) – by declaiming a farewell to him at the cemetery gates. As a politician, Infante had been sublimely irrelevant for many years, but his unrepentantly independent attitudes touched a chord with Bilbao's generation. Bilbao and several fellow students defied an instruction from the Instituto not to march with the funeral cortège.

Modern readers of "Sociabilidad chilena" might well feel puzzled by the furor it aroused. Bilbao's well-known essay is high-flown, with touches of lyricism, and is even semi-mystical in places. But no reader of the purple prose could fail to see that he was attacking the "medieval" Spanish colonial legacy, the Conservative regime and the Catholic Church. The recently founded *Revista Católica*, organ of the hierarchy, raised an immediate hue and cry, attacking Bilbao through no less than thirteen issues.[92] The secular press quickly took up the hue and cry. "How to explain such monstrous aberrations?" asked a contributor to *El Progreso*. Another longed for "the wise pen of a Fénélon, a Chateaubriand or a Bossuet" to refute the impudent youngster.[93] *El Mercurio* (over several issues) blamed the essay on "petty literary vanities" and on "romanticism," the vogue word of the moment.[94] A Catholic-inspired magazine indulged in some ponderous satire at Bilbao's expense. The best way to be a really famous author, wrote the would-be satirist, was to take "Luther and Calvin as . . . tutelary angels," to become a "disciple of Voltaire and Rousseau," and to "blaspheme and use latinate words, or gallicisms or anglicisms from the truly brilliant jargon of our enlightened century."[95]

Bilbao was prosecuted and condemned as "blasphemous" and "immoral" (although not "seditious," the other charge). "You want me to kneel," he told his accusers in court (it is a good example of his style), "so that Galileo can offer me his hand to raise me up. Thank you, Mr. Prosecutor." *El Progreso*

---

92 RCAT, Nos. 31–45, July 1–November 1, 1844. For an analysis of Bilbao's essay, see Varona, pp. 175–84.

93 PR, No. 503, June 25, 1844; No. 506, June 28, 1844.

94 MV, Nos. 4841, 4843–4844, June 27 and 29–30, 1844.

95 *Juguetillo*, No. 4, June 10, 1844.

congratulated the prosecutor, the caustic, hard-line *pelucón* Máximo Mujica, on his "noble patriotism and decisiveness."[96] Bilbao's fine (1,200 pesos) was immediately paid by his friends, who assembled (with several hundred others) outside the courtroom to stage an impromptu demonstration. "I never believed there could be such enthusiasm," reported *El Mercurio*'s Santiago correspondent.[97] The offending issues of *El Crepúsculo* were rounded up and burned, in private – the government wanted no more demonstrations. Bilbao himself was expelled from the Instituto Nacional, and four months later left for a lengthy stay in France. Despite a few further fulminations from the church, the brouhaha soon faded.

The Montt Cabinet and the 1846 Elections

In September 1844, soon after the Bilbao commotion, President Bulnes took a leave from the presidency on the grounds (genuine) of ill health. Irarrázaval stood in as vice president, placing Manuel Montt in charge of the Interior ministry. Manuel Rengifo having lately died, the Finance ministry was taken by José Joaquín Pérez. The moderate Irarrázaval and the authoritarian Montt had never found it entirely easy to work together. But Irarrázaval, like Bulnes, needed a rest, and when Bulnes resumed the presidency six months later (March 1845), he agreed to lead a delegation to Rome in pursuit (vain, as it turned out) of a concordat between Chile and the Papacy. Montt retained the Interior ministry, bringing his closest friend (and protegé), the twenty-eight-year-old Antonio Varas into the cabinet as Justice minister. Irarrázaval had been respected by Liberals, but they were suspicious of Montt. A Liberal newspaper suggested that Varas's appointment was part of Montt's underlying design "to renew the absolute domination . . . of Portales."[98]

Such comments spelled trouble. The Bilbao episode had shown that there was a reserve of general if diffuse liberalism among the educated youth of the upper class – the generation born in the years to either side of 1830. The names of some its most conspicuous figures will figure in this narrative before long. At the senior end of the generation were the future Liberal presidents Federico Errázuriz and Domingo Santa María (both born in 1825), followed by the brothers Manuel Antonio and Guillermo Matta (1826 and 1829), Angel Custodio and Pedro León Gallo (1827 and 1830), and Miguel Luis and Gregorio Amunátegui (1828 and 1830). The year 1830 saw the birth of a cluster of future intellectuals: the historians Diego Barros Arana and Ramón Sotomayor Valdés, the publicist Ambrosio Montt,

96 *Crepúsculo*, Tomo 2, No. 3, July 1, 1844; PR, No. 503, June 25, 1844.
97 MV, No. 4835, June 21, 1844.
98 *Gaceta del Comercio*, No. 1010, May 10, 1845.

and the novelist Alberto Blest Gana. The tail end of this extraordinary generation included Pedro Félix Vicuña's remarkable son Benjamín Vicuña Mackenna (1831), Marcial Martínez (1833), Isidoro Errázuriz (1835), and Vicente Reyes (1835). Not all of these men would become partisan Liberals, but all without exception can be described as liberal. They had no memories of the fragile political experiments of the 1820s, and had never known a world not dominated by the Conservatives. It was a world against which the naturally rebellious feelings of youth were bound to react, or at least had to be defined.

Most of this generation was still too young to play a part in the politics of 1845–6. For the Montt cabinet, the situation was made somewhat more fraught by the closeness of the next congressional and presidential elections, which would both (for once) fall in the same year. Two newspapers, the pro-Irarrázaval, anti-Montt *El Siglo* in Santiago, and the Liberal *Gaceta del Comercio* in Valparaiso, were already trying to rally opposition, as were more ephemeral news-sheets such as *El Republicano*, one of many such publications by Pedro Félix Vicuña, who was eager to reenter the fray. In many ways Vicuña typified the opposition of the mid-1840s, which was less a full-scale Liberal movement than a stubborn effort by a handful of unreconstructed *pipiolos* to make things difficult for a regime they still regarded as illegitimate. Colonel Pedro Godoy, who fully shared this aim, had contributed some impassioned antigovernment articles to *El Siglo* before it ceased publication in mid-1845. Godoy next went on (July 1845) to found a new *Diario de Santiago*, in which he caustically attacked not merely the regime in general but Montt in particular, as well as many leading figures known for their support of the government – Sarmiento, Andrés Bello, Portales's old henchman Victorino Garrido, and so on.

A slander on the Municipality of Santiago (alleging that councilmen had diverted money for police wages into their own pockets) brought Godoy a prosecution under the press law. He organized broadsides and posters summoning his supporters to the scene of the hearing (September 12–13, 1845). A crowd collected, broke through the police, and invaded the courtroom. Godoy was narrowly acquitted. *El Progreso* afterward alleged that a dozen or so agitators outside the court were coaching the crowd with slogans such as "Down with the cabinet!" or "Long live the sovereign people!" ("Long live the Constitution of the year 1828!" apparently proved too much of a mouthful).[99] Two particular agitators, Martín Orjera (an Argentine) and Pascual Cuevas (Peruvian-born), both of them well known to the authorities, whipped up the crowd to a frenzy. A timely rainstorm enabled the police, their swords drawn, to restore order. Orjera and Cuevas were arrested. Some of Godoy's followers converged on Pedro Félix Vicuña's house. *El Progreso*

99 PR, No. 837, September 15, 1845.

expressed disgust at the "imbecile rabble" that had gathered there, and compared Vicuña himself to Philippe Egalité – inciting "the people" from above.[100] Indignant about this description of his following, Vicuña Égalité dashed off an open letter to President Bulnes: "It was not a rabble," he protested; "everyone had a frock-coat, a cape and a silk umbrella, which ought to console the minister [Montt] and his aristocrat friends."[101]

Street scenes and agitation of this kind, after several years of somnolence (the Bilbao incident apart), put heart into authoritarian *pelucones*, and showed them there was still work to be done. Montt, writing to the Intendant of Valdivia, told him that the near-riot had inspired "great alarm in all those who have something to lose," and he claimed that "the parties boil down to haves and have-nots, frock-coated people and people with coarse shirts."[102] Montt evidently managed to communicate his alarm to others. Whether it was real or feigned we will never know, but Montt was a master tactician who never disdained scare tactics and who sometimes used them (as we shall see) when they had lost much of their efficacy. On this occasion they worked. The Godoy incident prompted a number of Conservatives and Liberals to rally round the government with a hastily created *Sociedad del Orden* (Society of Order). At its opening meeting, the Society's president, the aging Ramón Errázuriz, alluded to the need for governments to hold firm during "those terrible popular fevers" that marked elections in Spanish America. The fluent Domingo Santa María, with all the pomposity of youth, urged the Society "to make a solemn call to the sensible part of the people to raise a dike against that torrent of immoralities that is being poured on the masses."[103]

Vicuña and his followers retaliated by founding their own *Sociedad Demócrata* (Democrat Society), in which Vicuña himself, Juan Nicolás Álvarez and Manuel Bilbao (Francisco's younger brother) were all prominent. Both Societies (on different days) attended the opera and demanded that the cast sing the national anthem. Vicuña, however, did not stop there. He was already trying actively to mobilize artisan support, for the usual reasons.[104] He now sponsored a second "society," the *Sociedad Caupolicán*, placing it in charge of a vehement young Liberal, Manuel Guerrero. Probably no more than a few dozen artisans ever joined.[105] The Society of Order quickly organized propaganda of its own among the artisans, attacking

---

100 PR, No. 896, September 27, 1845.
101 *Republicano*, No. 11, October 1, 1845. *Gaceta del Comercio* (No. 1120, September 15, 1845) reported that the crowd at Vicuña's house included "young men from all the [upper-class] families of the capital."
102 Montt to Salvador Sanfuentes, September 24, 1845. Amunátegui Reyes, *García Reyes*, II, 274.
103 *Orden*, No. 1, October 20, 1845.
104 See Vicuña, *Vindicación*, pp. 40–41.
105 Barros Arana, *Decenio*, II, 75.

Vicuña and attempting some character assassination of his father, the ex-president.[106]

The Montt cabinet did not take long to react (almost certainly overreact) to this spasm of agitation. But the arrests it ordered on November 1, 1845 (Colonel Godoy, Manuel Guerrero, Nicolás Álvarez, half a dozen others), and the "investigations" that lasted for months afterward (nothing was ever proved) merely exacerbated the feelings of the opposition. A Concepción news-sheet claimed that the imprisonments simply showed that "our persons, lives and haciendas are completely unsafe."[107] The Society of Order's artisan news-sheet instantly riposted: "Poor people go to prison all the time, and nobody says a word; but as soon as a well-heeled type has to pay the price, they start screeching and invoking liberty and demanding guarantees."[108]

In January 1846, the opposition created a Directory and called for provincial delegates to assemble in Santiago to designate a presidential candidate. As in 1836 and 1841, the names of General José María de la Cruz and General Ramón Freire (now back in Santiago) were mooted. The delegates never left home. The agitation in Santiago suddenly intensified. A typographer, Santiago Ramos ("El quebradino Ramos") had been publishing (on his own account) a radical news-sheet, *El Pueblo*, vaguely supporting General Freire. The typographer-radical is a very familiar type in labor history. Ramos's trade enabled him to acquaint himself with political writings and to fashion his own democratic and egalitarian outlook. In its seventh issue (scheduled to appear on Sunday, March 8), *El Pueblo* issued a confused call for an insurrection or at least a disturbance of some kind, and summoned "the people" to the Alameda.[109] Interior minister Montt immediately secured a meeting of the Council of State, brandished a copy of *El Pueblo*, No. 7, and sketched a lurid picture of an imminent disaster provoked by a licentious press and unscrupulous agitation among the poor.[110] A 180-day state of siege was declared in Santiago Province. The police made thirteen arrests (Vicuña, Guerrero, and four artisans among them); all thirteen men were "relegated" or banished. Order was quickly restored in the capital, where, indeed, it was never seriously menaced. The streets were ostentatiously patrolled for several days by the Yungay Battalion. The Society of Order congratulated the government on its exemplary firmness.[111]

106 *Artesano del Orden*, Nos. 7 and 8, December 14 and 21, 1845.
107 *Penquisto*, No. 16, November 19, 1845.
108 *Artesano del Orden*, No. 5, November 30, 1845.
109 *Orden*, Nos. 42–43, March 13 and 17, 1846. Ramos's ideas are valuably explicated in Wood, pp. 223–37.
110 Montt, *Discursos*, II, 241–45.
111 PR, No. 1041, March 16, 1846.

Unsurprisingly, in the circumstances, the opposition made only a feeble showing in the congressional elections (March 29–30, 1846), winning in only three districts. In San Felipe, a young Liberal tried to bribe a militia officer, and was instantly jailed; a more senior Liberal rode his horse into the plaza and briefly harangued the crowd before surrendering.[112] In Valparaiso, however, the election led to tragedy. The opposition could count on sympathy in the port, but needed to neutralize the Intendant's hold over four battalions of civic guards. Its efforts began early, with dinners for artisans[113] and propaganda from both the Liberal *Gaceta del Comercio* and a special newssheet, *El Artesano de Valparaíso*, in favor of the opposition candidate, Pedro Félix Vicuña. "Artisans of Valparaiso!" trumpeted the *Gaceta*, "choose between the illustrious and popular Vicuña and the candidate the cabinet imposes on you!"[114] (Vicuña himself was still under arrest at the time, on a ship in the bay.) The government countered with a lavish distribution of liquor, some of which found its way down the throats of opposition artisans.[115] The first day's voting favored the government. The opposition hastily circulated two handbills urging a bigger effort on the second day.[116] When the next day came, the government's agents began buying votes for 12 *reales* and a glass of liquor. An alcohol-primed mob tried to prevent voters from approaching the table in the Almendral district.[117] As the crowd swelled, civic guardsmen from an adjacent barracks moved in to restore order. The editor of the *Gaceta del Comercio*, Juan Nepomuceno Espejo, tried unavailingly to calm the crowd,[118] which destroyed the voting table and attacked the militiamen with sticks and stones, and then retreated to a bridge across a nearby creek, where it improvised barricades. Sticks and stones were no match for the guns of militiamen and soldiers. At the end of the affray, at least a score of rioters were dead.[119]

The progovernment press swiftly capitalized on the tragedy, placing all blame on the opposition, although also criticizing the Intendant of Valparaiso, ex-president Joaquín Prieto, whose conduct was seen as less than firm.[120] The now somewhat subdued *Gaceta del Comercio* did little more than

112 *Orden*, No. 48, April 2, 1846.
113 See *Gaceta del Comercio*, No. 1244, February 14, 1846.
114 *Gaceta del Comercio*, No. 1258, March 2, 1846.
115 *Gaceta del Comercio*, No. 1297, April 30, 1846.
116 Described as inflammatory (which they were not) and reprinted in *Orden*, No. 49, April 6, 1846.
117 See the reports in "Crónica electoral," *Gaceta del Comercio*, Nos. 1296–1297, 1305, and 1307–1308, April 29–30, and May 12 and 14–15, 1846.
118 Barros Arana, *Decenio*, II, 91–95.
119 The only figure published (22) was in the *Gaceta del Comercio*, No. 1363, July 8, 1846. It could easily have been higher.
120 *Orden*, No. 48, April 2, 1846. For Prieto's view of the agitation, see his letters to Manuel Montt, February–April 1846, in León and Aránguiz, pp. 75–106.

suggest that the tragedy had been due to "the bad use of force."[121] *El Mercurio* accused the opposition of exploiting "drunken and hallucinated *rotos*."[122] "The Opposition has imposed a sacrifice on the artisans of Valparaíso," thundered the Society of Order, "and the bloodshed will be an indelible stain that will distinguish and shame the opposition forever!"[123] In his ministerial report for 1846, Montt made sure that this version of events became part of the official record. The opposition, he claimed, had set out to seduce "the most abject classes of society . . . and they tried . . . to inspire in them a hatred of the well-to-do classes," with the help of the press – "a workshop of calumny and defamation."[124]

With the congressional elections over, the government foresaw no difficulty with President Bulnes's reelection. It rather pointlessly paid the Argentine publicist Juan Bautista Alberdi (then living in Chile) 500 pesos for an eighty-four-page "campaign biography." The opposition, or part of it, persisted in pursuing the will-o'-the-wisp of a Freire candidacy. It *was* a will-o'-the-wisp: General Freire showed no interest in abandoning his tranquil retirement, although he was not above offering discreet encouragement to the opposition. *El Diario de Santiago* "proclaimed" him as its candidate, while the other Liberal newspaper, the *Gaceta del Comercio*, although not endorsing him, happily printed a five-part manifesto on his behalf.[125] The election passed off without serious incident. When the result of the Santiago vote became known, there was a small demonstration outside Manuel Montt's house. To most Liberals and at least some *pelucones*, the agitation of 1845–6, even if not actually orchestrated by Montt, as was sometimes claimed,[126] was certainly something he had exploited for his own ends. Montt became a figure to be watched very carefully, as the most formidable authoritarian on the political stage.

His cabinet added one final item to its legacy in the weeks before it resigned, at the end of Bulnes's first presidential term. It decided to push through a new and tougher press law to replace the law of 1828 – the (recently dead) Mariano Egaña's frustrated dream of 1840. Analyzing the new law, Juan Bautista Alberdi did not find it radically different from its predecessor: "If that one had gaps, this one has excesses."[127] The excesses – the stiffening of penalties for abuses of the press, and the enhanced powers given to the judges presiding over the traditional "press juries" – were what perturbed both Liberals and moderate *pelucones*. Despite their strongly

121 *Gaceta del Comercio*, Nos. 1282–1283, March 31 and April 1, 1846.
122 MV, No. 5477, March 31, 1846.
123 *Orden*, No. 48, April 2, 1846.
124 *Memoria* of Interior minister, September 12, 1846. DP, II, 421.
125 Nos. 1324, 1326–1329, June 4 and 6–10, 1846.
126 For example, *Eco Nacional*, No. 6, March 26, 1846.
127 Alberdi, *Legislación*, appendix, p. 3.

progovernment sympathies, both *El Mercurio* and *El Progreso* attacked the new law. The essayist José Joaquín Vallejo told his friend Manuel Antonio Tocornal that it smacked of "the discipline of the schoolroom," suggesting that it was "a monument of inexperience and childishness, if not of ambition and bad faith."[128] The government naturally secured favorable votes in Congress, but the debates in both houses highlighted, yet again, the division between authoritarian and moderate *pelucones*. Governments in Spanish America, claimed Antonio Varas, stoutly defending the law, "rest on the support of the enlightened class and on the acquiescence of the unenlightened." It was only too easy to stir up the "the uncultured and gross passions" of the people, which was the road to anarchy. He was answered by the moderate *pelucones* Manuel Antonio Tocornal and Antonio García Reyes, whose parliamentary performances on this occasion greatly enhanced their reputations. Anarchy in Spanish America, argued Tocornal, was not due to the press. Its causes were "inherent in the infancy in which we find ourselves, the product of our customs, customs inherited from the Spaniards," and he pointed to recent upheavals in Spain to underline his argument.[129] It should probably be remarked here that the 1846 law had no real effect on restraining the press at times of political excitement. Its ardor could only be damped down by the imposition of emergency powers, which had a sobering effect on newspapers when they were not actually closed down by the authorities. The Conservative regime was frequently described as tyrannical by its opponents, but it tolerated a surprising amount of abuse from the opposition press, which it was perfectly able to pay back in kind.

128 Vallejo to Tocornal, August 19, 1846. Vallejo, *Obras*, p. 501.
129 CN/D, August 3, 1846.

4
The Liberal Challenge, 1846–1851

The Rise and Fall of Manuel Camilo Vial

President Bulnes seems to have wished to start his second term in the same way as his first, in a relaxed atmosphere. His new Interior (and temporary Finance) minister, the ambitious, sometimes bad-tempered but also broad-minded Manuel Camilo Vial, one of the younger *filopolitas* of 1835, was a cousin. The poet Salvador Sanfuentes took the Justice portfolio. All those arrested and punished during the recent spasm of repression were freed or allowed to return from exile. Vial almost certainly had his eye on the presidential succession in 1851, as was sometimes alleged in the press.[1] Before it closed down in 1847, the Liberal *Gaceta del Comercio* in Valparaiso conducted a running battle with *El Mercurio*, which maintained that Vial was merely continuing the work of the Montt cabinet. The *Gaceta* denied that the new cabinet was "retrograde," hailing it as both "liberal" and "progressive."[2] In November 1847, Vial abruptly withdrew the government's subsidy to (and started withholding Customs information from) *El Mercurio*. The administrator of the Customs House, Fernando Urízar Garfias, told *El Mercurio*'s owner, Santos Tornero: "It's true, Don Santos, that we haven't been able to ruin your enterprise, but . . . we shall cause you all the difficulties we can."[3] Unsurprisingly, *El Mercurio* began to be openly critical of Vial.

At first it was the only newspaper that was. It took time for the renewed good feelings of Bulnes's second term to show signs of dissipating. But Vial had an Achilles heel: an ill-disguised passion for accumulating offices for himself and his relatives. A limited amount of nepotism was tolerated by the political class (inevitably, given the importance of family networks), but Vial's behavior was clearly seen as going beyond legitimate bounds. Vial himself continued to cling to the Finance portfolio. Three of his brothers

1 See PR, No. 1759, July 6, 1848.
2 *Gaceta del Comercio*, No. 1503, December 22, 1846.
3 Tornero, pp. 81–88.

received public contracts or good public jobs, one the Intendancy of Talca, near some of the family haciendas. In June 1848, while the Chamber of Deputies was discussing its traditional formal reply to the president's annual address, the young deputy for Copiapó, Miguel Gallo, launched a sharp attack on Vial. He criticized him for tolerating repressive acts like the gratuitous imprisonment of the editor and head printer of the newspaper *El Copiapino* by the Intendant of Atacama, which had caused a public furor earlier in the year, and for the "system of *nepotism*" he was practicing.[4] Manuel Antonio Tocornal, supporting Gallo, persuaded the Chamber to urge Vial to "integrate" (i.e., complete) the cabinet by appointing a new Finance minister.

In October 1848, during the budget debates, there were further signs of *pelucón* disaffection. Tocornal challenged the government's claim that there was a 2-million-peso budget surplus. His own calculations showed it to be twenty-eight thousand. Along with his moderate *pelucón* friend Antonio García Reyes, Tocornal returned to the attack over specific items in the budget. It was clear by now that a respectable cohort of deputies was turning against the minister. Vial soon made matters much worse for himself by cajoling Justice minister Sanfuentes into appointing him official attorney (*fiscal*) to the supreme court. He kept this secret, but the news soon leaked to *El Mercurio*, which printed it in ever-larger type over a whole week (December 7–13, 1848). By the end of the week the announcement of Vial's appointment was the size of a small poster.

The anti-Vial groundswell cut across the traditional divide between moderate and authoritarian *pelucones*, uniting moderates such as Manuel Antonio Tocornal and Antonio García Reyes and authoritarians such as Manuel Montt and Antonio Varas. Throughout January 1849, *El Progreso* (the Vial family newspaper) reported that the cabal was spreading rumors against the cabinet. Meanwhile Vial maintained strict secrecy about his "lists" of candidates for the forthcoming congressional elections. *El Mercurio* learned that he wanted to elect "a young Chamber." *El Progreso* suggested that "new men, perhaps with different backgrounds and diverse ideas" were needed in government.[5] Two dissident *pelucones*, Francisco Ignacio Ossa and Victorino Garrido, asked President Bulnes about Vial's intentions. They learned that while Montt and José Joaquín Pérez (a slightly older dissident) were on the list, Tocornal, García Reyes, and Varas were not. Montt then approached Bulnes and requested a more balanced slate. After a difficult three-hour interview, Montt was left with the impression that (as he told Varas) "this poor country risks going to the devil, and soon."[6] Bulnes,

4 CN/D, July 12, 1848.
5 MV, No. 6374, January 15, 1849; PR, No. 1911, January 2, 1849.
6 Montt to Varas, April 21/26, 1849. *Revista Chilena*, No. 28 (1919), p. 304.

offended by Montt's *démarche*, strongly backed his Interior minister and gave firm instructions that the elections should be won *"a todo trance"* ("whatever it takes"), telling Domingo Santa María, the Intendant of Colchagua (where there had been talk of a government-opposition deal) that this was "an *unalterable resolution*."[7]

Santa María did his job. Bulnes congratulated him afterward on his "splendid triumph" in keeping Antonio Varas out of the Chamber by means of his rough tactics – "Menaces, dismissals, imprisonments . . . , without economizing on floggings either," as Montt indignantly described them.[8] But three of the dissidents defeated the machine, and their natural ally, José Joaquín Vallejo, proclaiming his devotion to regional interests, won brilliantly in the Huasco valley.[9] Miguel Gallo had an easy victory in Copiapó. García Reyes surreptitiously switched his candidacy to a district where the governor was caught off-guard. The success of Tocornal's campaign in Valparaiso owed much to the attitude of Intendant Blanco Encalada, whom the opposition persuaded to abandon his plans for intervention and to allow the civic guardsmen to vote freely, to the annoyance of some of their officers. In theory Blanco Encalada controlled 1,060 of the 1,300 or so *calificaciones* in Valparaiso. Tocornal won a majority of 155.[10] From the government's viewpoint, Blanco Encalada's behavior was an outrageous dereliction of duty. The old hero's eminence placed him beyond official sanction, but not beyond vilification.

The anti-Vial faction was pleased with its limited electoral success. García Reyes even considered the possibility of turning the faction into a new political party, a party that would marginalize the older *pelucones*, who were tied, he thought, to "their fears and meannesses" rather than to principles. A "new party" might combine "timidity in political reforms . . . with the progressive fever of the Liberals, both old and new." Manuel Montt could well be the leader of the new party. García Reyes talked at some point with Bruno Larraín, a prominent Liberal, and got the impression that there was at least a chance that the two parties might work together at some stage.[11] As it happened, a number of well-known Liberals (Bruno Larraín among them) had recently met in Santiago to see what could be done to revive their half-dead party.[12]

---

7 Bulnes to Santa María, March 20, 1849. Varas, *Correspondencia*, III, 4–5n.

8 Bulnes to Santa María, March 28, 1849, printed in Amunátegui Solar, *Teatro*, p. 101; Montt to Varas, April 21, 1849. *Revista Chilena*, Año III, Tomo IX, No. 28 (1919), p. 304.

9 For a description, see "Elecciones de Huasco," Vallejo, *Obras*, pp. 359–68.

10 MV, No. 6436, March 27, 1849. See also the vigorously written account by Fernando Urízar Garfias, *Los ministeriales*.

11 García Reyes to Rafael García Reyes, April 15, 1849. Amunátegui Reyes, *García Reyes*, III, 81–86. For a valuable study of García Reyes's political thought in general, see Brahm García, pp. 21–146.

12 MV, No. 6440, March 31, 1849.

It is unlikely that Montt ever thought in García Reyes's terms, but he certainly played a leading part in the maneuvers against Vial. "Our opposition [to Vial] is almost completely organized," he told Varas in April 1849, "and it will soon have its directing committee and . . . a newspaper."[13] The "newspaper" was the small-format *El Corsario*, printed on a press happily supplied by Vial's old foe Santos Tornero. Directed by Juan Pablo Urzúa, a future editor of distinction, it ran from April to September 1849. Its satire at the expense of the Intendant of Santiago almost immediately won it a monstrous 1,200-peso fine and two years in jail for the editor, a sentence quickly rescinded by the supreme court. The anti-Vial opposition widened its attack in a new (and somewhat more moderate) daily paper, *La Tribuna*, edited by Tocornal and García Reyes, with some help from Sarmiento. It poured continuous scorn on the Vial cabinet as "uncertain, vacillating, indefinite."[14]

With Congress in his pocket, and his eye still on the presidency, Vial sought ways of consolidating his position. He had long been cultivating the younger generation, and was well aware of the excitement aroused among younger Chileans by the news of the French Revolution of 1848, to which even President Bulnes paid a graceful compliment when opening Congress that year, saluting France as one of the great sources of "civilization and freedom."[15] News of the revolution prompted a number of celebratory banquets. Andrés Bello called on the French minister (an instant adherent of the new government in Paris) to express his pleasure.[16] Within a month or so, however, certain doubts were creeping in. Everyone now talked of the People, the Republic, and Liberty, reported *El Progreso*, but what did *people* mean in Chile? The only "people" that counted consisted of "the men who think, who discuss . . . , who understand liberty without license," while "the imbecile mass" needed education before it could become a real "people" like the French.[17] *El Progreso* also speculated that in Europe the revolution might unleash "unrestrained licence" and "the fierce instincts of an emboldened multitude."[18] Such warnings had little or no effect on the younger generation. The demonstration effect of the 1848 revolution was to play an important part in politics over the next few years.

José Victorino Lastarria, who had been supporting Vial in a new literary magazine, *La Revista de Santiago*, urged the minister to create a new "progressive" following, and to distance himself from the older *pelucones*.

---

13 Montt to Varas, April 21/26, 1849. *Revista Chilena,* No. 28 (1919), p. 305.
14 TRI, No. 1, May 1, 1849.
15 DP, III, 103.
16 PR, No. 1725, May 27, 1848; J. Edwards, "Decenio," p. 20.
17 PR, No. 1728, May 31, 1848.
18 PR, No. 1751, June 27, 1848.

Vial lacked the nerve to do so. More seriously, rumors began to spread that, infuriated by its exoneration of *El Corsario*, he intended to purge the supreme court. By now his opponents were becoming seriously alarmed. They worked on Bulnes through his father-in-law, ex-president Pinto. In the end Vial, who was always inclined to hubris, met its usual counterpart. We do not have details of his final *démarche* to Bulnes, but he clearly wished the president to abstain from involvement in the presidential succession, to agree to changes in the supreme court, and to allow a reform program of some kind. Bulnes was unwilling to enunciate these points in public. By the time he opened Congress (June 1, 1849), it was an open secret that the cabinet had fallen. Vial withdrew from active political life and settled happily into the supreme court attorneyship he had arranged for himself. His adversaries celebrated his downfall effusively. "Good principles," declared *El Mercurio*, "have attained a splendid victory through the sheer power of opinion." *El Corsario* hailed the end of the Vial era as a "splendid manifestation of public opinion," and felt that the "cabalistic . . . , monkish, jesuitical spirit" of the deputies Vial had placed in the new congress did not matter.[19] As things turned out, it did.

The Beginnings of Liberal Renewal

President Bulnes's feathers had been badly ruffled by the tone of the anti-Vial press. Yet, it was from the anti-Vial faction that the new cabinet had to come. José Joaquín Pérez took the Interior portfolio, with his fellow *pelucón* rebels Antonio García Reyes and Manuel Antonio Tocornal at Finance and Justice respectively. Tocornal and García Reyes, both in their early thirties, did not have a high opinion of the middle-aged Pérez, a man "without soul or thought," according to García Reyes, who felt that he and Tocornal were the only ones driving "the coach of State."[20] Early in November 1849, there were rumors that Tocornal and García Reyes would quit the cabinet, but the crisis (if that is what it was) soon passed. Observing the scene from Copiapó, José Joaquín Vallejo described Pérez as "that frivolous parakeet with all his stupid calmness."[21] Vallejo did not live long enough to see how supremely useful Pérez's "calmness" would one day prove to the republic.

In different circumstances, the Pérez cabinet might have attracted the cohort of young deputies Vial had elected to the Chamber. Tocornal and García Reyes were among the most popular members of the rising generation. Both were effective parliamentarians. García Reyes's powerful intelligence was

19 M(V), No. 6515, June 29, 1849 (M(V) was not yet separately numbered); *Corsario*, No. 49, June 13, 1849.
20 García Reyes to Rafael García Reyes, September 8, 1849. Amunátegui Reyes, *García Reyes*, III, 128.
21 Vallejo to Tocornal, November 21, 1849. Vallejo, *Obras*, p. 509.

widely admired. (His premature death in 1855 deprived Chile of one of her more serious politicians.) Both men were liberal-minded. "What clear and tangible dividing-line separates [Salvador] Sanfuentes from Tocornal, Lastarria from García [Reyes]?" asked the newspaper *La Crónica*.[22] It was a fair question. García Reyes did in fact explore an alliance with Lastarria, the most prominent Liberal in the newly elected Chamber. Lastarria found him impossible to pin down to specific deals.[23] Deals were probably unlikely in any case. Given the fact that the Pérez cabinet had displaced their bene-factor so abruptly, the deputies Vial had packed into the Chamber had no intention of supporting it. Indeed, they not only presented the Conserva-tive regime with its first serious parliamentary opposition, but in so doing revived Liberalism as a political force in Chile.

The Pérez cabinet, facing immediate hostility from the majority in the Chamber, did not shrink from organizing rowdy attendances in the public gallery, a tactic the opposition soon copied. The *de facto* majority leader, Lastarria, introduced several bills (on the press, emergency powers, and elections), none of which stood a chance of passing, but which exempli-fied the new liberal thrust he was eager to organize. Lastarria had more than his fair share of vanity, but he put his intelligence to good tactical use in Congress. This was his finest hour. The first major tussle of wills between government and opposition came in August 1849, when the pro-Vial Municipality of Santiago illegally dismissed its municipal attorney, a deputy who had been voting for the cabinet. Five pro-Vial deputies (all Santiago councilmen) formally moved the impeachment of Pérez for de-creeing that the dismissal was illegal. Lastarria proposed a censure motion to accompany the impeachment. A crowd invaded the floor of the Cham-ber, and the sitting was suspended.[24] Manuel Montt, in a speech next day, claimed that all the opposition wanted was to bring down the govern-ment, and that anarchy loomed. The anarchy, riposted Lastarria, lay in the "open and unwise conflict" the cabinet was provoking in the Chamber. His censure motion was approved, by 20 votes to 16.[25] The government retaliated by prosecuting the Santiago councilmen who had dismissed the attorney. They were never brought to trial. The Chamber refused to waive the congressional immunity enjoyed by the five who were deputies, but it did not persist with the impeachment, knowing that it would fail in the Senate.

The press played its part in keeping political emotions at a high pitch. *El Mercurio* predictably supported the cabinet, as did *La Tribuna* (edited for

22 *Crónica*, No. 32, September 2, 1849.
23 Lastarria, *Diario*, pp. 26–29.
24 *Aconcagüino*, No. 5, August 29, 1849.
25 CN/D, August 24, 1849; TRI, No. 97, August 25, 1849.

a while by Bartolomé Mitre, the future Argentine president). *El Progreso* and the equally pro-Vial *Comercio de Valparaíso* (founded in 1847) were unremittingly hostile, as were a number of news-sheets, notably the Liberals' *El Timón*. Early in August 1849, *El Progreso* printed a sixteen-point "Program" (agreed by the opposition deputies), advocating a whole raft of reforms covering the press, elections, the emergency powers, education, the municipalities, and taxation.[26] On August 31, shortly after the agitated congressional sessions just mentioned, the newspaper announced that the opposition (or most of it) was proposing Ramón Errázuriz (then vice president of the Senate) as its presidential candidate for 1851. The sexagenarian Errázuriz, the president of the Society of Order in 1845–6, hardly seemed the ideal candidate for a reviving Liberal party. *La Tribuna* happily reminded its readers that he had once belonged to the cream of the Conservative party "under the discipline of Portales,"[27] not mentioning Portales's role in removing him from the Interior ministry in 1832 or the fact that he had been a *filopolita*. He was reluctant to accept his new role, and was only persuaded by a letter from General Ramón Freire (still the Liberals' "lost leader"), who publicly endorsed his candidacy.

The name "Liberal" was not yet being consistently attached to what *El Progreso* called "the militant party . . . , a great national party," which it defined as consisting of "the Liberals of the year 1828, the *filopolistas*, [*sic*] the majority of the Chamber, [and] many members of what has been called the *pelucón* or Conservative party."[28] Only on October 9 did the newspaper refer for the first time to "the great PROGRESSIVE PARTY,"[29] a label that remained in use for a few months. *La Tribuna* referred to its congressmen as "the Deputies of the left"[30] – not an expression used very much at the period. The *Club de la Reforma* (Reform Club) formed in October 1849 under Salvador Sanfuentes's presidency may possibly have helped to consolidate the new Progressive identity. It set up two bureaus to handle correspondence with the provinces, one for the north, one for the south, but does not appear to have been a hive of activity.

The Progressives renewed their struggle with the cabinet in the "extraordinary" sittings of Congress (October 1849–January 1850), when battle was joined over the budget and taxation laws. By this stage, succumbing to government pressures, often exercised through families, opposition deputies were beginning to abandon ship. For the final debates, the contending forces were weighted fairly evenly. On January 7, 1850, the Liberal

26 PR, No. 2098, August 4, 1849.
27 TRI, No. 106, September 5, 1849.
28 PR, No. 2141, September 29, 1849.
29 PR, No. 2148, October 9, 1849.
30 TRI, No. 199, December 31, 1849.

Bruno Larraín proposed deferment of the tax laws. Both Montt and Lastarria rose to the occasion with memorable speeches. Larraín's proposal, said Montt, was nothing less than an attempt to make the president the instrument of the Chamber. If successful, the maneuver would induce "an upheaval in all constitutional principles." The "terrible right of suspending taxation," Montt concluded, could only be justified in "extremely extraordinary cases" such as tyrannical actions by a government, which "would make a revolution legitimate.... Public execration should fall on revolutions, and on actions that lead to them."[31] The vote on Larraín's motion was 21 to 21. Two days later, Lastarria, who had been absent because of sickness, reopened the debate with a lengthy reply to Montt, pointing out (correctly) that there had been no pattern in the past for the annual approval of taxation, rather petulantly complaining of attacks that had been made on him in the press, and strongly resisting the implication that the Progressives were bent on fomenting revolution: "Revolution! Civil war! *Why* – when the Constitution leaves us the freedom to obtain the reforms we desire through peaceful means?"[32] The deputies voted again, to resolve the previous tie, and Larraín's motion was defeated (24–16) – a sign of the cabinet's successful pressure on opposition deputies. *El Progreso* reported Lastarria's speech as having "terrified the supporters of the cabinet." The report was written by Lastarria. *El Progreso* also printed a very complimentary account of Montt's speech, but chided him for his "absolutist ideas."[33]

The cabinet's parliamentary victory did little to calm political passions. As they enjoyed the summer recess on their haciendas, the politicians simply awaited (as *El Progreso* put it) "the sound of the bugle to call them once again to battle."[34] The bugle sounded soon enough. There was a new pretext for battle. Manuel Montt's supporters, impressed by his recent parliamentary performances, began to press his claim to the Conservative presidential candidacy. Portales's old henchman Victorino Garrido acted as what would nowadays be called his campaign manager. (Over the ensuing months the principal pro-Montt *pelucones* were often referred to as the "Garrido Club.") In January 1850, Garrido and a small group of Conservatives considered an approach to President Bulnes on Montt's behalf, but decided to postpone it, since other *pelucones* objected to this preemptive strike,[35] and Bulnes was still disinclined to accept Montt as his anointed successor.

The rumors of Montt's candidacy provoked *El Progreso* to make clear that the entry of "his circle" into the cabinet would mean a "signal

31 CN/D, January 7, 1850.
32 CN/D, January 9, 1850.
33 PR, No. 2226, January 11, 1851; Lastarria, *Diario*, pp. 58–61; PR, No. 2223, January 8, 1851.
34 PR, No. 2228, January 14, 1850.
35 PR, No. 2235, January 22, 1850; No. 2240, January 28, 1850.

of alarm ... throughout the Republic."[36] Montt was certainly seen as a formidably impressive figure: "he stands out ... ," noted an 1849 newssheet, "for a serious and frank character, for rectitude of judgement, for infinite clarity and simplicity of expression ... and even for the retiring and modest life he has always led ... ; a real genius."[37] But for Liberals the memory of the Montt cabinet of 1845–6 was only too fresh. *El Progreso* accused him of harboring "regressive designs." His policy," the paper explained, "was a second edition of Portales's," but where Portales's despotism had been "necessary," Montt's was merely "capricious."[38] The comment may or may not have been fair, but it spelled trouble if Montt became the official candidate.

For his part, Lastarria felt that the opposition badly needed someone like Montt – "energetic, decisive, systematic, tenacious." On March 20, 1850, impatient with what he saw as the incoherence of the opposition's tactics, he read its leading members a lengthy memorandum. It was in his best didactic style. Their directing committee, he told them, was "lax [and] ... indolent." They needed to raise money, to launch a new, aggressive newspaper, and to concentrate on a central purpose: "to overthrow" the twenty-year Conservative regime.[39]

The *Sociedad de la Igualdad*

Even as Lastarria was lecturing, others were widening the campaign against the government. The formation of the *Sociedad de la Igualdad* (Society for Equality) stands out as an unusual moment in that age of upper-class politics. Historian Cristián Gazmuri sees the Society as the great precursor of a new type of political and social organization that was to become standard in Chile from the 1860s onward. It certainly anticipated the more widely based agitation of 1858, and there was some continuity of personnel. There is no reason to doubt the testimony of contemporaries that the Society began as an idealistic venture to educate the Santiago artisans and to make them aware of their political rights. Its founder, the Chilean-born Santiago Arcos, had moved back in 1848 to his birthplace from Paris, where he had grown up. At a meeting of the *Club de la Reforma*, he had expressed the view that what was needed was less a presidential campaign than "to raise the people" from its "shameful tutelage."[40] The return to Chile in February 1850 of Francisco Bilbao, who had witnessed dramatic scenes of revolution in Paris, gave him a partner in the enterprise.

36 PR, No. 2171, November 5, 1849, and No. 2180, November 15, 1849.
37 *Independiente*, No. 5, May 25, 1849.
38 PR, No. 2043, June 7, 1849.
39 Lastarria, *Diario*, pp. 62–69.
40 Zapiola, *Sociedad*, p. 6.

Bilbao had lost none of the fervor he had displayed at the time of his famous article in 1844. Arcos had a clearer head. In March 1850, the two young men recruited both upper-class Liberals and a number of artisans for their Society. Among its more zealous members were the young poet Eusebio Lillo and the musician José Zapiola. They eventually produced a suitable marching song for the Society, "*La Igualitaria.*"

> *¡Independiente, Chile,*
> *somos ya ciudadanos,*
> *pero hay nuevos tiranos*
> *y triunfa la maldad!*

> Chile is independent
> and we are citizens now,
> but there are new tyrants,
> and evil is triumphing!

Arcos and Bilbao were both enraptured by the epic story of the French Revolution, enthusiasm for which had been heightened among the younger generation by a recent serialization of Lamartine's *Histoire des Girondins*, a book suffused with revolutionary sentiment. (If the book has a hero, it is Robespierre.) Members of the Society called each other "citizen," and its leaders adopted suitable nicknames. Bilbao, whose flair for speechifying recalled the great Girondin of 1791–3, became Vergniaud. Arcos, rather less appropriately, was Marat.

Within weeks the Society had organized a small number of branches and was planning classes in mathematics, tailoring, music (taught by Zapiola), ancient history, Chilean history, political economy, and English. The Liberal leadership, however, quickly appreciated the Society's potential as a more systematic means of mobilizing artisans for electoral purposes than had ever been attempted before, and deputed the active Manuel Guerrero (Pedro Félix Vicuña's collaborator of 1845–6) to become a leading *igualitario*. The Society's newspaper *El Amigo del Pueblo* (the name copied Marat's *L'Ami du Peuple*), was, for Lastarria, the aggressive newspaper he had called for in his March memorandum.[41] It openly proclaimed its hostility to Montt (and support for Ramón Errázuriz) from its very first issue (April 1, 1850). Arcos, never less than skeptical of the Liberal leadership, began to play a less conspicuous role in the Society, leaving Bilbao as its most prominent figure.

The government certainly had its spies among the *igualitarios*. As José Joaquín Vallejo reported in June 1850, "the police know from A to Z

---

41 Lastarria, *Diario*, p. 71.

everything that is said and done."[42] The "social" edge of the Society's propaganda scandalized authoritarian *pelucones*. Montt's supporters, coordinated by Garrido, saw it as an excellent pretext for pressing his claims to the "official" presidential candidacy. Their chance came with a cabinet crisis in early April 1850. Tocornal and García Reyes had been pinning their presidential hopes on General José Santiago Aldunate (a well-liked former War and Navy minister), "whose election," as García Reyes put it, "can . . . be achieved without bloodshed."[43] Interior minister Pérez, for his part, wanted wider discussions among *pelucones*. President Bulnes refused to commit himself, and Tocornal and García Reyes quit the cabinet. Montt's supporters needed a cabinet that would further their main aim, and almost certainly pressured Pérez to step down. Montt's protégé Antonio Varas then decided to take a hand. It was a preemptive move. He was well aware that Ramón Luis Irarrázaval (still on his travels in Europe) was gathering support among moderates as a possible president, as well as General Aldunate, whom Bulnes possibly favored. The president's preferences were still not known. Some believed that he entertained hopes for his cousin, General José María de la Cruz,[44] the popular Intendant of Concepción, who had been spoken of as *presidenciable* often enough in the past.

Varas was duly appointed as Interior (and temporary Justice) minister, with Finance entrusted to Jerónimo Urmeneta, a leading trader, and one of the few Chileans to have studied in the United States (at Brown University). It was at this point (toward the end of April 1850) that the wayward, strong-willed Fernando Urízar Garfias (as vehement for the opposition as he had once been for Portales), approached Varas on his own initiative with a proposal for a deal between government and opposition on the basis of the promise of an "open" presidential election (and the removal of three unpopular Intendants). Varas did not seem hostile. The Liberal leadership was clearly tempted. The Liberals, however, wanted a formal statement of the deal, and this Varas refused.[45] Varas next sent a flurry of letters to the provinces to ascertain opinion on the presidential question. Reports on the political preferences of prominent families flowed back to him.[46] Varas found that there was a groundswell of interest in Montt, but that the provinces were waiting for a lead from the president. As one of

42 To Nicolás Munizaga, June 28, 1850. Vallejo, *Obras*, p. 514; cf. Zapiola, *Sociedad*, p. 17.
43 García Reyes to Tocornal, April 3, 1850. *Revista Chilena*, Año I, Tomo II, No. 6 (1917), p. 84.
44 PR, No. 2321, May 10, 1850; *Amigo del Pueblo*, No. 30, May 4, 1850.
45 Lastarria, *Diario*, pp. 74–79; García Reyes to Tocornal, May 13, 1850. *Revista Chilena*, Año I, Tomo II, No. 6 (1917), p. 86; see Urízar Garfias's letters in PR, No. 2320, May 8, and No. 2325, May 15, 1850; PR, May 1850, *passim*.
46 Varas, *Correspondencia*, Vol. III, *passim*.

his correspondents put it, "President Bulnes will decide for the strongest candidate."[47]

The Liberal-*igualitario* opposition reacted fiercely to Varas's appointment. *El Amigo del Pueblo* mocked him in Horatian fashion: "The mountains have given birth to a mouse. Good God! It's Don Antonio Varas!" But it also adopted a more threatening tone: "Varas cabinet! The republicans of Chile declare war on you!"[48] *El Progreso* declared that the new cabinet implied the danger of "a frightful civil war."[49] "Varas in the cabinet means revolution," trumpeted an opposition newspaper in Talca.[50] Every week now brought a new excitement, rousing the somnolent society of Santiago to continuous attention. Francisco Bilbao chose this moment to add fuel to the flames by publishing some translations from *Paroles d'un croyant* by the then world-renowned dissident French Catholic Félicité-Robert de Lamennais, whom he had got to know in Paris. Pope Gregory XVI had condemned the book in his encyclical *Singulari nos* (1834), and the appearance of the translated extracts in *El Amigo del Pueblo* provoked a furious response from the Church. This scared the Liberal leadership, which included two prominent priests. *El Amigo del Pueblo* published no further extracts and found it advisable to close down. It announced the creation of a new newspaper, *La Barra*, to continue "the war . . . on the mummies of the cabinet and the chorus-masters of the retrograde party."[51] *La Barra* mostly refrained from anticlerical provocations. Bilbao himself could not so refrain, and he published (May 1850) a further effusion, *Los boletines del espíritu*, ostensibly in the Lamennais idiom. *La Revista Católica* denounced the pamphlet as an incitement to "socialism and communism . . . , those two great heresies of modern times."[52] Archbishop Valdivieso of Santiago condemned the *Boletines* and excommunicated Bilbao. These antics prompted Manuel Guerrero to propose Bilbao's expulsion from the *Sociedad de la Igualdad*, but the artisan membership rallied to his side.[53]

The government was not slow to counter the propaganda of the Liberals and *igualitarios*, as usual paying particular attention to the artisans.

> *Viva Chile, viva el orden,*
> *Viva el artesano honrado*
> *Que vale más que el malvado,*

47 Tomás Zenteno to Varas, La Serena, August 7, 1850. Varas, *Correspondencia*, III, 136.

48 No. 4, April 4, 1850 (cf. Horace, *Ars Poetica*, line 139); No. 18, April 20, 1850.

49 PR, No. 2292, April 4, 1850.

50 *Talquino*, No. 4, June 26, 1850.

51 *Amigo del Pueblo*, No. 50, May 29, 1850. The *barra* was the public gallery (not actually a gallery, as it was at floor level) in the Chamber of Deputies.

52 RCAT, No. 208, June 1, 1850. For an analysis of the *Boletines*, see Varona, pp. 184–88.

53 Zapiola, *Sociedad*, pp. 18–20.

Aunque use levita o frak:
¡Compañero! sin la paz
Mandarían los pipiolos,
Y ya sabeis que ellos solos
Nos quieren alucinar.

Long live Chile, long live order,
Long live the honorable artisan,
Who is worth more than the wicked man
Even if he wears a frock-coat:
Comrade! without peace
The *pipiolos* would govern,
And you know they're the only ones
Who want to bamboozle us.[54]

Taking its cue from the Church, the news-sheet printing this verse denounced the "ideas of socialism, of communism"[55] being preached by Bilbao and Arcos. These terms were less precise in meaning than they later became (and wildly inaccurate as a description of the thinking of Bilbao and Arcos), but they already had the power of alarming the reading public,[56] and were much invoked over the next few months. The newspaper *La Tribuna*, now fully behind Montt, accused Bilbao of transforming the presidential issue into "a question of socialism, of struggle between rich and poor," and suggested that this would provoke "the reaction nobody wants." A few weeks later the newspaper published several hostile articles on the subject of "socialism," emphasizing its inapplicability to a country like Chile.[57] Another Conservative publication argued the same point: "it would be ridiculous for Chile, with its scanty population, the ignorance of its masses, the lack of knowledge among its higher classes, to launch itself into a complete subversion of institutions the civilized world accepts as good."[58]

Conservative propaganda quickly began to sound a note of warning. One news-sheet observed that "Voltaire, D'Alambert [*sic*], Dideró [*sic*], etc." had spread their subversive writings to the "artisan's workshop" and

---

54 *Verdadero Chileno*, No. 9, May 24, 1850.
55 *Verdadero Chileno*, No. 22, June 25, 1850.
56 This was not the first time the terms had been used in Chile. In 1845 the *Revista Católica* published seven articles (by "J.B.") on socialism, mostly a hostile examination of the ideas of Robert Owen (Nos. 69–83, July 15–December 11, 1845). Even earlier, in July 1842, *El Mercurio* printed some rather favorable observations on socialism – "that is to say, the need to combine science, art and politics in the aim of improving the fate of peoples, of favoring liberal principles, of combating retrograde prejudices, of rehabilitating the people." (No. 4163, July 28, 1842). This is the first use of the word "socialism" I have found in *El Mercurio*.
57 TRI, No. 352, July 8, 1850; cf. Nos. 344–49, June 27–July 4, 1850.
58 *Consejero del Pueblo*, No. 6, October 19, 1850.

"peasant's shack," and had thus provoked "the catastrophe of the bloody revolution in France." Another accused the *Sociedad de la Igualdad* of being "a European import, a vile plagiarism of French customs," likely to bring about "really terrible effects."[59] Partly to counteract the government's increasingly alarmist propaganda, Arcos insisted that the *Sociedad de la Igualdad* issue a "Solemn Act" (written by himself) to underline its essentially peaceful purposes. The declaration specifically repudiated "upheavals, [and] the use of force" as pointless, and rejected "the tyranny of popular caprice as well as the tyranny of the ruler."[60]

This disavowal cut no ice whatever. The government's attitude hardened by the week. In July 1850, Bulnes filled the vacant Justice ministry with the authoritarian *pelucón* Máximo Mujica, Francisco Bilbao's prosecutor of 1844. The Liberal-*igualitario* opposition immediately saw this as a provocation. Bulnes had still not accepted Montt's candidacy, but the opposition was now sure that he had, and redoubled its agitation, not least in the Chamber of Deputies. In fact, the 1850 sittings were slightly less stormy than those of 1849, and were by no means unproductive. Both the Chamber (by 40 to 5) and the Senate (11 to 1) voted to abolish flogging, and there was a memorable debate on education, with Montt and Lastarria once again staging a notable rhetorical battle. Both Lastarria and the young Federico Errázuriz tried and failed to press the matter of constitutional reform, which later became the main plank in their *Bases de la reforma*, a Liberal "manifesto" issued (despite certain Liberal misgivings) in October 1850.[61] In July–August, during debates on the abolition of the old colonial *mayorazgos*,[62] the Liberal deputy Juan Bello (son of Andrés) launched an attack on the entire Conservative system, imposed, he said, "when our political atmosphere was still darkened by the smoke from the fratricidal cannon of Lircay."[63] Colonel Justo Arteaga, although an opposition deputy, praised the victors of Lircay for destroying anarchy, a remark that provoked an emotional eulogy of the 1828 Constitution from Bruno Larraín and a tart comment from Colonel José Francisco Gana to the effect that far from destroying anarchy, the triumphant army of Lircay had created it.[64] The uproar was such that the sitting had to be suspended.

There were one or two further furors before the "ordinary" sessions ended. On August 9, Federico Errázuriz put down an *interpelación* (parliamentary

59 *Verdadero Chileno*, No. 13, June 4, 1850. *Porvenir*, No. 4, June 22, 1850.

60 Zapiola, *Sociedad*, pp. 22–23.

61 Lastarria, *Diario*, pp. 89–90.

62 Strict entails, abolished in 1828, restored under the 1833 Constitution, and finally abolished in laws passed in 1852 and 1857. Although an emotional issue in the 1820s, they were of no real economic importance, and their abolition in the 1850s occasioned very little debate.

63 CN/D, July 31, 1850.

64 CN/D, August 12, 1850.

question) to Interior minister Varas over the recent abolition of the autonomy of the Academia de Leyes (Academy of Law), a school dating back to
colonial times where aspiring lawyers honed up their forensic skills. Its ul-
trareactionary director had expelled the eighteen-year-old Benjamín Vicuña
Mackenna for protesting a congratulatory message the director had sent to
the new Justice minister Mujica.[65] Later that month, the opposition proposed the impeachment of the Intendant of Aconcagua, José Manuel Novoa,
for arbitrarily imprisoning the editor of a local opposition news-sheet. On
this occasion (unlike the previous year), the Chamber voted to send the case
to the Senate, the first time this had occurred under the 1833 Constitution. Hastily inventing some rules, the Senate (predictably) exonerated the
Intendant.

By the time the Chamber voted on the impeachment, the political
temperature had suddenly been raised by several degrees. The *Sociedad de
la Igualdad* had already been subjected to harassment by the authorities.
On August 19, 1850, after a general meeting of the Society attended by
eight hundred, the executive committee, still in the hall, was assaulted
by "a band of men in ponchos armed with clubs,"[66] some of them obviously police agents. Seven *igualitarios* (including Bilbao, Guerrero, and
Zapiola) were bloodily beaten. The affray caused an instant sensation in
Santiago. It was rumored that a dismayed Manuel Montt offered to with-
draw his name as a presidential contender. If he did, the impulse soon
passed. Moderate *pelucones* were still hoping against hope for a suitable alternative to Montt, who still needed, as José Joaquín Vallejo put it, "to
rehabilitate himself in the opinion of the country."[67] García Reyes had
once again been floating the name of General Aldunate, and Lastarria and
a number of other Liberals welcomed the idea. But Bulnes still refused
to commit himself, and García Reyes's scheme faded away.[68] José Joaquín
Vallejo was by this stage certain that "the highest-caliber *pelucones*" favored
Montt.[69]

For the opposition, the attack on the *igualitarios* was a shot in the
arm. Those Liberal leaders (nearly all) who had kept their distance from
the *Sociedad de la Igualdad* now joined it *en masse*, although the artisan
membership remained high.[70] Pedro Ugarte, the judge investigating the
August 19 assault, was suspended by the government, largely because he

65 I. Errázuriz, *Historia*, pp. 429–32.
66 Zapiola, *Sociedad*, pp. 27–28.
67 To Nicolás Munizaga, July 13, 1850. Vallejo, *Obras*, p. 515.
68 Lastarria, *Diario*, pp. 95–96.
69 To Nicolás Munizaga, July 13 and June 28, 1850. Vallejo, *Obras*, pp. 514–15.
70 Gazmuri, *El "48" chileno*, pp. 97–99.

was a vehement Liberal who was heard to murmur that the trail of evidence might soon reach Montt and Varas. By this stage, the tension in Santiago was growing by the day, almost by the hour, and it provoked some curious responses. Jacinto Chacón, an independent-minded liberal, circulated a handbill proposing General Francisco Antonio Pinto as a candidate of national salvation and attacking Bulnes as "tied to the carriage of the Monttists."[71] Pinto himself issued a printed statement (August 25), gently pointing out that his time had passed.

Halfway through September 1850, a *birlocho* loaded with cartridges was intercepted on its way to San Felipe, capital of Aconcagua Province. The old agitator Martín Orjera and the compulsive activist Fernando Urízar Garfias had been planning an insurrection.[72] Urízar Garfias had already been bought off by the government with an appointment as inspector of Customs. Orjera was arrested. With lurid rumors spreading like wildfire, the political atmosphere was now explosive. On September 18, twenty-nine leading figures in the opposition (including Ramón Errázuriz, Bruno Larraín, Lastarria, Federico Errázuriz, Salvador Sanfuentes, Manuel Camilo Vial, Juan Bello, and Domingo Santa María) published a handbill denying that they had any desire for revolution, but squarely blaming the tension on the government. *El Progreso*, printing the statement, left its third and fourth pages blank, apart from pithy one-line messages denouncing the regime.[73]

Montt's following, mobilized by the ever-useful Garrido, now decided that the time had come to "proclaim" his candidacy. Bulnes had finally acquiesced. "The Conservative Party designated señor Montt," he told General José María de la Cruz a few weeks later, in an unenthusiastic tone, "and I adhered to a candidacy that I saw was generally supported."[74] Antonio García Reyes and Manuel Antonio Tocornal, among others, refused to attend the meeting (October 19) at which Montt was formally nominated. García Reyes was informed by a friend that "none of those present dared to pronounce the magic name, Montt," and spoke of him indirectly. "It's Montt or bust," he told Tocornal. "With other men it would have been something else. What's done is done."[75] In hindsight, it can probably be said that the efforts of moderates such as García Reyes and Tocornal were pursued too half-heartedly to counter the rising tide of support for Montt among the

71 *La salvación está . . .*
72 See Domingo Santa María to Isidoro Errázuriz, June 20, 1878. *Revista Chilena,* Año V, Tomo XIII, No. 45 (1921), pp. 502–04; Lastarria, *Diario,* pp. 100–01.
73 PR, No. 2427, September 18, 1850.
74 Bulnes to Cruz, February 24, 1851. BACH, No. 74 (1966), p. 31.
75 PR, No. 2464, October 21, 1850. García Reyes to Tocornal, October 21–22, 1850. *Revista Chilena,* Año I, Tomo II, No. 6 (1917), pp. 90–94.

pelucón magnates. The news of his candidacy spread quickly through the provinces.

Even as Montt's candidacy was clinched, the *Sociedad de la Igualdad* staged a large demonstration (October 14) along the Alameda, Bilbao at its head, bearing an unconvincing replica of a tree of liberty. The Conservative press mocked the "Jacobin procession" and denounced the marchers as "a mixture of all that is worst in the different classes of society."[76] "A large number of Conservatives and their ladies also attended, to watch the extravagant march," reported Antonio García Reyes, "and they laughed fit to kill over such simplemindedness."[77] The Intendant of Santiago, Matías Ovalle, did not laugh. He promptly issued a decree regulating all future demonstrations, which merely provoked the Society to stage another. The Intendant fined those he identified as ringleaders, and then in an abrupt about-face withdrew the fines. Vicente Sanfuentes, deputy for Valdivia, went to the Intendancy to reclaim his money, did not even remove his hat,[78] and spat in the Intendant's face, afterward running off at great speed to the offices of *El Progreso*, where a crowd prevented the police from seizing him. He was later jailed for six months.

Matters quickly came to a head. At the start of November, a self-created copy of the *Sociedad de la Igualdad* in Aconcagua Province – "we are not abject Helots but undaunted Aconcaguans!" it proclaimed[79] – briefly seized control of San Felipe and deposed the Intendant.[80] Soldiers and civic guardsmen swiftly dispersed the rebels. The government had the pretext it needed. Fernando Urízar Garfias suggested to Montt that the suppression of the *Sociedad de la Igualdad* might detonate a popular explosion. "You don't know Chileans," Montt told him. "There would be a bit of a commotion, a few shots would be fired, three or four people would die, and everything would be sorted out."[81] On November 7, 1850, the government placed Santiago and Aconcagua Provinces under a sixty-day state of siege and ordered numerous arrests. It banned the *Sociedad de la Igualdad* and shut down the newspapers *El Progreso* and *La Barra*. There was no reaction, no spontaneous uprising in the poorer districts of Santiago – or anywhere else. The extraordinary agitation of 1850 melted away. In January 1851, when a few *igualitarios* announced the reopening of the *Sociedad de la Igualdad,* they were fined by the Intendant, and paid their fines rather than go to jail.

76 *Verdadero Chileno*, No. 67, October 15, 1850. TRI, No. 432, October 15, 1850.
77 García Reyes to Tocornal, October 21/22, 1850. Amunátegui Reyes, *García Reyes*, IV, 32.
78 A detail that incensed TRI (see No. 447, November 2, 1850).
79 *Aconcagüino*, No. 25, September 21, 1850.
80 See Sarmiento, *Motín de San Felipe*. A very shrewd account was printed in the French-language *Courrier des Mers du Sud*, No. 2, January 11, 1851.
81 *Reforma*, No. 37, November 21, 1850.

General Cruz, the Easter Rising, and the Election of Montt

"The year 1851 could be a difficult one," Antonio García Reyes told his friend Tocornal during the state of siege.[82] The summer brought the usual lull in political activity. In April 1851, when Lastarria returned from temporary banishment in Peru, he found that "the opposition did not exist. The leaders of the Progressive party . . . had abandoned their posts, and . . . all the other proselytes were disheartened, without hope and without ideas."[83] His assessment was not completely accurate. There were still Liberals who wished to act, but their thoughts turned increasingly toward armed insurrection. In January 1851, a conspiracy in the Valdivia Regiment was nipped in the bud. Rumors of subversion in the Army and in the prisons reached the press.[84]

The hopes of the Liberal opposition were suddenly revived by an entirely unexpected event. On February 10, 1851, around one hundred citizens of Concepción proclaimed General José María de la Cruz, their popular Intendant since 1846, as presidential candidate. Cruz announced, with grandiloquent vagueness, that his platform was "to enhance the greatness of the country."[85] President Bulnes immediately notified his cousin of his firm support for Montt. To others, he expressed the view that the family relationship would be "a powerful obstacle" to Cruz's candidacy; the presidency would be seen as a "hereditary monopoly."[86] Insofar as Cruz had political ideas (his old O'Higginism was long since irrelevant), they were conservative. His nomination was more an expression of provincial pride and resentment of Santiago than of deep hostility to the regime. But the general had a streak of stubbornness. He set about consolidating his support in Concepción and throughout the South. The Intendant of Ñuble told Interior minister Varas that Cruz's candidacy was gaining ground with "extraordinary speed," suggesting that army units be moved from Concepción to the safety of Chillán.[87] Hoping that the pen was mightier than the sword, Varas dispatched a printing press for the use of the Conservatives in Concepción.

In their detestation of Montt, the Santiago Liberals were immediately tempted to adopt Cruz as their standard-bearer, despite the fact that their recent proposals for constitutional reform included a prohibition on

82 García Reyes to Tocornal, November 25, 1850. Amunátegui Reyes, *García Reyes*, IV, 53.

83 Lastarria, *Diario*, pp. 107–08.

84 See *Album*, No. 4, January 25, 1851.

85 *Voto Libre*, March 5, 1851.

86 Bulnes to Col. Eugenio Necochea, February 20, 1851. BACH, No. 74 (1966), p. 31.

87 Juan Ignacio García to Varas, February 28, 1851. Alb. Edwards, *Gobierno*, pp. 422–24. José Toribio Medina MSS, Vol. 369 (Biblioteca Nacional) contains a collection of pro-Cruz statements from communities all over the south.

incumbent presidents' relatives from running for the presidency. Liberal emissaries were sent to discuss matters with the general. Cruz would not accept a full-scale Liberal program, but agreed to support the principle of electoral freedom. This was enough. At the end of March 1851, the Liberal leadership persuaded Ramón Errázuriz to stand down in favor of Cruz. He did so with no great reluctance.

The government realized immediately that Cruz's emergence was suddenly energizing the opposition.[88] Some of the younger, more impetuous Liberals, including Benjamín Vicuña Mackenna and his friend José Miguel Carrera, along with the inevitable Francisco Bilbao, were already busy suborning the military, pinning their hopes on armed insurrection. On Saturday, April 19, *La Tribuna* confidently declared that Chile was no longer "an appropriate field for the triumph of an undisciplined soldiery."[89] On the very next day – Easter Day – a rebel colonel, Pedro Urriola, usurped command of the Valdivia Regiment and launched an attack on the Artillery barracks at the foot of the Cerro Santa Lucía, the rocky hill that rises over downtown Santiago. There was fierce street-fighting for an hour or two before the rebels gave up, leaving around two hundred dead, among them Urriola. Liberal deputy Juan Bello's defiant speech at the colonel's funeral next day won him instant banishment to Peru. With other rebels, Francisco Bilbao sought sanctuary in a monastery, and soon afterward quit his native land for ever. Vicuña Mackenna and Carrera were imprisoned, but soon escaped, in feminine disguise, with the help of two society ladies. Lastarria, who played no part in the rising, was stripped of his professorship at the Instituto Nacional and expelled from the Chamber of Deputies – an act of pure vindictiveness and spite. A collection was taken for the families of civic guardsmen who had died. Montt was one of five who contributed the highest sum: 103 pesos, 4 *reales*.[90]

"It is the South that seriously frightens me," wrote García Reyes soon after the Easter rising. "They say Cruz is horribly prejudiced against the Cabinet."[91] "Many of the young men engaged in the affair of the 20th have fled to his camp," the American minister in Santiago Bailie Peyton reported, "and there is intense anxiety manifested to hear from him."[92] Throughout April and May, *La Tribuna* repeatedly reported that the South was "quiet." The government summoned General Cruz to Santiago. What it hoped to gain is not clear. Cruz was not easily intimidated. He arrived

88 Bulnes to Necochea, February 20, 1851. BACH, No. 74 (1966), p. 30.
89 TRI, No. 583, April 19, 1851.
90 *Diario de Avisos*, No. 19, May 12, 1851. The fullest narrative of the Easter rising remains Vicuña Mackenna, *Jornada.*
91 To Rafael García Reyes, April 27, 1851. Amunátegui Reyes, *García Reyes*, IV, 102.
92 Peyton to Daniel Webster (Secretary of State), April 19 (?29), 1851. Manning, p. 189.

on May 12. On the road from Valparaiso he encountered (and talked with) prisoners who were being sent into exile, as well as some sergeants from the Valdivia Regiment on their way to the Magellan Strait penal colony. The sergeants cheered him. In Santiago, he received demonstrations of support from students at the Instituto Nacional (headed by the sixteen-year-old Isidoro Errázuriz), from delegations of artisans, from young Liberals, and from sixty or so society ladies dressed in mourning, led by the widow of the notable patriot José Miguel Carrera, whose son and namesake, as we have seen, was in trouble.[93] At the opening of Congress on June 1, when Interior minister Varas, reading the presidential message, alluded to the Civic Guard as a "guarantee of peace," Cruz was observed to smile knowingly at a relative in the gallery. Afterward, a large crowd cheered him back to his lodgings.[94] Antonio García Reyes found him a man of "innocent credulity."[95] According to some accounts, Cruz proposed that he and Montt abandon the election in favor of a compromise candidate, perhaps Ramón Luis Irarrázaval, who had returned to Chile from Europe on the day of the Easter rising. But the authoritarian *pelucones* had the bit between their teeth, and would not countenance any such deal, although they must have known that it would save their country bloodshed. Irarrázaval visited General Cruz and asked him to seek a settlement. Cruz urged Irarrázaval to talk to Ramón Errázuriz and Salvador Sanfuentes. Sanfuentes told him that it was too late. No deal was possible between the two sides.[96]

The presidential election at the end of June was preceded by a veritable flood of propaganda from both camps, far more extensive and intense than the propaganda of 1841. President Bulnes had already circularized the Intendants, declaring Montt to be the choice of all "the men of judgement and following" as the only candidate offering "positive guarantees of order and stability."[97] The Conservative party issued a manifesto stressing Chile's progress over the previous twenty years; 510 prominent citizens issued a statement of support for law and order.[98] Montt's friend Sarmiento wrote a vigorous manifesto of his own, to complement an earlier, equally vigorous pro-Montt pamphlet of November 1850.[99] *La Tribuna* backed Montt shrilly. So did *El Mercurio*, in its more measured way. *El Progreso*, printing General Cruz's name at the head of its editorial column, rivaled *La Tribuna* in shrillness. These newspapers and the ephemeral news-sheets

93 TRI, No. 610, May 21, 1851; No. 631, June 16, 1851.
94 TRI, No. 619, June 2, 1851. *Sud-América*, Vol. II, No. 7, June 9, 1851.
95 García Reyes to Manuel Antonio Tocornal, July 21, 1851. *Revista Chilena*, Año I, Tomo II, No. 6 (1917), p. 100.
96 García Reyes to Tocornal, July 21, 1851. *Revista Chilena*, Año I, Tomo II, No. 6 (1917), p. 99.
97 Circular to Intendants, February 20, 1851. L. Montt, *Recuerdos*, pp. 745–47.
98 *Manifiesto del Partido Conservador*; *Manifestación*, June 10, 1851.
99 *Don Manuel Montt* (1851); *¿A quién rechazan y temen?* (1850).

of the election campaign show the two sides appealing to very much the same sentiments, attacking each other in essentially the same fundamentally liberal language. A Conservative news-sheet in Concepción, for instance, defined the candidates as follows:

> THE PEOPLE DOES NOT WANT CRUZ
> BECAUSE HE REPRESENTS:
>> Will over intelligence.
>> Aristocracy over the people.
>> The sword over peace.
>> A dynasty over the Republic.
>> Ultraconservatism over progress.
>
> THE PEOPLE WANTS MONTT
> BECAUSE HE REPRESENTS:
>> The citizen as leader of peace.
>> The government of the people through law.
>> Wisdom in power.
>> Democracy in the Republic.
>> The prosperity of the country.[100]

An election time broadside praised Montt as "the first Republican and the apostle of liberty," and damned Cruz as a man with "monarchical ideas," as a "despot by character and pride."[101] A short-lived newspaper, *Los Avisos*, pitched Montt's case to the artisans: "Montt . . . will improve the condition of the workers. He will introduce new industries, open up careers hitherto unknown for the working class, and he will bring in the railroad, to supply the poor with all the products they need, at low prices and in the greatest abundance." The paper even pledged that Montt would make service in the civic guard "less onerous."[102]

The opposition hit back as hard as it could. The old *pipiolo* Nicolás Pradel accused Montt of wishing to heighten the centralization of Chile "to the apogee it had during the blessed regime of the colony."[103] A broadside circulated in Valparaiso claimed that Cruz would revive "our public spirit, buried for twenty years in the darkness of a barbarous despotism."[104] A Valparaiso news-sheet insisted that a Cruz government would be in harmony with the "advanced principles of the century," which on closer inspection turn out to be a conflation of the preambles of the United States Declaration

---

100 *Conservador*, Nos. 5–6, May 21 and 29, 1851.
101 *¡Chilenos! Viva la República – Viva Montt.*
102 *Los Avisos*, No. 55, June 25, 1851.
103 Pradel, p. 25.
104 *A los artesanos.*

of Independence and Constitution.[105] Civic guardsmen in Santiago were urged to defy their officers and vote for Cruz, "because he is the friend of the poor and protector of the civic guardsman."[106] An election day handbill in Santiago (signed by "100 civic guardsmen") predicted that Montt's victory would mean "the absolute and perpetual loss of liberty and the Republic." Another news-sheet printed a skull and crossbones to show what Chile would be like under Montt.[107] Yet another published a poem declaring that Montt *"Siempre fue un tigre, nunca hombre"* ("Was always a tiger, never a man.")[108] This also was the view of Pedro Félix Vicuña, his hour come round at last, fulminating against Montt from both Valparaiso and Concepción: "Even if Montt became an angel, even if his circle of friends all became saints," he trumpeted, "nobody would believe they were anything other than tigers in sheep's clothing."[109]

Nobody doubted that the tiger would win the election, which he did everywhere except in Concepción Province, where Cruz reportedly received five thousand votes, compared with Montt's 179.[110] All the Concepción *electores* favored Cruz, as did five out of sixteen in Maule Province and three of the twelve in Coquimbo. In Santiago, the government fended off a respectable challenge from the opposition, as can be appreciated from the figures.

	Montt	*Cruz*
June 25	2,137	1,004
June 26	2,886	469[111]

Because of the intensity of the election, especially in Santiago, the recriminations afterward were far more savage than usual. An opposition manifesto, listing election abuses in lurid detail, was countered with a government manifesto (written by Sarmiento) with exactly the same title, only in quotation marks.[112] Antonio García Reyes, indignant over opposition charges, wrote his friend Tocornal: "Whatever they say, the [Conservative] party showed itself to be strong, and colossally, against its adversary, which it has beaten in proper form; by opinion in some places; by money in others; by family relationships and influences in still others."[113] García Reyes's view of "proper form" was a common one, and he can be pardoned for

105 *Voto Libre*, No. 2, March 27, 1851.
106 *Los cívicos de Santiago a sus compañeros.*
107 *Libertad*, No. 4, March 21, 1851.
108 *Pescador*, No. 4, June 19, 1851.
109 *Reforma*, No. 40, July 4, 1851.
110 *Reforma*, No. 40, July 4, 1851.
111 TRI, No. 638, June 27, 1851.
112 *Manifiesto del partido de oposición; "Manifiesto del partido de oposición."*
113 García Reyes to Tocornal, July 21, 1851. *Revista Chilena*, Año I, Tomo II, No. 6 (1917), pp. 98–99.

believing that the elections had been fair. Some of the opposition's outrage was synthetic, but much of it simply stemmed from sheer frustration with the government's heavy-handed interventionist tactics over the previous twenty years.

General Cruz stayed in Santiago during the elections. Shortly before he returned to the South at the end of July, Varas relieved him of the Intendancy of Concepción. Cruz had told Varas of his wish to step down, but had not submitted a formal resignation, and felt aggrieved. "General Cruz will never be a caudillo of revolts," he had assured Varas in February.[114] The government half expected him to break his word. Its eyes turned nervously to the south, though *La Tribuna* reassured it that since Concepción was now moving from the "political" to the "industrial" era, a revolution there was unthinkable.[115] On August 31, Montt was proclaimed president-elect to the sound of trumpets, but an American observer noticed that "there was neither enthusiasm nor cheering" from the crowd.[116] By the time he was inaugurated on September 18, word had reached Santiago that La Serena was in revolt. The next day, as the new president made his way to the traditional military parade, a messenger galloped into the city with the news that Concepción had followed suit. Laying down the presidency, Manuel Bulnes became a general on active service again, riding south three days later (in a convoy of *birlochos*) to save the Conservative regime in its hour of maximum danger.

Manuel Montt's First Civil War

The revolt of La Serena (September 7, 1851) was staged by local Liberals, led by the rich and respectable Nicolás Munizaga and figures like the journalist Juan Nicolás Álvarez (of *El Diablo Político* fame) and the "tribune" Pedro Pablo Muñoz, active in the local *Sociedad Patriótica*, which bore a resemblance to the *Sociedad de la Igualdad*. The *serenenses* were supported by Liberals who had earlier fled from Santiago, among them José Miguel Carrera (who became revolutionary Intendant of Coquimbo) and Benjamín Vicuña Mackenna. The rebels neutralized the Yungay Regiment, stationed in the city, by inviting its officers to lunch and taking them prisoner. Colonel Justo Arteaga, Colonel Urriola's second-in-command during the Easter rising, traveled from his exile in Bolivia to offer his services. The revolutionaries sent small forces in the direction of Santiago, one of them captained by the twenty-year-old Vicuña Mackenna, who later dramatized his role in the kind of lyrical prose historians are no longer permitted to use.

114 Cruz to Varas, February 18, 1851. *Revista Chilena*, Año V, Tomo XII, No. 44 (1921), p. 39.
115 TRI, No. 699, September 10, 1851; cf. No. 684, August 22, 1850.
116 Gilliss, p. 309.

His expedition got no further than Illapel, where on September 18, dressed in his little brief authority, he presided over a dignified celebration of the national holiday. A later expedition under Colonel Arteaga was routed at Petorca, further south, by government troops commanded by Colonel Juan Vidaurre Leal. Fifty or sixty rebels died. Vidaurre Leal then laid siege to La Serena, assisted by the ever-useful Victorino Garrido. The morale of the city's defenders remained high. Ad hoc news-sheets such as *El Periodiquito de la Plaza* raised their spirits with vividly malicious attacks on Montt.[117] They kept Vidaurre Leal and Garrido at bay for weeks.

The north was a distraction, although not a trivial one. The south was a different matter. General Cruz was a national figure, a veteran of independence and a hero of the 1836–9 war second only to Bulnes. Much fêted on his return from Santiago in July, Cruz had thrown himself into a vigorous social round. "He gave a second ball last Saturday," reported the young judge Rafael Sotomayor to Varas on August 26, "and he will offer a banquet to the artisans. Perhaps everything will stay on the level of banquets and Bacchic feasts."[118] It did not. The prime movers of the revolutionary movement in Concepción were the tireless *pipiolo* Pedro Félix Vicuña and a well-known soldier, General Fernando Baquedano, helped by an elderly but eloquent local priest, Father Sierra. On September 13, Vicuña and Baquedano persuaded ninety-five prominent citizens to sign a revolutionary *acta*, refusing to accept Montt as president and asserting Concepción's independence of Santiago. Vicuña became interim Intendant. Cruz, meanwhile, had secluded himself on one of his haciendas, and hesitated for several days before deciding to cross his personal Rubicon. His position seemed strong. He had about two thousand infantrymen at his disposal, and at least as many potential cavalrymen.

The rhetoric of both the northern and southern rebellions was in some ways a strange throwback to the independence period. "Using the imprescriptible rights of the Sovereignty of the People," states the Concepción *acta* of September 13, "we declare the social pact broken, resuming our powers and withdrawing those we had delegated to the authorities established in the Constitution of 1833."[119] There was a similar declaration in La Serena. The only program offered by the revolutionaries was the creation of a provisional government pending the summoning of a constituent assembly.[120] It was not to be expected that General Cruz would contribute much in the way of ideological coherence. He merely stressed that it was necessary to "overthrow the despotism now enthroned," and that his cause

117 For example, *Periodiquito de la Plaza*, No. 4, December 14, 1851; No. 6, December 23, 1851.
118 Sotomayor to Varas, August 26, 1851. Ruz T., p. 47.
119 See *Boletín del Sur*, No. 9, October 24, 1851.
120 *Boletín del Sur*, No. 2, October 8, 1851.

was "that of the Republic, the cause of the people."[121] He declared that he would rid Chile of "that parody of a government" and "the sinister figure of Manuel Montt, whose unrestrained ambition has compromised the peace of the country."[122]

One of the rebels' first actions, both in north and south, was to seize two small steamships, one of them British-owned (and used by the Franco-British mining magnate Charles Lambert), with the aim of keeping the two wings of the revolution in contact. The tiny Chilean Navy had no steam-powered warships. With the consent of the government, and the enthusiastic backing of the British minister in Chile, Stephen Sulivan (a ne'er-do-well nephew of British foreign secretary Lord Palmerston),[123] the British naval squadron stationed off Valparaiso recaptured both the ships and placed Coquimbo under blockade.[124] "If those infamous gringos rob us at sea, we should cut off their heads on land!" expostulated Pedro Félix Vicuña,[125] – who, after the Easter rising, had fled aboard a British warship. In fact, the rebels were angrier with Montt, for sanctioning foreign intervention in a Chilean quarrel. There was nothing much they could do about it. Nor were their efforts at fomenting popular risings in the cities very successful. In Valparaiso, four months earlier, the authorities had stopped a British freighter from landing a consignment of arms, wounding its captain in the affray.[126] The insurrection in the port (October 28) was quickly suppressed by Intendant Blanco Encalada, with the help of his naval adjutant, Lieutenant-Commander Patricio Lynch, who was wounded in the fighting and promoted to the rank of Commander for his pains. A French pharmacist living in Valparaiso describes the episode in a vivid letter.

A band of tattered men seized a [civic guard] barracks and rifles, cannon and ammunition; there were six hundred or so who packed the top of our street . . . Blanco

121 Cruz, *Compatriotas!*
122 Cruz, *Soldados del ejército.*
123 Sulivan was transferred to Chile in early 1850 by his eminent uncle, from a diplomatic posting in Munich, where his taking of a mistress had caused scandal. His Italian wife was a former mistress. In Santiago he took yet another mistress. His reports to the Foreign Office were full of bilious contempt for Chileans. Palmerston moved him to Lima at the end of 1852. During General Manuel Ignacio Vivanco's rebellion in Peru (1856–8), the Royal Navy seized a rebel ship that had attacked a British steamer. Sulivan authorized its handover to the government. At dinner on August 11, 1857, with his secretary and a new mistress, Nicida Vidal, Sulivan was shot by an intruder at close range with a blunderbuss, and died within two days. The British (including Palmerston) apparently accepted it as a political murder, inspired by Vivanco's partisans. It is more likely that either Sulivan's estranged wife or Nicida Vidal (by all accounts a high-class gold-digger) were behind it. See Kenneth Bourne, ed., *The Letters of the Third Viscount Palmerston to Laurence and Elizabeth Sulivan, 1804–1863*, Camden Fourth Series, Vol. 23 (London, 1979), pp. 24–26.
124 For information on the British involvement, see Mayo, pp. 68–74.
125 Quoted in Ag. Edwards, *Cuatro Presidentes*, I, 82.
126 Intendant Blanco Encalada to Interior minister, June 24, 1851. AMI, Vol. 265.

[Encalada] . . . arrived at the head of 150 soldiers of the line and was received by a discharge which killed several of his men. A fusillade began, and in half an hour they (the insurgents) were repulsed. There were about forty dead. The bullets whistled over our house, but as they were firing high, nobody in the house was wounded; we spent the night with some doctors and others dressing the wounded before they were taken to the hospital. . . . The crews of warships . . . were landed to stop pillaging if the [government] troops were defeated; the French, the English and the Americans each had a company ashore. Everything was back in order the next day.[127]

Early in November, having assembled an army of more than thirty-three hundred men, General Bulnes advanced to the Ñuble river. The first clash of the two armies, at Monte de Urra (November 19), was an indecisive cavalry engagement. Cruz marched northward with reinforcements, but Bulnes managed to overtake him, and the key battle of the campaign, grim and ferocious, was fought on December 8 at the confluence of the Maule and Loncomilla rivers. Bulnes himself rode into the thick of battle. Cruz's soldiers, however, resisted fiercely, and after several hours of fighting Bulnes withdrew. Technically, neither side won the battle of Loncomilla. No official figures were published, but at least eighteen hundred (and conceivably over two thousand) soldiers died either on the battlefield or by drowning in the Loncomilla river. Cruz discovered that two of his colonels (and their men) were treacherously abandoning him – a suspicion was voiced that the government had bribed them – and reluctantly accepted Bulnes's conditions for peace. On December 16, the two cousins lunched together and duly signed an agreement, the Treaty of Purapel, embodying honorable terms. In exchange for Cruz's surrender and recognition of Montt as president, rebel soldiers were allowed to rejoin the national army with their ranks (and pensions) unaltered. Bulnes also undertook to try to secure a general amnesty. Cruz returned to his estates and lived his remaining twenty-two years in peace and quiet.

Meanwhile, at La Serena, disagreements within the rebel camp (mostly between Colonel Arteaga and José Miguel Carrera) and news of the Purapel capitulation finally undermined the will to continue the struggle. Arteaga fled aboard a French warship, Carrera into the mountains. General Vidaurre Leal quickly took possession of the city (December 31, 1851). This was not quite the end of disturbances in the north. Atacama Province, loyal to Montt, had been denuded of government troops, which had gone to help besiege La Serena. At the end of October the mining camp at Chañarcillo was comprehensively sacked by its mine workers, to the cry of "Long live Cruz!" The tumult was suppressed by a hastily mustered force from Copiapó under

127 Joseph Miran to Joseph Miran (brother), January 25, 1852. Roudié, pp. 67–68.

José Joaquín Vallejo's command. A further revolt ostensibly in favor of Cruz suddenly broke out in Copiapó itself at the very end of the year. Victorino Garrido soon quelled this brief final spasm of rebellion, in a skirmish to the west of the city on January 8, 1852, the last action of the civil war. Only three days later, however, news reached Valparaiso of a horrific mutiny in the Magellan Strait penal colony, where a sadistic lieutenant, Miguel José Cambiaso, had imposed a sanguinary reign of terror on the settlement, again ostensibly on behalf of Cruz. Cambiaso and seven of his henchmen were hung, drawn and quartered in Valparaiso in April 1852. They were never claimed by Liberals as heroes of liberty.

The crisis of 1851 was the worst faced by the Conservative regime in its twenty years of power. But the government weathered the storm, overcoming the dramatic efforts of Liberal revolutionaries and the military muscle of General Cruz. Manuel Montt, his adamant will to rule thus demonstrated, was left in unchallenged command of the republic. It may be doubted whether he agreed with the view of the civil war taken by the newspaper *El Copiapino* – that after twenty years of peace "it was necessary for us to suffer an eruption, so as to be able to await more bounteous and lasting peace and quiet."[128] The next eruption, as it happened, came eight years later, with Manuel Montt's second civil war.

---

128 *Copiapino*, No. 1203, December 11, 1851. Vicuña Mackenna, *Historia de los diez años*, remains the most comprehensive narrative of the civil war.

PART III

Mid-Century Attitudes

5

Progress and Its Instruments

The political struggles within Chile's governing class during the making of the republic seem, on the face of it, to have been clear enough – defeated (and reviving) Liberals at loggerheads with victorious Conservatives, the champions of liberty versus the upholders of order. In many respects, however, Conservatives and Liberals always laid claim to rather similar ideological terrain, despite their fierce struggles, and used a common language when attacking each other, as we have noted in the electoral propaganda of 1851. Certainly the great keywords of the period – "liberty," "reform," "democracy," "progress," "civilization," and so on – were used with comparable frequency by the two sides, although the use made of them by Conservatives and Liberals was sometimes slightly different.[1]

There were many ways in which disagreements did not run along party lines at all. This was especially true of the practical reforms and improvements both sides wished to see in the Chile of the period. All the evidence we have suggests that the political class *as a whole* rather clearly favored policies such as (to take the two outstanding cases) the promotion of education and the encouragement of European immigration. When there were differing approaches to the practical application of such policies, Conservatives and Liberals were always to be found on both sides of the argument. The solvent was the idea of *progress.* We do not need to remind ourselves here how this essentially modern concept took shape (after its first seventeenth-century stirrings) during the European Enlightenment (especially the later Enlightenment) and came to underpin the nineteenth-century's version of modernity, the vision of which swept the entire Western world. In

---

1 Most of the keywords used by Chilean writers and politicians at this period have more or less the meanings they retain today. Some had greater novelty value, and perhaps more of an emotional charge, than they do nowadays. "Progress" (in its principal modern meaning) and "civilization" are eighteenth-century words, inseparably associated with the Enlightenment, and "Liberal" (in its partisan sense) is a label from the Cadiz Cortes (1810–13) in Spain, from where it spread to the rest of the world. "Democracy," in Chile at least, seems to have lost all its earlier negative connotations by the mid-nineteenth century and was essentially a synonym for representative government.

its nineteenth-century form, the idea of progress, tied to the notion of a permanent evolutionary process (later reinforced by Darwin's revolutionary insights) and often associated with political liberalism, can be described as relatively uncomplicated. In the twentieth century, with all its apocalyptic violence, the idea (although it certainly retained much of its hold over the popular mind) inevitably became (indeed, had to become) more qualified, or at any rate a good deal more nuanced.

Progress

Almost all educated Chileans in the early republic seem to have believed that progress was the key to (indeed the "master-narrative" of) the times they were living through. The concept had been assimilated into the Chilean political outlook during the independence period, often in the form of glowing visions of the national future,[2] but it became a more frequently articulated theme in the decades that followed. It is revealing that Santiago's first daily newspaper chose to call itself *El Progreso* – far and away the most popular title for newly founded Chilean newspapers over the next century. How did Chileans see progress? "If gravity is the universal constitution given by the Creator to all his worlds," *El Progreso*'s first editorial declared, "it can be said that progress is the internal rule for each of them."[3] A Conservative newspaper of 1853 defined it as the "spontaneous fermentation and natural elaboration of the elements inherent in society; the constant succession of human affairs on an ever-ascending highway."[4] In the age of Tennyson (with his "vision of the world and all the wonder that would be") and Victor Hugo (with his *"Nef magique et suprême"* sailing toward a sublime and majestic future), it was possible to be altogether more rhapsodic than this. Jacinto Chacón, in a long poem of 1846, presented a vision of progress in which sixteenth-century Europe was the starting point, with its gift of "liberty and independence to the world." America, because of the Spanish conquest, had been less fortunate – "Great Philip II! / Your sepulchral spirit stains a world!" However, "Albion, genius of the North," with its "industrious cohort," had planted democracy in the American continent. Finally, thanks to France, "the modern Eagle," Spanish America was reviving. Chile had entered the world of progress: "Advancing Humanity enrolls you!" Chileans needed to study "the book of history," whose laws were even now being uncovered by noble European spirits like Guizot and Hegel.

2 Collier, *Ideas*, pp. 183–85.
3 PR, No. 1, November 10, 1842.
4 *Mensajero*, No. 119, November 22, 1853.

Oh Patria! en ese libro tu porvenir medita.
En gérmen una lucha en tu interior se agita,
Lo viejo va muriendo, lo nuevo va dentrando,
Tu gótico edificio la Europa va minando.

Oh homeland! contemplate your future in that book!
Within you, the germ of a struggle is agitating,
The old is dying, the new is coming in,
Europe is undermining your Gothic edifice.[5]

In a later poem, Chacón (a man much given to versifying) lengthened his historical perspective, starting this time with the fall of the Roman Empire and the birth of its successor-nations, a process now being repeated in Spanish America.

Así gira la máquina del mundo,
Pueblos cayendo, pueblos levantando,
Así a la humanidad va renovando
De tiempo en tiempo, espíritu fecundo;
Y así vas realizando
¡GEÓMETRA CREADOR! tu plan profundo.

Thus turns the machine of the world,
Peoples falling, peoples rising,
And thus you renew humanity
From time to time, oh fertile spirit.
And thus you are fulfilling
CREATOR-GEOMETER! your profound scheme.[6]

By no means all educated Chileans would have appreciated the nebulous spiritual component in Chacón's picture. (His cast of mind *was* strongly metaphysical.) Yet, most of them would probably have seen history as heading (to quote a disquisition on legal education) in "an indefinitely progressive direction." As the disquisition's author explained, "the route traced for humanity by the grand plan of creation is not, as Vico thought, a circle, but a straight line."[7]

Yet the straight line often encountered obstacles. The reason for this, according to Liberal poet Salvador Sanfuentes, was the interaction of two social impulses planted by the "Supreme Regulator": "the need for advance" and "the instinct to preserve what already exists." The "definitive triumph"

---

5 Chacón, *Discurso*, pp. 32–39.
6 Chacón, "Himno a la Providencia por la libertad de América," *Revista del Pacífico*, Vol. III (1860), p. 323.
7 Fernández Concha, p. 9.

of progress, Sanfuentes believed, was still many ages away.[8] But whatever the setbacks, there was good reason for hope. "The past weighs on men's shoulders, the present is slippery," observed *El Progreso*, "but the future is always smiling." Even catastrophes like the French Revolution, according to *El Progreso*, had their place in the onward march: "Behind, to be sure, you will see corpses and blood, but ahead you will see life, splendor and perfection."[9] Perfection, in fact, was often described as the ultimate goal of progress. For Martín Palma, a distinguished journalist (later a controversial anticlerical novelist), perfectibility was the key impulse in humankind, "an invisible hand" that pushed the human race onward and upward.[10]

However they conceived of progress in abstract terms, most educated Chileans would have agreed that it took a visible and material form. "*Material progress* is the fascinating term of the moment," reported the *Revista Católica* (not very approvingly) in 1852, "the term that feeds the illusions of journalists and fills their hearts with enthusiasm."[11] It certainly did. Those who opposed material improvement were denounced by the pro-government *El Ferrocarril* as believing "that . . . barbarism is worth more than civilization, poverty worth more than riches, the ignorant man worth more than the educated man, the Kaffir or the Hottentot worth more than the Englishman or the Frenchman," and Manuel Miquel, in one of the few serious economic treatises to be written during the early republic, sounded the same note. To oppose machines, he insisted, was "to defend ignorance, routine, idleness, and barbarism."[12]

One reason for the nineteenth-century triumph of the idea of progress, as we know, was its continuous reinforcement by manifest scientific and technical advance. Chilean newspapers, caught up in the Western world's enthusiasm for technological innovations, often took note of new developments, even some that were abortive, like W. H. Henson's steam-powered "aerostat" in England, which provoked a lyrical editorial in *El Mercurio* on the "immense future offered by aerial navigation."[13] The coming of the steamship and the railroad were greeted with unfeigned delight. One or two of the captivating essays of José Joaquín Vallejo reveal the obvious pleasure he felt when traveling aboard the new P.S.N.C. paddle-steamers. Commenting on the construction of the Caldera-Copiapó line, an 1851 almanac hailed the railroad as "the glorification of human genius."[14] President Bulnes, in his farewell address (1851), praising "the marvels our age

8 "Chile desde la batalla de Chacabuco hasta la de Maipó," in Vicuña Mackenna, *Historia general*, III, 15.
9 PR, No. 260, September 18, 1843.
10 Palma, *El cristianismo político*, p. 1.
11 RCAT, No. 284, November 20, 1852, p. 457.
12 FE, No. 1223, December 3, 1859; Miquel, p. 138.
13 MV, No. 4485, July 3, 1843.
14 *Almanaque pintoresco*, p. 32.

has witnessed," was proud to number railroad building plans as "one of the emblems" of his government.[15]

It is difficult to find serious criticism of material improvement among Chilean writers of the time. A dissenting voice, it is true, was sometimes heard from the Catholic Church. Its house journal, *La Revista Católica*, repeatedly pointed out that progress was not everything. It inveighed against the "senseless materialism" obviously invading Chile, and protested that "the idea of indefinite progress" and the elimination of the "miseries afflicting humanity today" was no more than a fantasy "in the delirious heads of certain philosophers of our time."[16] Slightly anticipating Pope Pius IX's *Syllabus*, the *Revista Católica* openly identified "*modern civilization*" as the main enemy. But although it denied that "unbelieving and materially progressive men" could ever be truly civilized,[17] it usually paid at least lipservice to technological progress. The archbishop of Santiago, we might note, was on hand at the inauguration of the Santiago–Valparaiso railroad in September 1863. He blessed the locomotive and made the keynote speech before the president and his party left for their sumptuous banquet at Llay-Llay, halfway down the line. Suitably deferential to this grand achievement of high technology, he could not resist deflating the assembled politicians and engineers by pointing out that God could have revealed the steam engine much earlier if he had felt like it.[18] This was not a point that occurred to anyone making the speeches at Llay-Llay.

Capitalism and the State

Progress, according to the Conservative newspaper of 1853 quoted earlier, was "achieved independently of all human effort."[19] This was a convenient doctrine, but most Chileans assumed that there were ways of spurring progress onward with specific *improvements*. "Improvements are good . . . ; they demonstrate the nation's progress," as Senator Manuel José Balmaceda[20] put it in 1860.[21] There also was widespread recognition that Chile's poverty positively demanded the touch of progressive reforms. Chile, for *El Ferrocarril*, was "an hacienda which, though fertile, is completely uncultivated . . . , an estate where we must begin by making great improvements."[22] But what improvements? What would nowadays be called

15 DP, III, 787.
16 RCAT, No. 436, April 26, 1857.
17 RCAT, No. 284, November 20, 1852.
18 Rivera Jofré, pp. 115–19.
19 *Mensajero*, No. 119, November 22, 1853.
20 Manuel José Fernández de Balmaceda y Ballesteros, the father of José Manuel Balmaceda (President of Chile, 1886–91).
21 CN/S, August 20, 1860.
22 FE, No. 735, May 6, 1858, editorial.

economic development was obviously fundamental. "Trade, industry, population, immigration, public education," suggested *La Crónica* in 1849, were "the true interest of the people and the aim of a wise, just and advantageous policy."[23] Trade and industry,[24] according to *El Mercurio*, had "a highly moralizing influence. . . . To strengthen . . . the commercial spirit is to civilize."[25] The main instrument of progress, therefore, was seen to be private enterprise — what Interior minister Manuel Montt called in 1845 "the spirit of association, the germ of great and useful enterprises."[26] Editorializing on the need for highways, *El Mercurio* emphasized that "These works are always done more perfectly and at lower cost when they are done by private enterprise, whose interested parties watch over them with greater assiduousness and effort than the subaltern agents of the government."[27]

And yet, as *El Mercurio* admitted almost in the same breath, the "spirit of enterprise" was sadly lacking in Chile. This was a recurrent theme among politicians and writers, who were often frustrated at the slow growth of the proper capitalist ethos.[28] "Without association, no great enterprises," moaned *El Ferrocarril* in 1859, "and without them, no rapid and tangible growth in the life of a nation."[29] The Santiago–Valparaiso railroad, complained Interior minister Antonio Varas in 1855, was opposed by "men without faith in the future of the country . . ., dominated by a spirit of routine," while an earlier Interior minister, Ramón Luis Irarrázaval, deplored the fact that "in Chile . . ., society still demands everything from . . . authority."[30] Given such inertia, it was widely agreed that the government needed to *stimulate* enterprise. Speaking in 1851 on the railroad issue, Senator Diego José Benavente compared countries like England or the United States, where private enterprise had produced "magnificent results," with those (like Germany) whose developed "administrative regime" enabled the state to act as entrepreneur. Chile, Benavente maintained, fell into

23 *Crónica*, No. 7, March 11, 1849.

24 The word *industria*, "industry," was used at this period to cover *productive work* in general, with no necessary connotation of manufacturing industry as such, which was often referred to as *industria fabril*.

25 MV, No. 4651, December 18, 1843.

26 DP, II, 353.

27 MV, No. 3380, March 20, 1840.

28 In fact, there was some quite vigorous entrepreneurship in the early republic, mostly in mining and trade, by figures such as (to name only half a dozen) José Tomás Urmeneta (copper), José Ramón Ovalle (copper), Francisco Echeverría (copper), Matías Cousiño (coal), Agustín Edwards (trade), and Emeterio Goyenechea (mining, land, trade). We need a comprehensive survey of such entrepreneurship as existed. The general perception seems to have been that there simply was not enough of it.

29 FE, No. 1135, August 20, 1859.

30 DP, V, 268; DP, II, 221. For the arguments against the railroad in the 1847 Senate, similar to those used in many countries, see Barros Arana, *Decenio*, II, 160–62.

neither category. He therefore recommended "a mixed system" in which "government cooperation" combined with "private interests."[31] Looking back on the Santiago–Valparaiso railroad venture after the government bought out the private shareholders (as it did in 1858), *El Ferrocarril* agreed that government abstention from economic involvement could accomplish marvels in advanced countries, citing (perhaps not altogether happily) "the political and economic domination of India by a single commercial company." But could private interests alone complete the Santiago–Valparaiso railroad? Obviously not. There were certain material improvements for which "the entire nation" had to assume responsibility.[32] There was something like a consensus on this point. Manuel Miquel's economic treatise of 1863 distinguished between "the spontaneous action of individuals" he saw as the main key to progress, and the role of government, which was "to facilitate that action" by maintaining order, and by "multiplying railroads, improving where possible the means of communication, and extensively diffusing primary education."[33] This certainly accorded with the role the Chilean state took in real life.

Our concern here is less with the economic decisions of the Conservative period than with what seems to have been the general climate of ideas. Governments from independence onward pinned most of their hopes for prosperity on the expansion of foreign trade. Their policies, however, were highly pragmatic, and did not neglect the protection (or attempted protection) of what were seen as vital national interests. Yet, it is also fairly clear that the economic *outlook* that developed among educated Chileans (in the abstract) was favorable to free (or freer) trade even before the arrival in 1855 of the French economist Jean-Gustave Courcelle Seneuil, who is often credited with spreading liberal economic doctrine. (He did, but in much more moderate form than the legend has us believe.) *El Mercurio*, which was usually well attuned to the commercial ethos of Valparaiso, claimed in 1856 that "the theories of free trade have been proved among us, and we have seen that in practice they are good, they are of easy application, [and] give sure results."[34] A year later, the same newspaper declared that in economic theory Conservatives and Liberals were completely at one: "Free trade is now a national doctrine . . . : in England the Torys [*sic*] were partisans of protectionist laws and the Whigs of the emancipation of trade; amongst us, everyone is for the good principle."[35]

In respect of the general drift of ideas, *El Mercurio* may well have been correct, but it exaggerated the degree of consensus. As Sergio Villalobos and

31 CN/S, August 8, 1851.
32 "El estado. Sus funciones económicas," FE, No. 735, May 6, 1858.
33 Miquel, pp. 239–40.
34 MV, No. 8789, November 4, 1856.
35 MV, No. 9142, December 26, 1857.

Rafael Sagredo have shown, both protectionist measures and protectionist ideas had their exponents in the early republic.[36] Such ideas were by no means ignored in the press. The progovernment *El Mensajero*, for instance, claimed in 1854–5 that Spanish American manufacturing was in a state of "true dependence [and] slavery" with respect to Europe, and urged the creation of a state textile industry.[37] Ten years earlier, the highly intelligent Conservative, Antonio García Reyes, objecting to concessions made to Britain in a recent commercial treaty, sketched (rather eloquently) a plan for an "American Commercial League" to develop manufacturing industry and markets so as to free Spanish America's economy from "the European yoke that oppresses it." Given a long period of peace, he believed, manufacturing could well develop strongly in Spanish America. But "the rude and gross artefacts of our own industry" were poorly placed to compete with "all the inventions" now arriving from Europe, so that Spanish American manufactures were drowned "at the moment of birth." A protected Spanish American free trade zone, García Reyes believed, could provide a framework for the growth of manufacturing at least to the point where it could satisfy most domestic needs.[38]

The issue of protection and free trade was sometimes debated in Congress. A proposal to lower duties on silks in 1854, for instance, provoked Interior minister Antonio Varas to ask why Chile should not emulate the United States, which protected its industries. "In our country," he argued, "there are only two self-sufficient industries: agriculture and mining. Take away the protective system, and what future do we leave to the artisan, the man of the workshop . . . who does not have a piece of land to farm? Will we leave open to him simply the career of a casual laborer?" Varas was acutely conscious of the tension between the ideal and the practical in commercial policy. In a debate in 1852 on the raising of duties on exported minerals, which had been denounced as unmodern and "antieconomic," he observed: "Oh that we could free the products of national industry from all imposts! but . . . it is one thing to write a book, and quite another to apply its doctrines to . . . a state."[39] Varas may well have seen free trade as an ultimate ideal, but he was not prepared to abandon the intelligent pragmatism that had been the hallmark of policy from Manuel Rengifo's time onward.

36 Villalobos and Sagredo, *El proteccionismo*, pp. 33–59. See the essays by Andrés Bello, Pedro Félix Vicuña, Vicente Sanfuentes, Juan Bello, Marcial González, and Cristóval Valdez in Villalobos and Sagredo, ed., *Ensayistas*, pp. 29–231. Economic ideas in the early republic deserve deeper investigation. An excellent study in this line, for Peru, is Paul Gootenberg, *Imagining Development. Economic Ideas in Peru's "Fictitious Prosperity" of Guano, 1840–1880* (Berkeley, Calif., 1993).

37 *Mensajero*, No. 241, March 9, 1854; No. 598, May 22, 1855.

38 Minority report, Government Committee, Chamber of Deputies, December 20, 1844. SCL, XXXIV, 661–63.

39 CN/D, August 8, 1854; CN/D, September 24, 1852.

Education

A memorandum on primary education submitted to the University of Chile in 1856, taking a glance at the United States, asked whether Spanish Americans were simply unfitted for modern industry. Yet had North Americans been so different "three centuries ago?" It concluded that it was "not the race, but education, that produces the admirable industrial aptitude of certain peoples in the other hemisphere."[40] Education was seen by upper-class Chileans as the key to both material progress and eventual democratization. "Our present institutions are only a promise," editorialized *El Mercurio* in 1841, "the framework or skeleton which it is necessary to fill up:" preparation for liberty through education should therefore be the "primordial occupation" of government and people alike.[41]

The hopes pinned on education were sometimes utopian. "There is not, perhaps, a single good quality that is not enhanced, or a single vice that cannot be extirpated," declared *El Mercurio*, "when exposed to the beneficent influence of education."[42] A treatise on the subject by Francisco Díaz Prado (1856) went further than this by asserting that education would bring "individual self-perfection, and with it the complete regeneration of society." With proper education, a Chilean's life would become "a continuous progress, a ceaseless apprenticeship, and, as the years go by, his qualities will become ever more recommendable," so that in the future the country would "present a magnificent spectacle of good customs."[43]

The 1833 Constitution (Article 153) described education as "a matter of preferential attention" for the state, and mandated Congress to produce "a general plan for national education." In his ministerial report for 1836, Interior minister Diego Portales eloquently (indeed, strikingly) underlined the government's priorities.

It is not necessary to tell legislators of the immense ground we still have to cover to give education all its appropriate scope, which is to say putting it within reach of the poorest class in even the remotest corners of the Republic; nor do I think it necessary to remind you of the difficulties we must overcome to reach that point, which is certainly what we should propose to ourselves, however distant its achievement.[44]

The difficulties *were* extreme. It was beyond the power of any Chilean government of the time to achieve Portales's vision. But it remained the standard vision. In 1849–50, when the first serious primary school bill

40 *Memoria sobre instrucción primaria*, pp. 34–36.
41 MV, No. 3770, June 22, 1841.
42 MV, No. 3164, July 3, 1839.
43 Díaz Prado, pp. 77–78.
44 *Memoria* of Interior minister (1836). DP, I, 93.

came before Congress, Portales's disciple Manuel Montt stated firmly that his basic principle was "the right the inhabitants of the State have to be given free primary education, and the consequential duty of the State to give them that education." Proposing two schools (one for boys, one for girls) for every two thousand Chileans, he claimed that "it is the least we can demand if we have pretensions to call ourselves a civilized people."[45] Montt's great adversary Lastarria agreed with him, viewing primary education as an "indispensable condition for the development of society, and therefore a right the State should satisfy."[46] Montt's proposed bill, however, was doomed by his insistence that primary education should be locally organized and funded from a locally levied tax, ideas he had assimilated from his Argentine friend Sarmiento, who had himself assimilated them during a recent visit to the United States. The Chamber of Deputies defeated the bill (30 to 13) and it was ten years before it returned to Congress, with centralized state control written in, but no method of financing proposed.

While Montt, when president, was assiduous in creating new primary schools, the "immense ground" of which Portales had spoken remained almost as immense as ever, something reflected in official rhetoric. As Justice minister Silvestre Ochagavía reported in 1853, nine tenths of the population reached working age "without having acquired any kind of knowledge, any germ of civilization." This was one reason for "the inferiority of our means of production and the backwardness of our industry." Ochagavía was well aware of a certain public skepticism about educating the poor, and asked, with heavy irony:

Our men on the city-outskirts and in the fields . . . , wallowing in liquor and in abject degradation – *are they vicious because they know how to read?* Have they perchance *just come out of school* . . . ? No: they are men who do not distinguish good from bad, because they are uncultured, abandoned to instincts and wild passions which education alone can correct – by capturing their hearts, enlightening and strengthening their reason until its precepts triumph.[47]

As Sol Serrano has shown, in an excellent study, there was a remarkable degree of consensus within the political class over both the *control* and the *content* of education. Article 1 of the 1860 law stated that primary education should be open to everyone "under the direction of the State." (Antonio Varas thought the provision had "a certain flavor of socialism," and feared that if the state was obliged to teach on the grounds that education was an "essential element of society," it might eventually be obliged to feed the

45 CN/D, October 19, 1849.
46 CN/D, June 12, 1850.
47 *Memoria* of Justice minister (1853). DP, IV, 325.

population on the same grounds.)[48] The state's indirect control of private schools (through the University of Chile) was similarly uncontroversial. As for the content of education, nobody questioned the principle that it should include an element of religious instruction,[49] although there were sometimes debates on the role of the clergy in imparting it.[50] The consensus would only break down in the 1870s, when education became a divisive political issue for the first time. This emphatically does not mean that there were no criticisms of the *state* of education. Díaz Prado's treatise identifies seven serious difficulties: a lack of suitable teachers, a lack of textbooks, low salaries for teachers, the tendency of some teachers to refuse to admit poorer children, the dispersed nature of the population, the lack of will by the poor to receive education, and inadequate funding. To resolve the last two problems, Díaz Prado proposes a special property tax, and suggests that primary education be made obligatory. The 1860 law did no more than establish the *principle* of free primary education. Not until 1920 did it become obligatory.

There were also doubts as to whether the *kind* of education being given in the early republic was appropriate. Manuel Miquel's economic treatise, one of the more intelligent discussions of this theme, took for granted that a country's prosperity depended on "development of its productive forces," and that the "primordial" way of stimulating these was education. But education lacked a technical orientation. It was easy enough to find "men of letters and lawyers who have become celebrities," but far more difficult to find "enlightened farmers, engineers [or] financiers." Miquel blamed his compatriots' predilection for taking up legal careers before entering trade or agriculture: "Possessors of great fortunes, they have no idea how to use them for their own profit or the good of the country in general."[51]

Immigration

There was a second instrument of progress about which there was no real disagreement: immigration, by which was meant European immigration. There existed "a unanimous conviction," according to a periodical of 1856, that it was "the mainspring of our social transformation."[52] The fundamental presupposition here was stated in a treatise by Marcial González (1848): immigration, he asserted, brought "more civilization than the best books, more wealth than a thousand ships laden with

48 CN/D, June 7, 1859.
49 Serrano, *Universidad*, pp. 81–89.
50 For example, CN/D, June 1860.
51 Miquel, pp. 118–19.
52 *Mensajero de la Agricultura*, "Prospecto," October 1856.

manufactures." Noting "the quasi-fabulous development" of the United States, with its hordes of immigrants, González suggested that Chile did not need additional manpower so much as examples of work and skill that would help train the poor, "the useless, ignorant and idle rabble."[53]

Certainly there seems to have been a widespread belief that foreign immigrants automatically spelled progress. Reporting on the arrival of four hundred Australians (attracted by news of the big fire in Valparaiso in March 1843 and the reconstruction it would entail), *El Mercurio* applauded the "introduction of foreigners, industrious and of good morals" as a means of spreading modern arts and crafts.[54] One of Antonio García Reyes's hopes, in the document quoted earlier, was that immigration might bring "useful men" for Chilean manufacturing.[55] The point was made in more homely fashion by Interior minister Antonio Varas in 1854. The foreign artisan, he said, had a positive effect on Chilean artisans: "In his workshop the Chilean apprentice begins to train himself so as to become a boss or entrepreneur on his own account, as has often happened with industrious and honorable artisans, who by studying in those foreign workshops have been able to make a way for themselves among the multitude."[56] The same point, although applied to rural workers, was made by Diego José Benavente in a Senate debate the same year. Every immigrant settler on the land, he said, would need to hire "a certain number of peons," and the peons would learn how to be "good farmers."[57]

How many people seriously believed that Chile was a promising destination for mass immigration is hard to say. The country's first colonization law (November 18, 1845), allowing immigrants to settle on state lands, obviously did not contemplate a huge flood. Vicente Pérez Rosales, the tireless sponsor of the small German immigration that took place in the south (around Valdivia and later around Lake Llanquihue) from the end of the 1840s, was well aware that there was no suitable land available for immigrant farmers in the hacienda-dominated Central Valley, although he suggested (vain hope!) that hacendados might reserve a part of their estates for permanent foreign tenants – a good way, he believed, of mixing "foreign inquilinos" with Chilean inquilinos.[58] Juan Bautista Alberdi, the Argentine whose ideas on immigration were so influential in his native land, also favored the introduction into Chile of "European inquilinos."[59] Interestingly, Pérez Rosales also advocated the use

53 González, *Europa*, pp. 18, 41.
54 MV, No. 4665, January 1, 1844.
55 As note 38.
56 CN/D, August 8, 1854.
57 CN/S, September 11, 1854.
58 Pérez Rosales, *Memoria*, p. 135.
59 Bulnes, "Alberdi y Chile," p. 24.

of penal colonies as the basis for future settlement. He evidenced Sydney, Australia, "a fraction of Europe transplanted, as if by magic, 5,000 leagues away."[60] Surely Chile could develop the Magellan Straits penal colony in the same way? Its strategic position was important, as had been shown by "England, occupying the Falkland Islands and promoting . . . a colony there."[61]

While the general view of immigration was positive, there were some who questioned whether it should be indiscriminate. *El Mercurio*, in one of many articles on the subject, speculated that uncontrolled immigration might awaken "the sleeping monster of fanaticism."[62] It did. When the first contingents of Germans arrived in the south, the *Revista Católica* noticed immediately that there were far too many Protestants among them: Valdivia was clearly destined to become a "focus of Protestant propaganda."[63] Discussing a particular colonization plan in the Senate in 1852, Pedro Nolasco Mena proposed that only Catholic immigrants should be admitted. This provoked the caustic Diego José Benavente to riposte: "Are we going out to look for Spaniards? Worse still, Italians? Or Irishmen? God help us! They are as miserable, oppressed, vexed, and ignorant as we are."[64] Interior minister Varas agreed in a later debate that "The Government's interest is that Catholics should come," but also suggested that the idea should not be pressed too far.[65] Nor, in practice, was it.

The church did not give up. It inveighed at regular intervals against the Protestant menace, suggesting that Chile ran the risk "of completely losing its nationality . . . and perhaps also its religion."[66] The *Revista Católica* emphasized that it did not oppose immigration as such: "what we do not want . . . is settlement by Protestants, and by Protestants of a race so different from ours."[67] (As Vicente Pérez Rosales tells us, the church's view was to some extent influenced by a disgruntled German immigrant posing as a "persecuted Catholic.")[68] The *Revista Católica* did its best to put the fear of God into its readers by pointing out the well-known "alliance" between Protestantism and the "sinister systems of communism and socialism."[69] Noting the obvious expansionist plans of what it called "the

60 Pérez Rosales, *Memoria*, p. 152.
61 Pérez Rosales, *Memoria*, p. 154. For his recommendations on the Magellan Strait colony, see pp. 154–72.
62 MV, No. 4281, November 29, 1842.
63 RCAT, No. 270, July 2, 1852.
64 CN/S, September 15, 1852.
65 CN/D, September 15, 1853.
66 RCAT, No. 338, November 26, 1853.
67 RCAT, No. 270, July 2, 1852.
68 See Pérez Rosales, *Recuerdos*, pp. 430–31.
69 RCAT, No. 329, October 15, 1853.

colossus of the north," it maintained that "Catholic unity preserved by Catholic immigration" was the best defense against foreign domination.[70]

Religious Toleration?

The political class had mixed feelings about such arguments. It was not too sure whether religious toleration was an instrument of progress. The positions taken on the issue never corresponded precisely with the Conservative-Liberal divide, although before the 1850s the main proponents of religious liberty tended to be Liberals rather than Conservatives, many of whom were strongly attached to the Church. Article 5 of the 1833 Constitution made Catholicism the republic's official religion and prohibited public worship by other churches. The government, however, always turned a blind eye to the foreign Protestant congregations in Valparaiso. (There were no Spanish-language Protestant services in the country before the late 1860s.) In many ways, the demand for formal religious toleration in Chile grew rather slowly. *El Mercurio*, always sympathetic to the foreign trading communities, became the first newspaper to advocate toleration, although very cautiously at first. Commenting in 1839 on a message by Ecuadorian president Vicente Rocafuerte to his country's congress, it singled out "the eloquent part" – his plea for freedom of worship – as especially commendable.[71] Two years later, it printed an anonymous essay in favor of religious freedom by a student at the Instituto Nacional, which created a minor furor.[72] *El Mercurio*'s continued allusions to religious tolerance sometimes provoked hostile comments from other newspapers. Responding to criticism in the *Gaceta del Comercio*, it claimed that it was doing no more than suggest that the matter might be discussed in the future, although it added: "We know of no country where tolerance of worship has produced the ruin of the state."[73]

Newspaper-reading Chileans were kept well abreast of religious controversies overseas. The opposition *El Siglo*, for instance, ran a series of articles in 1844 on religious cults in the United States, not failing to give an explicit account of the doctrines of Unitarianism.[74] Incidents stemming from mixed marriages – in 1845, the church's forcible seizure of a woman who had married an Englishman aboard a British warship; in 1848, an American *chargé d'affaires* virtually expelled from the country by pressure from the

---

70 RCAT, No. 338, November 26, 1853; cf. RCAT, No. 269, July 2, 1852 for similar arguments.

71 MV, No. 3128, May 20, 1839.

72 MV, No. 3622, January 9, 1841. See also Amunátegui Solar, *Instituto*, pp. 169–83.

73 MV, No. 4290, December 8, 1842. *El Mercurio* was normally deferential to Catholic Christianity *as a religion*, and in July–August 1844 ran a lengthy series of articles on its beneficent effects on Spanish America: "Del cristianismo católico considerado como elemento de civilización en las repúblicas hispanoamericanas," MV, No. 4847, July 3 to No. 4902, August 27, 1844.

74 *Siglo*, Nos. 1–6, April 5–11, 1844. On Unitarianism: No. 3, April 8, 1844.

archbishop after his Protestant marriage to a Chilean – became *causes célèbres*.[75] The press began to take note of instances of Catholic intolerance. *El Progreso* roundly condemned the prohibition by the bishop of La Serena of a long list of books – including the entire works of Voltaire, Rousseau, Diderot, and Lord Byron, selected works by d'Holbach, Condorcet, and Lamennais, nearly all Madame de Staël's novels, and Gibbon's *Decline and Fall of the Roman Empire* ("both in English and French").[76] The *Revista Católica*'s consistent opposition to religious freedom sometimes touched a raw nerve. A short-lived magazine of 1845 took it to task for its rigid attitudes: "Are we living in the nineteenth century," it asked, "or under the pontificate of Alexander VI?"[77] Although it is hard to chart, there was, by the middle and late 1840s, a rising current of anti-clericalism in Chile.[78] It would, as we shall see, play its part in politics before long.

With the revival of Liberalism as a political force at the end of the 1840s, the demand for religious toleration became more public. *El Mercurio* once again led the way, conducting an endless running battle with the *Revista Católica*, whose position remained consistently intransigent. From its earliest issues, the *Revista* had regularly reiterated the view that toleration, whether justifiable or not in the United States or England, was simply inappropriate in a Catholic country like Chile.[79] "The tolerance incessantly preached by *El Mercurio* and the *Diario de Valparaíso*," it thundered in 1852, "is the same preached by Luther and his followers, and taught by Voltaire and his gang . . . ; it is the moral bewitchment that leads directly to irreligion, materialism and atheism."[80] In response to the exposure given by Francisco Bilbao to Lamennais's sinister ideas in 1850, its position hardened into extreme dogmatism: "All Chileans have the obligation," it stated in July 1850, "to believe and profess, both inwardly and outwardly, the Roman, Catholic and Apostolic religion, the only one there really is." It followed from this that Chileans did not even have the *right* to "ask for tolerance of other forms of worship."[81] In a disquisition to the Theology Faculty of the University three years later, Father Pedro Ovalle Ibarra went so far as to claim that the church's unique position in history and "its exclusive character" were such that "it is impossible for it to be tolerant." Father Ovalle even had kind words for the Inquisition.[82]

75 I. Errázuriz, *Historia*, pp. 229–31; Barros Arana, *Decenio*, II, 557–63.
76 PR, No. 948, November 27, 1845.
77 *Entreacto*, No. 1, May 11, 1845.
78 See Collier, "Religious Freedom," pp. 312–14.
79 E.g., RCAT, No. 32, July 9, 1844.
80 RCAT, No. 272, July 27, 1852.
81 RCAT, No. 212, July 24, 1850.
82 "Discurso . . . ante la Facultad de Teología . . . ," September 12, 1853. AUCH, Vol. X (1853), pp. 307, 325–29.

The rising demand for toleration soon found a sympathetic hearing in official circles. Discussing the immigration question in 1854, the heavily subsidized progovernment *El Mensajero* described religious intolerance as an obvious "absurdity." Interior minister Varas certainly sympathized with this view, opposing restrictions on immigration in the Senate as "a kind of public notification of a spirit of intolerance."[83] This in no way deflected the church from its self-imposed mission to defend Chile against the imminent arrival of "the mosque of the Mohammedan, the synagogue of the Jew, the chapel of the Protestant, the pagoda of the Chinese, etc."[84] A provincial news-sheet supported the Church's position somewhat backhandedly, claiming that if Islam were allowed in Chile, all Chileans indulging in *de facto* polygamy would immediately assert that they were Muslims.[85] In the mid-1850s, the new newspaper *El Ferrocarril* joined *El Mercurio* in its advocacy of religious freedom – indeed, its articles on the topic rapidly became a spate. The fact that the church was by then trying to distance itself from the state (see Chapter 9) intensified the *Revista Católica*'s attacks on the apostles of toleration. It regularly (and sometimes luridly) reiterated the "religious principle" as the only barrier to the "purely materialist civilization"[86] that would stem from the inroads of Protestantism in Chile: "Deism, atheism, skepticism, rationalism, pantheism, communism and socialism: these are the seven heads of the great beast engendered by Protestantism, which threatens to devour societies and plunge the world into barbarism."[87] In 1858, the *Revista* began, for the first time, to direct its fire at freemasonry, speculating that England ("which makes such ferocious war on Catholicism everywhere") was behind the freemasons, who, along with the "South American Protestants," were most likely instruments of "the policy of Lord Palmerston."[88] Most literate Chileans (and not merely the handful who by that time were freemasons) had a better opinion of "Pam" than did the *Revista Católica*.

Stung by repeated accusations that the clergy were "fanatics," the *Revista Católica* invited its readers to remember the Paraguay of the Jesuits – "A handful of priests establishing a republic so perfect that the most brilliant imagination could not create it."[89] It may be doubted whether this argument cut much ice. While the feelings of the political class on religious toleration were still moderately ambivalent in the 1850s and 1860s, the tide was flowing strongly in its favor. In 1858 *El Ferrocarril* urged a new

83 *Mensajero*, No. 230, February 22, 1854; CN/S, September 28, 1853.
84 RCAT, No. 387, January 31, 1855.
85 *Emisario*, No. 7, September 4, 1857.
86 RCAT, No. 579, April 4, 1859.
87 RCAT, No. 518, October 24, 1857.
88 RCAT, No. 566, October 16, 1858.
89 RCAT, No. 560, September 4, 1858.

law to "interpret" Article 5, which, it alleged, was being used as a "weapon of fanaticism" by "certain professional Catholics."[90] At the very end of our period, the congressional sittings of 1865 addressed the matter head-on, with debates on the amendment of Article 5, possibly the highest-quality debates the Chilean Congress had yet seen.[91] Even so, the constituency mobilized by the Church and its lay supporters in 1865 was still strong enough to persuade the Pérez government to sponsor an "interpretative law" (as *El Ferrocarril* had suggested), rather than a constitutional amendment as such. It was enough. The interpretative law established for all time the principle of religious freedom in Chile. It also showed clearly that most of the political class had no real wish to live in a Jesuit Republic, however brilliant. Quite apart from anything else, Jesuit Republics had no place for politics. It was politics that excited Chileans most of all, and it is to their political differences that we must next turn.

90 FE, No. 753, May 27, 1858.
91 See Collier, "Religious Freedom," pp. 314–18.

6
Political Argument

Now tell us all about the war,
And what they fought each other for.

The question Old Kaspar could not answer in Robert Southey's poem could well be applied to the early republic in Chile. What divided the political class, given its social and economic homogeneity, other than the eternal competition of "ins" and "outs" to be found in most political systems? That particular competition can frequently provoke fierce partisanship even in the absence of strong ideological differences. In essence, the divisions among Chileans stemmed mostly from conflicting views of how best to conduct the government of Chile, Conservatives believing above all in firm control, with repressive measures when needed (in their view), and their Liberal opponents arguing for a more relaxed approach, with proper respect for civil liberty. While a similar ideological tussle can be observed in many forms in the governing classes (and sometimes at a more popular level) all over nineteenth-century Latin America, the main issues in the political debate in Chile were rather clear. Unlike their counterparts in neighboring Argentina, for instance, Chilean politicians did not have to address the tangled themes of caudillo rule or the conflicting claims of sharply disparate regions. General Cruz and Pedro León Gallo, Chile's would-be caudillos (if it is right to call them that) in 1851 and 1859, did not aspire to dictatorship and firmly associated themselves with *national* visions of reform and liberty, very moderate in Cruz's case, more radical in Gallo's. As for regionalism, it certainly existed (both in north and south) on the level of resentment and complaint, but it was not articulated as a coherent political program. The somewhat artificial "federalism" of the mid-1820s was not revived in the early republic (or later). In most respects, therefore, the prime political arguments among Chileans focused on the classic issue of order and liberty and the balance between them.

There is an underlying sense in which both Conservative and Liberal outlooks fell well within the boundaries of nineteenth-century liberalism. There is nothing paradoxical about this. Nineteenth-century liberalism was, as we know, a very broad church, embracing congregations that were, ide-ologically speaking, moderate-conservative, middle-of-the-road, and radi-cal, and, socially speaking, aristocratic, middle-class, and popular. Both major British political parties of the nineteenth century were liberal, but only one of them came to call itself Liberal. This was also true of politi-cal parties in the United States, none of which used (did they even think of using?) the label. Assimilated comprehensively at the time of indepen-dence, liberalism – its essence, politically, can be defined as representative government and civil liberty – provided the framework of virtually all political thinking in Chile for the remainder of the nineteenth century and in most ways (leaving aside a few rather unimpressive excursions into authoritarian nationalism and Marxism-Leninism) throughout the twenti-eth. Nineteenth-century Chilean Liberals and Conservatives sat on opposite sides of the aisle, but they belonged to the same capacious church.[1]

It is true that the Conservative rebellion of 1829–30 was a reaction to the perhaps naively optimistic *partisan* Liberalism of the 1820s. But we need to remember that the new Conservative order, at least as defined for public consumption, was not based on a truly *reactionary* outlook of the kind visible enough in Europe in the post-Napoleonic period. Diego Portales could be harsh, but his long-term vision for Chile was a liberal one. He was no Metternich or King Bomba, despite his admiration for the Duke of Wellington, not exactly the most liberal-minded of British politicians. For all his hankering after European-style Legitimism, Mariano Egaña, perhaps the only genuinely reactionary Chilean intellectual of the period (and definitely an admirer of Metternich), never contemplated a reversion to monarchy (whether absolute or constitutional), in the manner of Lino de Pombo in New Granada or some Mexican Conservatives. Chilean Conservatives certainly did not express nostalgia for the colonial era, as did the great Mexican historian-politician Lucás Alamán. It is true that the militantly progovernment newspaper *La Civilización* (1851–2) urged a return to the "Spanish spirit," as a means of countering the wicked French influence it detected in the recent upsurge of Liberalism, but this was not in any sense a standard Conservative view. The Conservative regime, in fact,

---

1 Adoption of "Liberal" and "Conservative" as party labels by Latin American liberals and conservatives was not universal. Aside from Chile, the names established themselves firmly in Mexico, Venezuela, Colombia, Ecuador, Bolivia (in the late nineteenth century), and Brazil, although, prior to the late 1840s, partisan Brazilian conservatives styled themselves the *partido de ordem*, "Party of Order" (see Jeffrey D. Needell, "Provincial Origins of the Brazilian State: Rio de Janeiro, the Monarchy, and National Political Organization," *Latin American Research Review*, 36:3 [2001], pp. 132–44). In Argentina, Uruguay, and Peru, the names were not used. It might be remarked here that English Tories did not really become Conservatives before the 1840s, and it was not much before the 1860s that English Whigs began to refer regularly to themselves as Liberals. Chile can thus claim to have had Conservative and Liberal parties before Great Britain.

invariably paid lip-service to liberal, republican, even democratic ideals. Conservative behavior was sometimes clearly illiberal. Such ideals were often honored more in the breach than in the observance, but they *were* honored. In terms of political argument, what distinguished Conservatives from their Liberal adversaries? What did Chilean Conservatism really amount to?

Conservatism: Order and Progress

"Order and progress should be our motto," declared *El Mercurio* in 1841,[2] fifty years before the first Brazilian republic adopted it. The concept of order is familiar in most conservative traditions. The Conservatives' role in government after 1830 inclined them to emphasize its virtues, for their strongest claim to legitimacy was keeping the peace. Liberty, the great liberal keyword, was firmly embedded in Conservative rhetoric, but liberty, in the *pelucón* view, depended essentially on a firm structure of order. In 1851, president-elect Montt expressed his belief in "not liberty at the expense of order or . . . order at the expense of liberty, but the just harmony of these two saving principles."[3] Most *pelucones* would probably have accepted this formula, but it is possibly true that their emotions were engaged more fully with order than with liberty, especially in the earlier years of their regime, when the consensus of the majority of the political class accepted the need for repressive measures when necessary. "Order," trumpeted a Conservative news-sheet of 1840, " – our sole aspiration, the most sacred idol of our hearts."[4] The "sacred idol" frequently appeared in presidential messages or ministerial reports to Congress. *"Public order,"* for Interior minister Irarrázaval in 1841, was "that source from which emanates all social good, without which we cannot expect happiness or progress."[5] The president's annual addresses to Congress often included a phrase or two of self-congratulation on having got the country through another year without civil commotion – or, on rarer occasions, self-congratulation on having suppressed civil commotion.

Order, for Conservatives, definitely embraced a conception of social hierarchy. Every level of the hierarchy had a stake in order. "In all the societies of the world there are rich and poor," declared a news-sheet of 1844, "for so it is ordained by Providence. There is no individual so poor that he does not have something that can be stolen or that he can lose when the social order experiences some upheaval. Thus the preservation of order is

2 MV, No. 3701, April 10, 1841.
3 TRI, No. 698, September 9, 1851.
4 *Conservador*, No. 17, September 30, 1840.
5 *Memoria* of Interior minister (1841). DP, I, 118.

in everybody's interest."[6] It did not follow that all levels of society should participate in government. The Conservative manifesto of 1851 makes it perfectly explicit that the "ignorant masses" are incapable of governing,[7] a task properly reserved to those President Bulnes (unconsciously echoing Edmund Burke?) once termed *"los hombres de juicio y séquito,"* "the men of judgment and following."[8]

Insistent as Conservatives were on the need for a governing class (themselves), their propaganda was never "aristocratic" as such. Individual *pelucones* were quite able to spring to the defense of the titled and *mayorazgo*-holding families of colonial times when Liberals mocked them as "retrograde." Manuel Antonio Tocornal reminded the Chamber of Deputies in 1850 (inaccurately) of the prominent role taken by "the *mayorazgo*-holders, the Marquises and the Counts" in the revolution for independence: "If that noble conduct is now to be called antiquated, if those who observed it were retrograde, well, I too am like them."[9] Conservative propaganda did not appeal to sentimental traditionalism of this sort. It preferred to stress (especially when courting artisans) that "the rich by inheritance are very few in comparison with those who have become rich through work,"[10] even though this was no truer of Chile than anywhere else, then or now.

The Conservative emphasis on order implied a discernible tendency to view almost any opposition movement as potentially conducive to chaos. The image of *dis*order so often evoked by *pelucones* seems to have been real enough in the minds of some. For the more cynical, it was little more than a useful card to play against the opposition. "The social order is like one of those great dikes that hold back a torrent," warned the progovernment *El Mensajero* in 1853, "and in which a crack . . . is the beginning of its collapse and ruin."[11] This graphic image was repeated in many forms, especially in times of agitation, when the Conservative press often became extremely harsh. A news-sheet of 1840, for instance, condemned the Liberals for promoting "commotion and disorder, mutinies and upheavals, licence and anarchy," and their inoffensive leaders as "a gang of daring *sans-culottes*."[12] Such rhetoric was not confined to the press. Colonel Bernardo Letelier, masterminding the government's electoral efforts in Talca in 1840, sedulously

---

6 *Artesano del Orden*, No. 15, March 15, 1846.
7 *Manifiesto del Partido Conservador*, p. 6.
8 Circular to Intendants, February 20, 1851: L. Montt, *Recuerdos*, p. 745. Bulnes's phrase, *hombres de juicio y séquito*, is strikingly reminiscent of Burke's "the men . . . of light and leading [in England]": *Reflections on the Revolution in France*, ed. C. C. O'Brien (Harmondsworth, 1969), p. 200.
9 CN/D, August 5, 1850. In fact all the holders of titles and most *mayorazgo*-holders had welcomed the Spanish "reconquest" of Chile in 1814.
10 *Artesano del Orden*, No. 15, March 15, 1846.
11 No. 188, January 3, 1854.
12 *Mundo*, Nos. 1–2, February 11/15, 1840.

(and absurdly) put it around that a Liberal victory there would lead to "the most frightful revolution."[13] When emergency powers were imposed, Conservatives sometimes greeted them ecstatically. The November 1850 state of siege, for example, was hailed as putting an end to "all the fears for the fate of the Republic. . . . The *state of siege* will rescue the country from a *complete social dissolution.*"[14]

As this specimen of hyperbole suggests, there is little doubt that the Conservatives' fears of disorder included the fear of social upheaval, but they did not believe that such an upheaval would occur spontaneously. As the newspaper *La Tribuna* claimed in 1850, it was not "a revolutionary movement" that was feared, for "you do not make revolutions with *rotos.*" What was at stake was "a threat to property" from "the masses of vagabonds who lurk on our city-outskirts."[15] Such anomic explosions, in the Conservative view, were invariably provoked by opponents of the regime, by definition unscrupulous. After the mine workers' rebellion at Chañarcillo in 1851, it seemed obvious to the local *subdelegado* that the "authors" of the tumult "had something political in mind, but in their stupidity they did not see that it would be impossible to rein in the rabble they were using to promote the disorder."[16] During the 1858 elections, the Intendant of Valparaiso noted that "the industrious and lovers of work" were always outnumbered by the "destitute class, especially in this port full of transients," and that such people could be "deluded in an instant and start up a commotion, on the most frivolous pretext."[17]

As time passed, the Conservatives' concept of order came to occupy the key place in their vision of Chile's own recent history. By 1850, after all, there had been twenty years of peace. The contrast between Conservative order and the Liberal "anarchy" of the 1820s was an obvious theme for propaganda, and the more effective for containing a grain of truth. Conservatives often made use of the "before-and-after" contrast. Everything before 1830, suggested a newspaper of 1852, had been "uncertain and precarious," with trade and agriculture "destroyed and paralyzed," and the national finances "bankrupt."[18] Happily, the Conservatives had sprung to the rescue, and "the people, taught by their own calamities," or so said an 1840 newssheet, "learned to understand their true interests, [and] closed their eyes to the insidious suggestions of the anarchists."[19]

The "argument from success" was a strong one in Conservative propaganda. The 1851 manifesto emphasizes that "the Conservative party . . . does

13 *Alcance al No. 3 del Liberal*, February 11, 1840.
14 *Verdadero Chileno*, No. 78, November 9, 1850. Emphasis added.
15 TRI, No. 409, September 14, 1850.
16 Subdelegado of Chañarcillo to Intendant of Atacama, November 3, 1851: AI(V), Vol. 86.
17 Intendant of Valparaiso to Interior minister, March 18, 1858. AMI, Vol. 283.
18 *Verdadero Chileno*, No. 88, May 22, 1850.
19 *Conservador*, No. 16, September 9, 1840.

not need programs to reveal its spirit. The country has seen it march on-
wards for twenty years, imperturbable before the tempests ... of anarchy."[20]
Self-congratulation of this kind was linked to a growing sense of national
pride, as educated Chileans became aware of the positive reputation Chile's
stability was winning in the outside world, for which the Conservatives
were the first to claim credit. In 1841, Interior minister Irarrázaval, noting
the "lamentable picture" offered by other Spanish American republics, suggested that Chile was "a new spectacle in these regions."[21] Obviously the
upheavals of 1850–1 briefly undermined this sentiment of pride. Fears were
expressed that Chile might be reduced to the level of the other "discredited
and semisavage states" of Spanish America.[22] The government's victory in
the civil war soon dispelled such downbeat feelings. Soon after it ended,
a Conservative newspaper proudly proclaimed that "Chile will once again
march in the vanguard of the American nations, will once again be what
she was before."[23]

When reflecting on their success in maintaining order, most *pelucones*
agreed that it stemmed from the institutions imposed after 1830, and
in particular the excellence of the 1833 Constitution. Conservative reverence for the constitution grew discernibly greater as the years passed.
The 1851 manifesto declared that it was widely considered the "most perfect Code known in Spanish America" – the reason why Chileans were
the only Spanish Americans to be "perfectly constituted."[24] Whenever
Liberals suggested amending the Constitution, the Conservative reaction
was to circle the wagons, the standard argument being that constitutional
change was simply premature. Was it credible, asked Interior minister
Irarrázaval in 1844, that after the "immense duration of three centuries"
and only a short period of "popular representative government," a "democratic spirit" had really taken root in Chile?[25] The question was rhetorical. Chile was not yet ready for drastic political change: "Our outward
appearance and our institutions are democratic and republican," observed
El Mercurio in 1843; "our habits, our minds, and ... our current situation are not."[26] The news-sheet *El Orden*, one of the best written of its
type, insisted in 1845 that Conservative institutions gave the country
"the only democracy possible."[27] Occasionally Conservative propagandists went further than this, even suggesting (as was done in 1850) that

20 *Manifiesto del Partido Conservador*, p. 3.
21 *Memoria* of Interior minister (1841). DP, I, 118.
22 *Verdadero Chileno*, No. 78, November 9, 1850.
23 *Civilización*, No. 98, January 12, 1852.
24 *Manifiesto del Partido Conservador*, p. 4.
25 *Memoria* of the Interior minister (1844). DP, II, 221.
26 MV, No. 4663, December 30, 1843.
27 *Orden*, No. 5, November 1, 1845.

Chile was "the freest people on earth, perhaps."[28] The "perhaps" is very Chilean.

Conservatives were not hypocritical in using terms like "freedom" and "democracy." Whatever their practice, their self-image was not authoritarian. For all their emphasis on order, their propaganda shows no trace of an authoritarian *philosophy*. Ambrosio Montt, writing in 1859, may possibly have been right in claiming that the true Conservative approach was Machiavelli's "it is better to be feared than loved,"[29] but this was not a viewpoint Conservatives chose to express. The terms "left" and "right" would not become part of the Chilean political vocabulary for many decades to come, but many *pelucones* would probably have placed themselves near the center of that particular spectrum. "We . . . want to be regarded . . . as liberals and republicans," revealingly declared a Conservative newspaper in 1851; "moderate progressives" was how supporters of President Montt defined themselves in 1853, while a pro-Montt news-sheet of 1851 even used the term "Progressive Conservative Party,"[30] although qualifying adjectives of this kind were rare. Vicente Pérez Rosales, in an essay published in French, referred to *"le parti modéré, connu au Chili sous le nom de parti conservateur."*[31]

This moderate, centrist position was often justified rhetorically in terms of the undesirable alternatives. An article in *El Orden* in 1845 presents Conservatism as following a middle course between "exaggerated doctrines of liberty" stemming from the French Revolution, which tried to raise humanity "on wings of imaginary theory" to "beautiful utopias," and, on the other side, retrograde "colonial" ideas that tried to keep humanity in a "stationary state."[32] A similar positioning of Conservatism can be found in a contribution to *El Progreso* that same year. According to its author, two parties had striven for mastery after independence. One tried to subject "the facts," in other words Chilean social realities, to "European philosophical ideas," while the other tried to proscribe all such ideas and to maintain "the facts, however shocking these might be to reason." Conservatism, on this view, had emerged through a dialectical process, with the aim of "preserving the results obtained by the revolutionary spirit [of independence]" while respecting "the facts that recall the old regime . . . , modifying them bit by bit."[33]

Statements like these show that the Conservative claim to legitimacy was not based *simply* on keeping the peace. Conservative propaganda never

28 *Verdadero Chileno*, No. 70, October 22, 1850.
29 A. Montt, *Gobierno*, p. 23.
30 TRI, No. 605, May 15, 1851; *Mensajero*, No. 3, May 24, 1853; *Los Avisos*, No. 50, June 18, 1851.
31 *Essai*, p. 213.
32 *Orden*, No. 3, October 26, 1845.
33 PR, No. 910, October 14, 1845.

appealed to a vision of timeless tradition, still less Hispanic tradition, and never implied that society was static and unchanging. The 1851 manifesto contrasts the Conservative theme of "order and gradual progress" with the Liberal theme of "revolution and regression."[34] This was monstrously unfair to the Liberals, yet it marks the way in which Conservatism had assimilated the idea of progress. Keeping the peace was necessary, but necessary "in order for the onward march of society to reach its goal – perfection."[35] This seems oddly unconservative language, and certainly the perfectibility of humankind was an idea more often articulated by Liberals. Yet there is no doubt that Conservatives constantly deployed the concept of progress in their rhetoric. Opening Congress in 1855, President Montt affirmed that a "progressive onward march, regulated by prudence," was the "normal situation of the Republic," which was adapting itself "to a law of societies never more imperious than in the present times: *advance!*"[36]

Easily the most eloquent "campaign literature" for Montt in 1850–1 was written by his Argentine friend Sarmiento, who presented Montt (in seductive prose) as a true progressive in his zeal for material progress.[37] The image was one Montt was evidently fond of projecting. At a banquet just before his inauguration, he said:

What you celebrate today, gentlemen, is the triumph of a principle, the principle of the Conservative party, the triumph of those institutions in whose shadow will be worked the moral and material improvement of the people through industrial arts and public education. . . . You have wished to place me at the head of a phalanx of workers, so that together . . . we may build in the republic a temple to *peace* and a monument to *prosperity*. . . . God be with the workers![38]

A remarkable gloss on this speech was given a few weeks later in a fiercely progovernment newspaper:

What we should seek, then, is the creation of a workers' society, of what might be called an *industrial nation*. . . . What we will call *industrial nation* is one in which the dominating classes end up by recasting themselves as working classes, or in which the working classes have acquired a decisive mastery over the dominating classes; in which the population, instead of disputing and struggling to take possession of existing wealth, applies its force simultaneously to create new wealth.[39]

34 *Manifiesto del Partido Conservador*, p. 6.
35 *Orden*, No. 3, October 26, 1845.
36 DP, V, 259.
37 See his three pamphlets: ¿*A quién rechazan y temen? a Montt. ¿A quién sostienen y desean? a Montt. ¿Quién es entonces el candidato?* Montt (1850); *Candidato a la presidencia de Chile para 1851, D. Manuel Montt* (1851); *Manuel Montt, su época y sus adversarios políticos* (1851).
38 TRI, No. 691, August 30, 1851.
39 *Civilización*, No. 21, October 11, 1851.

It may be doubted whether all *pelucones* would have understood such a statement, but it is striking that it should be part of their public stance.

Yet, however much Conservatives invoked the idea of progress, it was never allowed to override their emphasis on order. The phrase "gradual progress," cited earlier, is itself revealing. Reforms (of the kind espoused by both Conservatives and Liberals) were desirable, but needed to be put into effect with due caution. The Conservatives' reform timetable was altogether slower than the Liberals', and took into account the strength of tradition (Diego Portales's "weight of the night") in a way Liberals perhaps did not. As a Conservative newspaper of 1853 put it, reforms "demanded . . . by opinion, discussed and purified in the laboratory of sensible and reasoned discussion, sanctioned by the support of the public spirit," could be introduced without the "distrust" or "the opposition and resistance" that excessively bold measures would probably provoke.[40] Perhaps the most lucid expression of the Conservative position on this point in the entire literature of the period is to be found in an essay in *El Orden* in 1846:

There are in nations certain habits, prejudices and facts to which there is much attachment, and only the slow and gradual action of civilization can make them disappear. If one tries to uproot them by force, a perilous reaction can supervene, which slows down or paralyzes the movement of progress they bear. The Conservative hand only touches such circumstances with prudence. . . . So it is that no abuse, no prejudice which seems to have played its part in the common well-being will disappear or be destroyed until the generality [of people] is ready for this. . . . The Conservative system favors the gradual organization of the social body; it respects the constitutive elements of the association; and it prepares by direct and indirect means the progressive development of the whole.[41]

With its references to abuses and prejudices, this paragraph strongly reminds us of Edmund Burke. There is no evidence that Burke's political writings were well known in the Chile of that time.[42] Yet the more thoughtful *pelucones* seem to have been Burkeans of a kind.

Liberalism: Republic, Liberty, Revolution

The Liberal party, when it existed at all in any credible sense, could not (and mostly did not) claim the impressive continuity the Conservatives evoked in their propaganda. Cowed by Portales, reconciled (up to a point) to the

40 *Mensajero*, No. 2, May 23, 1853.
41 "Sistema conservador," *Orden*, No. 3, October 26, 1845.
42 The only work of Burke in the National Library in 1860 was his *Philosophical Inquiry into the Origin of Our Ideas of the Sublime and Beautiful* (see *Catálogo alfabético* [1860]). This obviously does not preclude copies of other works being in private hands.

regime by Bulnes, the Liberals only showed real signs of revival at the close of the 1840s, with the *vialista* excision, which gave them a substantial new cohort. The "new" Liberals, though drawn into rebellion in 1851, were led by the younger generation (the future presidents Federico Errázuriz and Domingo Santa María were prototypical figures) whose project in the 1850s became the winning of power as a respectable political force. Prior to the unexpected political realignment of 1857–8, their chances seemed slim.

Both Conservatives and Liberals often indulged in hyperbole in their propaganda. An interesting study could probably be made of the colorful and insulting epithets they flung at each other, at times with reckless abandon. In this particular competition, it would be hard to say who won. Possibly the Liberals. If their hyperbole tended to be more drastic, it was probably simply out of desperation. A news-sheet of 1850, for instance, described the *pelucones* as "that sinister, liberticide, bloody, treacherous, hypocritical, egotistical, machiavellian, antirepublican, antisocial, terrorist faction of [the last] twenty years."[43] On the eve of Montt's inauguration, *El Progreso* absurdly asserted that "Chile today offers the singular spectacle that must have been offered by the peoples of Rome or China when, invaded by the barbarians of Attila or the hordes of Genghis Khan, they were subjected to the harsh law of the conqueror."[44]

Such picturesque statements should not distract attention from the perfectly serious Liberal critique of the Conservative regime. It was symbolized in a single word. In their manifesto of October 1849, Federico Errázuriz and José Victorino Lastarria asserted that the "progressive party" (the temporary Liberal label) had as "its highest aspiration the ACHIEVEMENT OF THE REPUBLIC in Chile."[45] The "Republic," sometimes called the "True Republic," was an expression that so often appeared in Liberal pronouncements that (in 1859) the novelist Alberto Blest Gana indulged in some gentle leg-pulling at its expense: "This thing *the true republic* . . . is rather like the Huemul on our coat of arms, which almost nobody has ever seen and whose very existence the majority doubts. Nonetheless, on hearing that word, everyone feels electrified."[46] It was, therefore, a code word with a strong emotional charge. "The Republic is the City of God," proclaimed *El Progreso* in 1850, "and our duty is to work so that . . . [it] descends to earth and lives in every soul and people."[47] The code word was used in a great variety of contexts. "The republic . . . is disposed to refuse an angel," professed an opposition news-sheet of 1850, discussing presidential candidates, "if the

43 *Aconcagüino*, No. 29, October 28, 1850.
44 PR, No. 2625, August 8, 1851. XXXX.
45 Lastarria and Errázuriz, *Las bases*, p. 3.
46 *Semana*, No. 12, August 6, 1859.
47 PR, No. 2429, September 18, 1850.

government proposes one," and Diego Barros Arana, at the "protest banquet" held in October 1858, affirmed resoundingly that "no compromise
is possible between the republic and the present government."[48] Examples
could easily be multiplied.

What "republic" in this sense meant was simply the Liberal program,
which aimed, essentially, at the elimination of the authoritarian practices
of the regime, the reduction of executive power, and (always a *sine qua non*
for Liberals) the reform of the 1833 Constitution. "Chile desires nothing
so much as the reform of the Constitution...," Federico Errázuriz told
Congress in 1850, "for it prevents the Republic from marching forward
up the path of civilization."[49] Lastarria and Errázuriz suggested in their
manifesto that five rights should be seen as constituting the core Liberal
demand:

1. equality before the law, including an equal tax on property and capital with the
   aim of "abolition of customs duties," and also the democratization of the civic
   guard;
2. individual liberty, including freedom of movement, of association (not mentioned in the 1833 Constitution), "of professing a religious belief," and of the
   press "without prior censorship or ... subsequent legal accusation;"
3. "inviolability of all properties" ("Current dispositions on this point should be
   preserved," the authors note here);
4. "Free primary education and the freedom of scientific instruction," including
   "free, superior industrial education for the poor";
5. "the protection of industry," with the authors insisting here that industry itself
   should always be "free and independent," not directly run by government.[50]

Many Conservatives would have had little difficulty in accepting points
3, 4, and 5, with some argument, possibly, about 5. The essential Liberal
demand, in fact, was for greater political freedom – points 1 and 2.

It must be stressed here that it was not a deeply radical demand. While
Liberals may have been emotionally somewhat less attached than Conservatives to the idea of social hierarchy, their view of the franchise was
substantially similar. In the course of fierce attacks on the government in
March 1846, the Liberal *Gaceta del Comercio* devoted a two-part article to
denouncing universal suffrage, which gave "supremacy to ignorance," and
was both "a powder-magazine with a bonfire at its door" and "a popular lot-
tery."[51] For their part, Lastarria and Errázuriz advocated what they termed
"intelligent universal suffrage." Their explanation of this expression, their

48 *Reforma*, No. 32, August 28, 1850; ACT, No. 222, October 21, 1858.
49 CN/D, August 28, 1850.
50 Lastarria and Errázuriz, *Las bases*, pp. 23–26.
51 *Gaceta del Comercio*, Nos. 1272 and 1273, March 17 and 19, 1846.

mixture of general and instrumental arguments, is worth quoting at length:

> We accept universal suffrage, but only when this universality is that of men (without distinction of class) who are capable of exercising their political rights. . . . All men are equal. . . . But in the political order not everyone can have equal participation, for the good of society is not achieved . . . unless the men who participate in power have a proper sense of social questions and the will to resolve them in the general interest. In Chile, if the day-laborers and servants of the haciendas were to exercise the electoral right, the result of the election would be very different from the result of an election voted in by the artisans of the towns and other citizens who are legally qualified to vote. In the first instance it is the landowners, the bosses of that multitude without a will of its own, who would do the electing; in the second case, the election would give us a free expression of the national will.[52]

The Liberals' view of recent Chilean history was a mirror-image of the Conservatives'. For Liberals, 1829–30 marked a turning point not for the better, but emphatically for the worse. It was then, as Liberal activist Manuel Antonio Carmona wrote in 1846, that "the counterrevolutionary reaction . . . cut off, in short order, the . . . glorious progress the republic was making."[53] "We were detained in mid-career," asserted Pedro Félix Vicuña in 1849, "but nobody is capable of annulling the revolution we began in 1810."[54] Instead of the True Republic, Chile now had a highly authoritarian system under a president who (according to an 1840 Liberal news-sheet) was "an omnipotent colossus invested with limitless powers."[55] An editorial in an opposition newspaper for the *dieciocho* of 1858 presents an imaginary conversation between the Liberals of 1858 and the fathers of independence: "We have betrayed the revolution," wail the 1858 Liberals, "and . . . we have thrown ourselves into the arms of the political system you overthrew. . . . Material interests, it is true, have developed in the shadow of that system" – *but nothing else has*; "The republic does not exist." The fathers of independence tell them: "You are not worthy to be our children."[56] One of the first political cartoons in Chilean history, printed in the fourteenth issue of *El Correo Literario* in 1858, shows two drawings: the first, captioned "Republic of 1810," displays a female figure taking flight above a vaguely Andean landscape, her left hand (anachronistically) clutching the Chilean flag. The second, "Republic of 1858," shows the same woman, her hands in chains, sitting by a broken column (part of which has fallen to the ground) bearing the inscription "Liberty."

52 Lastarria and Errázuriz, *Las bases*, pp. 12–13.
53 Carmona, *Manifiesto de Aconcagua, Cuaderno 2°*, p. 58.
54 Vicuña, *Recuerdos*, p. 27.
55 *Nuevo Maquiavelo*, No. 1, June 23, 1840.
56 ACT, No. 196, September 18, 1858.

The Liberal distaste for the 1833 Constitution, with its "ideal of centralism and repression,"[57] was accompanied by nostalgia for its ill-starred predecessor of 1828 – "a monument," according to Manuel Antonio Carmona, that symbolized "the final triumph of liberty."[58] A few Liberals conceded that it might not have been perfect. An obituary of ex-president Francisco Antonio Pinto (responsible for the 1828 constitution) even admitted that it was "the emblem of a political party that perhaps got too much ahead of its time."[59] This was almost certainly a minority view. Liberal nostalgia for the 1828 Constitution achieved its most serious expression in a historical essay (1861) by Federico Errázuriz. Errázuriz chose the years 1828–30 as his topic, believing that it would cast light on "the legality, justice and convenience of our fundamental institutions." Although impeccably observing the canons of narrative history, he made sure that it did. For Errázuriz, the 1828 constitution had been based on "the healthiest principles of democratic science," and its overthrow had been a reactionary curtailment of liberty. The 1833 document, by contrast, gave "an excessive preponderance to the executive," which in practice "annulled ... the other powers of the state."[60]

A final aspect of Liberal propaganda that stands out in any analysis is its indulgent attitude to disturbances and upheavals, a position diametrically opposed to the Conservatives' strict emphasis on order. This particular attitude was surely enhanced by the frustration of being condemned to apparently eternal opposition. Many Liberals seem to have believed that upheavals were inevitable whenever governments set their face against Liberal aspirations. Nor were upheavals necessarily unwelcome. Diego José Benavente, who never entirely shed his earlier liberalism, once praised the quality of *"revolutionary enthusiasm,"* suggesting that "The energy of this feeling sustains *revolutions,* and makes them fertile in illustrious deeds."[61] Juan Nicolás Alvarez similarly believed that "revolutions that spring from a people's development should not be feared but desired, as benefits conferred by Providence ... ; they announce to us ... the presence of DIVINITY on earth."[62] It was natural for Liberals to invoke the classic right of rebellion (with its perfectly respectable ancestry in European political thought) not only to "contain the abuses of power," as *La Reforma* put it in 1850 (citing the cases of England's Charles I and James II, and France's Louis XVI, Charles X and Louis Philippe) but also "to overthrow bad legislation when tyranny has managed to organize it in its own interest."[63] The same paper,

57 I. Errázuriz, *La emigración*, p. 14.
58 *Manifiesto de Aconcagua, Cuaderno 2*, p. 58.
59 ACT, No. 144, July 20, 1858.
60 F. Errázuriz, *Chile*, pp. 5, 268, 280.
61 *Cartas Patriotas*, No. 5, n.d. ?1839, p. 61.
62 *Diablo Político*, No. 15, October 14, 1839.
63 *Reforma*, No. 30, August 13, 1850.

a year earlier, had approvingly cited Jefferson's view of the need to water the tree of liberty with blood from time to time.[64] Even civil wars were not without their positive side. According to *El Progreso* (in its Liberal phase), a civil war "awakens generous feelings, lights up the country with glorious deeds, and almost always conquers solid gains for humanity."[65] This almost casual attitude to upheaval was perhaps most vividly summarized in Diego José Benavente's remark in the Senate in 1852 that the recent civil war had been rather like a "duel between gentlemen." He was reproved by future president José Joaquín Pérez, who told him that civil wars were infinitely more rancorous than duels between gentlemen.[66]

The Radical Fringe

Liberalism's radical fringe first became politically significant with the *Sociedad de la Igualdad* of 1850, and it reemerged in the agitation of 1858–9. What, if any, were its distinctive arguments? As we saw, the campaign of Arcos and Bilbao to promote the education of the Santiago artisans was quickly merged into the general opposition to the candidacy of Manuel Montt, which became the consistent line of the newspapers *El Amigo del Pueblo* and *La Barra*. *El Amigo del Pueblo* does not refer to the *Sociedad de la Igualdad* under that name, and only rarely alludes to the French Revolutions of 1789 and 1848. In its final issue it claims to have focused "almost exclusively" on the specific needs of artisans, and while it certainly prints a fair sample of artisan complaints, a reading of its fifty-three issues does not wholly bear out the claim. What it does is to sound a distinctively radical note – a note of intensified Liberalism tinged with an egalitarianism unusual for that era.

José Zapiola tells us that those who sought admission to the *Sociedad de la Igualdad* were required (in a formula suggested by Bilbao) to "Recognize the sovereignty of reason as the authority of authorities; the sovereignty of the people as the basis of all politics; and universal love and brotherhood as the morality of life."[67] The *igualitarios* certainly made a great deal of play (in the circumstances, dangerous play) with the term "revolution." "Let us proclaim revolution at the top of our voice," declared the opening issue of *El Amigo del Pueblo*, "and let us accept the title of revolutionaries." The newspaper explained, however, that this did not mean "violent revolution," and that its sole object was "the progress of ideas, with the help of written and spoken propaganda."[68] "Revolution," like

64 *Reforma*, No. 19, May 25, 1849.
65 PR, No. 2468, October 25, 1850.
66 CN/S, September 10, 1852.
67 Zapiola, *Sociedad*, p. 9.
68 *Amigo del Pueblo*, No. 1, April 1, 1850.

"Republic," was thus no more than a metaphor for the implementation of the Liberal program, albeit a Liberal program with an additional edge of social reform.

The *people* of today, with the working class [i.e., the artisanate] marching at its head, awaits its day of triumph . . . to throw on to the bonfires of liberty barbarian codes of law, institutions that oppress the poor, the pharisees' fanaticism, the prejudices that stem from ignorance, the pride of the aristocracy, the indolence of the servants of the Republic, and even the memories of the epoch of [colonial] absolutism. With the triumph of the people there will arise a Republic with humane and equitable laws, with institutions that open the way to education and prosperity for the poor, with reason as sovereign, with equality before the law.[69]

There were times, too, when *El Amigo del Pueblo* could sound a note almost of class war, as when it described Chile as

A country where the law is meted out severely and rigorously to the poor and softly and lightly to the rich. A country where, despite the fertility of its soil, hundreds of families live poverty-stricken, their work badly recompensed by their *señores.* . . . A country where talent does not spring up unless it has been reared in a noble cradle. . . . Tyranny does not exist for the powerful, does not exist for those who can afford frock coats and understand the rights the Republic grants to them as citizens; but it does exist, with intolerable weight, for those neglected classes, who in their poverty are ignorant of the guarantees they enjoy from having been born in a country with democratic institutions.[70]

What specific policies does *El Amigo del Pueblo* actually recommend? It deplores the scarcity of small-denomination coins and the tokens that shopkeepers use to tie customers to their stores, and urges the government to introduce a full-scale decimal currency.[71] It advocates a comprehensive clean-up of the poorer districts of Santiago.[72] It denounces police brutality toward the poor.[73] It consistently argues in favor of a widespread expansion of education.[74] Predictably, it urges the democratization of the Civic Guard.[75] It also backs tariff protection for artisans. It notes that when the Moneda palace was refurbished as the seat of the president,[76] 20,000 pesos

69 *Amigo del Pueblo*, No. 52, June 1, 1850.
70 *Amigo del Pueblo*, No. 28, May 2, 1850.
71 *Amigo del Pueblo*, No. 49, May 28, 1850.
72 *Amigo del Pueblo*, No. 38, May 15, 1850.
73 *Amigo del Pueblo*, No. 39, May 16, 1850.
74 For example, *Amigo del Pueblo*, No. 42, May 20, 1850.
75 *Amigo del Pueblo*, No. 10, April 11, 1850.
76 The neoclassical Moneda palace (more simply "the Moneda") had been the royal mint in colonial times. President Bulnes moved in there in 1846 and it has been the presidential palace ever since, although not (since the 1950s) a residence.

were spent on imported furniture and materials from Europe, when the work could have given Chilean artisans "a lucrative occupation for a long time." What is needed, therefore, is a "considerable rise" in import duties on "any manufactures that compete with the work of national industry." (German and English furniture is seen as especially competitive.) The newspaper admits that protectionist tariffs should only be used "in an extreme case," but argues that the position of the artisanate *is* a special case.[77] All of the points made by *El Amigo del Pueblo* were important to artisans, certainly, but nowhere are they incorporated into a truly coherent vision of social reform. Except in the vaguest of senses, Francisco Bilbao's romantic utterances never really added up to one. As we shall see, however, his friend Arcos proved more than capable of providing just such a vision – concrete, radical, and powerful.

Five Political Treatises

Several Chileans during the early republic tried their hand at political treatises. The choice of the five to be examined here is not arbitrary. A good case can be made for considering them as the best of the period. Let us start with José Victorino Lastarria (1817–88), the leading Liberal publicist of his time. His works have been extensively studied over the years, but they need to be included, if only as a mark of respect. His *Elementos de derecho público constitucional, teórico, positivo y político* (1847) is a straightforward primer or textbook in "political science," based fairly heavily on a text published in Brussels in 1837 by the German Heinrich Ahrens (1805–74), and about as interesting as such books usually are. Lastarria follows Ahrens's advice not to mix theoretical discussions with "questions of the day," although he naturally points out that "the liberal system" is the tendency of the nineteenth century. In his next extended (and much more interesting) political work, *La Constitución política de la República de Chile comentada* (Valparaiso, 1856), Lastarria's own political thought is more openly displayed. He interprets the Conservative scheme of 1830 as "that of rehabilitating the Colony, of perpetuating its spirit, by containing social regeneration,"[78] though he sides with the 1833 Constitution in preferring the formula "sovereignty of the nation" to "sovereignty of the people," since "the people" can mean everyone, and in Spanish America "the rabble . . . lacks a will of its own."[79] He therefore approves of the constitution's limitation of the suffrage to "active citizens." Universal suffrage simply means "entrusting the exercise of sovereignty to those who offer no guarantee of their good intentions, of

77 *Amigo del Pueblo*, No. 51, May 31, 1850.
78 *Constitución*, p. xxvii.
79 *Constitución*, p. 8.

their independence, and of their interest in society."[80] At the same time, Lastarria finds the 1833 constitution highly defective in its protection of civil liberties: "personal freedom has no guarantee except the will of public officials."[81] Nor is Congress "a real power."[82] Lastarria's severest criticism is reserved for the executive, which enjoys "a *supremacy* that has few parallels in republican constitutions."[83] Finally, he notes, it is far too difficult to amend the Constitution – "the current perfection" of the British constitution is attributable to the fact that it can be amended without "great solemnity."[84]

Juan Manuel Carrasco Albano's *Comentarios sobre la Constitución Política de 1833* (Valparaiso, 1858) is less a critique of the Conservative regime than a blueprint for the liberal future. A younger Liberal, Carrasco Albano (1834–73) is more daring than Lastarria. Chile, he tells us, "is in a certain way only half a Republic."[85] Unitary government, he believes, is "natural" for the Latin peoples, in contrast to the local autonomy favored by the Anglo-Saxons. Spanish Americans must struggle "against the background of their race, their past over thousands of years," and only "time . . . , civilization, and . . . the liberal action of governments" can create "the Saxon element, local autonomy, the only guarantee of freedom."[86] Carrasco Albano advocates religious liberty, the separation of Church and state, and easier naturalization laws, for "Chile needs immigration, above all Protestant immigration."[87] A failure to attract immigration goes "against the manifest future of our continent, called to be the new homeland of regenerated humanity."[88]

Carrasco Albano sees Lastarria's view of the franchise as too timid. If elections are truly an expression of national sovereignty, he argues, then all "social persons" (i.e., heads of family) should vote. Existing property and financial qualifications mean that "the great majority of the nation is subject to the tutelage of the minority. . . . The mass of the Chilean people foreigners in their own country!" Carrasco Albano is a true nineteenth-century optimist. He is confident that to confer the vote on the poor will serve as an enormous stimulus to literacy and education: "The great landowners and enlightened men . . . would happily tax themselves to instruct and civilize the ignorant people that would govern, would create laws . . ."[89] Only eight years earlier,

80 *Constitución*, p. 22.
81 *Constitución*, p. 37.
82 *Constitución*, p. 40.
83 *Constitución*, p. 89.
84 *Constitución*, p. 221.
85 *Comentarios*, p. 190.
86 *Comentarios*, pp. 16–17.
87 *Comentarios*, p. 32.
88 *Comentarios*, p. 40.
89 *Comentarios*, pp. 45–48.

the landowners and enlightened men in Congress, voting down Montt's education bill, had shown extreme unwillingness to do any such thing.

Carrasco Albano is perfectly aware that Congress is dominated by public officials and "the big landowners." To counteract their influence he advocates "a respectable salary" for congressmen. True, the British do not pay their members of parliament, but that is not the case in "the wise, republican and never sufficiently praised Constitution of the United States."[90] Like Lastarria, like any Liberal, he regards the powers of the presidency as excessive. The president is "a single individual acting as estate-manager of the entire nation";[91] his influence is so "overwhelming and omnipotent" that opposition to him is given a stark choice: "Either it resigns itself and abdicates, or it rebels and fights: either a shameful withdrawal or a revolution."[92] What is needed, therefore, is vigorous parliamentary life and democratic municipal government, about which Carrasco Albano is especially eloquent. Even the Mapuche, he maintains, have better local government than is allowed for in the 1833 Constitution: "That Araucanian people . . . , though barbarous, can give us more than one lesson in good government, or *self-government*, which is the same for them as it is for the North Americans."[93] Notwithstanding such fanciful assertions, Carrasco Albano was a vigorous and lucid thinker; his premature death deprived Chile of a serious intellectual presence.

Given its importance in the national life, it is hardly surprising that both Lastarria and Carrasco Albano should have anchored their political reflections to the 1833 Constitution. In his *Ensayo sobre el Gobierno en Europa* (Paris, 1859), Ambrosio Montt (1830–99), Manuel Montt's son-in-law, abandons Chile altogether as his focus, choosing to examine politics much more broadly, and in a mostly European context. His treatise hinges on the contrast between the successful Anglo-Saxons (England and the United States) and the altogether less successful "Latin" nations. What explains the "immense preponderance" of England? In part, it is "the homogeneity of men, institutions, and customs," that makes English society "the most serious, the most ingenious, and the most practical in the world."[94] The mark of the Anglo-Saxons – steamships, telegraphs, banks, insurance companies – can be seen in ports such as Rio de Janeiro or Valparaiso ("English cities par excellence"); the cities of the South American interior have not yet felt "the beneficent influence of England."[95]

90 *Comentarios*, pp. 88–91.
91 *Comentarios*, p. 121.
92 *Comentarios*, p. 125.
93 *Comentarios*, p. 200.
94 *Ensayo*, pp. 270–74.
95 *Ensayo*, pp. 284–87.

Unlike the British, however, the British constitution does not travel. Montt believes that it exemplifies certain fundamental political truths: that government is "a historic, traditional fact," that absolute freedom is illusory, and that laws should rest on custom rather than be determined *a priori*.[96] By contrast, the French political tradition suffers from a fatal tendency to place all power in the hands of a strong ruler, who "absorbs the nation, dominates it, tyrannizes it."[97] In general, and citing Joseph De Maistre, Montt believes that countries get the governments they deserve. Russia needs the Czar and "pure absolutism," and the Germans a government that is "intelligent, patriotic, wise, but indifferent to liberty." The Latin nations are full of "doubt, uncertainty," and are destined to oscillate between despotism, constitutional monarchy, and republicanism.[98] The Latin races need to revitalize themselves by an "honest and fertile emulation" of the Anglo-Saxons, who in the meantime should be welcomed in Spanish America. Indeed, "the peaceful invasion of the Anglo-Saxons, far from being a cause of fear, is a true guarantee of peace for the Latin peoples," since the Anglo-Saxons will be *hostages*. When men and goods are universally exchanged, war becomes impossible. "In our age, England would never destroy New York, the sister of London and Liverpool."[99] The most urgent political need for the Hispanic peoples is "to organize themselves, to constitute themselves on a firm and durable basis, to introduce administrative morality, to make the law respected, to strengthen authority; in short, to form a government."[100] Of the Latin American nations, only Brazil and Chile have gone a reasonable distance in this direction, partly because they have resisted "the beautiful but treacherous theories of publicists and philosophers," and have established "a regular and serious regime" grounded in "history, the facts, customs, the education of the people."[101]

In contrast to Ambrosio Montt's intelligent soundings in European history, *El porvenir del hombre* (Valparaiso, 1858), by Pedro Félix Vicuña (1805–74), a remarkable if stylistically lackluster book, focuses its attention on the future of democracy, the old *pipiolo* Vicuña's ideal. Democracy, he insists, requires a proper economic and social base. Vicuña sees an unholy trinity – authority, aristocracy, the clergy – holding back "the impetuous current of civilization and democracy" in Spanish America, and fears that a destructive revolution might overwhelm this "anti-social league."[102] His self-imposed task as a theorist is to find a way between "those who,

96 *Ensayo*, pp. 337–41.
97 *Ensayo*, p. 354.
98 *Ensayo*, p. 335.
99 *Ensayo*, p. 290.
100 *Ensayo*, p. 399.
101 *Ensayo*, p. 399.
102 *Porvenir*, p. xxiv.

made fanatical by their power . . . , will not accept any improvement that affects their pride," and "those who are delirious for the Communism of the future, which would only bring barbarism to the world."[103] Property, Vicuña tells us, is an institution for which society needs to have "an inviolable respect."[104] But the "unlimited freedom of property" has led to "the most complete social inequality," to "a new feudalism."[105] The value of land in Chile has risen by threefold since the colonial era; the wages paid to inquilinos have remained static.[106] What is needed is a "radical reform of the organization of property." This will be difficult, Vicuña realizes, if it is to be done voluntarily by landowners, but not impossible.[107] Landowners could perhaps pay a proper wage to their workers, or lease land to them over a thirty-year period. If this failed, haciendas could be expropriated (with compensation) by the state.[108] Expropriated land could then be distributed to inquilinos, along with a state mortgage. Vicuña follows Locke in arguing that an individual has an absolute right to what he can cultivate. Beyond that, "greater extension of land" is a *social* right, subject to social control, although "extension" has deep roots in society and should be respected, provided it does not conflict with the rights of laborers.

Vicuña's vision of Chile's future, however, is not at all agrarian. Chile is destined to become "a manufacturing and industrial people," since it has abundant mines and "the raw materials for the richest manufactures."[109] The key to progress and independence is not so much foreign trade as *internal development*: "When we are producers we will also become traders and navigators, and not, as now, subaltern agents of the foreign factories that have established themselves among us."[110] Here Vicuña comes to his prime obsession. The capital for national development, he believes, must come from a central bank completely independent of political control; political control can too easily become an instrument of tyranny.[111] Public credit, Vicuña explains, is the key to the history of England, which had once been peculiarly grim – Henry VIII, after all, "had five of his seven wives executed"(!). But with the foundation of the Bank of England, the country has risen and flourished in "the most extraordinary effort known up to

103 *Porvenir*, p. 25.
104 *Porvenir*, pp. 38, 58.
105 *Porvenir*, pp. 38–41.
106 *Porvenir*, pp. 59–60.
107 *Porvenir*, p. 65.
108 *Porvenir*, pp. 89–91.
109 *Porvenir*, p. xv.
110 *Porvenir*, p. 236.
111 *Porvenir*, pp. 117–18. For a similar although less well-articulated view, see Palma, *Cristianismo*, pp. 71–93.

our times."[112] England, sadly, is blighted by her aristocratic tradition. Chileans would do better to emulate the more democratic United States, whose possible expansionist tendencies can only be resisted by a Spanish America that is both democratic and prosperous.[113] Indeed, and here we reach the outer edge of Vicuña's political vision, a Spanish America which has discovered the proper organization of property and the secret of public credit might well find itself "at the head of civilization."[114]

None of the political treatises mentioned so far caused much of a stir, although Andrés Bello described Ambrosio Montt's as "the most notable Chilean production published up till now"[115] – from that source, praise indeed! Perfectly respectable specimens of political thought, none of the treatises really deserves the immortality that has rightly attached to some of the major Argentine writings of the period. One that does made almost no stir at all when first printed in 1852. Santiago Arcos's thirty-two-page pamphlet, *Carta a Francisco Bilbao*, written in prison while Arcos was awaiting his final banishment from Chile, takes the form of a letter to his recent comrade-in-arms, and arises from their experiences in the *Sociedad de la Igualdad*. Like Vicuña, Arcos (1822–74) focuses on economic and social realities rather than institutional questions. From his perspective, it does not matter who is President of Chile – "A Washington, a Robert Peel, the Archangel Michael himself in Montt's place would be as bad as Montt."[116] There is no prospect of democracy in Chile, Arcos tells us, until attention is paid to "the condition of the people, the poverty and degradation of nine tenths of our population."

Arcos divides Chilean society into three classes: the Poor, the Rich, and the Foreigners. "The Poor man is not a citizen," he argues, for even if he votes he does so on somebody else's orders.[117] In the recent civil war, the Poor "fought for Boss Bulnes or Boss Cruz – fought for food, clothes, pay."[118] The Rich – descendants of colonial officials, "mayordomos who enriched themselves two or three generations back," newly rich mining magnates – are the "Chilean aristocracy." This aristocracy is neither "cruel and energetic" as in Italy, nor "industrious and patriotic" as in England, but merely "ignorant and apathetic," although it has produced some great men – including Portales and "this Manuel Montt." The political division between Liberals and Conservatives simply reflects the classic story of "ins" and

---

112 *Porvenir*, pp. 192–99, 223.
113 *Porvenir*, pp. 264–65.
114 *Porvenir*, p. 265.
115 Andrés Bello to Juan Bello, March 28, 1859. Jaksić, *Bello: pasión*, pp. 284–85. I thank Professor Jaksić for giving me an advance transcript of this letter.
116 *Carta*, p. 7.
117 *Carta*, p. 9.
118 *Carta*, p. 10.

"outs." The Liberals, because they are the permanent "outs," attract losers: "Any fool in Chile who has not been able to prosper, any bankrupt peddler, anyone of modest means who has lost a lawsuit, any cheated gambler – all describe themselves as Liberals."[119] Liberalism does, however, contain a valuable element: young men such as Francisco Bilbao, Eusebio Lillo, Benjamín Vicuña Mackenna – "a youth full of future promise, courageous, generous, patriotic." This youthful cohort needs to come together in a "new party, the big party, the democratic-republican party."[120] The new party should take particular note of Arcos's third class, the Foreigners, who, whether traders or immigrants, want both freedom of worship and freedom of trade. A declaration of rights to include both freedoms should be the first priority of a revolutionary government on coming to power. Free trade and immigration will work wonders, especially in the underpopulated South. Valdivia and Chiloé, Arcos speculates, might become culturally more advanced than the rest of Chile and then (he fantasizes) split off as "new Ionian Islands under the protectorate of England." The Ionian Isles were still under British rule at the time he wrote; twelve years later they were transferred to the new Kingdom of Greece.

However, the democratic-republicans achieve power – "by a military mutiny, or a strong popular insurrection, or both things at once" – the first step of the "new, All-Powerful, Revolutionary Government" must be to guarantee all civil rights *except one*, which it will reserve to itself, the right "To dispose of private properties that might be useful to the Republic and to fix the compensation due to the dispossessed."[121] Strong measures are needed to transform the "old Chile" of the Central Valley. Arcos's core proposal is starkly simple: "Take their lands away from the Rich and distribute them among the Poor."[122] The agrarian reform he sketches is far more drastic than anything ever attempted in Chile by later generations. The countryside will be divided into lots (Arcos specifies no size) "without reference to any previous demarcation," and each lot will be supplied with livestock. The tenants or owners of each lot will pay 1 percent of their product to the state for fifty years. Current landowners will be guaranteed eleven lots. The land they lose will be valued, the state paying compensation, also over fifty years. Around one fifth of lots will be reserved for immigrants.[123] Arcos confidently expects the Rich to describe the land reformers as "thieves [and] communists," but the measure "must be taken in order to save the

---

119 *Carta*, p. 15. The same view, presented more humorously, can be found in José Joaquín Vallejo's essay "El Liberal de Jotabeche," Vallejo, *Obras*, pp. 305–10.

120 *Carta*, p. 15.

121 *Carta*, p. 21.

122 *Carta*, pp. 26–27.

123 *Carta*, pp. 27–29.

country." The rich will be saved from a future *jacquerie* – "the fate of the Whites of Saint Domingue [Haiti]" – and foreign traders will benefit from an enormously expanded market.[124] Why has the United States progressed so "admirably"? Because of its even distribution of property. Arcos expresses the hope that by "attacking the evil head-on" Chile can avoid the agrarian upheaval France went through in the 1790s: "Let us raise the cry of BREAD AND LIBERTY, and the Star of Chile will become the morning-star that announces the light that is coming for Spanish America."[125]

It cannot be denied that Arcos's thinking is utopian. The traditional hacienda system was far tougher than he supposed. His "generous, patriotic youth," when it took charge of Chilean affairs later in the century, showed no great inclination to adopt his agrarian reform. Nor did the Chilean tradition, as it developed, have much place for All-Powerful Revolutionary Governments. Yet, the force and directness of Arcos's pamphlet and its ruthless underlying realism make it the most imaginative of the political treatises of the time, and one of those rare pieces of political writing that persuades us, for a bit, to think of what might have been.[126]

124 *Carta*, p. 30.
125 *Carta*, p. 31.
126 For an intelligent recent reading of Arcos, see Gazmuri, "Pensamiento."

7
Model Republic

What can be described as the Chilean worldview (educated Chileans' *cosmovisión* or *imaginario*, as Spanish-speakers sometimes call it nowadays) has obvious connections with the ways in which both political ideas and political behavior developed in the mid-century years, not to mention the program of reform espoused by both Conservatives and Liberals. For this reason alone, it needs to be examined as part of the general pattern of ideas and politics. What kind of a country did educated Chileans of the early republic think they were living in? How did they "imagine the nation"? What were their feelings about it? How did they see its future and interpret (or start to interpret) its past? Since they often looked beyond their own frontiers, we need to ask how they saw their country fitting into the postcolonial Latin American pattern. What were their attitudes to the great world beyond South America, especially Europe and the United States? To what extent did they take Europe or the United States as models for their own future? The following two chapters illustrate the multitude of answers Chileans gave to these questions.

The Chilean Superiority Complex

Qué escena tan sublime
Oh Patria ves hoy día!
Una era en agonía
Y otra era que te imprime
Su sello constructor!

What a sublime scene,
Oh homeland, do you see today!
One era of agony
And another era which imprints
Its constructive seal.[1]

1 *Crepúsculo*, No. 4, September 18, 1843.

So runs part of a poem from 1843. Governmental self-congratulation on Chile's growing stability, although often reiterated, was invariably couched in a distinctly dignified and sober tone. This was largely because of the powerful influence of Andrés Bello on the style of official documents, many of which he drafted. The press, however, labored under no such constraints, and abounded in highly positive evaluations of the country by writers and politicians. It was already being suggested in 1835 that Chileans were "excessively appreciative of the things of their country."[2] They more than proved the point in their expressions of self-approval, which added up to a superiority complex when they compared themselves with other Spanish Americans, as they seem to have done fairly often. Chile, declared a newssheet of 1839, was "an object of admiration and praise for its present state of civilization and tranquillity," a happy state of affairs attributable to the Conservative government and "to the soft character . . . [and] unequaled patriotism" of Chileans.[3] Such themes were to be sounded again and again throughout the early republic – and well beyond. A newspaper of 1841 put Chile at the "head of South American civilization."[4] *"There is no doubt,"* asserted another in 1857, *"Chile is the first among South American nations."*[5] Interior minister Irarrázaval told Congress in 1841 that Chile was "a splendid lesson" for other countries.[6] This note was often struck in newspaper editorials or articles marking the *dieciocho*. For the holidays of 1842, Santiago Lindsay preceded a suitably patriotic poem with the epigraph: "The sun shines in the sky: Chile shines in South America."[7]

As time went on, such self-congratulation almost became a chorus. As a country, Chile was obviously becoming "the most advanced, indubitably" in South America, "the vindicator and regenerator of our race," even perhaps *"the England of South America."*[8] The young Diego Barros Arana, a far from uncritical judge, summed up the universal consensus in 1853, when he wrote that what had once been a "wretched province" of the Spanish Empire was now "a wisely and stably constituted republic," admired even in Europe: "Forty years ago we were nothing in the eyes of the world or to ourselves, and today we call ourselves *Chileans* with pride and dignity."[9]

2 *Repertorio chileno . . . 1835*, p. 3. For Bello's influence on the "public" Chilean style, see Serrano and Jaksić, pp. 441–42.
3 *Época*, No. 2, September 14, 1839.
4 *Estrella del Norte*, No. 11, September 25, 1841.
5 *Conservador*, No. 64, October 16, 1857.
6 *Memoria* of Interior minister (1841). DP, I, 118.
7 *Semanario de Santiago*, No. 11, September 22, 1842.
8 *Correo Literario*, No. 9, September 12, 1858; *Tren*, No. 7, June 6, 1859; *Copiapino*, No. 3103, September 14, 1858.
9 *Museo*, No. 15, September 17, 1853.

The Chilean superiority complex tended to be reinforced whenever Chileans traveled elsewhere in Spanish America. General José Francisco Gana, envoy to Ecuador in the mid-1850s, was flattered to be told by his hosts that in Peru and Ecuador Chile was seen as "the most advanced country in South America and a model all would like to imitate." And Gana felt pride when he contemplated "how political affairs proceed in these lands."[10] Admiral Manuel Blanco Encalada, on his diplomatic mission to Europe in the mid-1850s, reported that Chile was regarded there as "the model people" of South America, that the European press regarded Chile as "the exceptional country in South America," and that Venezuela's minister in France had told him: "Only Chile is doing well, thus saving the honor of Spanish America."[11] Domingo Santa María, writing in 1859 from New Granada (Colombia), declared that "on all this [west] coast down to Cape Horn there is only Chile."[12] The idea of Chile as a "model" was clearly a flattering one. The catchphrase *república modelo* ("model republic") was used with increasing frequency during the period, not to mention later. Not everybody found it appropriate. For *El Mercurio* (in one of its many moods) the claim betokened a "fictitious superiority."[13] "Everyone is shouting that Chile is the model Republic of South America," protested *El Copiapino* in 1858. "What can the others be like?"[14] A newspaper three years later denounced the use of the catchphrase as "a mania . . . , a rather quixotic pretension."[15] Quixotic? Maybe. A pretension? Definitely.

Evaluations of "national character," however, tended to be somewhat more skeptical. No attempt was made during the early republic to interpret Chilean nationality in ethnic terms: the first writings in that vein do not appear much before the start of the twentieth century. Nor was there much "sociological" description of the kind Sarmiento was so good at for Argentina – and indeed, to some extent for Chile, for Sarmiento's sketches of Chilean life are among the best of the period, stronger than texts such as José Victorino Lastarria's well-known "Manuscrito del diablo" (1849). There were some, certainly, who believed that Chile's historic isolation had been the main influence on national character. The oceans had stopped "egotistical and feudal Europe" from enslaving Chile; the giant barrier of the Andes prevented the "barbarian pastoral life" of Argentina from seeping in; the northern deserts fended off "the immorality and relaxation" of Peru.[16]

10 To Antonio Varas, Guayaquil, April 20, 1855. *Revista Chilena*, No. 100–01 (1928), p. 929.
11 Blanco Encalada to Varas, November 30, 1853, October 31, 1855, and May 14, 1856. Varas, *Correspondencia*, II, 24; II, 119; II, 05.
12 To M. L. Amunátegui, Panama, December 21, 1859. Amunátegui Solar, *Archivo*, I, 69.
13 MV, No. 7396, May 3, 1852.
14 *Copiapino*, No. 3021, June 5, 1858.
15 DIS, No. 77, February 22, 1861.
16 *Tren*, No. 12, June 11, 1859.

There were others who believed that isolation had given Chileans a "commonsense and moderate character," and had made them "the most sensible of South Americans."[17] Interior minister Tocornal noted in 1835 that a benign climate had endowed Chilean countryfolk with a "vigorous constitution," and that as many Chileans survived infancy as was the case in "not a few European nations."[18] A northern news-sheet identified "good judgment and mildness . . . , [and] docility of . . . character" as essential Chilean characteristics.[19] A writer in *El Ferrocarril* in 1860 suggested that Chileans combined traces of French impetuousness, Spanish hidalgo spirit, English pride, German pigheadedness, and Dutch phlegm: "We are by temperament cold, reserved, meditative – though with few ideas."[20] Vicente Pérez Rosales, sketching his compatriots (in French) for a European audience, thought they had an *"esprit plutôt réfléchi que brillant . . . , esprit éminemment conservateur."*[21]

This "reflective" and "eminently conservative" character, however, had its negative side. An 1835 almanac, describing Chileans as more taciturn (but also more hospitable) than other peoples, identified their main vice as a "pernicious . . . lassitude . . . which they themselves call *apathy*," a quality that depressed "their public or religious spirit."[22] A magazine of 1855 blamed its low sales (and rapid closure) on Chilean "apathy and indifference," adding for good measure that Chileans were "the most insipid and monotonous people in the world."[23] Chileans might be physically robust and intelligent, suggested Francisco Javier Rosales, but they also had "a marked lack of ambition."[24] Such assertions often were made in discussions of the slow progress of the capitalist spirit. "We Chileans," Ramón Luis Irarrázaval wrote in 1853, commenting on the construction delays on the Santiago–Valparaiso railroad, "will not be the ones to hasten to make innovations or improvements – or anything."[25] There was, however, general agreement that this "apathy of the national character" and "indolence of spirit," as *El Mercurio* put it, could be blamed fairly and squarely on the Spanish colonial legacy.[26]

If there was one particular national trait that tended to be singled out by writers of the time it was the Chilean love of wandering. "Chileans,"

---

17 Manuel Guillermo Carmona, "Fastos sangrientos de América," *Revista del Pacífico*, Tomo II (1860), p. 511; *Conservador*, No. 65, October 17, 1857.
18 *Memoria* of Interior minister (1835). DP, I, 81.
19 *Estrella del Norte*, No. 11, September 25, 1841.
20 FE, No. 1411, July 12, 1860.
21 *Essai*, p. 192.
22 *Repertorio . . . 1835*, p. 7.
23 *Revista de Santiago*, Tomo I (1855), p. 821.
24 Rosales, p. 41.
25 To Manuel Blanco Encalada, June 29, 1853. Ovalle Castillo, p. 86.
26 MV, No. 3671, March 6, 1841; No. 3815, August 7, 1841.

claimed a military news-sheet of 1838, "are the English of South America in more than one way, but especially because of their inclination to travel."[27] Certainly Chileans *were* inclined to roam, when they could. The young officer Patricio Lynch, seconded to the Royal Navy in 1840, and relishing action on board H.M.S. *Calliope* in the First Opium War, was astonished to find a compatriot fighting for the Chinese.[28] Jacinto Chacón, in a "historical fantasy" of 1849, has the Angel Uriel tell the Genius of Chile: "In all the regions of Europe my Spirits have visited, they have found those sons of the Andean mountains, always with their customs and popular songs." Yet, the Angel Uriel adds, they are also prone to "a fever that induces in them a homesickness that saddens them, consumes them, makes them restless to return to their own skies."[29] It is certainly not hard to find touching expressions of patriotic feeling among Chileans far from home. "My country is not the world," wrote Benjamín Vicuña Mackenna, from the exile into which he was unceremoniously flung in 1859. "My country is Chile, in the combination of its love, its creation, its light, its sky, the sand of its beaches, its name, its flag; and the more I see her outraged and unhappy, the more I feel that country is mine."[30]

The Chilean Future

Whatever the possible blemishes on their national character, most educated Chileans were convinced that progress would give their country a bright future. The first history book written after independence, by Father José Javier Guzmán (1834), speculated that Chile could well become "worthy of ... representation and place among the most celebrated associations of the human theater."[31] *El Mercurio* in 1840 was confident that the country was "called to become, at a time we do not think far off, both opulent and happy."[32] A guide for foreigners printed in 1841 was even more buoyant, claiming that Chile was on "an ascendant and rapid march" of progress, and an opposition newspaper ten years later believed that the country was "destined by the divine hand to be a paradise of common happiness."[33] Optimism about the future (a very nineteenth-century mood) was standard in official rhetoric. President Montt, opening Congress in 1854, referred to Chile's "constant march towards the high destiny without doubt reserved

27 *Boletín del Ejército Restaurador*, No. 2, December 21, 1838.
28 Balbontín, pp. 35–37.
29 "Fantasía histórica en 1849," *Revista del Pacífico*, Tomo II (1860), p. 778.
30 Vicuña Mackenna to A. C. Gallo and G. and M. A. Matta, Paris, August 25, 1859. Vicuña Mackenna et al., *Montt presidente*, p. 27.
31 Guzmán, II, 448.
32 MV, No. 3454, June 20, 1840.
33 *Guía de forasteros*, p. 48; *Talquino*, No. 45, April 4, 1851.

for her."[34] "The country's prosperity will never be upset by a bad year," wrote Montt's Interior minister Antonio Varas, after the serious drought of 1853, "and it will go on rising."[35] Chile's obvious advantages were itemized by *El Semanario de Santiago* in 1843: "A population almost without a mixture of races . . . ; a temperate climate favorable to active and industrious life; a territory with sources of wealth that are as varied as they are inexhaustible."[36] An 1860 almanac, under an engraving of a female figure taking flight from a murkily indeterminate landscape, observes that all nations have good or evil stars. What is Chile's? "She lacks for nothing: magnificent ports, rich and abundant mines, an active trade, progress, enlightenment, civilization. What more could she desire? Her horoscope does not lie: her star is a happy one."[37] Such confident assertions were markedly different in tone from the gloomy national assessments common in the "Parliamentary" period, half a century later.

Estimates of Chile's future position could sometimes be fanciful. "The horizon of our future is immense," declared a provincial news-sheet in 1859. True, from Australia and New Zealand "the Anglo-Saxon race" might become contenders for the "dominion of the Pacific," but Chile had "all the conditions to become a real power. . . . A million and a half Chileans in the position they occupy today, and with the direction they can be given, are worth more than three hundred million Chinese, or two hundred million Indians, or fifty million Frenchmen."[38] As this statement shows, visions of the future could include an element of national assertiveness and power. In 1862, *El Mercurio* called for Chile to "take the lead" in a "crusade of civilization and prosperity . . . , [to] assert her importance amongst the nations on the Pacific Ocean."[39] But while there were some who wanted Chile to achieve "a high external preponderance over the other republics,"[40] this was not necessarily an aggressive *military* aspiration. Indeed, the newspaper article just cited takes it for granted that the key to future national power is *trade*. There were those who believed that progress alone was already giving Chile "supremacy . . . over the whole of Spanish America."[41] On one occasion, *El Progreso* self-servingly attributed the "expansion of Chilean

34 DP, V, 15.
35 To M. Blanco Encalada, August 13, 1853. Varas, *Correspondencia*, II, 8.
36 *Semanario de Santiago*, No. 27, January 5, 1843.
37 *Almanaque enciclopédico*, p. 6. The republic was always visually depicted in female form, although (unlike France's Marianne) the symbolic woman never received a name. The precedents were classical. It should also be remembered that the Patron of Chile was female, the Virgin of Carmen. See Cruz de Amenábar.
38 *Tren*, June 4 and 11, 1859.
39 "Review for Foreign Parts" (in English), M(V), No. 192, July 20, 1862.
40 *Civilización*, No. 208, May 27, 1852.
41 TRI, No. 473, December 3, 1850.

civilization over the other states" to the superiority of its newspapers. The same newspaper, after the failure of the European revolutions of 1848, even suggested that Chile assume the messianic role of "head of the universal progressive movement."[42]

There was, it is true, the occasional saber rattling in literary form. Jacinto Chacón, for instance, wrote a stirring marching song, set to music by a visiting Austrian-French pianist, Henri Herz. It made a definite impression in the Santiago of February 1851, as well it might have done, since it was performed by a brass band, double orchestra, and no less than eight pianos.

> *Marinos en el Pacífico,*
> *En la América guerreros,*
> *Sois Chilenos los primeros*
> *En la tierra y en el mar.*
> *Chilenos, marchad! marchad!*

> Sailors on the Pacific,
> Warriors in America,
> Chileans, you are first
> On land and sea.
> Chileans, march! march![43]

It is hard to find such martial sentiments on any level other than the rhetorical. A pamphleteer of 1845, refuting the idea (evidently a popular one) that the Army was "an odious charge on the nation," urged the government to raise military pay,[44] but there was never a serious political demand that the Army should be expanded. Nor was military opinion (insofar as it can be traced) particularly bellicose. *El Eco Militar*, a military magazine that published thirty-two issues in 1845, speculated in a definitely nonbelligerent way on the size of an army needed to repel either Peru or Bolivia, but judged such a conflict highly unlikely. In the 1849 Congress, a deputy even proposed the abolition of the Military Academy. "Chile is not a country bent on conquest," he said, "nor can she be; she is not at war with anyone, and she is not threatened by any nation." In times of real peril, he argued, the people would spring to arms, as they had done at the time of independence.[45]

It is conceivable, however, that public opinion favored a stronger Navy. Chile's Navy during the early republic consisted, at most, of three or four ships, not all of which were seaworthy.[46] There were a few who

---

42 PR, No. 43, December 30, 1842; No. 2168, November 1, 1849.
43 TRI, No. 477, December 7, 1850; Pereira Salas, *Música*, p. 113 and *Biobibliografía*, p. 84.
44 Ramírez, *Breves ideas*, p. 2.
45 CN/D, December 26, 1849.
46 Its first steam-powered warship, the 850-ton English-built corvette *Esmeralda*, later to win immortality at the battle of Iquique (1879), joined the fleet in 1856.The Navy had previously had

even advocated its outright abolition, as Antonio García Reyes disapprovingly pointed out in his historical essay (1846) on the first Chilean naval squadron,[47] itself a plea for a revamped Navy and a flourishing merchant marine. Chile's destiny, argued García Reyes, was the ocean, across which could be extended "the empire of our laws and interests in all the regions of the globe."[48] Chileans, according to *El Mercurio* (in numerous editorials), were natural seafarers.[49] In 1847, a senator demanded "a squadron that will maintain our independence and trade . . . , but not," he added, "a squadron to fight the old nations of Europe," which would be crazy, "but certainly to sustain ourselves against any of the neighboring nations." He believed that the Navy deserved higher priority than the Santiago–Valparaiso railroad.[50] Despite the Navy's poor state in the early republic, its warships could sometimes make a good impression. In 1853 the Valparaiso-built 644-ton corvette *Constitución* put in at Guayaquil in Ecuador: "Competent judges are saying," wrote Carlos Bello (son of Andrés), who was there at the time, "that not even a warship of Her Britannic Majesty is more beautiful or better commanded and crewed."[51]

As with the Army and Navy, so with foreign policy. Chile's foreign policy in the early republic can be described (generously) as minimalist.[52] The maltreatment of Chileans abroad (or episodes like William Walker's filibustering in Central America in the 1850s) sometimes brought demands for a more active stance, even armed intervention.[53] This was pure fantasy. Such pleas always fell on deaf ears. In 1850, Lastarria, criticizing the government's claim to have a *prescindente* ("detached") foreign policy, charged that *prescindente* was a euphemism for "inactive," and demanded a more coherent approach consciously "based on a single principle, *trade*." Marcial González,

two steam-powered vessels, the Valparaiso-built *Maule*, used as a tug, and the *Cazador*, a French freighter fitted out as a transport. Both had sunk, in the case of the *Cazador* (January 1856) with the loss of 460 lives.

47 García Reyes, "Memoria sobre la primera escuadra nacional," in Vicuña Mackenna, *Historia general*, IV, 20. See also the indignant article in *Mensajero*, No. 728, October 29, 1855.
48 García Reyes, "Memoria," IV, 15–17.
49 See, for instance, "Marina Nacional," No. 4491, July 9, 1843 to No. 4498, July 16, 1843.
50 Juan de Dios Vial del Río, CN/S, July 12, 1847.
51 To Varas, January 18, 1853. Varas, *Correspondencia*, V, 362.
52 Chile had only five permanent legations abroad during these years: in London, Paris, Washington, Lima and (after the peace treaty of 1844) Madrid. (The London legation was vacant between the mid-1850s and the War of the Pacific.) Between the 1836–9 war and the little war with Spain in 1865–6, Chilean diplomacy covered the handling of specific claims from foreign powers, an attempted mediation between Peru and Bolivia in the early 1840s, the negotiation of Spanish recognition, a failed mission to Bolivia (1853), and three failed missions to Rome (1847–8, 1852, and 1855–6) in order to resolve the question of the *patronato*.
53 See, for example, MV, No. 5899, June 28, 1847 (Ecuador); *Mensajero*, No. 702, September 28, 1855 (Bolivia); FE, No. 334, January 20, 1857 (Nicaragua).

in the same congressional debate, saw no point at all in diplomacy of any kind: "among other things it gave us the war with Peru, where we lost 300,000 pesos and 3,000 pairs of hands."[54] Some found Chile's inert diplomacy a useful stick with which to beat the government. President Montt's adversaries, for instance, castigated him for having forfeited "the justified prestige Chile had won abroad," and for doing nothing to raise Chile to "the high position" she obviously deserved, while indulging in meaningless gestures such as his declaration of Chilean neutrality in the Crimean War.[55] In 1860, the journalist Manuel Blanco Cuartín strongly attacked the tradition of "absolute detachment," which might be appropriate for San Marino or Andorra or "the barbarous tribes of the Orinoco," but not for Chile, which needed to play a "decorous and dignified role" in Spanish America. "Detachment" in the cases of Bolivia and Argentina, he argued, was singularly inappropriate in that the Chilean boundaries with those countries had still not been fixed – forty years after independence![56]

An Incipient National Memory

History became an unusually prominent part of the cultural panorama of the early republic, partly because it had an official stimulus. In the law creating the new University of Chile, Article 28 (not even discussed in the Chamber of Deputies)[57] stipulated that there should be a solemn annual session of the University Council, in the presence of its patron (the president of the republic), to hear a scholarly essay or *memoria* on a particular facet or episode from Chilean history. At the first such session, in September 1844, José Victorino Lastarria, at Andrés Bello's invitation, presented a *memoria* entitled "Investigaciones sobre la influencia social de la conquista y del sistema colonial de los españoles en Chile"("Investigations into the Social Influence of the Conquest and the Colonial System of the Spaniards in Chile"). Lastarria delivered his paper only a few weeks after Francisco Bilbao's famous trial, and his line of argument was in many ways reminiscent of Bilbao's, although articulated more soberly. (Even so, the audience greeted his words with an icy silence.) His arguments in favor of a "philosophical" approach to history, by which he meant broad generalizations underpinning his Liberal political agenda, provoked a serious polemic between himself and Bello, which Bello can be said to have won.[58] The Chilean historians who

54 CN/D, August 21, 1850.
55 ACT, No. 199, September 24, 1858; CHAM, pp. 244, 253.
56 "Nuestra política en el exterior," *Mosaico*, No. 21, December 8, 1860. The Chile-Bolivia boundary was fixed at 24°S in 1866. Chile and Argentina agreed (1856) to recognize the old colonial border, which had never been demarcated, only fixing it more precisely in 1881.
57 SCL, XXX, 174.
58 See Jaksić, *Bello: Scholarship*, pp. 133–42; Woll, pp. 29–48.

began to make their mark in the 1850s and 1860s (a brilliant generation) all followed Bello in their strict adherence to document-based research and narrative. In their political views, most of them were closer to Lastarria than Bello.[59]

This is not the place to examine the growing historical literature of the time, much of it still easily accessible, but it clearly both mirrored and influenced the incipient "national memory" of educated Chileans. A point at issue between Bello and Lastarria in 1844 (questions of method apart) was Lastarria's deeply negative view of the Spanish colonial legacy, which Bello defended in his usual measured way.[60] The fierce anticolonial and anti-Spanish feelings that had welled up at the time of independence[61] may have abated somewhat in the ensuing decades, although they could be revived only too easily, as in 1865 with the Spanish naval squadron's aggressions on the Pacific coast. At the time of the Chilean-Spanish treaty of April 1844, they were perhaps latent rather than active. Sometimes, indeed, there could be proud assertions of Chileans' Spanish lineage. "We are Spaniards, legitimate heirs of our forefathers in their racial pride, their religious fanaticism, their political intolerance and all their defects," declared *El Ferrocarril* in 1857, "but we are also their heirs in intelligence, in patriotism, and in an innate love of our liberties."[62]

In general, however, the Chilean view of the colonial past remained highly jaundiced. Father Guzmán's history book of 1834 contains the standard litany of charges: the atrocities of the conquest, the sufferings of the Indians, the Spanish commercial monopoly, discrimination against creoles, and so on.[63] A University-approved school textbook by Miguel de la Barra (1858) pictures the "cold and calculated avarice and despotism" of the colonial era, and the "maintaining of the masses in ignorance, and the inequality of classes."[64] The academic historical works that began to appear in the 1850s and 1860s reflected much the same view, as did the very limited amount of historical fiction that appeared in these years. (Prior to the mid-1860s, novels and short stories in this genre can easily be counted on the fingers of two hands.) There were plenty of more private expressions of dislike for the colonial legacy. Eusebio Lillo, contemplating the fortresses at Corral during his relegation to the south in 1851, marveled at "the energy and power of the Spanish race," and regretted that it had not been spent on "monuments of use to industry and humanity."[65] Pedro Félix Vicuña, writing up a temporary

59 Woll, pp. 49–66.
60 Jaksić, *Bello: Scholarship*, pp. 135–36.
61 Collier, *Ideas*, pp. 192–201.
62 FE, No. 121, May 1, 1857.
63 Guzmán, II, 489–553.
64 De la Barra, *Compendio*, p. 18.
65 "Apuntes de un viaje al sur de Chile en 1851," *Revista de Santiago*, Tomo 1 (1855), p. 32.

banishment in Peru, could not resist the reflection that "the Almagros and Pizarros" had destroyed the Inca empire, "an empire created more by civilization than arms," replacing it with a "military despotism" that had enslaved "a peaceful race."[66] One of Guillermo Matta's poems castigated Francisco Pizarro as an *"alma de piedra y corazón pigmeo, / indigno aventurero sin conciencia,"* a "spirit of stone with a pygmy heart, / unworthy adventurer without a conscience."[67]

Chileans were always, however, prepared to make an exception for their own local conquistador, Pedro de Valdivia. In 1842 *El Semanario de Santiago* urged the erection of a monument to "this illustrious Spanish caudillo," its sympathy for the Araucanians outweighed by admiration for the conqueror. Father Guzmán's history book, while praising Araucanian resistance, describes Valdivia as "gifted with an incomparable spirit and great political and military talents." In 1850, when the government allocated money to buy and preserve Valdivia's house in Santiago, the congressional debate evinced considerable respect for him.[68]

The political title deeds of Chilean nationality, of course, were to be found in the heroic struggle for independence, which would remain the prime focus of the republic's national memory. For *El Mercurio*, the 1810 revolution "shone for us with a light as pure as the first day of creation."[69] The heroes of independence, wrote Hermógenes Irisarri, had given "the most unequivocal proofs of valor and boldness," and the battle of Maipó had conferred "an unwithering aura of glory" on Chile's tricolor flag.[70] Anniversaries of all the major battles of independence became part of the month lists printed in the roughly ninety popular almanacs published in Chile between 1830 and 1864. A glance at a representative sample of these gives the impression that patriotic anniversaries (as compared with saints' days, always the major component of the lists) increased in number in the 1840s and 1850s. In some earlier almanacs, there are none at all.[71] Even in later ones, the anniversaries of the independence period are mixed in with a bewildering miscellany of other dates.[72] The saga of independence, we might note, did not have much effect on the naming of ships. Of the 190 registered vessels of the merchant navy in 1848, only seven had patriotic names, four of which came from the wars: *Independencia, General Freire,*

---

66 Vicuña, *Ocho meses*, p. 3.
67 Matta, *Poesías*, II, 274.
68 *Semanario de Santiago*, No. 7, August 25, 1842; Guzmán, I, 150; CN/D, August 26, 1850.
69 MV, No. 3857, September 18, 1841.
70 Desmadryl, I, ix–xi.
71 For example, *Almanak Chileno, útil y curioso, para el año de 1843, XXXIV de nuestra libertad* (n.d. ?1842).
72 See *Almanaque chileno para 1854* (n.d. ?1853); *Almanaque para el año bisiesto de 1856* (1856); *Almanaque popular e instructivo para el año de 1857* (1857).

General O'Higgins, and *Lord Cochrane*.[73] As philatelists know, Chile's first postage stamp (1856) shows the head of Christopher Columbus rather than one of the country's own heroes.

It was several decades before the heroes of independence were commemorated in statuary. The story of the first statues in Santiago is intertwined with that of the political rivalries of the moment. The first patriot leader to be immortalized in bronze (September 1856) was General Ramón Freire, whose nemesis, of course, had been the Conservative regime. Sculpted and cast in England, the remarkably handsome statue was paid for by subscription, most (although certainly not all) of the subscribers being opponents of President Montt. Freire was a reminder of the abolished Liberalism of the 1820s. The poem Guillermo Matta declaimed at the inauguration drove the point home. Unlike the detested Montt, Freire was

> *Déspota, nunca! siempre ciudadano,*
> *No fue su vida la ambición menguada.*
> *Los espectros que acechan al tirano*
> *Nunca durmieron en su pura almohada.*

> Never a despot! always a citizen,
> His life was not one of wretched ambition.
> The specters that lie in wait for tyrants
> Never slumbered on his spotless pillow.[74]

The government responded in kind. The Municipality of Santiago tried to organize a public subscription for no less than five statues – Bernardo O'Higgins, José Miguel Carrera, José de San Martín, the colonial savant Juan Ignacio Molina, and Diego Portales – but fell short of its target. In August 1857, the Chamber of Deputies agreed (on a 36 to 7 vote) to add 20,000 pesos to the fund. In the Senate, Pedro Nolasco Mena suggested in Periclean fashion that the effort, although praiseworthy, should be deferred for "a time more appropriate than the present; let us content ourselves for now by knowing that the names and the deeds of these illustrious men are preserved in the hearts of the citizens."[75] Despite Mena's objections, the Senate approved (9 to 5) the 20,000-peso subsidy, and added another 10,000 pesos to the budget for a new public clock. The only statues to be erected over the next few years were those of José Miguel Carrera (September 1858) and Diego Portales (September 1860), whose reputation was being magnified by the government at the time. The Carrera statue seems to have

---

73 *Registro de la marina.*
74 Desmadryl, II, 75. The inscription on the statue puts Freire's death in 1853; it was in September 1851.
75 CN/S, October 5, 1857.

been largely uncontroversial. Portales was a different matter. Domingo Arteaga Alemparte, for one, questioned whether a man who still aroused hatred as well as veneration should have priority over greater heroes.[76] The solemn inauguration of the Portales statue was as much a political demonstration as the Liberals' homage to General Freire.

By the time the first statues went up, there was a growing awareness that the generation that had fought for independence was fast dying out. As an act of patriotic *pietas*, there appeared in 1854–6 a superbly printed two-volume compendium of engraved portraits and brief biographies of the principal patriots, the engravings done (excellently) by Narciso Desmadryl, a French artist then working in Chile, and the minibiographies by well-known Chileans. The liberator O'Higgins's death in 1842, needless to say, had been marked by suitable tributes in the press,[77] after years of rather shameful silence. The passing of others was duly noted. With the demise of ex-president Francisco Antonio Pinto in 1858, Guillermo Blest Gana commented: "Only a few are now left, the last of the generation of the great ones."[78] The death (in 1860) of Juan Agustín Alcalde, the last surviving participant in the historic *cabildo abierto* of September 18, 1810, did not pass unnoticed.[79] Newspapers occasionally compiled lists of survivors from the heroic era: thirty-six officers from the battle of Chacabuco, for instance, or fifty or so from the battle of Maipó, or fifty-nine veterans of the 1820 expedition to Peru (in this case with a note of their current whereabouts).[80] The return to Chile in 1858 (after a twenty-five-year absence) of General William Miller, the liberator General José de San Martín's English aide, seems to have sparked a certain amount of curiosity.[81]

Not all the figures from the heroic age were necessarily seen as uncontroversial. O'Higgins's political role "stained his laurels," according to a news-sheet of 1843,[82] and the title of *La dictadura de O'Higgins* (1853), Miguel Luis Amunátegui's historical essay on his regime, is sufficiently revealing of Amunátegui's approach, although his real target was probably less O'Higgins than Manuel Montt. A guidebook of 1847 took the view that it was understandable that the wars of independence should have made O'Higgins "a sort of dictator," but his "healthy heart" meant that

76 "Ecos de la semana," *Semana*, No. 48, June 2, 1860.
77 Good examples include MV, No. 4272, November 20, 1842; *Telégrafo de Concepción*, No. 1, December 15, 1842.
78 *Revista del Pacífico*, Tomo I (1858), p. 128.
79 FE, No. 1520, November 20, 1860.
80 ACT, No. 11, February 12, 1858 (Chacabuco); *Voz de Chile*, No. 22, April 5, 1862 (Maipó); *País*, No. 22, August 20, 1857 (1820 expedition).
81 ACT, No. 249, November 22, 1858.
82 *Observador Político*, No. 3, August 16, 1843.

he had never been a genuine "tyrant."[83] Memories of the deadly rivalry of O'Higgins and the Carrera brothers still lingered on. (In muted form, they still do.) José Miguel Carrera tended to be venerated more by Liberals than Conservatives. A passionate (and controversial) defense of him was included in the second of the university *memorias* (1845), by the old *carrerino* Diego José Benavente. Benavente was not above altering the text of one of O'Higgins's letters in order to smear him, something not found out until 1916.[84] Alberto Blest Gana made gentle fun of the rivalry in his hilarious 1859 sketch of political banquets:

"Gentlemen," says Don Tito. "A health to Carrera, O'Higgins, San Martín, those great . . ."

"Those three names should *never* go together," exclaims a partisan of Carrera; "the last two of those you named were *tyrants*."

"Carrera was ambitious and wicked," shouts an O'Higginist, "and there's the battle of Rancagua to prove it."

"San Martín was an Argentine crook," cries another *carrerino*, climbing on to his chair.

"And O'Higgins was a tyrant and a *bastard-orphan*," adds another *carrerino*, his eyes inflamed.[85]

Guillermo Matta, writing up the patriot guerrilla Manuel Rodríguez ("an adventurer of genius") for the Desmadryl albums of 1854–6, could not resist a few barbed comments about O'Higgins, but also pleaded for an end to the rivalry: "Let every man bring his laurels," he wrote; the two heroes together were "the monument of our independence."[86] By the 1860s, O'Higgins and Carrera were well on their way to becoming national myths.

Diego Portales was not, or not yet. One reason for this was that (unlike O'Higgins or Carrera) he was still only too well remembered. At the time of his death, as we saw, he was given a full measure of tribute. *El Mercurio*, as befitted a Valparaiso newspaper, was fairly assiduous in keeping his memory green, often (although not always) marking the anniversary of his death with salutes to "the illustrious Portales, honor and glory of the Chilean people" (in 1838), or Chile's "cleverest statesman" (1843), and so on – and *El Mercurio* sometimes chided other publications for not doing the same.[87] Yet, comments on Portales in the press (or in Congress) in the years that followed are surprisingly scanty and intermittent. President Prieto's

83 *Guía general 1847*, p. 57. The wording of the comment is identical in Briseño, *Memoria* (published later), pp. 86–87.

84 Woll, pp. 53–56. See also Luis Valencia Avaria, *Bernardo O'Higgins, el buen genio de America* (1980), p. 134.

85 "Los banquetes patrióticos," *Semana*, No. 12, August 6, 1859.

86 Desmadryl, I, 138.

87 MV, No. 2848, June 9, 1838; No. 4458, June 6, 1843; No. 4114, June 8, 1842.

farewell message in 1841, surveying the 1830s, mentions him only (and not by name) as the "illustrious victim" of the 1837 mutiny, not as the organizer of the republic.[88] An obituary in 1842 of the *filopolita* Manuel José Gandarillas, recounting the events of 1829–35, passes over Portales's role in silence,[89] as does Ramón Rengifo's short biography (1846) of his brother Manuel, the Finance minister. A schooner was named after Portales, but it was one of the smallest ships in the merchant fleet.[90] (No Chilean warship has ever borne his name.) His biographical note in the Desmadryl album (by his old henchman Fernando Urízar Garfias) was just about the shortest in the collection.[91] It is too much to say that there was a conspiracy of silence about Portales, but the absence of comment *is* rather striking.

Only in the 1850s was the silence broken, largely because President Montt and his Interior minister Antonio Varas tended to present themselves as continuing Portales's work. In Congress in 1853, Varas praised Portales as the man who "devoted himself to fighting against faction . . . and to establish order, to give stability to our institutions and to prepare the present situation of the Republic."[92] Appreciations of Portales in the government press became more frequent in the later 1850s than before – "that man whom all recognize as the founder of the present state of things," or so he was eulogized by *El Ferrocarril*, which also saw him as developing "a vast political plan, and, in our concept, a liberal plan."[93] The Montt-Varas self-identification with Portales was inevitably drawn into the propaganda of their adversaries, for whom "the present state of things" was far from ideal. The opposition, or some of its writers, adopted an unpredictable tactic. Instead of condemning Portales, as they would have done earlier, they accepted his greatness: "he was a genius . . . , he was bold . . . ," said Domingo Santa María in 1857; "he had rare will-power, and . . . exemplary selflessness in the public service."[94] Several leading Liberals (including Santa María and Federico Errázuriz) subscribed to his statue.[95] Greatness, of course, could easily be compared with its opposite. An opposition newspaper in 1858 firmly denied that Montt was the "continuer of Portales," contrasting Portales's "genius" and "patriotism" with Montt's supposed "ineptitude."[96] Another newspaper described Montt as simply a "caricature" of Portales.[97]

88 Sotomayor Valdés, *Historia*, IV, 257.
89 PR, No. 22, December 5, 1842.
90 MV, No. 4059, April 14, 1842.
91 Desmadryl, II, 171–73.
92 CN/D, October 13, 1853.
93 FE, Nos. 392 and 421, March 28 and May 1, 1857.
94 Speech on reception into the University Law Faculty. FE, No. 387, March 23, 1857.
95 FE, No. 300, December 11, 1856.
96 ACT, No. 199, September 24, 1858.
97 DIS, No. 195, July 12, 1861.

The contrast became the theme of four remarkable articles by Benjamín
Vicuña Mackenna, published in the news-sheets *El Ciudadano* and *La
Asamblea Constituyente*, and left unfinished when both were shut down by
Montt. For Vicuña Mackenna, Portales had "the instinct for the great," and
his government had been fertile in achievement. Montt was an altogether
smaller man, "the school inspector, the university professor."[98] In 1860, to
mark the inauguration of the statue, Manuel Blanco Cuartín published a
rather good poem on this theme:

> *Tu genio, pues, se opuso a la corriente,*
> *Y la nave triunfante de repente*
> *De los escollos y hondo remolino*
> *A izar volvió orgullosa*
> *La bandera gloriosa,*
> *Signo inmortal de nuestro gran destino;*
> *Y caminando alegre, viento en popa,*
> *Cruzó el mar del Pacífico admirado,*
> *Y fijó las miradas de la Europa*
> *Sobre un pueblo ignorado . . .*
> *Moriste, pues, Portales,*
> *Y la nave preciosa*
> *Sin más piloto que tu mismo empuje*
> *Siguió atinada; más al cabo ruge*
> *La tempestad airada, arrecia el viento,*
> *Los mastiles deshace, al fin zozobra,*
> *I rota ya tan portentosa obra,*
> *Encalla en la ribera.*

> Your genius, then, went against the current,
> And the triumphant ship suddenly
> Through the reefs and whirlpools
> Once again proudly raised
> The glorious flag,
> Immortal sign of our great destiny;
> And moving merrily, wind in the sails,
> She crossed the Pacific, admired by all,
> And fixed the gaze of Europe
> On an unknown people . . .
> Then you died, Portales,
> And the beautiful vessel,
> With no pilot except the push you had given,

---

98 "Portales y Montt," *Ciudadano*, No. 80, November 13, 1858; No. 81, November 17, 1858; No. 82,
   November 20, 1858; No. 83, November 24, 1858.

Sailed on, on course; but eventually
The storm rages, the wind rises,
The masts are split, and at last the ship founders,
The portentous work broken,
She runs aground ashore.[99]

It should be added in the interests of accuracy that by no means all Liberals (Blanco Cuartín was a Conservative) shared such positive assessments of the "omnipotent minister." Lastarria's well-known essay on him (1861) was unremittingly hostile, and strongly negative accounts of him would continue to appear in Liberal writings, to set against the special reverence for him in Conservative writings.[100] It was perhaps Vicuña Mackenna's large-scale, vivid, fair-minded biography of Portales (1863), still mesmerizingly readable, that did most to place him above party, above the still-remembered conflicts and persecutions of his own time, and to lodge him in the Chilean imagination as the equal of the heroes of independence. This process was still incomplete in the 1860s – the biography sparked criticism from several Liberals[101] – but the seed planted by Vicuña Mackenna would prove a fertile one.

Indomitable Araucania

In 1854, Father José Manuel Orrego, who had recently visited the trans-Bío Bío territory of the Mapuche (or Araucanians) recounted his impressions to the Sociedad Evangélica, a missionary society created by the Church five years earlier. He found it tragic that the Araucanians, so "robust . . . , lively, intelligent . . . and hospitable," should be vegetating "in idleness, in ignorance, in brutishness, the victims of the most absurd superstitions." What, he asked, had Christian Chileans ever done for a people "who could be so useful if they became civilized"? His answer: "nothing, or almost nothing."[102]

The Araucanians were very much a part of Chile's present as well as her historic past. Until the 1850s, the government continued the old colonial policy toward the Mapuche, with vigilance along the Frontier, contacts with the Indians through official intermediaries, and subsidies to friendly caciques such as Lorenzo Colipí, who in fact received the largest subsidy (204 pesos) in 1846.[103] The mid-century agricultural boom pushed new

99 "A la estátua de Portales," *Mosaico*, No. 12, October 6, 1860.
100 For example, I. Errázuriz (Liberal), *Historia*, esp. chapter VI; Sotomayor Valdés (Conservative), *Historia* and Carlos Walker Martínez (Conservative), *Portales* (Paris, 1879).
101 Donoso, *Vicuña Mackenna*, pp. 152–55.
102 Orrego, p. 39.
103 CN/S, August 12, 1846. Twelve other caciques received subsidies that year.

settlers (fourteen thousand by 1858) south of the Bío Bío. The new province of Arauco (Araucania), created in 1853, theoretically covered the whole Mapuche territory, while, further south, the arrival of German colonists warranted the establishment (1861) of a second new province, Llanquihue. How to handle the Araucanian enclave, lying as it did between the Frontier and the new southern settlements, thus became one of the inevitable political issues of the day.

The resistance of "indomitable Araucania" to the Spanish conquistadors had given the patriots of independence a suitable myth to inspire their struggle against Spain. To some extent they identified themselves *as* Araucanians.[104] The habit died hard – in some ways it never died at all. (A popular song of 1962 claimed that Chile's success in the World Cup that year thrilled "our red Araucanian blood.") When the victorious General Bulnes arrived at Valparaiso from Peru in November 1839, one of the welcoming addresses was read by a schoolboy "dressed like an Araucanian in the most costly and excellent manner."[105] The government's official newspaper was given the name *El Araucano.* As War and Navy minister José Javier Bustamante put it in 1835, "Every Chilean feels in his heart the keenest pleasure in hearing of the ancient and modern prowess of the Araucanian heroes."[106] "Look at our brothers in Araucania," urged a clandestine opposition news-sheet of 1859, "who never bent their neck to the ferocious Spaniard: LET US IMITATE THEM ALL."[107] For many, the Araucanians remained a potent symbol of freedom. Father Guzmán's history book presents them as such,[108] as does a poem of 1853 by Hermógenes Irisarri:

> *Libre es el león en las quebradas hondas*
> *Y libre entre sus riscos el huemul,*
> *Y el araucano libre es en su tierra*
> *Cuál cóndor libre en la región azul.*

> The lion is free in the deep ravines,
> The huemul amongst the crags,
> And in his land the Araucanian is as free
> As the condor in the regions of the blue sky.[109]

There were some, admittedly, who had no patience with such attitudes. "We are *not* Araucanians," insisted *El Ferrocarril*, "as some claimed in the

104 See Collier, *Ideas*, pp. 212–17.
105 MV, No. 3289, November 30, 1839.
106 *Memoria* of War and Navy minister (1835). DP, I, 321.
107 *Razón*, No. 1, October 18, 1859.
108 Guzmán, I, 399.
109 *Museo*, No. 2, June 18, 1853.

bewilderment of the revolution."[110] There were others who believed that the Mapuche were no longer the noble warriors of old. A German traveler passing through Araucania in 1859 was convinced that they had degenerated into a "state of barbarism and stupidity."[111]

There was no trace whatever of "cultural relativism" in Chilean perceptions of Araucania. According to *El Mensajero*, Chile was "a cultured, European republic," while Araucania had been "savage" from the first days of Spanish colonization.[112] A guidebook of 1841 praised Araucanian physique and love of freedom, but noted that "as well as being superstitious, they are marked by all the vices that arise from [their] savage state."[113] For War and Navy minister Bustamante, they were "a bloodthirsty, enemy race."[114] There were occasional serious outcries in the press over supposed Mapuche atrocities, the most famous case being the wreck of the brig *Joven Daniel* on the Araucanian coast in 1849, which inflamed feelings in Santiago, and which probably marked the start of the "Araucanian question" as a political issue. The ship's passengers and crew were said to have been murdered by a local cacique, but in all likelihood drowned.[115] Those few who actually traveled through Araucania were often more evenhanded in their judgments. Ignacio Domeyko, for instance, found that in respect of domestic life and material comfort, "the Araucanian Indians are not *savages*, and are perhaps more civilized than many plebeian Chileans and many of their civilizers on the frontier."[116]

There was general agreement that it was impossible simply to leave the Mapuche alone. Antonio Varas, commissioned by Congress to study the political arrangements on (and across) the Frontier, concluded that it was "inhuman, immoral" to leave them "in the darkness in which they lie." He saw no evidence that the Mapuche lacked "the perfectible character of our species." It was the duty of modern states, he believed, to "civilize and convert . . . , to prepare those barbarians for the introduction of constitutional government. . . . Anything else would upset the order of things. We would not be fulfilling our civilizing mission."[117] Others saw

110 FE, No. 121, May 1, 1857.
111 Treutler, *La provincia*, p. 64.
112 "Reducción de indígenas" (part of a series), *Mensajero*, No. 79, August 23, 1853.
113 *Guía de forasteros*, 1841, p. 50.
114 *Memoria* of War and Navy minister (1835). DP, I, 323.
115 Barros Arana, *Decenio*, II, 337–42; Bengoa, pp. 163–64. The *Joven Daniel* episode was enhanced by the story of a young mother, Elisa Bravo, allegedly captured and taken to live among the Mapuche. The tale lived on. The French artist Raymond Quinsac Monvoisin, who worked in Chile between 1842 and 1858, painted (when back in Paris) a picture of her among the Indians, an engraving of which became very popular.
116 Domeyko, *Araucanía*, p. 103.
117 Varas, *Informe*, pp. 27, 8, 42.

the issue in starker terms. It was an immutable law, according to *El Progreso*, that "imperfect races . . . incapable of culture" should be replaced by others with "the powerful germ of development."[118] A progovernment newspaper of 1854 called for a "crusade of Chilean civilization against indigenous barbarism."[119]

When it came to practical ideas for incorporating the Mapuche into what Domeyko called Chile's "republican-Catholic nationality,"[120] there was less agreement. Straightforward military invasion had its advocates – at various times, newspapers such as *El Mercurio, El Progreso, El Ferrocarril* or, among politicians, Diego José Benavente, who urged this course of action in the Senate in 1853. Benavente was confident that Araucanians would not be killed or despoiled of their lands – "in four or five years' time we will have managed to civilize them, while any other way will do no more than continue the miserable state . . . of those Indians." Senator Pedro Nolasco Mena suggested that the "proverbially bellicose character" of the Mapuche would make killing inevitable. Prisoners might have to be taken, admitted Benavente, and that was barbaric – but was it not more barbaric "to keep them in a savage state for three hundred years"?[121]

For Antonio Varas, it was unthinkable that a modern republic should organize a full-scale military assault on Araucania.[122] Father Orrego, likewise, thought it would almost be better to leave the Indians alone rather than "civilize them by means of sword and cannon."[123] The most consistent opposition to the idea came from the Church. "Let us not be socialists and communists," urged the *Revista Católica*. "Nor let us civilize the barbarian by starting with the theft of what he has justly acquired." This was too much like telling the Araucanians: "Either I will civilize you or I will kill you."[124] The church pinned its hopes on missionary activity and the gradual conversion of the Mapuche. Government policy supported this aim. Justice minister Mariano Egaña stated in 1840 that it was part of the government's "great plan" to "incorporate the Indians into the bosom of the homeland."[125] The formation of the Sociedad Evangélica in 1849 was seen by the church as a "project very worthy of Christian and patriotic hearts," as a result of which, "perhaps in a few years," the Mapuche would be won over by "the peaceful religion of Jesus Christ."[126]

118 PR, No. 117, March 29, 1843.
119 *Mensajero*, No. 739, November 12, 1855.
120 Domeyko, *Araucanía*, p. 106.
121 CN/S, August 24, 1853.
122 Varas, *Informe*, p. 6.
123 Orrego, p. 5.
124 "Independencia de Arauco" (part of a series), RCAT, No. 558, June 4, 1859, p. 90.
125 *Memoria* of Justice minister (1840). DP, I, 221. See González and Retamal.
126 RCAT, No. 188, August 17, 1849.

The evidence that the Mapuche responded well to missionaries was not copious. Traveler after traveler in the south testified to the church's failure to convert more than handfuls of Araucanians, and almost never those who were well away from the Frontier. Father Orrego, on his visit to Araucania in 1854, was perplexed by the Indians' stubbornness in resisting Christianity. He attributed this in part to the "not very edifying lives" of Chileans who had settled among them (between fifteen hundred and two thousand, he estimated) and who were hardly a good advertisement for civilization. But Orrego also put his finger on a more fundamental reason: "They do not, it is true, hate civilized people, but they are very suspicious of them, fearing that they want to usurp their territory and enslave them. As they have told me, they knew from the tradition of their elders that the Spaniards had done this in another time."[127]

Those who thought most seriously about the question – Varas and Domeyko among them – tended to agree that it was vital to improve the state of "the frontier Christian population,"[128] perhaps, as Varas suggested, by planting "military-agrarian" colonies, in which veterans would be allotted land, and at a later stage (here the old arguments in favor of immigration come into play) "industrious foreign settlers," whose example would "stimulate more activity and better habits" among Indians – and Chileans. Varas advocated strict control of cross-frontier trade, to eliminate the large number of shady merchants who operated there, and a government monopoly on all purchases of Indian land, to prevent the manipulation of Indians by unscrupulous local hacendados. He also envisaged a new political structure, with caciques becoming state officials, albeit under "paternal" supervision.[129] Domeyko shared Varas's views on trade and land purchases, but was more skeptical about industrious foreign colonists. He advocated a series of mission settlements, in which both religious instruction and respect for the national authorities could be imparted. Each settlement would begin with a church, a priest's house, quarters for a judge or *capitán de amigos* (traditional liaison officer), and soon enough there would be a trader's store, a blacksmith's, a carpenter's shop.[130]

Those with hands-on Frontier experience tended to think in similar fashion. One of them, Father Victorino Palavisino, shared Domeyko's skepticism about foreign settlers, but strongly endorsed the idea of a state monopoly on land purchases. This, in Palavisino's opinion, was where the civilizing of the Mapuche had to begin. By purchasing land (fairly) and then selling it to settlers, the government could begin to mix the Araucanian and Chilean

127 Orrego, p. 7.
128 Domeyko, *Araucanía*, p. 123.
129 *Informe*, pp. 29–30, 19.
130 Domeyko, *Araucanía*, p. 154–55.

population of the south.[131] A resident of the new Arauco Province, publishing his thoughts in 1861, pushed this idea further, by suggesting a gentle process of infiltration, with colonies (perhaps military at first) being established on land purchased from the Indians by the government. The Indian population would thus become dispersed, and "instead of Araucanian enemies, we shall have Chilean subjects."[132] The one voice lacking in all of these discussions, of course, was that of the Mapuche themselves. Nor would it be heard in the 1860s, when official policy started shifting the Frontier southward (a new phase of the story that cannot appropriately be followed up here) and so, twenty years later, ending the long saga of Araucania's proud independence.

131 Palavisino, pp. 9–22.
132 J. M. Morales, "Indicaciones sobre la reducción de indígenas y colonización de la Araucanía," *Revista del Pacífico*, Tomo IV (1861), p. 417.

8

Looking Outward

Chile and the "Semisavage" Sister Republics

If the Araucanians were "savage" for educated Chileans of the early republic, their Latin American neighbors were at least "semisavage," according to an 1850 news-sheet.[1] Chileans' views of the other Latin American countries were invariably tinged by the superiority complex we have noted. Spanish America, for *El Mercurio* in 1841, was a "universal shipwreck ... from Mexico to Buenos Aires," and for a magazine of the following year, "a gladiatorial circus."[2] According to *El Ferrocarril* in 1859 (not a good year for Chilean boastfulness on this score), every steamship brought news of "revolutionary chaos" in the sister republics.[3] The general perception was often confirmed by foreigners living in Chile. Sermonizing in Santiago cathedral during the *dieciocho* of 1854, an Ecuadorian priest drew a lurid picture of the sister states – "many ... with more resources than you" – and the "stormy waves of anarchy" that battered them, not to mention their "nameless tyrants."[4] Father Noboa's point was fair. The other Spanish American republics were all passing through turbulent times, their histories regularly punctuated by palace revolutions, civil wars, regional struggles, dictatorial governments, and, in some cases, repressive atrocities that made Chile's Conservative regime seem a paragon of benevolence. Educated Chileans could read news reports from virtually every part of Latin America (although many more from Europe) in the press. Most of their attention (to judge from press articles and congressional debates) was focused on their immediate neighbors: Argentina, Peru, and Bolivia. Mexico aroused a certain amount of interest (and sympathy) at the time of its war with the United States, and in the mid-1850s, William Walker's filibustering in Central America provoked much comment – though less about Central America

1 *Verdadero Chileno*, No. 78, November 9, 1850.
2 MV, No. 3813, August 5, 1841; *Semanario de Santiago*, No. 4, August 4, 1842.
3 FE, No. 1183, October 18, 1859.
4 Noboa, pp. 22–23. I am grateful to Professor J. León Helguera for drawing my attention to Father Noboa's sermon.

per se than the menace of Yankee expansionism, a point to be examined later.

The neighboring country that loomed largest (by far) on the Chilean horizon was Argentina, which demanded, according to *El Mercurio* in 1839, "the preferential attention of all liberal writers."[5] The numerous Argentines exiled in Chile because of the long "federalist" dictatorship of Juan Manuel de Rosas were happy enough to ventilate their feelings about Argentine politics in the press. Domingo Faustino Sarmiento's classic book *Facundo* first appeared as a *folletín* in *El Progreso* (1845), under the title *Civilización y barbarie*, "Civilization and barbarism" (later its subtitle). The title quickly became a Chilean catchphrase, *El Progreso*, for instance, later describing the opposition's struggle against the government in 1850 as one of "civilization against barbarism."[6] Sarmiento's role in the Chilean journalism of the 1840s was important.[7] He almost became a Chilean citizen. He and the other exiles greatly magnified Argentina's image in Chile.

As a consequence, no foreign name was more consistently execrated in the early republic than that of Rosas – "bloody and atrocious," "the Nero, the Tamburlaine, the Robespierre of the nineteenth century," "the most bloody monster,"[8] and so on, ad infinitum. It was sometimes allowed that history might best determine whether he was "a vulgar tyrant, a monster . . . , or a marvelous hero."[9] His claim to marvelous heroism lay in his resistance to the French and Anglo-French naval blockades he attracted – "an eloquent lesson," according to one writer, of what governments could do when "supported and defended by the people."[10] The Valparaiso newspaper *La Gaceta del Comercio* was especially hostile to the blockades, arguing that tyranny was not a justification for foreign intervention, that intervention would merely strengthen Rosas's hand, and that Argentine *unitarios* (liberals) were remiss in supporting the foreigners.[11] Even here, though, solidarity with the sister nation was far from unanimous. "In the River Plate," pointed out *El Mercurio*, "Europe is exercising a ministry of civilization against barbarism."[12] The repeated claim of Rosas's propagandists that he was defending true "American" values against those of "foreign" Europe never

5 MV, No. 3307, December 23, 1839.

6 PR, No. 2452, October 7, 1850.

7 See Jaksić, "Sarmiento."

8 MV, No. 3312, December 30, 1839; *Museo de Ambas Américas*, No. 19 (1842), II, 263; *Civilización*, No. 33, October 7, 1851. The pro-Rosas articles printed in the *Diario de Santiago* in 1845–6 were designed to irritate the Argentine exiles, and did not reflect the standard Chilean attitude.

9 *Huelen*, No. 2, July 22, 1846.

10 *Justicia*, No. 3, March 18, 1841.

11 *Gaceta del Comercio*, Nos. 1374, 1381, and 1402, July 21 and 29, and August 22, 1846.

12 MV, No. 5567, June 30, 1846.

seems to have had much appeal in Chile. *El Mercurio* mocked his "ridiculous, ridiculous Americanism," contrasting it with "the true Americanism, liberty."[13] Rosas's name, needless to say, could be used in domestic political arguments. An opposition news-sheet of 1858 declared that it would not do President Montt the honor of comparing him with Rosas, whose despotism had been "daring and valiant," while Montt's was no more than "undercover and cowardly."[14]

The overthrow of Rosas by General Justo José de Urquiza at the battle of Caseros in February 1852 was greeted with evident delight in Chile. The progovernment *La Civilización* rejoiced that Argentina was no longer "expunged from the list of cultured nations," and patronizingly looked forward to watching its regeneration from Chile's "elevated position."[15] *El Mercurio* hailed Argentina's liberation from "more than twenty years . . . [of] frightful dictatorship."[16] General Urquiza became a toast at banquets,[17] although opinions about him were later more mixed. His constructive policies appealed to some,[18] but with the political division of Argentina that followed his triumph, Liberal opinion tended to side with the secessionist State of Buenos Aires rather than with Urquiza's Argentine Confederation, the only "Argentina" recognized by the Chilean (or any other) government. Urquiza, according to an opposition newspaper, was waging yet another "war of barbarism against civilization."[19] Buenos Aires attracted Liberals by the openness and vigor of its politics – so different from the atmosphere of Manuel Montt's Chile! Buenos Aires, as one writer tongue-in-cheekishly put it, had succumbed to "the extravagant mania . . . of organizing political *meetings*, [and] freely electing the public powers."[20] Liberals like Isidoro Errázuriz, banished to Argentina by Montt, longed for their own battle of Caseros.[21]

Although Chile made war on Peru and Bolivia in the 1830s, this never implied much interest in the internal politics of those countries, which were much less discussed than those of Argentina. The disputes between them in the early 1840s aroused pitying reactions. "Wretched peoples! When will they begin to understand their own interests?" sniffed *El Mercurio*.[22] Reporting a proposal from the citizens of Arequipa that Peru should become

13 MV, No. 5938, August 23, 1847.
14 *Ciudadano*, No. 13, March 13, 1858.
15 *Civilización*, No. 143, March 6, 1852.
16 MV, No. 7348, March 8, 1852.
17 For example, MV, No. 7353, March 13, 1852.
18 See *Copiapino*, No. 1310, May 19, 1852.
19 ACT, No. 101, May 31, 1858.
20 ACT, No. 156, August 3, 1858.
21 I. Errázuriz, *Emigración*, pp. 10–14.
22 MV, No. 3754, June 5, 1841.

a monarchy, a magazine of 1843 suggested that the country's "farce of republicanism" made it entirely understandable.[23] Chileans traveling in Peru were usually dismissive. A "wretched country," thought Victorino Garrido.[24] An exception was Pedro Félix Vicuña, banished there in 1846. He found Peru much more democratic, much less "aristocratic" than Chile,[25] but this was an eccentric view.

Bolivia was regarded as being an even worse case than Peru – a "land of inconsequence and fickleness," according to an 1841 news-sheet, and a country breathing "the poisoned atmosphere of anarchy," as an opposition newspaper put it in 1858.[26] During a brief stay in La Paz, on Chile's only diplomatic mission to Bolivia during the early republic (1853), José Joaquín Vallejo reported his impressions to Interior minister Antonio Varas. "You can have no idea . . . what this Government is like," he wrote, "if it really is a government at all." Bolivians, he told Varas incredulously, believed that Chile had been "corrupted and ruined" by Europeans, that Peru was even poorer than Ecuador, and that Rosas's tyranny was a model for Spanish America. On leaving Bolivia, Vallejo rejoiced that he was "once again in the civilized world," and pronounced a final, damning verdict on his recent hosts – "those *cholos* and Indians, infinitely more corrupt, wicked and fierce than our worst *rotos*."[27]

It cannot be said that Chilean views of the more remote sister republics were more flattering. Distance did not lend enchantment. Paraguay (hardly ever commented on) could be dismissed as "a people of the middle ages."[28] When a Bogotá newspaper claimed that New Granada (Colombia) was more advanced than Chile, *El Ferrocarril* bluntly riposted that "Chile is a century ahead of New Granada."[29] Domingo Santa María, passing through in 1859, found it a "preposterous republic."[30] New Granada's "ultra-liberal" phase (1849–53)[31] did nothing to enhance the country's reputation. Most of the comments made about it were hostile, especially in the Catholic press, which condemned "the reds" who were imposing "the most barbarous despotism in the name of liberty."[32] Manuel Ancízar, a distinguished *neogranadino*

---

23 *Semanario de Santiago*, No. 29, January 19, 1843.
24 To Manuel Blanco Encalada, December 30, 1854. Ovalle Castillo, p. 135.
25 Vicuña, *Cartas*, p. 17.
26 *Estrella del Norte*, No. 10, September 12, 1841; ACT, No. 203, September 29, 1858.
27 To Varas, April 28 and May 16, 1853. Vallejo, *Obras*, pp. 540–42.
28 MV, No. 4357, February 14, 1843.
29 FE, No. 570, October 23, 1857.
30 To M. L. Amunátegui, December 21, 1859. Amunátegui Solar, *Archivo*, I, 69.
31 For summaries, see David Bushnell, *The Making of Modern Colombia* (Berkeley, 1993), pp. 104–13, and Frank Safford and Marco Palacios, *Colombia. Fragmented Land, Divided Society* (New York, 2002), pp. 197–215.
32 RCAT, No. 251, August 27, 1851. Several articles in RCAT (August–December 1851) analyzed the New Granadan reforms in detail.

envoy to Chile, where he became a good friend of Andrés Bello, published a pamphlet to defend his country's reputation. A longer, anonymous Chilean pamphlet swiftly put him right.[33] A Valparaiso English-language newspaper ended a paean of praise to Chile with the entirely gratuitous comment: "What a contrast to *liberal* New Granada!"[34]

Mexico, which enjoyed a certain sympathy among Chileans during its war with the United States, was nearly always given bad marks for its politics: "a wretched country, incapable of giving itself a nationality" (according to a newspaper of 1849) to the point at which annexation by the United States was entirely possible: "one is inclined to want [it] for that country, given its incurable incapacity for self-government."[35] There were many similar verdicts, with Mexico being viewed as a land of "despotism, anarchy and unexploited riches," as an "immense festival of bloodshed, pillage and barbarism."[36] There was an inclination to blame the Gadsden Purchase (1853) on the "covetousness" of the United States, but it was also pointed out that the real culprit was the "criminal ruler" Antonio López de Santa Anna.[37] Benjamín Vicuña Mackenna, traveling in Mexico in 1853, visited some of the scenes of the recent American war. "My sympathies were with the conquerors," he wrote, "my admiration for the invaders."[38]

Why *was* Spanish America (Chile apart) in such a bad way? The answer nearly always given was the one often used to explain the obstacles to progress in Chile itself: the colonial legacy, which, as we have seen, was generally considered to have been highly defective. Spain had not been "one of the more cultured nations of Europe," in Pedro Félix Vicuña's opinion, so it was inevitable that her former colonies were "more backward" on the scale of civilization.[39] Spanish America, according to a Copiapó newspaper of 1856, had simply been enervated by the Spanish empire's "mixture of fanaticism and tyranny."[40] Reflecting more sociologically, the journalist Martín Palma suggested that the colonial aristocracy had been essentially backward-looking instead of forward-looking, and had rested too much on "the abjection . . . and effacement" of the people.[41] Others pointed to the militarization of Spanish America during the wars of independence: "If

33 Ancízar, *Anarquía y rojismo en Nueva Granada* (1853); *Observaciones a la "Anarquía y rojismo en Nueva Granada"* (1853); see also "Anarquía y rojismo en Nueva Granada," RCAT, No. 302, April 3, 1853.
34 *Valparaiso Echo*, No. 1, August 31, 1853.
35 TRI, No. 122, September 28, 1849.
36 *Mensajero*, No. 770, December 19, 1855; Manuel G. Carmona, "Fastos sangrientos de América," *Revista del Pacífico*, Tomo II (1860), p. 484.
37 *Mensajero*, No. 525, February 22, 1855.
38 Vicuña Mackenna, *Páginas*, I, 78.
39 Vicuña, *Único asilo*, p. 1.
40 *Cóndor*, No. 86, March 17, 1856.
41 *Revista del Pacífico*, Tomo III (1860), p. 496.

Europe's cancer is pauperism," wrote Justo Arteaga Alemparte, "Spanish America's cancer is – *killers!*" Until Spanish America curbed its military, Arteaga believed, there would be no end to civil wars and upheavals.[42]

A Latin American Union?

There was one possible cure for Spanish American ills that was ventilated intermittently, with varying degrees of confidence: the idea of a general Spanish (or even Latin) American union. References to the ideal of union occurred frequently in presidential messages and in the annual foreign affairs reports of Interior ministers. Colonial Spanish America had been a "common family, as Antonio Varas's report for 1860 noted; the new republics should obviously form "a great family of nations" in order to further "civilization and prosperity." Was not the German Zollverein a promising example of what could be accomplished?[43] Neither of the international conferences that met to further this idea – Lima (1847–8), Santiago (1856) – had any practical effect. The treaty signed at Santiago (September 1856) provided for a perpetual alliance between Chile, Peru, and Ecuador (with a regular Congress of Plenipotentiaries), but simply gathered dust on the shelf, though President Montt devoted some eloquent words to it when opening Congress in 1857.[44] But the will-o'-the-wisp of union continued to intrigue a number of educated Chileans. By the early 1860s, it had become something approaching an obsession.

It was an old idea, with important precedents from the independence period.[45] One of the earliest statements on the subject thereafter was a lucid pamphlet by Pedro Félix Vicuña (1837). His starting point was the obvious danger that Europe might take advantage of Spanish America's weakness and internal chaos. What was needed, to cure chaos and to deter Europe, was "an extraordinary power . . . , a moral lever stronger than the one Archimedes conceived of to move the world" – and such a power could only come from a Spanish American union. Vicuña cited the precedents of the Amphictyonic League of ancient Greece and the Germanic Confederation of 1815. Under his scheme, national delegations would form a "Grand American Congress," which would organize an "international code" and a supranational army to enforce the union's decisions. In Vicuña's view, a Spanish American union could well become decisive in "the destinies of the civilized world."[46]

42 *Semana*, No. 24, October 29, 1859.
43 *Memoria* of External Relations minister (1860). DP, VIII, 59.
44 M. Barros, pp. 155–57, 190–91; CN/D&S, June 1, 1857.
45 See Collier, *Ideas*, pp. 217–22.
46 Vicuña, *Único asilo*, pp. 39–43, 47.

The idea of union was regularly discussed in the press (and sometimes by politicians) over the years that followed. *El Mercurio*, for instance, both supported it and opposed it at different times, suggesting on one occasion that Spanish America would present a "by no means contemptible mass" to the rest of the world,[47] while also doubting, on another occasion, whether Spanish American needs would best be served by "the rowdy discussions" of a supranational congress.[48] Interior minister Manuel Camilo Vial, while favorable to the idea of some form of union, did not wish it to "undermine the independence and sovereignty of the Republic."[49] In 1849 *La Tribuna* pooh-poohed *El Progreso* (then an opposition paper) for its advocacy of a Spanish American Zollverein, on the grounds that it would do nothing for Chile's wheat exports: "Erasmus [*sic*] created his Utopia. . . . The opposition has created its 'Progressopolis.' " This was a topical put-down: Sarmiento, who frequently contributed to *La Tribuna* (and perhaps even wrote this comment), was about to publish his book *Argirópolis*, his political blueprint for the River Plate countries.[50]

Starting in the mid-1850s, a number of international episodes refocused Chileans' attention on the idea of union. Ecuador's apparent willingness to hand over the Galapagos Islands to an American entrepreneur and to place herself under United States protection (1855), the filibustering activities of William Walker in Central America (1855–7), the Dominican Republic's voluntary reincorporation into the Spanish empire, or what was left of it (1861), the French invasion of Mexico (1862) – all these events aroused much indignation, well reflected in the press. "America *en masse* should protest about what is happening in Mexico!" thundered *El Ferrocarril* in July 1862.[51] The Dominican Republic affair prompted one of the most serious foreign policy debates yet heard in the Chilean Congress (August 1861), with deputies demanding instant action by the government, and Justo Arteaga Alemparte wondering if other Spanish American republics might request annexation "by France, or England, or the Grand Turk."[52]

Juan Manuel Carrasco Albano, writing in 1856, saw the danger from Europe or the United States as "immediate, imminent." He sketched out an ambitious plan for a South American Congress (to include Brazil) that would help create "a South American nationality." Carrasco Albano did not think small: his union would have a common (decimal) currency, incentives to immigration (for the usual reasons), a common education system, a common

47 MV, No. 3216, September 3, 1839; No. 3126, May 17, 1839.
48 MV, No. 5016, December 20, 1844.
49 *Memoria* of External Relations minister (1848). DP, III, 127.
50 TRI, No. 90, August 17, 1849. For *Argirópolis*, see Jeremy Adelman, *Republic of Capital. Buenos Aires and the Legal Transformation of the Atlantic World* (Stanford, Calif., 1999), pp. 184–89.
51 FE, No. 2018, July 1, 1862.
52 CN/D, August 20, 1861.

"society of history and American antiquities," and, not least "a network of railroads . . . from Panama to the Magellan Straits, from Valparaiso to Rio de Janeiro" – governments would probably have to build the railroads. Which country should lead this noble venture? No prizes are offered for guessing the answer.[53]

The idea that Chile should take the lead was naturally appealing. In the early 1860s, the never-ratified 1856 treaty between Chile, Peru, and Ecuador became the pretext for a revived discussion of the whole idea of union. In Congress (June 1861), Interior minister Antonio Varas rejoiced that (because of the treaty) Chile would have "the glory of having initiated" a union of "American Republics." The most striking speech in this debate came from Ambrosio Montt. The main point of a union, he said, was to strengthen national feeling, to protect territory, and to prevent Latin Americans from inviting foreign powers (as had happened in Argentina) to intervene in their domestic quarrels and thus "to work the ruin of their country, their religion, their language." "We have astonished the world with our revolutions," he suggested, "and, what is worse, by our lack of . . . a strong and noble nationalism." Montt reminded the Chamber of Deputies that Simón Bolívar's Congress of Panama (1826) had been designed to fend off the Holy Alliance in Europe and to ensure republican government in America. Both aims had been guaranteed, he said ("with much satisfaction"), by the Monroe Doctrine (as it then was beginning to be called). Any treaty of union, Montt argued, should begin by setting Latin America's house in order. But he was skeptical of the likely effectiveness of any such scheme. To wish for a common currency or common professional standards was "doubtless beautiful and good," but he doubted whether it was feasible: "Local ideas, interests and passions will always prevail over any attempt at assimilation."[54]

So it would prove in real life, but not before "Americanist" sentiment among upper-class Chileans had reached its climax in the early 1860s, with politicians (even hard-headed skeptics such as Federico Errázuriz and Domingo Santa María) falling over themselves to embrace the idea of union, with the formation of an active *Sociedad de Unión Americana* (May 1862), with the solemn (and abortive) foundation of the new township of Unión Americana in the Aconcagua valley (October 1862), with "For the American Union" becoming one of the five points of the program of the new Radical party (December 1863), with ex-president Manuel Montt taking the chair at the American Congress in Lima (1864), convened in the shadow of Spain's

---

53 Carrasco Albano, "Memoria presentada," I, 261–72. Although he made no direct contribution to the debate in Chile, Francisco Bilbao also advocated a South American union, in the same year as Carrasco Albano, in his pamphlet *Iniciativa de América*, and for much the same reasons.

54 CN/D, June 22, 1861.

naval aggression in the Pacific – a conference that prompted Antonio Varas to remark that he had "such a poor idea of the governments of the sister Republics" that he was sorry Chile had to make common cause with them.[55] Varas's comment reflected the underlying Chilean attitude. Some have seen the "Americanist" wave of the early 1860s ("a collective delirium," the historian Mario Barros calls it)[56] as somehow weakening Chilean foreign policy. It is hard to see that it made a real difference, since, at the time, there was not much of a foreign policy to be weakened. In any case, when the little war with Spain came (1865–6), Chilean policy more or less had to be "Americanist."

Foreigners (Non-Spanish American)

Chileans' attitudes to non–Spanish American foreigners depended mostly on social class. Upper-class Chileans were welcoming to them, not least the foreign traders who flocked to Valparaiso. "The word 'foreigner,'" said Antonio Varas, "is an immoral word that should be erased from every dictionary."[57] Nonetheless, resentment could occasionally be expressed over the foreign warships that were a constant presence beyond the merchant vessels swaying at anchor in Valparaiso Bay. According to an 1838 news-sheet, the warships placed Chile in "an abject and degrading situation in the social scale of sovereign nations."[58] This was a comment made in wartime, when European partiality to the Peru-Bolivian Confederation was (rightly) suspected. For the most part, the warships did not usually arouse such reactions, although they were an irritant to the Intendant of Valparaiso, who was often asked to recapture deserters. (The French made their requests on a standard printed form.)[59] As for foreign traders, they were not only welcome, but their participation in the *supervision* of trade was thought perfectly acceptable. During a congressional discussion (1853) of new commercial tribunals on which foreigners could sit, Manuel Antonio Tocornal mildly observed that the foreign traders in Valparaiso included "some very honorable men, worthy of exercising such responsibilities." Nationality, he argued, was irrelevant in trade, which was based on "relationships of interest and mutual convenience."[60]

55 To Manuel Montt, December 1, 1864. Varas, *Correspondencia*, V, 48.
56 See M. Barros, pp. 209, 216–17.
57 Quoted by Vicente Pérez Rosales in *Época*, No. 1540, June 6, 1886.
58 *Eclipse en Paucarpata*, No. 4, February 24, 1838.
59 Correspondence in AMI, Vol. 213. The French seem to have been persistent. At one point the Intendant, ex-president Joaquín Prieto, mildly points out that he does not have problems with other foreign navies. In general, the authorities made no great efforts to catch deserters.
60 CN/D, July 3, 1853.

Chilean attitudes to foreigners, however, always included a strong element of national self-respect. Official policy, well defined privately by Portales in 1832 and publicly by President Montt in 1861, was that foreigners were fully entitled to "protection and security," but not "a special and privileged protection."[61] Noting in 1852 that the Valparaiso wharf commission consisted of three foreigners and one Chilean, a progovernment newspaper argued that foreigners, while indisputably a "civilizing element," should not be allowed to set up "a suffocating despotism . . . , a monopoly of thought." The newspaper suggested that an excessively visible role for foreigners could arouse very hostile reactions among "a people full of amour propre and jealous of its rights," and that demagogues could use this as "a terrible weapon that sooner or later could fall on the heads of the lovers of progress and the foreigners themselves."[62]

The point was an important one. Popular xenophobia certainly existed. In December 1829, for instance, during disturbances at the time of the Conservative takeover, a mob had sacked the French consulate in Santiago. It was easy enough, observed a newspaper of 1849, to arouse "the hatred of the multitude" against foreigners.[63] During the immigration debates of 1852, a deputy urged that settlers be dispersed rather than concentrated in one place, for "our people is envious, and inclined to look badly on any foreigner."[64] The public hanging of the probably demented American sea captain Anthony Paddock for multiple murder in Valparaiso in 1833, despite the pleas of the American consul and foreign traders, can only be interpreted as a means of placating the *porteño* populace. Certainly Portales, who was responsible, saw it in those terms.[65] That politicians did sometimes tap into xenophobia for their own purposes was shown in the Valparaiso election of 1846, when the opposition put it about that the English and the government were conspiring to deprive coachmen of their livelihoods by introducing the railroad, and also in one of the opposition news-sheets during the agitation of 1858. "The only ones who are afraid in Valparaiso are the English," it alleged, "for they fear the people and desire with all their heart a government like that of Rosas rather than lose a bottle of *aguardiente* or a length of cloth."[66] This was little more than a rhetorical flourish, although it is true that foreign traders (like traders everywhere)

61 See Portales to Tocornal, January 16, 1832 (EDP, I, 393); quotation from Montt, speech to Congress, June 1, 1861 (DP, IX, 7).

62 *Civilización*, No. 195, May 8, 1852.

63 *República*, No. 6, May 18, 1849.

64 Ignacio Valdez Larrea, CN/D, October 11, 1852.

65 Portales to Antonio Garfias, December 12, 1833 (EDP, II, 304–06) and to Guillermo Blest and Santiago Ingram, January 12, 1833 (EDP, II, 332–34).

66 Joaquín Prieto to Manuel Montt, February 26, 1846, in León and Aránguiz, p. 75; *Ciudadano*, No. 21, May 23, 1858.

hated disorder. Those who settled in Chile had little to complain about and for the most part lived satisfying lives. And even at the popular level, the civilization from which the foreigners came carried a definite cachet. In 1860, the consul of Hamburg complained to the Intendant of Atacama that several liquor stores in Caldera habitually displayed "the flag of Hamburg as a means of attracting the public."[67]

"Europe's Today Is Our Tomorrow"[68]

The Hamburg flags over the liquor stores of Caldera were symbolic. The one part of the outside world that really inspired educated Chileans was Europe. The politics of the "remotest corner of Europe," claimed *La Tribuna* in 1849, were better known in Chile "than those of, for instance, New Granada or Venezuela."[69] Reports from Europe (often reprinted from the European press) dominated the foreign news sections of Chilean newspapers. Chileans eagerly followed the great European events of the period – the 1848 revolutions, the Crimean War, the Italian Risorgimento, and so on. The Crimean War, the first serious European war during the early republic, roused a good deal of attention: "everyone is interested in the events in the East [i.e., the Crimea], which have been much commented on here," wrote Senator Juan de Dios Correa de Saa to a friend in Paris.[70]

Needless to say, Chileans sometimes criticized specific *actions* by the European powers. There was exasperation over European arrogance toward Spanish America, which was real enough – "an insufferable arrogance," thought the writer who disliked the foreign warships.[71] And Chileans sometimes complained that Europeans had "the most absurd and false beliefs" about Spanish America.[72] "Over there they still think we are savages who kill each other mercilessly," claimed *El Progreso* in 1843, suggesting that European knowledge of Spanish America had decreased since independence, largely because Spanish America had failed to produce the "political paradise" expected after the winning of freedom.[73] In his *Páginas de mi diario* (1856), the first real Chilean travel book,[74] the young Benjamín

---

67 E. W. Paulsen to Intendant of Atacama, September 5, 1860. AI(A), Vol. 181.
68 MV, No. 4924, September 18, 1844.
69 TRI, No. 45, June 23, 1849.
70 To M. Blanco Encalada, November 28, 1855. Ovalle Castillo, p. 190.
71 *Eclipse en Paucarpata*, No. 4, February 24, 1838.
72 FE, No. 1235, December 17, 1859.
73 PR, No. 223, August 5, 1843.
74 And as such well worth a close study in its own right. It was widely read and remains very readable. Vicuña Mackenna visited California, Mexico, the Mississippi valley, the eastern United States, Canada, Great Britain, Ireland, France, Italy, and Central Europe, and offers a lively and detailed account of his impressions. He was a highly inquisitive traveler, making sure he got closeup views of

Vicuña Mackenna recorded how his classmates at an agricultural college in England, learning that he came from Chile, asked him *"Is it very chilly?"* imagining him to hail from "some southern Siberia."[75] *El Ferrocarril* once even suggested that the new republics should jointly sponsor a publicity magazine (to be published in Paris) to counteract this kind of ignorance.[76]

Despite such irritations, most educated Chileans, unwittingly confirming the famous dictum of Karl Marx, were agreed that Europe was the image of their own future, the world's most advanced civilization – about two centuries more advanced than Spanish America, *El Mercurio* once calculated.[77] "However much we dislike it," predicted *El Progreso*, "there will come a day when we are Europeans to the marrow of our bones."[78] Europe was a "privileged continent, the current apogee of the human spirit," as Marcial González put it.[79] Interior minister Ramón Luis Irarrázaval thought it admirable that Chilean diplomats in Europe would have the opportunity "of contemplating, close-up, an advanced civilization."[80] Debating the pay of diplomats in 1852, another Interior minister, Antonio Varas, suggested that simply *being* in Europe should compensate for a modest salary.[81] The concerts of the internationally acclaimed Austrian-French pianist Henri Herz, who made a big stir in the Chile of 1850–1, were a chance, as *La Tribuna* pointed out, "to admire what the great ones of the earth accept and admire."[82]

Upper-class Chileans who experienced Europe for themselves (so much easier with the advent of the steamship) sometimes found a wide gap between their ideal and the reality. Carlos Bello, in Paris in 1847, noted that everyone talked of "the power and wealth of Great Britain," while the French newspapers were full of stories of "the people dying of starvation in Ireland and Scotland" and of murders and robberies in France.[83] "If this is the progress of the Protestant countries," wrote the young Manuel José Irarrázaval after seeing the factory workers of industrial Manchester,

---

Queen Victoria, Napoleon III, and the Emperor Franz-Josef of Austria, and visiting W. H. Prescott in Boston and Alexander von Humboldt in Berlin, as well as making a pilgrimage to Ireland in quest of Mackenna relatives. He found some. An ancient great aunt (who had last seen his long-dead grandfather, Colonel Juan Mackenna, in 1782) took one look at him and exclaimed: *"This is a Mackenna!"*

75 Vicuña Mackenna, *Páginas*, I, 399.
76 FE, No. 1235, December 17, 1859.
77 MV, No. 3731, May 13, 1841.
78 PR, No. 301, November 7, 1843.
79 González, *Europa*, p. 8.
80 *Memoria* of External Relations minister (1841). DP, I, 199.
81 CN/D, June 23, 1852.
82 TRI, No. 456, November 13, 1850. For Herz in Chile, see Pereira Salas, *Música*, pp. 112–14 and *Biobibliografía*, p. 84.
83 To Andrés Bello, February 14, 1847. Amunátegui, *Ensayos*, II, 268.

"for God's sake, forget it!"[84] "It is rare to hear an Englishman," commented Domingo Arteaga Alemparte in 1859, "who laments the horrible pauperism and degradation of the lower class of London."[85]

Although nothing like a full-scale debate ever arose in Chile about the superiority of Europe, there were certainly some who advanced a "republican" defense of America, contrasting it with monarchical decadence and corruption. "Europe! Decrepit Europe!" ran a letter to *El Mercurio* in 1843, "America does not want the brilliance of the purple. No . . . America prefers to remain savage with her elected presidents . . . rather than eminently civilized with your crowned heads."[86] Others cautioned against uncritical acceptance of everything European. "We must not *blindly* embrace foreign ideas," insisted a Concepción newspaper, "or embrace European civilization in a *servile way*."[87] The republic's intellectual mentor, Andrés Bello, clearly saw this as a danger in literary and cultural fashion. Addressing would-be historians in 1848 in often quoted words, he warned them against excessive servility toward Europe, urging them to think for themselves and to aspire to independence of mind – that was "the main philosophy we should learn from Europe."[88]

While Europe as a civilization was often invoked as a model, there were only two European countries that really excited educated Chileans: France and England. (The notable Chilean fascination with Germany only began after the unification of the Empire.) France and England, remarked *El Mercurio* in 1844, "are the head and the arms of humanity . . . ; they represent the two most powerful elements that decide the destiny of peoples, reason and money."[89] Jacinto Chacón did not fail to put it more resonantly:

> ¡*Grecia moderna, Francia!*
> ¡*Y oh, coloso romano, Gran Bretaña!*

> France, the modern Greece!
> And oh, Roman colossus, Great Britain![90]

The cultural and intellectual impact of France on nineteenth-century Chile could easily warrant a study in its own right. The level it had reached

84 To Joaquín Irarrázaval, January 16, 1859. BACH, No. 4 (1934), p. 90.
85 *Semana*, Año 1, No. 4, June 11, 1859.
86 MV, No. 4360, February 17, 1843.
87 *Telégrafo de Concepción*, No. 4, December 28, 1842.
88 "Modo de estudiar la historia," 1848. Bello, *Obras*, XIX, 250–51. See also Jaksić, *Bello: Scholarship*, p. 140.
89 MV, No. 4704, February 9, 1844. "By reason or money" would make an excellent motto for today's European Union.
90 "Himno a la Providencia," *Revista del Pacífico*, Tomo III (1860), p. 323.

by 1860 is amusingly illustrated in some remarks of a Chilean paterfamilias as imagined by Manuel Miquel:

I don't want Carlitos coming back to my house with the idea of furnishing it in the Louis Quinze style; I don't want him coming out with *"When I was in Paris"* every time he opens his mouth. . . . Now that we have hats from *Paris*, boots from *Paris*, furniture from *Paris*, neckties from *Paris*, clothing from *Paris*, let us at least not have children from *Paris*![91]

The press's serialization of French novels was very popular. Even the radical *El Amigo del Pueblo* and *La Barra* ran Dumas *père*'s recently published *Le Collier de la Reine*. A high proportion of the books offered for sale by a Santiago bookstore in 1849 were French, while Santiago theater audiences in 1860, reported *El Ferrocarril*, wanted "More France and less Spain!"[92] Female dress, furniture styles, literary fashion, viticulture, devotional practice in the Catholic Church – all were affected and altered by the French. So was politics, according to Ambrosio Montt (writing in a French-language newspaper in Valparaiso), who claimed to see French influence in the Chamber of Deputies, where *"mesures libérales"* were *"débattues avec la noblesse d'esprits éclairés."*[93]

France was seen as in many respects "the first nation in the world," as "unquestionably the most civilizing nation on earth," even as "the focus of all light [whose] reflections . . . are to guide us on the path to perfection."[94] Writing to Chile's envoy in Paris in 1854, Antonio García Reyes told him: "You are at the very peak of the human race . . . , surrounded by everything that is greatest in the arts and sciences."[95] There was certainly resentment, however, over the French blockade of Buenos Aires in the late 1830s. *El Mercurio* even mocked one of French commander Rear Admiral Louis-François-Jean Leblanc's *ordres du jour* as pure bombast – the sound from his ships was less likely to be gunfire than "a few uncorkings of bottles of good Champagne."[96] And while Chilean Liberals may have been enthused by the Revolution of 1848, they never had much time for Napoleon III: "we do not envy [France] her government," *El Progreso* declared in 1853; "we *do* envy her civilization."[97] As it happened, Chile's minister in France in the 1850s, Admiral Blanco Encalada, was a popular figure at *Napoléon le Petit*'s vulgar court. Napoleon and Empress Eugénie

91 *Semana*, No. 46, May 19, 1860.
92 *Catálogo general*; FE, No. 1401, June 30, 1860. French books were especially prominent in the History and Literature sections.
93 *Gazette des Mers du Sud*, No. 18, July 28, 1851.
94 *Album*, No. 1, January 4, 1851; MV, No. 4704, February 9, 1844; PR, No. 1725, May 27, 1848.
95 To M. Blanco Encalada, August 14, 1854. Ovalle Castillo, pp. 97–98.
96 MV, No. 2857, June 21, 1838.
97 PR, No. 2708, February 3, 1853.

stood as godparents to his daughter Teresa at her lavish Paris wedding in 1856.[98]

Because of the civilization, Chileans could sometimes overlook the grosser details of French society and politics. But not always. Ramón Luis Irarrázaval, in Paris in 1846, was shocked by "so much corruption, so much vice . . . alongside so much knowledge," and asked himself if Spanish America was really so much worse off.[99] Francisco Bilbao, too, was shocked by the poverty and inequality he found in the Paris of the 1840s, but remained touchingly confident in "the people, virginal and vigorous . . . , ever ready to rise up for freedom and glory at the sound of the trumpet."[100] Benjamín Vicuña Mackenna, arriving in Paris in 1853, felt that he had achieved "the dream of half a lifetime," that he was "in the capital of the world, at the heart of humanity." He did not doubt that Napoleon III was a tyrant of sorts, but could not reproach him for his belief in "the *Glory of France*," and wondered whether some twist of fate might prove him the true successor of his legendary uncle.[101] Vicuña Mackenna would never have given Manuel Montt the benefit of the doubt in this way. Montt, it is true, did not have a legendary uncle, merely a rich godfather who left him enough money to buy a prime hacienda.

France radiated culture and style. Great Britain radiated power, technological mastery, and economic strength. The British were more visible in Chile than the French. They were the most prominent foreigners in Valparaiso, where they kept up their quaint traditions, including cricket. Warships from the Royal Navy's South American Squadron were more or less permanently stationed off Valparaiso. Their officers enjoyed good relations with the local authorities, despite occasional frictions.[102] When a British rear admiral ended his tour of duty in 1844, *El Mercurio* saluted him as a "worthy representative of . . . *Old England*."[103] Educated Chileans

---

98 She married Francisco Echeverría, a rich Atacama miner (known locally as "the Count of Montecristo"), and it was near Copiapó, on February 18, 1864, that she was crushed to death by some ore-processing machinery, one of the most talked-about Chilean tragedies of the time.

99 To Andrés Bello, November 10, 1846. Amunátegui, *Ensayos*, II, 187.

100 To Andrés Bello, July 31, 1849. Amunátegui, *Ensayos,* II, 216.

101 *Páginas*, I, 281; I, 348–50.

102 The worst arising from the squadron's presence was in the mid-1840s, when the British used an abandoned warship, the *Nereus*, as a floating warehouse. The government saw this as an encouragement to smuggling, although there is no evidence it was ever used for this purpose. There were two threats of British intervention in Chile during this period. The first was in 1837–8, to force Chile to stop the war against Peru-Bolivia. This never came close to being carried out. The second was in 1863, to seek satisfaction in the case of a British subject, John Whitehead, allegedly wounded in the 1859 civil war. A powerful warship, H.M.S. *Sutlej*, was sent to Valparaiso. It is likely that the Chilean government never learned of the threat. Whitehead withdrew his claim. He was almost certainly bought off by the British trading colony.

103 MV, No. 5007, December 11, 1844.

were usually happy to express admiration for "powerful Albion . . . , that great theater of human progress," as "the nation the world calls illustrious *par excellence*," or, more simply, "the model nation."[104] The expanding British Empire commanded definite respect. *El Mercurio* found consolation in the fact that even if Britain disappeared from the map, there would still be "so many English nations all round the globe."[105] Comments on the Indian Mutiny of 1857, we should note, showed no trace of *tercermundismo* ("third-worldism") *avant la lettre*. *El Ferrocarril* printed a fulsome eulogy of Sir Colin Campbell, the hero of Lucknow.[106] Another (opposition) newspaper roundly affirmed that the British were "within their rights; with peoples like those of India only brute force should be used, for only force can impose respect."[107] There were some, however, who bemoaned the fact that India was "once again under the lash of the British trader," or who suggested that Britain should strive to become India's "protector" rather than her "jailer."[108]

Suspicions of British imperialism nearer home could sometimes be voiced. Joaquín Campino reminded the Chamber of Deputies in 1848 that the British had been "running around" the Magellan Strait for years, and that they had seized a colony from a neighboring republic.[109] British support for Rosas in Argentina (prior to the Anglo-French blockade) also was sometimes interpreted as having sinister implications. Could it be, asked *El Mercurio*, that the British were encouraging Rosas to make things so bad that they would have an excuse to intervene and colonize?[110] Highhanded actions by the Royal Navy could provoke negative reactions, as with the attack in 1859 on the Paraguayan steamer *Tacuarí* by H.M.S. *Buzzard* and H.M.S. *Grappler*. *El Mercurio* lamented that "intelligent and cultured England" was showing herself to be "more than despotic, arbitrary, and more than arbitrary, brutal with the weak States of South America."[111]

Chilean Conservatives, for their part, admired their British counterparts, even claiming once that "the Tory party of England" included some of "the highest spirits" of the human race,[112] not a comment all British readers will find entirely persuasive. British experience seemed to confirm the *pelucón* approach. The British took time over their reforms; they discussed them

104 M(S), No. 8228, January 11, 1855; Pérez Rosales, *Essai*, p. 209; FE, No. 1396, June 25, 1860.
105 MV, No. 4184, August 23, 1842.
106 No. 654, January 29, 1858.
107 *País*, No. 65, September 12, 1857.
108 FE, No. 1248, January 1, 1860; *Semana*, Año 1, No. 2, May 28, 1859.
109 CN/D, November 8, 1848.
110 MV, No. 4187, August 23, 1842.
111 MV, No. 9694, January 2, 1860.
112 *Consejero del Pueblo*, No. 7, October 26, 1850.

to the point of exhaustion, or so said Joaquín Villarino in 1860.[113] They trusted "in the fertile work of time . . . , believing more in work than in words," thus expanding "practical freedoms without upheavals."[114] Unlike the French, the British were not much given to revolutions. Liberals were not above pointing out that English liberty had in large part sprung from the "great revolution" that had followed John Hampden's protest of 1637.[115] Benjamín Vicuña Mackenna, whose year at the Royal Agricultural College in Cirencester gave him an unrivaled opportunity to study the English, had no difficulty in admiring "the Titan of modern history," or in praising its impact on Chile: "What signs of material progress in Chile in her half century as a nation . . . are not linked to England? *All are!*" But he found real-life English society deplorably unequal, and the condition of its industrial workers appalling (he went down a coal mine), so he concluded that no Chilean *huaso* or *roto* would wish to exchange "his ragged cloak" for British citizenship. Vicuña Mackenna's democratic politics compelled him to deny that the aristocratic British system was any kind of model for Chile. Nonetheless, he was also sure that Englishmen had a "pure and sublime patriotism" that gave them "inexhaustible resources of salvation and greatness."[116] With Vicuña Mackenna, hope always sprang eternal.

The Crocodile of the North

When educated Chileans looked northward, at that rising giant the United States, they did so with the admiration they had for France and England, although they did not expect Americans to set the tone for society in quite the way the French or even the English did. One magazine ranked the United States (with France and England) as one of the three countries that had reached "the highest level of enlightenment and power that will ever be reached by the human race."[117] There were many, indeed, who saw the United States as "certainly the most perfect model among modern societies," as "a sensible, industrious, democratic great nation," and, when Europe was in chaos (in 1848), as "an oasis of peace amidst the universal desolation."[118] Chileans were impressed, like everyone else, by the rapid growth of the United States, often identifying education and immigration (their own panaceas) as its keys. An article in the opposition newspaper

113 *Revista del Pacífico*, Tomo II (1860), p. 76.
114 TRI, No. 443, October 26, 1850.
115 *Cuestión administrativa-legal*, p. 24.
116 *Páginas*, I, 464–87.
117 *Museo de Ambas Américas*, No. 32 (1842), p. 321.
118 *Civilización*, No. 20, October 13, 1851; TRI, No. 249, March 2, 1850; *Crónica*, No. 32, September 2, 1849.

El País in 1857 noted that even *The Times* of London was now printed on American machinery.

> Hurrah for the Republic which is mentor to the world through its peace, its wealth, its population, its freedom, the education it gives to all its children. Hurrah for the Republic which is queen of the seas through its trade – and without naval squadrons! Hurrah for the Republic that buys up nations! Is Paraguay for sale? How much? Let's say 8 millions. And no more talk of a yerba maté monopoly, please.[119]

Chileans certainly sensed that the wealth and power of the United States were likely to increase still more, thanks to the "colossal, astonishing, marvelous thrust" of its people.[120]

For a few years after 1848, several thousand Chileans had personal experience of the United States, or at least California. Thousands more rubbed shoulders in the streets of Valparaiso with Americans on their way to the gold rush, and were not always impressed. (The Americans who operated the new Southern railroad in 1857 also attracted a certain amount of criticism as ill-mannered.)[121] Those Chileans who reflected on California did not find it hard to fathom the secrets of its success. It was not the gold, claimed Vicente Pérez Rosales, so much as the capitalist spirit, religious toleration, hard work, in short "the Anglo-British genius."[122] Episodes of discrimination against Chileans in California, however, somewhat tempered admiration for the United States. There were outcries in the press over "the brutal arbitrariness of the Yankees,"[123] and demands for action in the Chamber of Deputies. Coming on top of the Californian incidents, Ecuador's abortive attempt to become an American protectorate and William Walker's filibustering actions provoked further criticisms of the United States, and (as we have seen) revived interest in schemes of Spanish American union.

Anti-American feeling among educated Chileans never outweighed their admiration for American democracy, but unease about growing American power became fairly noticeable in the public rhetoric of the 1850s. There had been remarkably little Chilean hostility to the United States at the time of the Mexican war (more was expressed in retrospect), though some had regretted that the great republic was becoming a "military power" and thus imitating bad old Europe.[124] Others had feared the American annexation of Mexico, which (though Mexico probably deserved it) might lead

119 *País*, No. 35, September 4, 1857.
120 *Revista del Pacífico*, Tomo III (1860), p. 502.
121 See *País*, Nos. 78–79, October 27–28, 1857.
122 Pérez Rosales, *Diario*, pp. 60–63.
123 *Civilización*, No. 203, May 18, 1852.
124 MV, No. 5815, March 31, 1847.

to the "absolute dependence" of Spanish America on the United States.[125] Apparent American support for General Narciso López's "annexationist" expedition to liberate Cuba (1850) prompted a newspaper to ask whether the United States might not take advantage of countries "ruled by decrepit governments."[126] The events of the mid-1850s seemed to point to a definite expansionist tendency in the north.

Forecasts of American intentions could sometimes be lurid. "The crocodile of the north, its teeth stuffed with the meat of Mexico and Texas," alleged a Conservative news-sheet in 1857, "is now starting to gobble up Central America, and is advancing south, where our division and anarchy have prepared it a splendid feast."[127] There were many variations on this theme. *El Mercurio*, normally measured in its comments, ran a series of savage articles in 1855 on "The Yankee in South America," which suggested that Spanish America could well fall into "the claws of the rapacious bird of the North."[128] The author of these outbursts, whoever he was, was evidently well known as someone with a particular ax to grind. He was denounced in a letter to the editor (in English) as having "an ill-regulated brain."[129]

Maybe he did, but his views were to some extent representative. The *Revista Católica*, detecting (as usual) the insidious influence of Protestantism, condemned "the spirit of annexations and conquests" that obviously animated the entire American population.[130] Guillermo Matta, in a poem of 1857, jumbling his mythologies, saw the United States as "the Odin of the North, that awesome Hercules," now sending "pirates" to devour Spanish America.[131] Benjamín Vicuña Mackenna, traveling through the United States, came to the conclusion that "the mercantile spirit of the Saxon race, freed here from all barriers, will make this country the scourge of the earth, until some day a new Rome destroys this proud Carthage of the modern age."[132] The publication in Washington in 1855 of Lieutenant James Melville Gilliss's superb multivolume book about Chile (compiled during the American astronomical expedition to Chile he had led a few years earlier) sparked off some outraged comments in Santiago. Its comprehensively detailed picture of Chile ("warts and all") evidently offended some. According to *El Ferrocarril*, Gilliss had repaid Chilean hospitality with "disloyal" behavior that obviously stemmed from the "deep, invincible hatred" all Americans felt for Chile. A country that tolerated the

125 *Huelén*, No. 2, July 22, 1848.
126 *Consejero del Pueblo*, No. 5, October 12, 1850.
127 *Conservador*, No. 23, August 27, 1857.
128 "El Yankee en la América del Sur," M(S), No. 8253, February 13, 1855.
129 M(S), No. 8294, March 29, 1855.
130 RCAT, No. 438, May 10, 1856.
131 "A la América," FE, No. 416, April 25, 1857.
132 Vicuña Mackenna, *Páginas*, I, 247.

grossly immoral, polygamous Mormons had no right to criticize Chileans for religious fanaticism.[133]

The tide of anti-American feeling receded with the coming of the Civil War in the United States. *El Mercurio*, contemplating the imminent break between North and South in January 1861, castigated those who believed that Latin America might benefit from this turn of events.[134] *El Ferrocarril*, likewise, saw danger in the disintegration of the Union, given that an independent "republic of the South" was highly likely to sponsor annexation and filibustering.[135] The same paper later on, however, did speculate that there might be certain advantages in Southern independence, in that the North could then develop both its economy and "the liberal and democratic idea" without the encumbrance of slavery. Spanish America could then conclude agreements with the North, free from the "sinister suspicions" of recent years.[136] Later still, *El Ferrocarril* once again stressed the importance of a Northern victory, since the United States was still a potent force for maintaining the independence of "the weak States of Latin America" against possible European depredations. Because of the Civil War, it noted, Spanish American opinions of the United States had become altogether more favorable than in previous years.[137] In its editorial for the Fourth of July in 1862, *El Mercurio* confirmed this point, saying that nothing could really alter the common sentiments of all American republics, sentiments that would assure "our continental well-being."[138] The press and public opinion seem to have been unanimously in favor of the North and solidly against slavery. The American minister in Santiago, Thomas H. Nelson, an old friend (from Illinois and Indiana days) of President Lincoln, exploited such feelings to excellent effect. (He was, however, mildly surprised when a military band serenaded him with "Dixie" on the Fourth of July 1862; Chile's minister in Washington had sent the score to Santiago without explaining the piece's emblematic status among the Southern rebels.) The Confederacy's only friends in Chile appear to have been American consular officials, whose dismissal Nelson duly secured.[139] The victory of the North was greeted with elation in Santiago and in many provincial cities. Lincoln's assassination provoked a serious outpouring of public grief, with men weeping in the street and the pages of newspapers black-bordered.[140] "The expert

133 FE, No. 74, March 18, 1856.
134 MV, No. 10,016, January 17, 1861.
135 FE, No. 1673, May 18, 1861.
136 FE, No. 1819, November 8, 1861.
137 FE, No. 1965, April 30, 1862.
138 MV, No. 10,465, July 4, 1862.
139 See Guerrero Yoacham, pp. 185–91.
140 See Sater, pp. 23–24. For reactions to Lincoln's death, see Guerrero Yoacham, pp. 245–65. Guerrero Yoacham's detailed study provides copious evidence of Chilean attitudes to the Civil War.

driver has fallen," declared one magazine, "but the Yankee locomotive will continue its triumphal march."[141] It did.

Latins and Anglo-Saxons

A number of Chilean comments on the United States fell within the context of a more general discussion of the contrast between the "Anglo-Saxon" and "Latin" cultures, and this is worth just a brief mention. William Walker's Central American filibustering, for instance, was once described as a "war . . . between the Latin race and the Saxon race."[142] This particular terminology (imported from France) is largely absent before the later 1850s, but thereafter expressions such as "Americo-Latin" or "Latin America" begin to make their appearance.[143] As we saw, the Latin/Anglo-Saxon contrast was a minor theme of Juan Manuel Carrasco Albano's political treatise in 1858 and a major one of Ambrosio Montt's in 1859. According to Montt, Latin Europe had reached its peak with sixteenth-century Spain; the Anglo-Saxons had dominated since Waterloo. Neither race was intrinsically superior to the other, but they were certainly different. The Latin races had outstanding qualities "of creation, force, intelligence, passion." The Anglo-Saxons lacked a heroic or epic dimension in their conquests, which showed "cleverness without genius, valor without heroism, good soldiers but not great soldiers, wise organization but not creativity."[144]

Yet it was absurd, thought Montt, to criticize the Anglo-Saxons as materialists. England, the land of Bacon and Newton, was "an intellectual nation . . . where the lowest plebeian reads and writes." (Roughly one third of the population of England and Wales was still illiterate at the time Montt wrote.) As for the United States, no country with such a passion for education (not to mention its scholars shaming the Hispanic world with their books on Columbus, Cortés, and Pizarro) could seriously be called materialist.[145] Others, however, tended to stereotype the Latin-Anglo-Saxon divide in precisely those terms. The newspaper *El Mensajero* in 1855 contrasted

141 *Revista Ilustrada*, No. 1, June 15, 1865. A short-lived news-sheet of 1865 (supporting religious toleration) was called *El Lincoln*.

142 FE, No. 324, January 8, 1857 (supplement).

143 Ambrosio Montt once uses "Latin America" in *Gobierno* (1859), p. 85. Francisco Bilbao, who was closer to the source of the new terminology, used the term "América latina" (almost but not quite "América Latina") in 1856: *Iniciativa*, p. 12. For the French origins of the new terminology, see John Leddy Phelan, "Pan-Latinism, French Intervention in Mexico (1861–1867) and the Genesis of the Idea of Latin America," in Juan Antonio Ortega y Medina, ed., *Conciencia y autenticidad históricas* (Mexico City, 1968), pp. 279–98. It seems likely that the term "Latin America" was first coined by Colombian writer José María Torres Caicedo (1830–89), then in Paris. See Arturo Ardao, *Génesis de la idea y el nombre de América Latina* (Caracas, 1980).

144 A. Montt, *Ensayo*, pp. 251–62.

145 A. Montt, *Ensayo*, pp. 290–92.

the American love of material gain with the Spanish Americans' "life of the spirit." It predicted that some day, when modern industry had run its course, the United States would be left with "aridity and desolation," while Spanish America would flourish in prosperity.[146] This contrast between the "materialistic" United States and the more "spiritual" Latin America would have a long run in Spanish America, achieving its most celebrated expression in the Uruguayan writer José Enrique Rodó's essay *Ariel* (1900).

One or two Chileans took a pessimistic view of the future relationship between the Anglo-Saxons and the Latins. Domingo Santa María (in what must have been an uncharacteristic mood for him) forecast in 1859 that "the Latin race will disappear or become enslaved or be transformed into something different from what it has been and still is." Martín Palma, writing a year earlier, thought that all efforts at resistance to Anglo-Saxondom were useless. "Sooner or later we will be engulfed, because (though it hurts our amour propre to confess it) activity and civilization will always triumph over backwardness and sloth."[147] Yet, not everybody thought that the contest was either fixed or permanent. In June 1862, *El Ferrocarril* speculated that the future might actually see the races coming together, a

fusion between the Saxon-American and the Latin American. The latter needs more power of life, the former less asperity of action. The Latin American needs to come down to the terrain of the practical; the Saxon-American needs to rise towards the domains of intelligence; the Latin American needs to strengthen his body, the Saxon-American his soul. . . . The fusion of the two races has to be the great hope of the future.[148]

Who knows? Some of the population movements in the Western hemisphere in recent times make this speculation less far-fetched than it was in 1862.

146 *Mensajero*, No. 758, December 4, 1855.
147 To M. L. Amunátegui, December 21, 1859, Amunátegui Solar, *Archivo*, I, 69; Palma, *Cristianismo*, p. 87.
148 FE, No. 2012, June 14, 1862.

PART IV

Order and Liberty, 1851–1864

9
The Conservative Defection, 1851–1858

Montt's First Term, and an Omen from Atacama

The first two Conservative presidents had been generals, both of them heroes of independence. Manuel Montt, the first civilian to govern Chile for any length of time, had neither the military prestige of his predecessor nor the patrician detachment of his successor. He made up for it by sheer willpower. His slightly dark appearance (*el negro* was his widely known family nickname) was a target for the snobbery of some of the older upper-class families. Portales himself had spotted his capacity for hard work and his administrative talent, something Montt never forgot. He was a man of few words, outwardly unemotional and dry, although unfailingly polite in his private dealings. "All head and no heart" was his predecessor's private opinion.

The government's victory in the 1851 civil war guaranteed the triumph of the authoritarian *pelucón* tendency. British rear admiral Sir Fairfax Moresby toasted Montt early in 1852 (in language once applied to William Pitt the Younger) as "the good pilot" who had guided Chile through the storm.[1] The banquets held to mark the end of the civil war acclaimed Montt in similar terms but also rubbed salt in the wounds of the defeated opposition. The publisher Santos Tornero, attending a Valparaiso banquet in late December 1851, sensed a definite spirit of "rigor" in the air.[2] "I am the brother of all Chileans," declared Pedro León Gallo at a similar feast in Santiago. "I except the bad ones, for they cannot be brothers of the good ones." His brother Angel Custodio praised Montt in mawkishly religious language as "the first martyr of the Republic . . . , that republican Christ . . . sacrificed on the calvary of party."[3]

The Montt government's initial propaganda capitalized on the economic boom of the time by trumpeting its desire for material progress.

---

1 MV, No. 7346, March 5, 1852.
2 Tornero, p. 117.
3 MV, No. 7293, January 3, 1852.

In Valparaiso, in February 1852, Montt congratulated the port on its ea-
gerness to embrace "the great conquests of science and modern industry."[4]
Commercial expansion made it easier, perhaps, for the political class to
forget the recent upheaval. Montt was unwilling to test this proposition.
He refused the general amnesty Bulnes requested, as promised to General
Cruz at Purapel. In June 1852, Interior minister Antonio Varas asked the
Chamber of Deputies for a one-year extension of the emergency powers
in force. Former Justice minister Máximo Mujica proposed that the president be empowered to cashier officers reincorporated into the Army under
the Purapel treaty, adding that he personally would like to see them shot.
Both Manuel Antonio Tocornal and Antonio García Reyes spoke against
Mujica's amendment. Both had lent personal support to Montt in the civil
war, accompanying Bulnes to the south. Both saw Montt's refusal of an
amnesty as a betrayal of the spirit of Purapel. The Chamber upheld the
amendment (18 to 15), as did the Senate, despite Diego José Benavente's
pointed reminder that both Columbus and Cortés had quelled mutinies
through magnanimity.[5]

Soon after these debates a mutiny broke out at the Artillery barracks.
Its strictly nonpolitical aim was to seize the regimental funds. Eight of the
ringleaders were shot. The partisans of repression, Mujica to the fore, immediately proposed a fourteen-month extension of emergency powers, which
both chambers approved instantly. (*El Mercurio* printed the news, together
with the story of the recent reintroduction of flogging, in large, clear type
under the heading "THE PROGRESS OF THE COUNTRY.")[6] Montt
and Varas remained intransigent on the question of an amnesty. Montt's
messages to Congress in 1852, 1853 (when the emergency powers finally
lapsed), and 1854 never even hinted that one was forthcoming: "the consolidation of order," he said in 1854, was still a duty, and "faced with a duty,
it is necessary for feelings of benevolence to yield."[7]

Antonio Varas, Montt's truest of the true, remained Interior minister
throughout his first term. Physically, the taller Varas was Don Quixote to
the shorter and stouter Montt's Sancho Panza. His passionate (and sometimes vehement) nature may have complemented Montt's icy self-control.
Varas was an effective parliamentarian, although he took offence easily and
constantly fidgeted in his seat.[8] Montt's first Justice minister, Fernando
Lazcano, was well known for his piety: "His Castilian gravity, his firm
deliberate, serious stance, his square face, his ascetic glance," noted one

4 MV, No. 7351, March 11, 1852.
5 CN/D, September 6, 1852; CN/S, September 10–14, 1852.
6 MV, No. 7303, September 7, 1852.
7 Message of June 1, 1854. DP, V, 3.
8 Palma, *Oradores*, p. 9.

newspaper, "all reveal ... the mysticism of his soul."[9] One of Lazcano's immediate decisions was to place the "secondary" section of the Instituto Nacional under exclusively clerical control, with a zealous priest as Rector. The measure brought nothing but trouble. The students strongly resisted their new regime of prayers and rosaries. There were several minor disturbances, including an attempted attack on the Rector with a razor.[10] Although *El Mercurio* reported that "the ultra fraction" of the Conservative party was urging Lazcano's retention in the cabinet,[11] Montt replaced him in July 1852 with a less controversial figure, the pioneering viticulturalist Silvestre Ochagavía. Ochagavía gave way in turn (in May 1855) to Francisco Javier Ovalle, son of José Tomás Ovalle, the Conservative regime's first, short-lived president (1830–1). He was devoted to Montt.

The Lazcano episode symbolized a new fissure that was opening up in the Conservative fold, one which began to obfuscate the long-standing division between moderates and authoritarians. In ecclesiastical matters, both moderates and authoritarians had consistently upheld the government's "regalist" control of the church. The Papacy had never accepted Chile's right to the old colonial *patronato*, and had refused a concordat, but the *modus vivendi* between Santiago and Rome had operated smoothly enough. The Conservatives' justifications of their regime had never included a religious dimension. Their claims to legitimacy rested (as we saw in Chapter 6) on the keeping of the peace and the pursuit of progress. Many Conservatives, however, remained emotionally attached to the church, leaving anti-clerical attitudes to the Liberals. Arriving in Santiago in 1840, the immigrant Polish scientist Ignacio Domeyko attended both Conservative and Liberal *soirées*. The Conservatives, as he would recall, stood up and prayed at the time for the Angelus, while his Liberal hosts enjoyed "jokes against monks and nuns."[12] By the early 1850s, the more devout *pelucones* were gradually assuming "clericalist" attitudes, attitudes that inclined them to defend the rights of the church (as defined by the church) and, less automatically, to accept whatever lead it gave. Perhaps these attitudes should be termed "protoclericalist," for the Conservatives only really became Chile's "Catholic party" in a later incarnation. For the protoclericalists, the *patronato*, as one of their number provocatively pointed out in the 1852 Congress, was a "very special concession" to the Spanish crown, "which independent Chile cannot recover."[13] The other *pelucón* faction (especially

---

9 *Copiapino*, No. 1794, December 29, 1853.
10 See the interesting correspondence in FE, Nos. 414, 418, and 421, April 23 and 28, and May 1, 1857.
11 MV, No. 7449, July 6, 1852.
12 *Mis viajes*, I, 497.
13 CN/D, June 25, 1852.

Antonio Varas's following) remained strictly regalist. Some of these politicians were observant Catholics. Others were increasingly attracted to free thought. Montt was well aware of the growing divide between the regalists and protoclericalists (the latter well represented in the Senate), and almost certainly put Lazcano in his first cabinet as a means of balancing the two groups.

The balancing act might have worked had it not been for an increasingly militant temper within the Catholic Church, fostered by a compulsively active prelate, Rafael Valentín Valdivieso, archbishop of Santiago since 1845. Of distinguished colonial lineage, he was a man who enjoyed (in Justo Arteaga Alemparte's phrase) "the voluptuousness of struggle."[14] Archbishop Valdivieso was fully conscious of the winds of change then blowing through the Catholic Church, internationally, under the uncompromising leadership of Pope Pius IX.[15] With other "ultramontanes" (the word was in regular use as a term of abuse by the Church's critics by early 1853),[16] he took exception to the *de facto* ecclesiastical powers the government still exercised. Valdivieso's efforts to rally his flock form a fascinating chapter in the history of the Catholic Church in Chile. They included gratifying victories (both in 1848) over the local Provincial of the Franciscan Order (on a matter of internal discipline) and over the Intendant of Santiago (on the regulation of religious processions), and (between 1853 and 1856) a systematic program of archiepiscopal visitations. Valdivieso invited European religious orders to work in Chile. He also installed the first organ in Santiago cathedral.[17] Perhaps regrettably, we must concentrate on the political effects of his campaign, which were soon to become explosive.

We need to note, however, that the Catholic Church at mid-century was expressing repeated concern for what it saw as a rising tide of secularism. "Chile has lost much of the piety of her forefathers," claimed the *Revista Católica* in 1849; "indifference is day by day usurping the territory of faith."[18] Genuine freethinkers among politicians (Liberal or Conservative) were still fairly sparse, but there did exist a growing undercurrent of anticlericalism at all levels of society. Valdivieso himself noticed, in Colchagua Province, the unpopularity of a particularly devout Intendant.[19]

14 J. Arteaga Alemparte, *El desquite*, p. 25.
15 Pius IX, then a young priest, had visited Chile as secretary of the papal mission of 1824. Chileans who visited him in later years often observed the vividness of his memories of the sights and sounds of Santiago.
16 See RCAT, No. 296, February 21, 1853.
17 Vergara Antúñez, I, 281–84; I, 221–23 and ch. 20; for the foreign religious orders, see Serrano, *Vírgenes*, pp. 39–44; for the organ, Zapiola, *Recuerdos*, p. 77. The organ came from England (1849), and the first cathedral organist (until his death in 1860) was Henry Howell, an Englishman.
18 RCAT, No. 190, October 6, 1849.
19 Vergara Antúñez, II, 14.

In November 1853, he issued an edict denouncing all who were "suspect of heresy, excommunicated, or those who in any way pervert customs."[20] In Copiapó the local newspaper savaged the prelate as a modern Torquemada and blasted the "pharisaical Sanhedrin" surrounding him.[21] The newspaper exhorted *copiapinos* to gather at the railroad station to burn the edict. They did so, with unseemly enthusiasm, on Christmas Day 1853. The *Revista Católica* saw this as an "unprecedented outrage."[22]

As we saw in Chapter 5, the church was anxious to staunch the growing demand for religious toleration. It disliked the government's live-and-let-live attitude toward the foreign Protestant congregations in Valparaiso.[23] In its criticism of the church, the language of the press (by the early 1850s, progovernment newspapers as well as *El Mercurio*) was not always restrained. In October 1852, *El Mercurio* condemned "the emissaries of heaven" for their ultramontane views – "seditious [and] immoral" – while the progovernment *El Mensajero* took the Church to task for its role in the recent civil war, claiming that in many places priests ("crucifix in hand") had blessed "the revolutionary banners,"[24] which had certainly been true in Concepción and La Serena.[25] The *Revista Católica* eventually lost patience with *El Mercurio*, furiously attacking it (in large type) as "HERETICAL . . . , IMPIOUS . . . ," and as "A NOTORIOUS SLANDERER."[26]

There were several mildly contentious church-related issues that deepened the embryonic division in the Conservative ranks. The arguments over immigration mentioned in Chapter 5 were typical. The conversion of the old colonial *diezmo* (tithe), used to support the Church, into a land tax for the same purpose, occasioned lengthy debates in Congress. Although cleared by the government with the archbishop, it became the pretext for a few priests and protoclericalists to argue that the church was being persecuted. In 1854, former Justice minister Fernando Lazcano introduced a bill in the Senate to reestablish the Jesuit order in Chile with a state subsidy and the return of its main building in Santiago, the seventeenth-century church of La Compañía, soon to vanish in the holocaust of 1863. This alarmed the descendants of those who had bought the Jesuits' haciendas after their expulsion in 1767, although the question of returning the haciendas was

20 RCAT, No. 338, November 26, 1853.
21 *Copiapino*, No. 1787, December 20, 1853.
22 *Copiapino*, No. 1790, December 23, 1853; No. 1792, December 27, 1853; Treutler, *Andanzas*, pp. 165–70; RCAT, No. 344, January 2, 1854.
23 *El Mercurio* claimed in 1852 (No. 7553, November 6) that there were eleven thousand Protestants in Valparaiso. The figure seems far too high.
24 MV, No. 7525, October 5, 1852; *Mensajero*, No. 219, February 9, 1854.
25 See report of Intendant Rondizzoni of Concepción to Interior minister, May 7, 1852. Barros Borgoño, *Proemio*, pp. 224–45.
26 RCAT, No. 281, October 30, 1852, reprinted in No. 282, November 6, 1852.

not raised. The Chamber of Deputies firmly voted down Lazcano's motion (30 to 6). At this point, Montt, still anxious to balance the protoclericalists and regalists, considered reconstructing his cabinet, with Lazcano returning as Justice minister, and the more emollient Catholic Manuel Carvallo (for the previous twenty years, Chile's envoy in Washington) replacing Varas as Interior minister. Carvallo pressed for a general amnesty. Varas's following in the Chamber of Deputies made known its hostility to the idea. Montt had no wish to provoke further conflict, and abandoned his plan to reconstruct the cabinet.[27]

There were other factors that perturbed the *pelucón* fold. Montt's obstinacy over the amnesty after the civil war irritated the moderates. Montt also needed to mend his fences with the South – one reason why in February 1853 he undertook an ostentatious tour of the southern provinces, the first such tour made by a president, in some ways reminiscent of the *visitas* (visitations) of colonial governors.[28] How far it mended fences is unclear. An American traveler who saw Montt at Los Angeles noticed that "there was no outburst of enthusiasm. The people were sullen."[29] A further bone of contention for some Conservatives was the way Montt and Varas selected public officials, showing less interest in family connections than in competence. A prosopographical study of this group would be of the highest interest, for the "new men" promoted in this way were later to become arguably the most brilliant political generation in Chilean history. In the 1850s, however, many were both young and obscure. Considerations of snobbery by older Conservative families apart, there was also the suspicion that Montt and Varas were building up a powerful personal following with the aim of securing the next presidency for Varas, whose ascendancy loomed larger after Montt's failure to reconstruct the cabinet in 1854.

Despite these symptoms of trouble within the Conservative party, Montt's position throughout his first term seemed invulnerable. Politics was in temporary stasis. The Liberals had gone to ground. Not even the minor tremors in the Conservative party achieved much in the way of public expression. The press was altogether subdued. This makes it difficult to judge the mood of the political class. "The spirit of tumult has finished," Diego Barros Arana told an Argentine friend in August 1852.[30] *El Mercurio*, at the end of that year, saw nothing but "peace, tranquillity, confidence and the desire for prosperity."[31] The recently founded *El Ferrocarril*, usually a

---

27 Alb. Edwards, *Gobierno*, pp. 168–69.
28 Sagredo, "Las visitas," pp. 322–45.
29 Smith, pp. 330–32.
30 To Juan María Gutiérrez, August 14, 1852. RCHG, No. 94 (1939), p. 11.
31 MV, No. 7564, November 19, 1852.

reflection of Antonio Varas's views, suggested (January 1856) that Chile had reached a point where "revolutionary eventualities" could be disregarded.[32] Reporting to Congress that year, Varas himself claimed that Chile was showing that "the continuous malaise of political agitation" was not inevitable in Spanish America.[33]

All this was true up to a point, but where exactly did that point lie? "Is the country progressing?" asked the moderate *pelucón* Ramón Luis Irarrázaval in 1854.

> Yes, to certain degree, like the tree that rises through the spontaneous impulse of nature. Are we safe from a hurricane that might sweep away its fruits, branches and roots? I do not know, but my hope ... of a securer, more prosperous order of things, one more adequate to our needs and circumstances, is very distant from being ... a reality.[34]

A progovernment newspaper claimed in 1852 that the Montt presidency was "the most popular Chile has ever had."[35] This was hollow triumphalism. The defeated Liberals were not reconciled to the regime in the way the previous generation (or much of it) had been with Bulnes. The opposition did not bother to campaign in the elections of 1852 or, for the most part, 1855. The newspaper *El Copiapino* deplored the general apathy that surrounded the 1855 elections, attributing it either to the fact that "the country is satisfied with the direction it is taking," or to sheer laziness on the part of the citizenry.[36] *El Mercurio*'s steamship edition also regretted "the most total absence of all discussion" at election time. The comments on domestic politics in the steamship edition, intended for foreign consumption, were usually toned down. In its Santiago edition, the newspaper was more open, suggesting that the absence of discussion was "not healthy," that "complete calm is not the law of life either in the physical or moral spheres."[37]

But something *was* stirring. In 1855, three Liberals – Federico Errázuriz, José Victorino Lastarria, and the young Manuel Antonio Matta – were elected to the Chamber of Deputies. Errázuriz won with deftly mobilized inquilino votes. Lastarria and Matta ran in Copiapó, the capital of Atacama Province, which, suffused with its new prosperity, had become the most

32 FE, No. 9, January 2, 1856.
33 *Memoria* of Interior minister, September 6, 1856. DP, V, 465.
34 To M. Blanco Encalada, February 27, 1854. Ovalle Castillo, p. 89.
35 *Civilización*, No. 199, May 13, 1852.
36 *Copiapino*, No. 2152, March 23, 1855.
37 English Part, M(V), No. 23, April 14, 1855; M(V) No. 21, March 14, 1855; M(S), No. 8278, March 10, 1855.

independent-minded province in Chile. Its culture had always been more fluid than that of the hacienda-dominated Central Valley, which Copiapo's newspaper *El Copiapino* once described as "at least a century behind."[38] In its *dieciocho* issue for 1855, *El Copiapino* published a poem describing Copiapó as a *ciudad modelo* ("model city"): "*De los progresos de Chile, / Tú llevas el estandarte.*" ("You are the standard-bearer / Of Chile's progress.")[39] The north saw itself, not without reason, as the most industrious and progressive part of Chile. Atacama mining families such as the Mattas and Gallos (the latter connected by marriage to the Montts) had been among Montt's strongest backers in 1851, relating easily to his much-proclaimed desire for material progress. The government press sometimes instanced Atacama as an example to be followed by the rest of the nation.[40]

The newspaper *El Copiapino* faithfully reflected *atacameño* attitudes. Often outspoken on local issues, it once greeted the retirement of an unpopular *subdelegado* with a verse that began: "*Por fin te vas, ser odioso.*" ("You're off at last, you odious creature.")[41] Early in 1855, it reported in a rather saccharine way that Montt and Varas were enjoying their summer vacations on adjacent *chacras*, working hard for Chile "beneath the beneficent shade of leafy trees."[42] In the run-up to the elections, however, it suddenly shifted to a sharply critical tone, not attacking Montt frontally (he had "the best intentions") but condemning both Montt's loyalty to "his favorite Varas" and Varas's "extravagant and stupid caprices."[43] It did not explain what the caprices were. Its election day issue (on special blue paper) enthusiastically endorsed Lastarria and Matta, in language that had not been heard much during Montt's presidency.

> Long live freedom and order!
> Long live progressive reforms!
> Long live *Democracy*!
> Long live the *Republic*![44]

After the election, *El Copiapino* went further, describing the Varas cabinet as the most "odious, unpopular, and repulsive" in Chilean history, and it wondered why Montt, with his "notoriously high capacity," failed to realize this.[45]

38 *Copiapino*, No. 1787, December 20, 1853.
39 *Copiapino*, September 17, 1855.
40 For example, *Civilización*, No. 91, January 3, 1852.
41 "Adiós al Subdelegado de Tres Puntas," *Copiapino*, No. 2238, July 12, 1855.
42 *Copiapino*, No. 2100, January 19, 1855.
43 *Copiapino*, No. 2134, March 2, 1855.
44 *Copiapino*, No. 2151, March 22, 1855.
45 *Copiapino*, No. 2156, March 30, 1855.

Atacama Province was not the whole of Chile, but the opposition victory there was an omen: it indicated that a new mood was beginning to take shape. In early 1856, Diego Barros Arana wrote to his Argentine friend:

> The national prosperity is exorbitant. . . . All the industries are prospering. . . . In spite of all this, the country in general is not happy with the current administration. . . . There is not much sympathy for Minister Varas; he has proposed to interfere in . . . everything, and he has placed in important posts some of his own kinsmen and discreditable people. But do not think that there is any sign of revolution, or even of formal opposition. Everyone murmurs, but . . . for the majority, business is more than enough to take care of.[46]

Montt's reelection in June 1856 was inevitable. No gossip about alternative candidates has ever reached historians. *El Mercurio* declared that Chile had now definitely passed out of the "revolutionary whirlwind," but also (significantly) advocated "more latitude and tolerance . . . [a] more flexible, tolerant, and popular policy" for Montt's second term.[47] Antonio Varas, after well over six years as Interior minister (the longest continuous tenure of the portfolio in Chilean history), was happy enough to step down. *El Ferrocarril* listed three possible combinations for a new cabinet, none of which materialized.[48] Montt's eventual choice of new ministers pleased almost nobody. The new Interior minister, Francisco Javier Ovalle, was seen by many as his creature. Waldo Silva, the new Justice minister, also was criticized as being insufficiently independent. "The new cabinet has been badly received," reported Aníbal Pinto (ex-president Pinto's son and himself a future president) to his father-in-law, General Cruz. Silva's appointment, he noted, was proof of Montt's policy of promoting "people from the lower spheres."[49] By the time the Ovalle cabinet started work, however, the snobbish criticism of Silva was forgotten. Like a bolt from the blue, an unexpected crisis suddenly broke the Conservative party in two, and pointed the way to a new politics for Chile.

The Affair of the Sacristan

It began with an incident in January 1856. The young son of Pedro Santelices, a junior sacristan of Santiago cathedral, had recently been hired as a servant in the cathedral. He broke the glass in the sacristy's skylight and invited some of his young chums to drink the communion wine. He

46 To Juan María Gutiérrez, March 28, 1856. RCHG, No. 94 (1939), pp. 18–19.
47 MV, Nos. 8737 and 8739, September 2 and 4, 1856.
48 FE, No. 141, June 5, 1856.
49 Pinto to General Cruz, September 29, 1856. RCHG, No. 125 (1957), p. 303.

was fired. The indignant Santelices poured a half-hour's worth of insults on Francisco Martínez Garfías, the senior sacristan, who instantly dismissed him. We need to know the rest of the story, but it can be recounted briefly, without too many excursions into the fascinatingly complex legal terminology (both ecclesiastical and civil) used in the ensuing proceedings. The dismissal was overruled by the canons of the cathedral Chapter, which reinstated Santelices, but the Chapter in turn was overruled by the archdiocesan vicar, Archbishop Valdivieso being away on a visitation. Two of the canons, Juan Francisco Meneses and Pascual Solís, requested an extradiocesan appeal (standard ecclesiastical procedure) to the bishop of La Serena. Pending the appeal, the archdiocesan vicar banned them from saying Mass or hearing confessions. The public soon became mildly interested in what *El Ferrocarril* called (in March 1856) "the sacristans-canons-vicar question,"[50] but only as one of those entertaining rows that broke out in the church every so often.

Returning to Santiago, the archbishop upheld his archdiocesan vicar. On April 21, the canons, going outside the framework of ecclesiastical law, lodged an appeal to the supreme court with a writ known (since medieval Spanish times) as a *recurso de fuerza*. Archbishop Valdivieso and ultramontane opinion (and the Papacy itself) all regarded an appeal of this kind to the secular power with considerable disfavor. It did not square well with the Church's aspiration to greater independence. Valdivieso could well have been spoiling for a fight. Only a few weeks earlier, he had presided over the solemn celebrations of the new dogma of the Immaculate Conception. His sermon revealed an uncompromising vision of Catholicism, and praised Pope Pius IX for his role in "a time of struggle."[51] Did he want such a time himself?

The supreme court's procedures required the archbishop to submit the relevant evidence. He did so, also making clear his view that the matter fell outside the court's jurisdiction. The court asked its official attorney (former Interior minister Manuel Camilo Vial) to write a formal opinion. Vial took his time. Only in August 1856 did he deliver his opinion, finding for the canons in ostensibly pious but also provocatively regalist language.[52] The Affair of the Sacristan (as it would become known) began to spark wider public curiosity. At the end of August, the supreme court confirmed Vial's opinion. The way was cleared for the canons' ecclesiastical appeal to the bishop of La Serena, to whom Archbishop Valdivieso was required to remit copies (technically known as *apóstolos*) of the documentary evidence. Valdivieso ordered the *apóstolos* to be prepared, not revealing whether he

50 FE, No. 66, March 8, 1856.
51 Valdivieso, *Sermón*, p. 15. For the ceremonies, see Vergara Antúñez, I, 333–40.
52 FE, No. 211, August 26, 1856 and following issues.

would allow the appeal to proceed. The canons asked him to clarify their position. On September 16, Valdivieso issued an act of *no ha lugar* ("not granted"), signifying his denial of the appeal – and his defiance of the supreme court.

Neither the archbishop nor the two canons would back down. Public curiosity turned into excitement. Santiago changed overnight, *El Ferrocarril* reported, from "a great city" into "a great monastery."[53] The protoclericalist *pelucones* rallied to the archbishop's side. The regalists (Varas's following leading the pack) offered moral support to the canons. *El Mercurio* urged the government to uphold "the sovereign prerogatives of the Republic."[54] Valdivieso sent the government a note, calling on the president, as constitutional protector of the Catholic religion, to end the impasse. Interior minister Ovalle replied that the president was debarred from countermanding the supreme court. A second note from Valdivieso prompted a longer reply from Ovalle, full of constitutional arguments. There was yet a third note from the archbishop. The two canons returned to the supreme court, requesting enforcement of its ruling. The court once again asked Valdivieso for the relevant documents. Once again he complied, with a second assertion of the court's jurisdictional incompetence. On October 18, the court gave the archbishop three days to obey its decision under penalty of banishment and the seizure of his temporalities.[55]

Public excitement suddenly became feverish. There were other talking points in Santiago during those weeks (not least a retired army officer's murder of his faithless wife), but the threatened banishment of the archbishop roused deeper passions. *El Mercurio* praised the "patriotic firmness" of the supreme court.[56] A large crowd of the faithful gathered around the archbishop's house, with many society ladies dressed in mourning. One of them offered Valdivieso all her money (12,000 pesos) to let her accompany him into exile.[57] Some of the devout ladies (or so the story goes) visited President Montt, and one of them told him: "Look, if you banish the archbishop, we will cling to the wheels of his carriage, and he will only be able to leave by riding over our corpses."[58] For the *Revista Católica*, these demonstrations were "one of the most beautiful pages in the country's history."[59] Valdivieso himself, presumably to underline his authority, stripped

53 FE, No. 231, September 22, 1856.
54 MV, No. 8765, October 7, 1856.
55 Main documents are in *Relación documentada*.
56 MV, No. 8777, October 21, 1856.
57 Vergara Antúñez, II, 108n.
58 Silva Cotapos, p. 278. Whoever she was, she must have known Montt well, as she used the intimate *tú*.
59 RCAT, No. 470, October 27, 1856.

the defiant canons of their benefices and suspended them *a divinis*, that is, from exercising all priestly functions – an act "of anger and vengeance," declared *El Ferrocarril.*[60] It certainly intensified public emotions. More seriously, Federico Errázuriz, the archbishop's Liberal nephew, hastened from his Colchagua hacienda to Santiago, and (in the archiepiscopal residence, with some of his fellow Liberals) began plotting a *coup de main* on the strength of popular sympathy for Valdivieso and to coincide with his departure for exile. "You can imagine the thunderbolt that is going to fall on Santiago," wrote Aníbal Pinto to his father-in-law.[61]

The government was unaware of the plot, but only too aware of the public commotion. Attempts at compromise were already under way. Antonio Varas secured the good offices of the mining magnate Matías Cousiño and the veteran *pelucón* Joaquín Tocornal. The canons were persuaded to drop their appeal and to make "respectful demonstrations" to the archbishop. They did so on October 22, and Valdivieso then reinstated them.[62] Compromises, unfortunately, do not always allay bad feeling. This compromise was deeply dissatisfying to regalists (and anticlericals), who had wanted Valdivieso to be punished, while the protoclericalist *pelucones* were shocked by the government's attitude toward him. But the "real social alarm" detected by *El Ferrocarril*[63] quickly gave way to a calmer mood. *El Ferrocarril* and *El Mercurio* went on sniping at the Church for a couple of weeks, and continued to do so over the next few months. The young Vicente Reyes, then writing for *El Ferrocarril*, fanned the flames as best he could, as befitted a future distinguished anticlerical politician. By mid-November, *El Ferrocarril*'s "weekly reviews" were no longer mentioning the Affair of the Sacristan. *El Mercurio*'s roundup of the year's news on December 31 omitted all reference to the recent excitement.[64]

Deeper down, the Affair of the Sacristan had done irreparable damage. Early in the new year Vicente Reyes suggested that there had been a "truce" rather than a solution, and that "the principles . . . , the ideas . . . [and] the struggle" surrounding the Affair remained very much alive.[65] During the crisis itself *El Mercurio* went so far as to comment that "all of the politics of the future" might depend on its outcome.[66] Antonio Varas, for his part, speculated that Chile might soon be facing "a religious division" between "new Catholic and non-Catholic parties."[67] Both *El Mercurio* and Varas

---

60 FE, No. 257, October 22, 1856.
61 Pinto to Cruz, September 29, 1856. RCHG, No. 125 (1957), pp. 304–06.
62 Vergara Antúñez, pp. 109–12; *Relación documentada*, pp. 271–74.
63 FE, No. 257, October 22, 1856.
64 MV, No. 8838, December 31, 1856.
65 FE, No. 321, January 5, 1857.
66 MV, No. 8778, October 22, 1856.
67 Varas to Blanco Encalada, October 14, 1856. Varas, *Correspondencia*, II, 252.

were right. The seeds of clerical and anticlerical passions had been planted, passions that would color Chile's politics for the next half century and more.

The church itself reinforced the intrusion of the religious issue into politics. In August 1856, Archbishop Valdivieso created a new organization, the Society of Saint Thomas of Canterbury, whose eighty-two founding members (all priests) swore never to resort to secular courts in cases of ecclesiastical discipline. From Rome, Pope Pius IX expressed his approval, and complimented Valdivieso on his stand against President Montt.[68] The help of England's "holy blissful martyr" was sought, the Society's president explained, "to fight against the errors of the century under the banner of Catholic truth."[69] *Cantorberiano* became a term of both praise and (especially) abuse in the Chilean political vocabulary for the next decade (although not much beyond). The *cantorberiano* priests were Valdivieso's shock-troops, well able to influence Conservative politicians offended by the government's recent behavior. *El Ferrocarril* accused them, almost instantly, of harboring "seditious" ideas.[70] Antonio Varas's following seems at this point to have contemplated some sort of anticlerical opening to the Liberals. The maneuver (if that is what it was) came to nothing. However sympathetic Liberals (or some of them) might feel toward Varas's position, they could hardly overlook his authoritarian record. The Liberal high command (notably Domingo Santa María and Federico Errázuriz) counseled a wait-and-see attitude, believing that the confusion within the Conservative ranks might be turned to their advantage.

Events in 1857 were to show the wisdom of this approach. During the (as always) somnolent summer, in February 1857, the government suddenly arrested two well-known Liberals and several army officers and accused them of plotting a mutiny. One of the arrested officers implicated three other Liberals, including Federico Errázuriz (who went into hiding) and Benjamín Videla, for their planning of a *coup de main* at the time of the Affair of the Sacristan. Videla, additionally, was to be tried for the prominent part he had played in the Easter rising of 1851. Montt's scare tactics were beginning to lose their effectiveness. "A general laugh has been raised," reported *El Mercurio.*[71] The alleged plot was rapidly nicknamed the *"conspiración de los carneros,"* "conspiracy of the feeble-minded."[72] A month later, however,

68 Pope Pius IX to Archbishop Valdivieso, November 27, 1856 (in Latin). *Breve de S.S. el Papa,* pp. 49–53.

69 Fr. José Manuel Orrego, "Panegírico de Santo Tomás de Cantorbery," RCAT, No. 481, January 10, 1857.

70 FE, No. 222, September 8, 1856, and the indignant response of Fr. José Manuel Orrego in No. 224, September 10, 1856.

71 English Part, M(V), No. 69, March 15, 1857.

72 FE, No. 464, June 19, 1857.

the incident had grown into what *El Mercurio* called a "slight cloud that darkens our horizon."[73] The arrests, in fact, had the immediate effect of reviving the Liberal (and moderate *pelucón*) demand for a general amnesty, a demand supported by *El Ferrocarril*, thanks largely to insertions by Vicente Reyes and the historian Ramón Sotomayor Valdés, who was also writing for the newspaper.[74]

El Mercurio's "slight cloud" soon thickened. In May 1857, *El Ferrocarril* described the political situation as "alarming," with the government "surrounded by enemies."[75] President Montt, opening Congress on June 1, made no mention of an amnesty. Just over two weeks later, absolutely without warning, an obscure *pelucón* senator, Juan de Dios Correa de Saa, introduced a bill for a general amnesty. As Domingo Santa María remembered it, the senator had been impressed by the nervousness of a friend over the atmosphere of uncertainty now building up.[76] Correa de Saa appealed for an end to "past hatreds and rancors" and for the return to Chile of a "multitude of individuals who are highly useful to the country." His motion won unanimous approval.[77] In the Chamber, both Lastarria and Manuel Antonio Tocornal insisted on an immediate debate. Lastarria told the government that if it persisted in fostering old hatreds, "you will keep revolution simmering over." Tocornal, evoking the Treaty of Purapel, asked the government to have more faith in the "common sense, moderation and loyalty of the Chilean people." Antonio Varas accused the Senate of "a lack of thought." Interior minister Ovalle argued luridly that the return of exiles would inevitably produce "Societies of Equality, public agitation, and then another [battle of] Loncomilla."[78] The Chamber rejected the amnesty bill (30 to 18). Back in the Senate, Correa de Saa stuck to his guns. Alluding to Montt's annual declarations of Chile's "solid and unalterable peace," he asked: "What *is* going on? How can we know where we stand? Are we at peace or in a revolution?" The Interior minister's reply – that all countries were at peace until revolutions actually broke out – struck a very weak note, and the Senate insisted (13 to 3) on upholding the bill.[79]

The opponents of the amnesty in the Chamber did not have the two-thirds majority needed to nullify the Senate's decision. Montt did not veto the bill, but sent it back to Congress with two amendments. One allowed an amnesty for all those living in Chile who had taken part in the 1851 rebellion

73 English Part, M(V), No. 71, April 15, 1857. FE, Nos. 422 and 448, May 2 and 26, 1857.
74 Sotomayor Valdés, *Noticias*, p. 107. For Sotomayor Valdés's break with Montt, see Brahm García, pp. 185–96.
75 FE, No. 422, May 2, 1857.
76 Santa María to Isidoro Errázuriz, January 18, 1858. *Revista Chilena*, Tomo X (1920), pp. 157–58.
77 CN/S, June 17, 1857.
78 CN/D, June 20, 1857.
79 CN/S, July 4, 1857.

and for exiles who asked permission to return. The other gave the president discretionary power to amnesty those charged with political offences since 1851. These amendments failed to satisfy the supporters of a full amnesty. The debates in both houses were heated, Diego Barros Arana reporting to his Argentine friend that "a certain political agitation" was now definitely in evidence.[80] Alejandro Reyes, a deputy from Concepción, recounted a trip he had made round the south: "nowhere did I find symptoms of revolution, and all I saw was an Octavian peace." The progovernment deputy José Eugenio Vergara argued that a president was like a "head of household" who had a perfect right to deny entry to his house. In "a representative democratic State," furiously riposted Manuel Antonio Tocornal, the president should never be referred to as a "head of household" – the expression belonged to "the times of Louis XIV."[81] But the head of the Chilean household had his way, with a narrow victory (10 to 8) in the Senate and a much larger one (36 to 17) in the Chamber.

Historic Compromise

What the amnesty debates most strikingly revealed was that significant numbers of *pelucones* were opposing the government and aligning themselves informally with the Liberals. "A fraction of the party . . . that elected the current president in 1851," said the progovernment deputy Juan Esteban Rodríguez, "is now trying to thwart him." Manuel Antonio Tocornal admitted the "lack of unity" among Conservatives.[82] Montt himself was initially skeptical about the dissidents. "The day the *pelucones* hear a large box being dragged down the streets of Santiago and think there's a revolution," he is reported as saying, "they'll run as fast as they can to cling to my frock-coat."[83] The dissidents were made of sterner stuff. Reservations about Montt's inflexibility were eliding with the feelings aroused by the Affair of the Sacristan. Already in the autumn of 1857 there were rumors that efforts were under way to form a party of "moderate Conservatives,"[84] and during the amnesty debates, *El Ferrocarril* noted (interestingly) what it took to be the appearance of "militant parties" for the first time in Chile.[85] Antonio Varas saw clearly what was happening – a "decomposition of parties," as he put it, with an "ultra-*pelucón*" faction moving toward the suddenly reinvigorated Liberals, and the "progressive-Conservative party" sticking with

80 To Gutiérrez, July 14, 1857. RCHG, No. 94 (1939), p. 30.
81 CN/D, July 25, 1857.
82 CN/D, June 20, 1857.
83 Domingo Santa María to Isidoro Errázuriz, January 18, 1858. *Revista Chilena*, Tomo X (1920), p. 158.
84 FE, No. 446, May 24, 1857.
85 FE, No. 486, June 24, 1857.

Montt. Varas regretted the apparent defection of the "ultra *pelucones*," who were "a conservative element useful to the country."[86]

"Progressive-Conservatives" was a description the dissident *pelucones* felt applied to themselves, not Montt's supporters.[87] Their prototypical figure, Manuel Antonio Tocornal, although protoclericalist, had always been a moderate. Among the Liberals, Domingo Santa María and Federico Errázuriz did what they could to encourage the Conservative defection. "They are talking of fusion...," reported *El Mercurio* in June 1857, "of organizing a program acceptable among themselves."[88] Was it possible to overcome the historic antagonism? The antagonism, suggested a Conservative newspaper (very insightfully), lay less in principles than in "the means and timing of their execution."[89] Even constitutional reform might be accommodated, provided it was "in a gradual way..., in harmony with the spirit of the age."[90] A "historic compromise" was clearly in the making.

El Mercurio's steamship edition was soon openly reporting that Conservatives and Liberals had "come to an understanding...legally to oppose Government, and demand...a more frank and liberal line of policy."[91] This was still a long way from a formal alliance or "fusion." Aníbal Pinto thought (in August 1857) that the opposition was "not even half organized."[92] Yet both defecting *pelucones* and Liberals were already, in the customary way, establishing newspapers to sway public opinion – *El Conservador* and *El País*, edited by Ramón Sotomayor Valdés and Diego Barros Arana respectively. *El Conservador*, accepting that Conservative disaffection was "anomalous," urged the government to adopt greater "frankness and transparency," and suggested that politics had not benefited from Montt's "trumpeted six years of peace." *El País* saluted the flag of constitutional reform in decent Liberal fashion, but allowed that a proper operation of the existing constitution might be even more important: Liberals and Conservatives together needed to "rebuild our poor house."[93] Both newspapers displayed unremitting hostility to Montt. Given Montt's penchant for men of ability, mocked *El Conservador*, he should offer a post to the Mapuche cacique Culetrueque, who had recently visited the Moneda to complain about Frontier abuses.[94] *El Conservador* claimed that Montt had surrounded

86 Varas to M. Blanco Encalada, June 30, 1857. Varas, *Correspondencia*, II, 276.
87 See *Conservador*, No. 15, August 18, 1857.
88 MV, No. 8987, June 25, 1857.
89 *Conservador*, No. 5, August 6, 1857.
90 *Conservador*, No. 30, September 4, 1857.
91 English Part, M(V), No. 78, July 31, 1857.
92 Pinto to Cruz, August 28, 1857. RCHG, No. 125 (1957), p. 310.
93 *Conservador*, Nos. 1–2, August 1 and 3, 1857. *País*, Nos. 1–2, July 27 and 28, 1857.
94 *Conservador*, No. 6, August 7, 1857.

himself with "adulators" instead of "truly enlightened men . . . , respectable for their social position."[95] *El País* castigated Montt for his "iron will," which made him reject all compromise and govern like "a petty tyrant . . . of Africa."[96]

The petty tyrant was now faced with a serious opposition that threatened his command of Congress. To give himself maneuvering room, he decided to reconstruct his cabinet. The press speculated about his intentions throughout July 1857. *El Ferrocarril* saw a cabinet change as the best means of averting a "political storm," and *El Mercurio* wondered whether Montt might react by "entrenching himself in isolation."[97] The Senate immediately voted (11 to 7) to suspend discussion of the budget laws until a new cabinet was appointed. Fernando Lazcano, dangerously raising the stakes, even demanded that the Senate should *approve* the new cabinet. Diego José Benavente objected to this as "an infraction" of the constitution; Lazcano simply accused him of "demagogy."[98] *El Mercurio* saw Lazcano's proposal as conforming to the "parliamentary and constitutional system,"[99] but "parliamentary" ideas had still to take root in Chile. *El Ferrocarril's* insistence that Congress had no control over the composition of cabinets[100] reflected the much more standard view.

Montt's obvious difficulties in forming a new cabinet soon prompted wild rumors – the warship *Esmeralda* was fetching Ramón Luis Irarrázaval (then Chile's envoy in Peru) to head the new cabinet; Montt was going to take a leave from the presidency, and so on.[101] On August 5, Montt asked former Finance minister Jerónimo Urmeneta to cast around for a new team. Fernando Lazcano beamed his approval from the Senate.[102] Urmeneta's first choice as Interior minister, Matías Ovalle, would not serve without the obscure (although well-born) Alvaro Covarrubias at the Justice ministry. Montt rejected the combination, and overruled Urmeneta's nomination of the Liberal Francisco de Borja Solar as Finance minister, preferring José Joaquín Pérez. Pérez would not serve without Covarrubias. Covarrubias would not serve without Montt's agreement to greater electoral freedom and impartiality in public appointments. Urmeneta next proposed an Urmeneta-Pérez-Covarrubias cabinet, extracting a suitable verbal formula from Montt on Covarrubias's points. Montt refused to put it in writing. On

95 *Conservador*, No. 47, September 26, 1857.
96 *País*, No. 40, September 10, 1857.
97 FE, No. 499, July 30, 1857; MV, No. 8987, June 25, 1857. See also MV, No. 8998, July 8, 1857; FE, No. 482, July 10, 1857.
98 CN/S, August 10 and 12, 1857.
99 MV, No. 9029, August 14, 1857.
100 FE, No. 512, August 13, 1857.
101 MV, No. 9029, August 14, 1857; FE, No. 523, August 27, 1857.
102 CN/S, August 12, 1857.

September 7, Urmeneta abandoned his cabinet-making efforts, and soon published his reasons for doing so,[103] giving every appearance of having broken with Montt. Though details are obscure, Montt seems at this juncture to have made overtures to the dissident *pelucones*,[104] perhaps offering them seats in the next Congress. If he did, it was too late. As *El Mercurio* commented, in colloquial vein, *"when it's time to fry the eggs . . . , the butter has disappeared."*[105]

It is hard not to feel sympathy for Montt. He was overwhelmed at this point by domestic tragedy, with the death from apoplexy (mid-August 1857) of his eldest son, the fifteen-year-old Manuel. Many of Montt's adversaries went to the funeral. Not many clergymen did, as *El Ferrocarril* waspishly noted.[106] But the political truce was very short-lived. The opposition swiftly resumed its attacks on the government. Montt chose this moment to decree a full amnesty (September 15). Presumably designed to win favor from the opposition, the maneuver was a failure. *El País* described it as "a ridiculous slap in the face," and *El Conservador*'s reaction –"Better late than never" – was distinctly qualified.[107]

Weighed down by his bereavement, Montt himself was depressed to the point of contemplating resignation. Varas prepared several drafts of a resignation message to the Senate. By delaying the budget to pressure the government, the message affirmed, the Senate was on the "slippery slope" of mounting "an unconstitutional invasion of the rights proper to the President," thus imperiling the republic's future as an "organized State."[108] The message never became public. Once again there were wild rumors, this time that Varas and Máximo Mujica would form a "cabinet of resistance."[109] But Montt had recovered both his political nerve and his political touch. Jerónimo Urmeneta, urged by his millionaire brother José Tomás, agreed to try his hand once more at cabinet-making. By the end of September he had succeeded. He himself became Interior minister, with the Liberals Salvador Sanfuentes at Justice and Francisco de Borja Solar at Finance.

Urmeneta's earlier defiance of Montt had won him kudos from the opposition. The new cabinet was greeted with universal enthusiasm. *El Ferrocarril*, oozing with optimism, saw it as "the fusion of the different political parties," and hailed Sanfuentes and Solar as "the purest and noblest of the Liberal party."[110] *El Conservador* eulogized Montt as a "republican

103 *Conservador*, No. 39, September 15, 1857; see also MV, No. 9052, September 9, 1857.
104 *País*, No. 42, September 12, 1857.
105 MV, No. 9050, September 7, 1857.
106 FE, No. 514, August 17, 1857.
107 *País*, No. 45, September 16, 1857; *Conservador*, No. 39, September 15, 1857.
108 Barros Borgoño, *Proemio*, pp. 235–41.
109 *País*, No. 41, September 11, 1857; *Conservador*, No. 43, September 22, 1857.
110 FE, No. 549, September 29, 1857.

President" who had shown proper respect to the opinion of the Senate. *El País* declared its political mission over and closed down.[111] *El Mercurio's* steamship edition rejoiced that "a painful feeling of distrust" had been dispelled. With the "moderate liberal" party now prevailing, it noted, "the agitation mentioned in our former reviews may . . . be considered as terminated."[112] Unsurprisingly, the year's legislative business was conducted expeditiously. The budget laws passed smoothly. There were some, however, who were suspicious of the apparent mood of harmony. Some of the dissident *pelucones* had their doubts about Sanfuentes and Solar. Their newspaper continued to snipe at "the party of Government (which we shall call Montt-Varas)," repeating the old charges that Montt preferred "obscure persons" for public jobs. It fought a running battle with the pro-Varas *El Ferrocarril*, depicting Varas as being to the "severe, honorable, energetic" Montt of 1851 what the disastrous minister Manuel Godoy had been to King Charles IV of Spain.[113]

The illusion of concord soon faded. Toward the end of November, *El Mercurio* was reporting disagreements between cabinet and president,[114] and reporting accurately. Late that month, Justice minister Sanfuentes nominated two dissident Conservatives (one of them Tocornal) for vacant judgeships. Montt vetoed the appointments. Sanfuentes and Solar immediately resigned from the cabinet. Urmeneta did not, and replaced them with Rafael Sotomayor (Justice) and Matías Ovalle (Finance). "They gave me a poisoned chalice," Montt remarked, "and I have thrown out the poison and kept the chalice."[115] Had he simply been maneuvering all along, so as to ensure the passage of the budget? The news infuriated both Liberals and dissident Conservatives. *El Conservador* asserted that the breakdown was "a foreseen event," and laid the blame fairly and squarely on Montt.[116] The Conservative defection now seemed irreversible.

It is difficult not to see December 1857 as one of the nodal points of Chilean history, marking the genesis of what would become, in time, the multiparty system that has been a key feature of Chile's politics ever since. The realignment visible in the amnesty debates began to take final shape soon after the resignations of Sanfuentes and Solar. *El Mercurio* reported that "the two political parties" had named committees to discuss the possibility of "fusion."[117] The Liberals had already formed a committee for the forthcoming March 1858 congressional elections. *El Conservador* hinted that

111 *Conservador*, No. 78, November 2, 1857; *País*, No. 82, October 31, 1857.
112 English Part, M(V), No. 82, September 30, 1857.
113 *Conservador*, No. 98, November 25, 1857; No. 103, December 1, 1857.
114 MV, No. 9114, November 28, 1857.
115 Amunátegui Solar, *Democracia*, p. 141n.
116 *Conservador*, No. 115, December 16, 1857.
117 MV, No. 9133, December 15, 1857.

there might be a joint Liberal-Conservative effort.[118] But there were stumbling blocks on the way to the desired "fusion." The Liberals commissioned Benjamín Vicuña Mackenna to start a news-sheet to replace the defunct *El País*. When the first (and only) number of Vicuña Mackenna's *El Liberal* appeared, it contained a striking defense of the historical continuity of Liberalism, a sturdy denunciation of the "despotic" 1833 Constitution, a call for freedom of worship, and, worst of all, an attack on any attempt to "fuse" Liberal and Conservative principles.[119] Such ideas touched a raw nerve among Conservatives. *El Conservador* sprang to the defense of "the *Conservative* party, without which Portales, with all the greatness of his talent and civic spirit, would not have been able to achieve anything," and took strong exception to Vicuña Mackenna's remarks about the constitution and religious freedom: "A lot of people are saying that the Liberal party *cannot* be thinking like the *Liberal* newspaper."[120]

This temporary Liberal disarray made no difference. The government, for its part, now accepted the political realignment as a *fait accompli*. At the end of December 1857 prominent supporters of Montt and Varas (including the old maverick Diego José Benavente) issued a widely circulated handbill-manifesto, announcing their intention to work for "national" candidates in the 1858 elections, stating "liberty in order" as their guiding principle, and attacking the Conservatives as retrograde and the Liberals as utopian – themes to be sounded over and over again in the propaganda of what became known instantly as the National party. The Liberals, meanwhile, had shown barely disguised relief when the Intendant of Santiago ordered the suspension of Vicuña Mackenna's *El Liberal* on a legal technicality. They were after a bigger prize. *El Ferrocarril* mocked the idea of a Liberal-Conservative alliance as "a dream."[121] It was not. The Conservatives firmly rejected an olive branch extended to them by leading Nationals early in 1858.[122] In mid-January 1858, Liberal and Conservative leaders met at Ramón Subercaseaux' *chacra* outside Santiago, a favorite spot for Conservative confabulations. The Conservative delegation included Joaquín Tocornal (then staying at the *chacra*), Rafael Larraín and Francisco Ignacio Ossa. The Liberals were represented by Domingo Santa María, Federico Errázuriz, and Angel Custodio Gallo. As Santa María recounted it, Tocornal opened with a mild inquiry about the Liberals' opinion of the current political situation. The Liberals told him that their fundamental aim

118 FE, No. 611, December 10, 1857; *Conservador*, No. 111, December 11, 1857.
119 *Liberal*, No. 1, December 24, 1857.
120 *Conservador*, Nos. 125 and 125, December 28 and 29, 1857.
121 FE, No. 631, January 2, 1858.
122 MV, No. 9158, January 13, 1858.

remained constitutional reform. Tocornal was willing to concede this – "as the country gets more educated and advances," as he put it. The Liberals, for their part, agreed to defer such tricky matters as Article 5 and religious freedom until a future Congress debated constitutional reform in general.[123] Whether the politicians shook hands we do not know, but the historic compromise was made.

The news soon reached the public. On January 25, *El Mercurio* reported that the Liberal-Conservative "fusion" was "agreed and arranged." A northern news-sheet hailed this "perpetual alliance between order and liberty."[124] With the elections only two months away, the new alliance took immediate steps to publicize its cause. There was no longer any need for two opposition newspapers. One would do. *El Conservador* closed down on January 16, replaced two weeks later by a joint Liberal-Conservative newspaper, *La Actualidad*, the lion's share of the editing done by Diego Barros Arana and Ramón Sotomayor Valdés. From the beginning it attacked Montt remorselessly. *El Ferrocarril*, commenting on the appearance of this "opposition newspaper," declared that it could mean only one thing: "There *is* a fusion."[125] It was the first of many thousands of references *El Ferrocarril* would make over the years to the Liberal-Conservative Fusion.

The Elections and Congress of 1858

This was not a simple replay of the challenge to Montt in 1851. The government and its new National party were faced with more serious defiance from the Liberal-Conservative Fusion than the Liberals could have offered in 1851 without General Cruz. It is difficult to measure the strength of the two contending forces, and harder still to generalize about the nature of their support. No analysis along regional (still less class) lines seems to fit. Montt could count on many prominent families, on the public administration, on the "new men" whose careers he and Varas had promoted, and on some of the "new money" from the recent economic boom. The two most interesting contemporary analyses, those of Ambrosio Montt and Martín Palma, present the conflict in straightforwardly political terms. From different perspectives (pro-Montt and anti-Montt), both interpret the opposition as spearheaded by Conservatives, thwarted in their desire to control the president, egged on by the Church, and exacting their revenge with the help of essentially opportunistic Liberals. The Fusion almost certainly reflected a much wider

123 Santa María to Isidoro Errázuriz, January 18, 1878. *Revista Chilena*, Tomo X (1920), p. 162.
124 MV, No. 9168, January 25, 1858; *Norte*, No. 1, February 18, 1858.
125 FE, No. 657, February 2, 1858.

spectrum of the upper class than did the new National party. "Manuel A. Tocornal . . . is today united with Santa María . . . ," reported Diego Barros Arana later that year; "the Gallos and the Vials are in the same party. This extreme miracle has been worked by Montt." Ignacio Domeyko, writing to a Polish friend, described the opposition as consisting of "the majority of better-off people, the younger generation, the clergy, etc."[126] The Fusion could rely on what was certainly the majority of the old Conservative following, as well as the strength of the reviving Liberal party, although here there was an undercurrent of radical dissent, exemplified in Vicuña Mackenna and others who had not forgotten the revolutionary euphoria of 1850–1.

The Fusion could not realistically expect to capture the Chamber of Deputies, still less the Senate.[127] Interior minister Urmeneta made it known that he wanted to conduct "fair" elections, but this simply meant the avoidance of the more flagrant forms of intervention. The Fusion flung itself enthusiastically into the fray, propagandizing in various *ad hoc* news-sheets, some designed, as usual, to attract the artisan vote. The government countered with its own news-sheets and the powerful voice of *El Ferrocarril*, which filled page after page with attacks on the Fusion. A particular incident during these weeks inflamed political passions. In Copiapó an unpopular Intendant, Juan Vicente Mira, lost his temper with the opposition press, which had been baiting him – almost, it seems, blaming him for the recession now overshadowing the province.[128] He imprisoned three journalists and had them flogged. The public outcry was instant, and the government, which was anxious not to give too many hostages to fortune (as Justice minister Sotomayor privately admitted),[129] instantly dismissed Mira and put him on trial. *El Ferrocarril* warned the opposition not to make too much of the incident.[130] The Fusion took no notice, and attacked Montt for both appointing *and* punishing Mira.

Given the nature of the recent political realignment, we would not expect the propaganda for the 1858 elections to have been particularly coherent. As Manuel Guillermo Carmona wrote soon afterward, "Confusion reached such a level that it was very difficult to distinguish the banner of one party from another, since everyone was invoking *liberty* and nobody wanted to be seen

126 A. Montt, *Gobierno*, and Palma, *Reseña*; Barros Arana to Juan María Gutiérrez, December 15, 1858. RCHG, No. 94 (1939), p. 32; Domeyko to Wladislaw Laskowicz, January 14, 1859. Godoy and Lastra, p. 301.

127 After the election, the Fusion senators, a majority in the outgoing Senate, devised a legally dubious scheme to manipulate the results so as to guarantee a continued Fusion majority, but they resisted the temptation.

128 See *Copiapino*, No. 2955, February 19, 1858.

129 Ruz T., p. 59.

130 FE, No. 690, March 12, 1858.

as retrograde."[131] The remark is revealing about the general drift of political opinion. The Fusion issued a fourteen-point program that advocated economic measures (the removal of duties on exported metals and imported raw materials, cuts in public spending) with which many Nationals might have agreed. Its political demands (greater electoral and press freedom, greater powers for municipalities, reform of the civic guard) were somewhat more Liberal than Conservative in flavor.[132] For the most part, the arguments of both government and opposition were simply tactical and instrumental. The Fusion happily pointed out that while the Conservative and Liberal parties had "an important historical character," the National party was merely the instrument of Montt and Varas.[133] "The Liberal party . . . , progressive par excellence," declared one news-sheet, having its cake and eating it, had nobly joined forces with the "*pelucón* party, the primordial element in our independence and in our prosperity."[134] Opposition propaganda also sometimes raised the ominous specter of Antonio Varas as Montt's successor in 1861.[135] "If that candidacy required a Calvary to be raised in the public square," asserted a Fusion news-sheet, "Montt would raise it, and he himself would be the Longinus at that Calvary."[136] The language of the Fusion sometimes turned positively menacing. "The people has as many scaffolds as there are crossbars on gas lamps," the Valparaiso news-sheet *El Ciudadano* told Montt. "THE PEOPLE AWAITS YOU AT THE FOOT OF THE GAS LAMPS."[137]

The church weighed in behind the Fusion. "The clergy has been completely hostile to us," Justice minister Sotomayor told a friend, instancing the case of a priest who controlled some *calificaciones* and who excommunicated a citizen who dared to complain.[138] It was hardly a coincidence that Archbishop Valdivieso chose this moment to issue a pastoral (March 12, 1858) denouncing the existence of a Protestant chapel in Valparaiso that had been built a full three years earlier. A number of Catholics protested that the foreign worshipers were "honorable, industrious, moral," and deplored the archbishop's attitude.[139] The clergy, however, were not above circulating a handbill (signed by "various priests") attacking Montt and Varas for "protecting" the sinister chapel and describing them (wrongly

---

131 "Fastos sangrientos de América," *Revista del Pacífico*, Tomo II (1860), p. 511.
132 *Ciudadano*, No. 15, March 18, 1858.
133 ACT, No. 43, March 20, 1858.
134 *Ciudadano*, No. 20, March 23, 1858.
135 For example, *Norte*, No. 6, February 24, 1858; ACT, No. 41, March 19, 1858.
136 *Ciudadano*, No. 13, March 13, 1858. Longinus (or Longius): by tradition the Roman soldier who pierced Jesus's side after the Crucifixion (John 19:34).
137 *Ciudadano*, No. 20, March 23, 1858.
138 Ruz T., p. 60.
139 *Capilla protestante.*

in Montt's case, maybe less so in Varas's) as atheists. "By voting for the *opposition*," said the handbill, "you are working for the *Catholic religion*."[140] The message could not have been clearer.

National party propaganda, for its part, poured scorn on the Fusion as an artificial alliance, contrasting it with the National party, a true "union of moderates."[141] As one of its news-sheets had it, echoing a well-known satirical verse of thirty years earlier,

> *De liberales vendidos*
> *Al partido pelucón,*
> *Con el cual están fundidos,*
> *Sin conciencia y sin honor,*
> *Líbranos, Señor!*

> From Liberals who have sold out
> To the *pelucón* party
> With which they are fused
> Without conscience or honor,
> Deliver us, oh Lord![142]

It was easy, of course, to mock the Fusion as "the hermaphrodite," or as "the *peluco*-Liberals or Libera-*pelucones*," or as the "party of the renegades," or (with more traditional invective) as a "monstrous union born of fanaticism, vengeance and ambition."[143] *El Ferrocarril* denounced the Fusion's *pelucones* as no more than "the parasitical plant surrounding the moderate *conservative* party," while the Liberals also had a parasitical plant: "the demagogic or red or socialist or communist party." Given the Conservative persecutions of Liberals in past years, who could possibly believe in "the union of the victim with his executioner?"[144]

There was, interestingly, a mildly egalitarian (or perhaps populist) side to National propaganda. In what was obviously a stab at the Conservatives, one of the party's Valparaiso artisan news-sheets declared that "Equality in everything and for everything between the rich and poor" was the National party's "glorious stamp." The Nationals wanted individuals, "whatever their class," to raise themselves by merit, and not to fawn on "those who call themselves 'gentlemen' with no other claim but their parchments of nobility." The same issue of this news-sheet provides easily the most fascinating specimen of propaganda of all (from either side). With its mixture of religious

---

140 *Católicos!*
141 *Doce de Febrero*, Nos. 1 and 9, February 12 and 23, 1858.
142 *Doce de Febrero*, No. 29, March 18, 1858. Cf. Donoso, *Sátira*, pp. 19–20.
143 *Pueblo*, Nos. 3 and 4, February 25 and March 1, 1858; *Artesano,* No. 5, March 27, 1858; FE, No. 702, March 26, 1858.
144 FE, No. 696, March 19, 1858.

and liberal-democratic language, its almost total confusion of conventional political categories, it deserves to be quoted at length. It is an arresting little fable. An angel appears to Chileans in a time of disorder, bearing a flag marked "peace, order, fraternity." A second angel then appears, and tells Chileans to love one another. The angels are replaced by a celestial choir, which sings:

Democracy is the idea of God; it is the principle of social perfectability; do not profane this sacred principle.

    I. Love God the Creator above all; this is the principle of principles.

    II. Do not be perjurers or wicked.

    III. Render public worship to the divine idea.

    IV. Love your parents, your elders, and all men; respect others so that you may be respected.

    V. Do evil to nobody; may your lips pronounce nothing but peace, concord, love, and friendship.

    VI. Raise women to the dignity they should occupy in society, seeking in woman the tender mother, the beloved wife, the chaste friend, the adored sister, the innocent daughter, and the angel that sheds perpetual peace in this exile we call the world.

    VII. Live content with what you possess.

    VIII. Do not be false, or hypocritical or mendacious.

    IX. Respect the peace of families.

    X. And love the creative principle.

And then men understood how mischievous they had been, and understood what democracy was, and they were democrats, and they were happy.[145]

What the artisans of Valparaiso made of this is hard to imagine.

But the artisans were courted as avidly as they had been before. The clubs formed for them, *El Ferrocarril* suggested, unlike their predecessors of 1850, were not subversive, and were indeed "a great step forward in our political education."[146] There was no Bilbao or Arcos to radicalize the artisans. The upper-class politicians were firmly in control. In Valparaiso, where the contest was especially animated, the clubs (as the Intendant reported) attracted "an immense attendance, and, held in the most public places, they are becoming more crowded and turbulent every day."[147] The Valparaiso clubs were closed down a few days before the elections, Interior minister Urmeneta telegraphing the order from Santiago.[148] The opposition, however, was able to stage one or two large public meetings. Some six

145 "Visiones proféticas," *Pueblo*, No. 8, March 15, 1858.

146 FE, No. 697, March 20, 1858.

147 Intendant of Valparaiso to Interior minister, March 18, 1858. AMI, Vol. 283.

148 FE, No. 716, April 14, 1858; ACT, No. 43, March 22, 1858; CHAM, p. 114.

hundred artisans and others turned out on Sunday, March 7, in a Santiago theater,[149] though the authorities prevented a second mass meeting from taking place.[150] If the Fusion's campaign was thus mildly obstructed by the government, it was also undermined by the decision of the radical Liberal faction to run separate candidates in a number of districts. In Copiapó Manuel Antonio Matta ran as a "liberal," Tomás Gallo as a "*fusionista*." In other districts the radicals supported Fusion candidates. A speaker at the main artisan club in Santiago protested over "the list of the party that calls itself Liberal-Conservative," because "the people" had not been consulted, but he urged a vote for it in the interests of defeating the common foe.[151]

The elections themselves produced the usual crop of incidents: soldiers drawn up close to one of the voting tables in Santiago, falsified registers in Lontué, the votes of an entire parish ignored at Puchacay.[152] *La Actualidad* reported the purchase of five hundred *empanadas* and several gallons of chicha for the refreshment of Battalion No. 5 of the Santiago Civic Guard.[153] There was the customary jostling and intimidation around the voting tables.[154] In Santiago, as Domingo Santa María would recall, the Fusion spent 35,000 pesos and won the first day's vote.[155] On the second day, Antonio Varas was discovered directing the National party vote-buying effort from a house in Santa Ana parish. He was "obliged to fly for safety from the people's wrath, escaping through a gutter," reported *El Mercurio*. "In this tumult a policeman was killed."[156] When the dust settled, the Fusion had won fifteen of the seventy-two seats in the Chamber, the largest elected opposition contingent yet seen in Chile, and more than large enough to be disruptive.

The Fusion made it clear that disruption was intended. The opposition press (with *El Mercurio* now fully part of it) continued to pile abuse on Montt and Varas. "There is no doubt about it," asserted *La Actualidad*, "Chile is more oppressed than Russia"[157] – as if a newspaper like *La Actualidad* would have lasted five minutes in Czar Alexander II's empire! There were, it is true, some lighter moments in the midst of the political tussle. On May 2, for instance, the Liberals of Atacama hosted a ball in Copiapó. "People of all political colors," reported *El Copiapino*, "mingled like

149 FE, No. 687, March 9, 1858.
150 CHAM, p. 115.
151 ACT, No. 38, March 16, 1858.
152 Alb. Edwards, *Gobierno*, pp. 227–28.
153 *Suplemento extraordinario a la Actualidad No. 48 del domingo 28 de marzo de 1858*.
154 *Doce de Febrero*, No. 46, April 12, 1858.
155 Santa María to Isidoro Errázuriz, January 18, 1878. *Revista Chilena*, Tomo X (1920), pp. 163–64.
156 English Part, M(V), No. 94, March 31, 1858.
157 ACT, No. 67, April 21, 1858.

true democrats."[158] But in Santiago the war of words continued unabated. *La Actualidad* called Montt "the most pronounced and determined enemy" that "liberal principles" had ever encountered, a man whose morals were "daguerrotyped" (a word of recent coinage in Spanish) by his actions.[159] Not surprisingly, there were those who saw storms ahead. The government, declared *El Mercurio*, was "enclosed in an iron circle."[160] The Fusion was determined to tighten it.

When Montt delivered his address at the opening of Congress on June 1 – "the great annual lie" (*La Actualidad*); "more flattering than faithful" (*El Mercurio*)[161] – the Fusion deputy for Copiapó, Tomás Gallo, requested the right to reply. The request was unprecedented, and the session became an uproar. The 1858 "ordinary" sessions proved even more agitated than those of 1849–50, and more prolonged. They also saw an intriguing display of the kind of parliamentary maneuvering that would become commonplace a few years later. The government tried the tactic of introducing bills (on electoral and municipal reform) dear to Liberals and somewhat less dear to Conservatives but failed to drive the parties apart. Twelve Fusion deputies (Conservatives as well as Liberals) presented an easily defeated motion to reform the entire Constitution of 1833. Fusion deputies also resorted more often than ever before to the *interpelación*. For *El Mercurio* this parliamentary questioning of ministers was part of "the school of democracy,"[162] but cabinet ministers did not see it in that light, Interior minister Urmeneta once dismissing an *interpelación* by declaring that "he was not pleased to reply."[163]

One of the noisiest issues in the 1858 Congress concerned the Santiago–Valparaiso railroad, still far from complete. To finish the job, the government (with the 1857 Congress's approval) had raised a 7-million-peso loan in London (Chile's first foreign loan since 1822), and, to gain control of the company, now proposed to buy out the private shareholders. The opposition denounced the measure as a handout to Montt's supporters, although there is no evidence that it was. *El Mercurio*, despite its fierce opposition sympathies, saw it as an intelligent way of putting money into circulation in the recession that had now taken hold.[164] Such parliamentary tussles were conducted against the background of "the severest winter on record."[165] The copious rains did nothing to dampen the Fusion's mounting fury. "The people . . . is

---

158 *Copiapino*, No. 2995, May 4, 1858.
159 ACT, Nos. 72 and 73, April 27 and 28, 1858. The first daguerrotype machines reached Chile in 1841.
160 English Part, M(V), No. 97, May 15, 1858.
161 ACT, No. 103, June 2, 1858. M(V), English Part, No. 99, June 15, 1858.
162 MV, No. 9333, August 7, 1858.
163 CHAM, p. 122.
164 MV, No. 9305, July 6, 1858.
165 English Part, M(V), No. 101, July 15, 1858.

trying to secure institutions to make the republic effective," proclaimed *La Actualidad*, "and government puts forth all its energy to stop it. From such duels . . . come bloody revolutions. . . . The present is bad and the future dark. God save the republic!"[166]

"Independent Men and Patriots, Prepare Yourselves!"[167]

The agitation of 1858 can be seen in some ways as the real foundation of the Chilean political tradition as it developed from the 1860s onward: parties (two of them in a coalition and one of them with a fringe group), the vigorous use of the press, clubs that associated upper-class politicians and the artisanate in a less self-conscious way than had been true in 1850, large public meetings (not hitherto seen very much in Chile), some of them, in Valparaiso, attended by as many as five thousand people.[168] Only a few years later all this would be seen as unremarkable. The agitation of 1858, however, was clearly leading toward an explosion. "Rumours of a forthcoming *revolution* are whispered about," reported *El Mercurio*'s steamship edition in mid-October.[169] There seems little doubt that by this stage the Fusion leadership had set up a "revolutionary committee," with Santa María and Errázuriz among its leading members. Aníbal Pinto, visiting Santiago around this time to attend to the estate of his recently deceased father the ex-president, found that the government had "serious fears," but felt that the fears were unjustified, because the opposition was too weak to mount a revolution.[170]

Pinto underestimated the Fusion's determination. Its propaganda offensive did not slacken. The cruel political cartoons (the first in Chilean history) printed in the magazine *El Correo Literario* portrayed Montt very insultingly as diminutive and swarthy. "His Excellency should resign," editorialized *La Actualidad*, pointedly alluding to the liberator O'Higgins's abdication in 1823. "Abdication would prevent a war."[171] If Montt aspired to dictatorship, the paper warned, he should not rely on the Army[172] – was this a covert call for military support in a rebellion? As always, there were incidents that inflamed feelings still further. On October 14 Diego Barros Arana and an English friend, Robert Souper,[173] were suddenly arrested on

166 ACT, No. 147, July 23, 1858.
167 ACT, No. 213, October 11, 1858.
168 Manterola, "Revolución," p. 59.
169 M(V), No. 107, October 15, 1858.
170 Pinto to General Cruz, October 8, 1858. RCHG, No. 77 (1932), p. 64.
171 ACT, No. 219, October 18, 1858.
172 ACT, No. 231, November 1, 1858.
173 Robert (or Roberto) Souper (1818–81), born at Harwich (Essex), arrived in Chile in 1843 to manage a hacienda in the south. He later bought a property of his own near Talca and married

suspicion of assembling a cache of firearms. Souper had done no more than order a hunting rifle from a French gunsmith in Santiago, and he and Barros Arana were soon released. The episode was graphically written up by Barros Arana and wickedly caricatured in *El Correo Literario*.

The grand symbolic moment of the Fusion's mobilization efforts came a few days later, on October 19, 1858, when it staged a huge "protest banquet" attended by about seven hundred, including all the significant figures in the opposition – older politicians such as Manuel Camilo Vial and the now octogenarian Ramón Errázuriz, Liberal leaders such as Domingo Santa María, Conservatives such as Manuel Antonio Tocornal, Ramón Subercaseaux, and Francisco Ignacio Ossa. "There is not one of the old families in Santiago that was not represented," reported *La Actualidad*. "Almost all the great landowners were there."[174] The speeches breathed fire at Montt. Aníbal Pinto pointed to "a great discontent, a great indignation" throughout the republic. Diego Barros Arana drew a parallel with William Walker's recent filibustering in Nicaragua and exhorted the opposition "to fight the political filibustering that has invaded us." The Conservative Manuel Carvallo asked for a delegation to be sent to Montt, who was a good man "enclosed within a very tight circle of men whose interest is to hide the truth from him," to request a new cabinet. Carvallo's conciliatory words aroused no sympathy among the banqueters. All they wanted, they told him, was for Montt to go. At the end of the evening, Guillermo Matta (then winning renown as a poet) led a procession three blocks long to the statue of General Freire on the Alameda. His friends hoisted him on to the statue, where he proclaimed that "the man in the Moneda has trembled!"[175]

If he had, he was not showing it. He was, however, taking steps to prevent the revolutionary outbreak he knew was possible. Arrests (mostly of suspect civic guardsmen, policemen, and soldiers) were made in several cities – Concepción, Valparaiso, Talca, Copiapó, and Caldera (where the entire municipal council was detained) – although in Santiago, as we saw, the arrest of Barros Arana and Souper backfired. The arrests did nothing to deter the opposition. When Congress reconvened in November 1858

---

a *talquina*. A lifelong Liberal, he fought for General Cruz at Loncomilla in 1851. In 1856–7, as mentioned in Chapter 2, he served (at his own request) as *subdelegado* of Pelarco. When the War of the Pacific came, he sent his two sons into the Army and, although in poor health, himself volunteered, taking part in the naval battle at Cape Angamos and at the capture of the Morro of Arica. He was killed in the battle of Chorrillos (January 1881). He never took Chilean nationality: see the long note by his friend Diego Barros Arana, *Obras completas*, Vol. XII (1914), pp. 199–210. Souper's Chilean descendants were sometimes Army officers. One of them, another Roberto, led the abortive tank rebellion against President Salvador Allende on June 29, 1973.

174 ACT, No. 222, October 21, 1858.
175 For the banquet (and speeches) see Figueroa, *Historia*, pp. 80–98.

for its "extraordinary" sessions, the Fusion deputies resorted to systematic obstructionism to hold up the passage of the budget, scrutinizing every line in detail. Finally losing patience with the opposition, Interior minister Urmeneta, defying the Chamber's standing orders, requested a vote of confidence and the approval of the law on a simple reading of the text. The Fusion deputies walked out; the budget was approved 43 to 1.[176] The Fusion denounced Urmeneta's move as a de facto *coup d'état*.[177] In fairness to Urmeneta, we need to remember that the Chamber had no rules governing closure of debates before the 1920s; until that time, there was no answer to obstructionism. The novelty of Urmeneta's tactic in 1858 was great (only in January 1886 was it used again), and served to push political passions close to breaking point. One of *El Correo Literario*'s final cartoons showed Montt and Varas peering through a telescope at a comet (one had lately appeared in Chilean skies) marked "REVOLUTION. LIBERTY FOR THE PROVINCES."

It is possible, as Martín Palma speculated soon afterward, that Montt's failure to curb the opposition press (perhaps to show that he was *not* a tyrant) was interpreted as a sign of weakness.[178] By November 1858, the progovernment press was close to demanding a crack-down. *El Ferrocarril*, enraged by the tone of the opposition press, tried to point a moral, and one that certainly had a grain of truth. In the days of Portales, it noted, "a single line from one of the endless articles published in *La Actualidad*" would have occasioned "a noisy press trial" at least, or quite possibly the banishment of its author to Juan Fernández.[179] The newspaper's tone grew steadily more bad-tempered. The opposition's only aim, it declared, was to overthrow the government and replace it with "the leaders of the *fusion*." It described the Fusion delegation in Congress as the most negative in any period of history or any country in the world.[180]

A curious incident in mid-November showed how some of the Fusion's more youthful supporters tried to taunt Montt. A peasant with a remarkable physical resemblance to the president was dressed in a frock-coat and presidential sash and let loose on the Alameda at the time of the evening *paseo*. Two civic guard officers encountered him near the Moneda, and took him in to meet Montt. Montt conversed amiably with him, probing to find out who had perpetrated the joke. The peasant did not let on. Back in the street again, he was followed by large crowd to a church and later to the

176 CN/D, November 20, 1858.
177 CHAM, pp. 134–36.
178 Palma, *Reseña*, pp. 24–25. *El Mercurio* was fined but, apart from this, the press law of 1846 does not seem to have been used much.
179 FE, No. 870, October 13, 1858.
180 FE, No. 871, October 14, 1858; No. 905, November 23, 1858.

theater, where he was finally arrested. In fact, the peasant was a trusted retainer of the strongly *pelucón* Subercaseaux family, put up to the trick by its younger members.[181]

The final crisis of this agitated year was provoked less by the Fusion leadership than by the Liberal party's radical faction, the mostly younger Liberals who resented the pact with the Conservatives. Among them were Benjamín Vicuña Mackenna, Guillermo Matta and his brother Manuel Antonio, and Isidoro Errázuriz. In 1849–50, the radicals, as we saw, were inspired by reading Lamartine's history of the Girondins. As luck would have it, another Lamartine book, his *Histoire des constituents*, a depiction of the opening phase of the French Revolution, was being widely read by young Liberals in 1858. (*El Ferrocarril* serialized it between May and October.) Once again, the seductive story of the French revolutionaries played its part in Chilean politics. Montt "for us," asserted an opposition news-sheet, "is what the governor of the Bastille was for the French."[182] At the end of October, the radicals began publishing *La Asamblea Constituyente*, a news-sheet whose principal demand was implicit in its title: the immediate reform of the 1833 Constitution by a constituent assembly. The Fusion leaders and the Fusion press, far from distancing themselves from the radicals, welcomed *La Asamblea Constituyente* as an ally in the fight against the common enemy.[183] *El Ferrocarril*, predictably, found the news-sheet's program as "grandiose as Niagara Falls" – and as noisy.[184]

The radicals were determined to go their own way. On December 11, 1858, Interior minister Urmeneta closed the sittings of Congress by the simple expedient of placing a notice on the door. That same day, *La Asamblea Constituyente* summoned the citizens of Santiago to what it described as a "constituent assembly" at the premises of a club the radicals had recently founded. The Intendant of Santiago banned the meeting. The radicals distributed handbills repeating their invitation. Some two hundred young men turned up at the appointed hour. As the meeting began, Santiago's police chief entered the room and demanded its closure. The radicals agreed to disperse, but only after police and soldiers had made an appearance – to underline that they were yielding only to force. They locked the room and the soldiers had to break down the door to gain entry. A few scuffles ensued, and the young radicals insisted on being taken to prison. They marched there intoning the national anthem. All the young men, except the signatories of the original summons (Angel Custodio Gallo, Guillermo Matta and his brother Manuel Antonio, Benjamín Vicuña Mackenna, and

181 ACT, No. 250, November 23, 1858; Subercaseaux, I, 59.
182 *Ciudadano*, No. 79, November 10, 1858.
183 ACT, No. 230, October 30 1858; *Ciudadano*, No. 78, November 6, 1858.
184 FE, No. 885, October 30, 1858.

Isidoro Errázuriz) were released the following day. Most, according to *El Ferrocarril*, were "young men from school."[185]

Montt did not find this episode as picturesque as we probably do. He immediately imposed a ninety-day state of siege in Santiago, Valparaiso, and Aconcagua Provinces. The usual arrests were made. *La Actualidad* and *El Correo Literario* vanished from the streets for ever. Even the venerable *El Mercurio* was forcibly closed down, and did not reappear for three months. But December 1858 was not November 1850. The agitation did not melt away. Manuel Montt faced his second civil war.

185 FE, No. 922, December 13, 1858.

10
The Triumph of Liberty, 1859–1864

Manuel Montt's Second Civil War

This time the entire Army remained loyal to the government. With no national hero like General Cruz to help, the Liberal-Conservative Fusion's "revolutionary committee" had to improvise forces of its own. Its strategy was to bring the government to its knees by fomenting urban insurrections and sweeping the Central Valley with guerrilla bands (*montoneras*) organized by sympathetic hacendados. None of the urban risings achieved more than temporary success. On February 12, 1859, San Felipe was seized by local rebels, at the cost of the accidental death (from a stray bullet) of the Intendant's sister-in-law. The future Conservative politician Abdón Cifuentes, who lived there, contrasted the impeccable behavior of the revolutionaries with that of the civic guards and soldiers who recaptured San Felipe six days later and allowed it to be brutally sacked. Poor Cifuentes lost his first frockcoat in the tumult. A French nun arriving to work in the town's hospital reported eighty deaths.[1]

The rising in Santiago, staged by fifty mutinous civic guards, was snuffed out almost immediately. The Fusion's effort in Valparaiso (February 28) was entrusted to the poet Guillermo Blest Gana – "good for many things but not for running a revolution," wrote one of the rebels. He was almost immediately arrested. The rebels attacked the public warehouses and set fire to the main door of the Intendancy. There was not enough wind to spread the fire to the roof, as was noted with relief by the port's No. 3 Fire Company (whose corporate spirit outweighed the political divisions its members shared with the rest of the country).[2] The alleged chief arsonist at the Intendancy was shot the following day, by which time the revolt was over. Talca, a possible key to success in the Central Valley, was a different story – for a while. In January 1858, the small-time landowner Ramón

---

1 Cifuentes, I, 47–59; Sister Marie Deschamps to Mother Superior Devos, March 27, 1859. Serrano, *Vírgenes*, p. 286.
2 Manterola, "Revolución," p. 61; Ibáñez Santa María, p. 166.

Antonio Vallejos and a small guerrilla group seized the town. Vallejos set up a "governing junta," mobilized the local artisans, and imposed strict rule over (and financial exactions on) the better-off *talquinos*. Trenches and barricades were dug and raised in expectation of a siege. Government troops quickly surrounded and began bombarding Talca. In mid-February, Vallejos was fatally wounded. Under cover of a truce agreed with the War and Navy minister, General Manuel García, by then supervising the siege, the rebel leaders fled. On February 22, García occupied the town, taking three hundred prisoners.[3]

The government, armed again with emergency powers, acted swiftly to remove some of the more irritating thorns in its side. The *Asamblea Constituyente* group arrested in December 1858 received death sentences (not confirmed by the supreme court). Isidoro Errázuriz deposited a 20,000-peso bond and went into exile in Argentina. The other four men (the Matta brothers, Angel Custodio Gallo, and Benjamín Vicuña Mackenna) were taken to Valparaiso, where Intendant Jovino Novoa offered the captain of a British ship 3,000 pesos if he would dump them in Liverpool.[4] The captives pleaded to be put ashore in Peru, but the captain wanted his money. Given the four young men's flair for publicity, Montt would never hear the last of this episode. Another group of nine prisoners (one of them the Englishman Robert Souper) was bundled aboard a Chilean vessel, the *Olga*, and sent off to the Magellan Strait. The prisoners hijacked the ship and diverted it to Peru.

Although its urban risings failed, the Fusion could reasonably hope to tie down the government with its improvised guerrilla bands, its *montoneras*. The young historian Ramón Sotomayor Valdés was one of the more improbable agents organizing them.[5] The movement of these bands across the map is difficult to chart in detail, but the common pattern is one of active-minded hacendados (or surrogates they trusted) who mobilized the *huasos* of their estates and armed them rudimentarily. One such *montonera*, led by Víctor Antonio Arce, an hacendado from Chillán, thrust toward rebel-held Talca, but was soon dispersed by government troops. A more successful *montonera*, led by José Miguel Carrera, the rebel hero of La Serena in 1851, rampaged through Colchagua Province, targeting the haciendas of known government supporters. It merged with a band captained by the compulsively active José Dolores Fernandois. The two *montoneras* attacked Rancagua (February 16), only to be beaten off. Meanwhile General García, masterminding the siege at Talca, sent a force to rout another group recruited by Juan Antonio Pando

---

3 Figueroa, *Historia*, pp. 516–25. Figueroa, *Historia*, remains the most comprehensive narrative of the 1859 civil war. For more information on the Talca episode, see Daitsman.
4 The contract with Captain William Lesley of the *Louisa Braginton* is reprinted in CHAM, pp. 312–13.
5 Sotomayor Valdés, *Noticias*, p. 110.

(a rich grain trader ruined by the recession) and Pedro Ugarte (the former judge), both of whom were captured. The Carrera-Fernandois *montonera*, returning to the fray, was checked in two further skirmishes and decisively defeated at Pichiguao (May 2). Further south, the guerrilla threat was if anything more serious. Two *montoneras* seized Tomé and Talcahuano and mounted an attack on Concepción, only to be driven off after three hours of stiff fighting, leaving about sixty dead. Next day, as Aníbal Pinto recounts, the police were plied with drink and roamed the streets, firing wildly, sacking stores, and killing several women and artisans.[6] On the Bío Bío Frontier, veteran activists Nicolás Tirápegui and Bernardino Pradel enlisted the support of a number of Mapuche caciques. Pradel, Tirápegui, and cacique Juan Mañil, gathering about one thousand men, agreed to strike northward under Tirápegui's command. On April 12, at Maipón, near Chillán, the combined forces of the Intendants of Arauco and Ñuble Provinces dispersed Tirápegui's motley army.

The government's success in containing the guerrilla threat should not be underestimated. Had Concepción fallen, even if Talca had held out, the Fusion might have carried on the battle for months. But the most serious military threat lay less in the south than in the north, in Atacama Province. Here the Constituent Revolution (as the rebel movement came to be known) was largely outside the control of the Fusion's revolutionary committee, and was viewed ambivalently by the Fusion leadership. Here, in fact, the *illusion lyrique* of the radical Liberals was suddenly embodied in one of Chilean history's minor romantic epics.

As we saw, the mining magnates of Atacama had been among Montt's strongest supporters earlier on, identifying easily with his plans for material progress. Many of them turned against him as his presidency proceeded, finding his authoritarian approach gratuitous and outdated. Families such as the Mattas and the Gallos were attracted into the Liberal camp, and to its radical faction. They found a leader in Pedro León Gallo, who lived year-round in Copiapó. Something of a dreamer, he was an avid reader and would-be poet. As a Copiapó municipal councilman in 1858, he fought an ill-tempered battle with the Intendant of Atacama, Colonel José María Silva Chávez. After one particular provocation in August 1858 (arising from the gratuitous flogging of two policemen), Silva Chávez suspended Gallo from the council and prosecuted him (unsuccessfully) for *desacato*, "disrespect." By November 1858, Gallo was actively planning an insurrection, forming a local *Club Constituyente* as cover, and a second club to organize (and give military instruction to) the Copiapó artisans. The Fusion leadership proved unreceptive to these plans, urging Gallo to draw the line at capturing Copiapó. Gallo had something much more dramatic in mind.

---

6 Pinto to General Cruz, February 16, 1859. RCHG, No. 77 (1932), p. 68.

On January 5, 1859, the *copiapino* rebels seized the barracks and took control of the streets. Intendant Silva Chávez fled. Gallo was proclaimed Intendant of Atacama. The province (like Concepción and Coquimbo in 1851) declared itself independent pending a constituent assembly. Soon afterward, Gallo's brother Juan Guillermo arrived from Santiago with instructions from the Fusion to defer the revolution. Gallo took no notice. He sent small parties south to occupy the Huasco valley. Armor-plating some railroad wagons, he then prepared to attack a government force led by Silva Chávez which had taken up position along the Copiapó-Caldera railroad. Finding discretion the better part of valor, Silva Chávez withdrew to La Serena, abandoning Atacama Province to the rebels. Gallo set about organizing an army with great gusto, pouring his own fortune into the enterprise – and that of his mother, the feisty and radical-minded Doña Candelaria Goyenechea. His chief of staff, Ramón Arancibia (an army lieutenant earlier cashiered by Silva Chávez) was also a poet, and had already composed a suitable marching song, the *Canción Constituyente*.

> *Que el voto noble y santo*
> *Que pide una "Asamblea*
> *Constituyente" sea*
> *El canto popular.*

> May the noble and holy wish
> That asks for a Constituent
> Assembly become
> The song of the people.[7]

The rebels seized artillery pieces from ships at Caldera, and manufactured cannons in local foundries and ammunition in the railroad workshops. To remedy the shortage of coins for the soldiers' pay, "constituent pesos" were minted, silver coins with a star in the center – still the standard currency in Copiapó several months later,[8] and, later still, highly prized by numismatists. A larger prize escaped the rebels' grasp: the money (in gold) from the government's recent London loan, aboard a P.S.N.C. steamship southward-bound from Panama. The steamer put in at Caldera, but the captain, smelling a rat, ordered his crew to cast off immediately.[9]

By mid-February Gallo was poised to invade Coquimbo Province. The Constituent Army (more than one thousand soldiers) marched through the desert to La Higuera, a mining district about twenty miles from La Serena, and chased off a small government force. Here Gallo received an emissary

---

7 *Asamblea Constituyente*, No. 13, December 11, 1858.
8 See *Norte*, No. 18, June 18, 1859.
9 Treutler, *Andanzas*, pp. 251–52.

from the Fusion's committee, who advised him to call a halt, warning him of Silva Chávez's strength at La Serena. Undeterred, Gallo led his army into battle on the *meseta* just north of the city, soundly defeating Silva Chávez at Los Loros (March 14). The government troops lost around eighty dead, the Constituent Army around forty-five. Later that day, Gallo made a triumphal entry into La Serena.

Los Loros dismayed the government, restored (briefly) the flagging spirits of the Central Valley *montoneras*, and was a severe humiliation for Silva Chávez, who had recently described the Constituent rebels as "chickens." A rude rhyme was soon going the rounds in Santiago.

> *Sí, mi don Manuel {Montt},*
> *como te cercan escollos,*
> *pregúntale a Silva Chávez*
> *¿cómo le fue con los* pollos?

> Ah yes, don Manuel [Montt],
> Now that the crisis thickens,
> Go and ask Silva Chávez
> How he got on with the *chickens?*[10]

For different reasons, Silva Chávez's embarrassment was shared by the Fusion leadership. Photographs of Gallo were circulating throughout Chile. A quadrille for piano was composed in his honor. His actions had given him overnight heroic status and were, indeed, the stuff of which legends are made. But Liberal politicians such as Domingo Santa María and Federico Errázuriz also were uneasily aware that further triumphs by the audacious northerner might undermine both the Fusion and their own future leadership of the Liberal cause.

Could Gallo have reached Santiago? Probably not. The government, surmounting the southern guerrilla threat, had built up an army of more than seven thousand men, three thousand of whom set sail for the final reckoning with Gallo, commanded by General Juan Vidaurre Leal, with Finance minister Matías Ovalle also on hand. The Constituent Army entrenched itself on Cerro Grande, the low hill that looms to the south of La Serena. On April 29, 1859, Vidaurre Leal's soldiers assaulted the rebel lines. In a two-hour battle, the government forces lost around one hundred dead or wounded,[11] the Constituent Army presumably more. (Among the fallen was the soldier-poet Arancibia.) The gallant Constituent Army melted away. Gallo and many of his followers fled up the Elqui valley and across the mountains to Argentina. Vidaurre Leal occupied

10 Hernández, *Juan Godoy*, II, 284.
11 Rafael Sotomayor to Adolfo Larenas, May 2, 1859. Ruz T., p. 76.

La Serena next day, also dispatching troops to regain control over Atacama Province.

"The revolution has succumbed!" moaned a clandestine news-sheet in a final, black-edged issue. "Montt and Varas! You have triumphed."[12] The pacification of Atacama did not immediately dispel the disturbed atmosphere in the country. Valparaiso remained in a particularly agitated state. At the end of August, an attempt at mutiny there was detected and quashed.[13] On September 18, groups of armed men seized the rifles of the civic guardsmen posted outside the church where General Vidaurre Leal (temporarily in command of the port) was celebrating the *dieciocho*. The general, appearing in the doorway, was fatally wounded by a bullet – a spectacle that put a stop to the rising, if that is what it was. Vidaurre Leal's body was taken to Santiago and given a solemn state funeral, reminiscent in some ways of that of Portales in 1837. The parallel did not occur to *El Ferrocarril*, which described the tragedy as "the most infamous murder" in the republic's history.[14] The government immediately arrested five members of the Fusion's former revolutionary committee, Domingo Santa María and the Conservative Francisco Ignacio Ossa among them. Nothing could be proved, and they were soon freed. In the wake of the civil war, numerous death sentences were passed, and thirty-one (according to an opposition estimate) actually carried out.[15] The Fusion leaders the government could lay hands on were either exiled or self-exiled, and simply waited in Peru or Argentina (or in a few cases Europe) for better times. The better times came sooner than anyone expected.

Politics After the Civil War

Outward calm returned to the republic after May 1859. Inner calm among the politicians (on both sides) was more difficult to restore. Diego Barros Arana, watching from Buenos Aires, had recently speculated that Montt might turn to a "formal dictatorship" – a view shared by "hundreds of the most intelligent Chilean people," according to the American minister in Santiago.[16] Montt was too much a man of law to make himself dictator, but the emergency powers he kept in force did nothing to lighten the atmosphere of anxiety and discontent, which was heightened by the serious recession now gripping Chile. For the opposition there was the

12 *Libertad*, No. 19, May 14, 1859.
13 FE, No. 1144, August 31, 1859.
14 FE, No. 1160, September 21, 1859.
15 CHAM, p. 194.
16 To Juan María Gutiérrez, March 28, 1859. RCHG, No. 94 (1939), p. 36; John Bigler to Lewis Cass (Secretary of State), February 28, 1859. Manning, p. 246.

nightmare of Antonio Varas as Montt's inevitable successor. The Fusion made it known in different ways to Montt that despite his victory in the civil war he had still not conquered "opinion." Opinion was clearly undergoing something of a sea change. The consensus of earlier times in favor of repressive measures (when needed) was giving way to an altogether more tolerant mood. Why? It cannot be said that any particular section of the upper class, still less any particular regional element, was responsible for the sea change, although the role of Atacama Province is an interesting one. The most plausible explanation is generational. Upper-class Chileans born in the years around 1830 were more profoundly attached to the idea of liberalization than their seniors. Better educated, better traveled, and more receptive to European influences, they could hardly fail to notice that liberalism was the indisputable mark of nineteenth-century modernity. It also could well be true that the economic boom of the 1840s and 1850s had induced a more relaxed and confident feeling all round. As the younger generation matured, its more expansive political vision was communicated to the political class as a whole. A new and more tolerant consensus was in the making.

   It took the next three or four years for the politicians (or most of them) to work out how to articulate the new consensus in political terms, and to work it out in the rather novel framework of multiparty competition, the legacy of the realignment of 1857–8. For his part, Montt would dearly have liked to reconstruct the "old" Conservative party, reuniting his Nationals and the *pelucón* defectors, some of whom might possibly have been tempted. Montt certainly made overtures to a number of senior Conservatives (among them Fernando Lazcano) in mid-1859. Such a reconstruction was ultimately impossible. While they may have found it hard to shed their attachment to strong government, the Conservatives' protoclericalist outlook set them at odds with Varas's following, among which ideas of religious toleration (and even free thought) were spreading fast. (Many in later years would drift into the Liberal camp, as was true of *pelucones* such as Diego Barros Arana, who rejected religion altogether.) The Church, for its part, had no intention of smoothing the way to Conservative reunification. *El Ferrocarril*, always close to Varas, rarely lost an opportunity of sniping at the church, even taking it to task for its attitude during the civil war: "What did the clergy do to help the country to get out of its sorrowful situation? Nothing. . . . Perhaps it does not matter to religion if men tear themselves apart in fratricidal struggles?"[17] With language like this emanating from the government press, it is not surprising that the church and its *pelucón* champions remained unreconciled to Montt.

17 FE, No. 1169, October 1, 1859.

Soon after the civil war, Archbishop Valdivieso was advised by his doctors to take a long ocean journey. Before boarding the P.S.N.C. steamer *Bolivia* on July 1, 1859, rather than asking for permission (as he should have done), he simply informed the government that he was going. The government issued a decree granting the archbishop a fourteen-month leave, implying that he had requested it. Valdivieso undertook a vast tour of the United States, Europe, and the Holy Land, not failing to publicize his cause, especially in France, where the Catholic press had taken an interest in the Affair of the Sacristan. Writing to one of Pope Pius IX's counselors, he (by implication) compared his struggle to that of Pope Gregory VII in the Investiture contests of the eleventh century.[18] Montt, like Bismarck a few years later, was in no mood to go to Canossa. When the fourteen months expired, Valdivieso did not deign to tell the government he was staying abroad longer. This time the government failed to turn the other cheek, and suspended his archiepiscopal salary.

With political life once again at a very low ebb after the civil war, some of the more articulate members of the opposition sought consolation in literature. The young brothers Justo and Domingo Arteaga Alemparte (sons of the Colonel Arteaga of 1851 civil war fame) founded a lively weekly paper, *La Semana*, noted for its high-quality literary content as well as a conciliatory political tone. In August 1859, José Victorino Lastarria, ever the cultural entrepreneur, established a *Círculo de Amigos de las Letras* (Circle of the Friends of Letters). Historian Miguel Luis Amunátegui also established a small literary society. The poems and essays produced at meetings of the two societies had something of the flavor of the Liberalism temporarily excluded from the political arena.[19] Opening Congress on June 1, 1859, Montt positioned himself in the ideological terrain marked out by National party propaganda the previous year, ostensibly equidistant from the Liberals' "exaggerated doctrines" and the Conservatives' "spirit of resistance to all improvement" – a formula that was increasingly meaningless, given the creeping liberalization of "opinion." In political practice, as opposed to theory, he remained inflexible. The recent crisis, he claimed, had "partly undermined the morals of the masses and weakened respect for authority," and it was necessary for authority to be "strengthened in its means of action."[20] The emergency powers imposed at the start of the civil war remained in force to the end of Montt's presidency – and were used. Some of the Chilean exiles in Argentina who fled home after the devastating Mendoza earthquake (March 1861) were immediately "relegated" to the provinces.

18 Archbishop Valdivieso to Cardinal Franchi, Madrid, November 16, 1860. Valdivieso, *Obras*, II, 298.
19 Lastarria, *Recuerdos*, pp. 409–33; Santa Cruz, "Recuerdos," pp. 51–53.
20 DP, VII, 6–7.

In Congress, opposition voices were now few and far between. The old *pipiolo* Melchor de Santiago Concha tried to introduce a comprehensive constitutional reform, but the Chamber refused (38 to 2) even to discuss it.[21] When Francisco Vargas Fontecilla criticized the government for being too "harsh and inflexible" toward those defeated in the civil war, Finance minister Matías Ovalle firmly laid down the law, declaring that he was proud to belong to a government that punished those who had placed the country "on the edge of the abyss."[22] One or two deputies did at least question the need to extend the emergency powers. The fervent Liberal Francisco Marín told the Chamber that the opposition was prey to "a profound discouragement," and that the government had nothing to fear from "the defeated revolutionary party."[23] Santiago Gandarillas, revealing what can only be interpreted as an extraordinary detachment from political reality, even wondered why there had been a revolt against Montt in the first place. He had once visited him in the Moneda to lobby for the textile business, and had been struck by his courtesy, as well as by the tray of ice creams brought in at the end of the interview. Interior minister Urmeneta insisted that the emergency powers were essential. He pointed to the continued existence of *montoneras* (purely bandit gangs by this stage) and to the need to pacify the disturbed Araucanian Frontier. Ignacio Errázuriz (one of the deputies for Curicó) confirmed that there was "a panic terror" in Colchagua, and a widespread belief that guerrillas would soon reappear in force.[24] The evidence suggests that the government and its supporters were still fairly nervous. *El Ferrocarril's* editorials throughout August and September 1859 expressed unease about the effects of the *montoneras*, and speculated more than once whether the opposition might return to the attack, although in its *dieciocho* edition it affirmed that the time of *"calaveradas políticas,"* "wild political escapades," was over in Chile.[25]

Looming over all the lackluster debates of 1859 was the question of the presidential succession. Much as Montt wanted his friend Varas in the Moneda, he knew that the Fusion would oppose him bitterly. Interior minister Urmeneta saw himself as a logical candidate, but his authoritarian record offended Liberals and his views on religious toleration offended Conservatives. Rafael Larraín Moxó, one of the Conservatives with whom Montt conversed in mid-1859, put forward the idea of a third term for General Bulnes, a proposal greeted with icy silence by both Liberals and Nationals.

---

21 CN/D, September 22, 1859.
22 CN/D, June 16, 1859.
23 CN/D, August 25, 1859.
24 CN/D, August 23, 1859. For the disturbed state of the Frontier, see the letters from Vicente Pérez Rosales (Intendant of Concepcion) to President Montt, February–October 1860, in León and Aránguiz, pp. 387–425.
25 FE, No. 1159, September 17, 1859.

El Ferrocarril, picking up rumors of a possible deal between the government and the Conservatives, criticized the very idea of dealings between the government and specific parties: "The Government, dealing with a party, would make many people imagine . . . that there was equality between the two." *El Ferrocarril* was, however, perfectly willing for there to be compromises between *parties*.[26] The Nationals were not interested in compromises. They had their own simple agenda: to make Antonio Varas president.

In September 1859, Finance minister Matías Ovalle withdrew from the cabinet in favor of Jovino Novoa, the Intendant of Valparaiso. During the 1858 election campaign, Novoa had remarked that Chileans should go down on their knees when pronouncing the name of Manuel Montt, an observation that provoked particular derision from the opposition. (According to one report, Novoa actually knelt after making the remark, clasping his hands as if in prayer.)[27] Jerónimo Urmeneta was by this stage eager to relinquish the Interior ministry, perhaps to prepare a presidential bid for himself or his brother José Tomás, the mining magnate. His intentions were public knowledge by the end of 1859. The government's total silence on the matter unnerved *El Mercurio*: "the atmosphere is charged with electricity," it claimed, "and this absolute, suffocating silence . . . is very similar to the calm before the storm."[28]

Only in April 1860 did Urmeneta finally step down. With the presidential election only fourteen months away, it was obvious what a new Interior minister's main task would be. None of the leading Nationals showed any interest in the job; they were unwilling to promote any candidate except Varas. Silvestre Ochagavía, a National popular among Conservatives, entertained presidential illusions of his own, and declined to serve for that reason alone. Although it was nowhere written, Interior ministers did not prepare their own election to the presidency – one reason why Joaquín Tocornal had withdrawn from the office in July 1840. The usual rumors spread: Francisco Javier Ovalle as Interior minister? Manuel José Balmaceda at Finance?[29] As usual, they were unfounded. In his hour of need, Montt turned to the one man he could always depend on. Antonio Varas's reappointment as Interior minister (April 19, 1860) was instantly interpreted as the renunciation of his claim on the presidency. Fulsome tributes were paid to his action, particularly in the progovernment press. "The clumsy whispers about an official candidacy have been thrown into confusion . . . ," memorably declared *El Ferrocarril*, "by this clear, decisive, unanswerable fact. Authority has taken a great step forward on the path of

26 "Transacciones," FE, No. 1178, October 10, 1859.
27 "Revolución de Valparaíso en 1859" (anonymous). Figueroa, *Historia*, p. 488.
28 MV, No. 9742, February 27, 1860.
29 MV, No. 9766, March 26, 1860; No. 9778, April 11, 1860.

sincere politics, and señor Varas [has given] a proof of his selflessness. The spirit of [George] Washington has knocked on Señor Varas's door."[30] The newspaper pinned great hopes on Varas's decision: "The political situation of the country has changed completely. An entire peaceful revolution has just been worked."[31] *El Mercurio* was "agreeably surprised."[32] The opposition was much more guarded, mocking the Varas-Washington equation, and half-suspecting a ruse of some kind. It was not a ruse. Justice minister Sotomayor, writing to an Intendant soon afterward, asked him to spread the word among Nationals that Varas would definitely not run for president.[33]

Varas settled back into the Interior ministry as if he had never left it. Among his projects in the 1860 Congress was the so-called Law of Civil Responsibility. Introduced the previous year, it provided for financial penalties (including confiscation of property) on those implicated in revolutions or tumults, and all those associated with them. It is hard to find a historian who has ever had anything good to say of this measure. Even Montt's great admirer Alberto Edwards regards it as "impolitic."[34] As Jacinto Chacón observed at the time, it was quite wrong for repressive laws to touch "the sacred [right] of *property*."[35] In the Senate, the chief opponent of the bill, General José Francisco Gana (twice Montt's War minister), observed that it would simply prolong political hatreds. The emollient National senator José Joaquín Pérez suggested amendments to soften the measure slightly, and the Senate took his advice. In the Chamber, the law was opposed in good theoretical fashion by Lastarria, and more vehemently by Francisco Marín, who eloquently enunciated the traditional liberal appeal to the right of rebellion. He cited the French Revolution and the current "Italian revolution." The government press was constantly eulogizing Garibaldi. What if the King of Naples were to introduce a civil responsibility law? Would the government press start describing him as arbitrary and despotic?[36] Antonio Varas sprang to the bill's defense in one of his more memorable speeches, and the Chamber passed it by 33 votes to 6. We might note here that the law was never applied. It was repealed in 1865 by a unanimous vote in the Senate and a 38 to 1 vote in the Chamber.[37]

---

30 FE, No. 1340, April 20, 1860.
31 FE, No. 1344, April 25, 1860.
32 MV, No. 9788, April 23, 1860.
33 Rafael Sotomayor to Adolfo Larenas, May 10, 1860. *Revista Chilena*, Año II, Tomo IX, No. 27 (1917), pp. 162–64.
34 Alb. Edwards, *Gobierno*, p. 329.
35 *Revista del Pacífico*, Tomo III (1860), p. 266.
36 CN/D, November 18, 1860.
37 CN/D, July 20, 1865; CN/S, July 26, 1865.

Varas Reduvivus?

Notwithstanding the debates on Civil Responsibility in Congress, the Fusion leadership gradually began to realize that a silent revolution *was* occurring in politics. Opening Congress on June 1, 1860, Montt made it clear that his supporters should choose a candidate who could rise above recent conflicts, effectively admitting that the next presidency would mark a new beginning. Varas himself reiterated Montt's view in Congress soon afterward. With Varas's candidacy "patriotically eliminated," as *El Mercurio* put it,[38] the issue of the presidential succession now obsessed the politicians to the exclusion of virtually all else, except possibly the recession and the growing number of bankruptcies. The government's obsessive secretiveness meant that no indication of its intentions reached the public. The *pelucón* Rafael Larraín Moxó revived the name of General Bulnes – a proposal that some Conservatives (including Manuel Antonio Tocornal and Francisco Ignacio Ossa) were prepared at least to consider. The Liberals, or some of them, countered by floating the name of General Cruz. Domingo Santa María told a friend that Bulnes would almost certainly be the next president, and that his most serious rival might be José Joaquín Pérez.[39] By August 1860, according to *El Ferrocarril*, at least ten names were being spoken of as possible candidates, including those mentioned so far, along with Urmeneta, favored in La Serena, General Gana, favored in Copiapó, or Larraín Moxó or Manuel Antonio Tocornal, favored by other "oppositionists."[40]

In the spring of 1860, despite Varas's act of renunciation, the National party made a serious effort to revive his candidacy, an effort that both clouded and confused the political scene for several months. It can be dated fairly precisely to September 16, 1860, when Varas gave a superb keynote speech at the inauguration of the statue of Diego Portales, near the Moneda. He eulogized both Portales's "great work of calming the country and founding for ever a new and stable order of things" and the "great" 1833 Constitution – "the only one that can properly be applied in the epoch we are passing through."[41] Many of the Nationals listening found the speech inspirational. A few days later, President Montt and the cabinet took a ceremonial train ride to Rancagua and back, on a newly completed section of the Southern railroad – two of whose locomotives were named "Montt" and "Varas." Their return to Santiago was followed by a banquet at which Varas was required to speak more than once. His final words were a hope that Chile and South America would advance "on the road of the Republic, based on liberty, fraternity, progress and universal tolerance."

38 MV, No. 9795, May 1, 1860.
39 Santa María to Amunátegui, Paris, September 29, 1860. Amunátegui Solar, *Archivo*, I, 76.
40 FE, No. 1437, August 11, 1860.
41 MV, No. 9916, September 22, 1860.

This astonishingly liberal language prompted *El Ferrocarril* to declare that Varas had attained "the stature of a prophet of the future."[42] It now began publishing regular editorials exalting Varas, something that the newly founded opposition newspaper *La Discusión* interpreted immediately as a *de facto* "proclamation" of his candidacy[43] and treated with sarcasm:

Varas the great personality, Varas the unique, Varas without beginning or end, the eminent statesman, as great as the Andes, as disinterested and generous as Washington or Cincinnatus, as selfless as Jesus Christ. . . . Oh Redeemer of the Republic! Oh most humble Shepherd, ever solicitous for your flock! . . . The country does not want your sacrifice![44]

There were other names that came to the fore as possible candidates over the next few weeks, but the National leadership was now completely fixated on Varas. The Fusion's original fears of a ruse were suddenly and sharply revived. The editorials of *La Discusión* reflected deep suspicion of the government's intentions. On December 26, it reported a National party "shortlist" of José Joaquín Pérez, José Tomás Urmeneta, and Varas, and concluded that this was simply a stratagem for imposing Varas.[45] Given the new uncertainty, the Fusion could do little more than adopt a menacing tone in its propaganda. The tactic was logical, designed to scare the Nationals away from Varas. "If the Varas candidacy is a fact, as everyone is saying," wrote Manuel Blanco Cuartín in an opposition magazine, "the fact for us is *revolution*."[46] An article in *El Mercurio* also hinted at the possibility of "another civil war, more bloodshed, more tears," while *La Discusión* told the government that it would have only itself to blame "if a new revolution breaks out tomorrow."[47]

The Nationals were not scared. *El Ferrocarril* continued to present Varas as a "GREAT CITIZEN . . . , EMINENT STATESMAN,"[48] but the newspaper denied, in thirteen paragraphs, that it was formally "proclaiming" him as candidate. Seven of the paragraphs were a eulogy of Varas's "noble heart and high intelligence."[49] On December 15, 1860, the National party leadership met at Matías Cousiño's house, and reaffirmed its support for Varas. Varas, who was in attendance, reminded the leadership of Montt's words on June 1, and in effect said "no." He even had kind words for the Fusion ("if their ideas differ from ours, at least they know how to fight and die for them") and suggested that the next president should be neither a lawyer or a soldier,

42 FE, No. 1472, September 25, 1860.
43 DIS, No. 15, December 11, 1860.
44 DIS, No. 41, January 11, 1860.
45 DIS, No. 27, December 26, 1860.
46 *Mosaico*, No. 24, December 29, 1860.
47 MV, No. 9989, December 17, 1860; DIS, No. 21, December 18, 1860.
48 FE, No. 1541, December 14, 1860.
49 FE, No. 1539, December 12, 1860.

lawyers being "generally tricksters" and soldiers "plain ignorant."[50] The meeting nevertheless agreed to send a delegation to Montt to press Varas's claims. The president was adamant that Varas's position as Interior minister made his candidacy impossible.[51]

The Nationals would not take "no" for an answer. *La Discusión* was now certain that "a good part" of the National leadership "would insist on the Varas candidacy in spite of everything."[52] There was every sign that it would. On January 6, 1861, the Nationals staged a large banquet in Varas's honor, and the toasts made it clear that Varas's "no" had to be overruled.[53] *El Ferrocarril* praised the party's "perseverance in continuing to sustain his candidacy," and concluded: "There is no doubt about it. Antonio Varas is no longer the candidate of a party, but of the great majority of the nation."[54] Another banquet was held a week later, with the same sentiments expressed – albeit more alcoholically, according to *La Discusión*.[55] One National politician won applause at this second banquet by remarking that the country's welfare came before Varas's "individual repose."[56]

The campaign seemed unstoppable. "Proclamations" of Varas's candidacy (sometimes accompanied by banquets) were organized in several provinces, lists of supporters' names pouring like a huge flood into Santiago,[57] and duly printed by *El Ferrocarril*, for whom Varas had become "the embodiment of all the great principles of the Republic and democracy."[58] Analyzing the names attached to the Talca proclamation, *La Discusión* claimed to find a suspiciously high number of public officials.[59] Only a prosopographical study of a kind well beyond anybody's reach could tell us whether the newspaper's suspicions were fair. On January 4, 1861, *La Discusión* reported that Varas had definitely accepted the candidacy.[60] *El Mercurio*'s steamship edition announced it as certain that "Sr. Varas will be elected president, although contrary to the wishes of a great majority of the citizens," while its main edition for home consumption saw Chile as entering "on a perilous struggle which we hope will not bring a violent crisis."[61] A wild rumor went the rounds

50 DIS, No. 22, December 19, 1860.
51 DIS, No. 24, December 21, 1860.
52 DIS, No. 27, December 26, 1860.
53 DIS, No. 38, January 8, 1861.
54 FE, No. 1562, January 8, 1861.
55 DIS, No. 44, January 15, 1861.
56 MV, No. 10,014, January 15, 1861; FE, No. 1567, January 14, 1861.
57 Printed, usually in several columns, in FE, No. 1568, January 15, 1861 and issues following to mid-February. The list from Cauquenes (FE, No. 1577, January 25) filled six and a half columns.
58 FE, No. 1574, January 22, 1861.
59 DIS, No. 48, January 19, 1861.
60 DIS, No. 35, January 4, 1861.
61 M(V), No. 155, January 17, 1861; MV, No. 10,003, January 2, 1861. *El Mercurio* took the view that Varas should be accepted in the interests of peace.

that Pedro León Gallo was on the point of invading Chile with a powerful expedition.[62] The wish was clearly father to the thought. The Fusion could do little except continue its propaganda campaign, knowing perfectly well that the machinery of intervention alone could impose Varas as president.

In fact, the efforts of the National leaders fizzled out as quickly as they had begun. Varas evidently felt that enough was enough. On January 12, 1861, he sent a letter to the National committee, making it clear that his decision was irrevocable. He based his refusal on the fact that, as Interior minister, he would be required to "intervene" in the elections (such intervention would naturally be limited to the enforcement of the law, he said, although not everyone would see it that way), and this would hardly give a new government the "moral force" it would need.[63] The National leaders made one last effort, refusing to publish the letter and telling Varas that they would elect him against his will. Varas replied that if they did, he would leave the country.[64] The letter was published.

It was "a monument of truth, justice and patriotism," declared *El Mercurio*, which printed an English translation in its next steamship edition.[65] "The political situation seems to be changing its aspect absolutely . . . ," gushed *La Discusión*; "this letter . . . does much honor to señor Varas." The newspaper blamed its previous hostility to the minister on his "imprudent partisans," but made it clear that the opposition had been ready to "resist his elevation to the presidency at all costs."[66] *La Discusión*'s attitude irritated *El Ferrocarril*, for which Varas's "great act of abnegation" obviously qualified him for secular sainthood.[67] True, many Nationals were bitterly disappointed by their hero's withdrawal[68] and there was some loose talk of making Varas president through a "revolution," to which the Fusion leaders responded by quietly alluding to the new Civil Responsibility Law. The ever-loyal *El Ferrocarril* rather pointlessly announced that it would support Varas's candidacy until another candidate was chosen.[69] Varas himself had to ask its editor, Juan Pablo Urzúa, to tone down the eulogies.[70] In many ways the eulogies were deserved.

62 DIS, No. 24, December 21, 1860.
63 Antonio Varas to Domingo Matte, Manuel José Balmaceda, José Manuel Guzmán, and Manuel Alcalde, January 12, 1861. FE, No. 1577, January 25, 1861.
64 M(S), No. 10,023, January 25, 1861.
65 M(S), No. 10,024, January 26, 1861; M(V), No. 156, February 2, 1861.
66 DIS, Nos. 53 and 54, January 25 and 26, 1861.
67 FE, No. 1583, February 1, 1861; No. 1586, February 5, 1861.
68 See José Antonio Torres, "Crónica de la quincena," January 15, 1861, *Revista del Pacífico*, Tomo IV (1861), pp. 59–63.
69 FE, No. 1577, January 25, 1861.
70 See Domingo Santa María to M. L. Amunátegui, February 8, 1861. Amunátegui Solar, *Archivo*, I, 79–80.

There is little doubt that Montt and the Nationals could have made Varas president. We have no way of telling whether the Fusion would (or could) have opposed him by force of arms. By resisting the obvious temptation, Montt and Varas passed a real test of statesmanship.

The Rising Star of José Joaquín Pérez

The real task now facing Montt and the Nationals, all talk aside, was to find the next president. The name of General Bulnes was once again floated, as were Rafael Larraín Moxó's and Silvestre Ochagavía's, but none of them commanded enthusiasm among Nationals. *El Mercurio*, for whatever reason, ran a few articles vaguely supporting General Bulnes, and even printed some dreadful English doggerel in his favor by an American "poet," a certain James Jones, who ran a hardware store in Valparaiso and was known as a local "character."

> Hurrah! for General BULNERS
> He's covered with manly fullness.[71]

The Fusion, for its part, did not even bother to campaign in the congressional elections of March 1861. For nearly two months (March 14–May 8, 1861), *La Discusión* carried an announcement in large black type just below its masthead.

The Opposition to the present government, in agreement with its fellow members in the provinces, has resolved not to vote in the forthcoming elections, so as not to sanction with its suffrage a political system that completely annuls the rights of the peoples.

Both the congressional elections and the April municipal elections were the same story: "no member of the opposition even approached the voting tables," reported *La Discusión*, "and ... the government's triumph has been unanimous, stupendous."[72] This left the National party as more than ever the key to the presidential succession.

The government continued to maintain strict silence about its intentions. There was no shortage of suggestions from the press, especially the opposition press. *La Discusión* regularly put forward six or seven names over the next few weeks: Jerónimo (or José Tomás) Urmeneta, Melchor de Santiago Concha, José Joaquín Pérez, and Generals García, Aldunate, and Gana. The Fusion leadership apparently sent some "acceptable" names either to Montt

---

71 M(S), No. 10,072, March 23, 1861. For what little is known of Jones, see Guerrero Yoacham, p. 255. His incompetence as a versifier is shown by his choice of "Bulners" (presumably an attempt at jocular anglicization) rather than "Bulnes," which is a reasonable rhyme for "fullness."
72 DIS, No. 126, April 22, 1861.

or the National party, stressing that its objective was "to avoid a revolution by means of a change of policy that would inaugurate a government of conciliation and tolerance."[73] *La Discusión* adopted a tone of sweet reasonableness:

Is it a question of reforms? – Well, let us leave their solution to time, time which nothing can resist. – Is it a question of freedoms? They will be resolved by conciliation and good faith, by common sense and patriotism. – Is it a question of personal ambitions? – Has not Varas given us the example?[74]

Early in March 1861, *El Mercurio* reported that the National party had decided on José Joaquín Pérez.[75] *La Discusión* had already given Pérez a nod of approval, claiming that he would be accepted by "a great number of respectable persons of all the parties." It reported a small banquet at San Bernardo to promote his candidacy.[76] Two weeks later, the cabinet met with President Montt, to vote on a "shortlist" of two: Pérez and Silvestre Ochagavía. Montt, Justice minister Sotomayor, and Finance minister Novoa voted for Ochagavía; Varas and War-Navy minister General García voted for Pérez. Montt asked for further consultations with the National leadership.[77] *La Discusión* reported a rumor that government and opposition had come to an agreement on Pérez.[78] Whether there was ever a formal deal may be doubted, but it seems moderately certain that General García played a significant part in smoothing the way for Pérez.[79] There is remarkably little additional evidence of the way in which his name finally rose to the top of the pile of *presidenciables*, although it had been regularly mentioned since the end of 1860. As early as February 1861, Domingo Santa María, for one, had intuitively foreseen that he would be the official candidate.[80]

So it would be. On April 2, 1861, soon after the congressional elections, the National party leadership met yet again, this time at José Manuel Guzmán's house. Varas was asked whether he persisted in his attitude. He confirmed that he did. Domingo Matte then formally proposed José Joaquín Pérez as the National party candidate. A delegation visited Pérez next day at Las Higueras de Chena, his hacienda. "Gentlemen," the pleasant legend has him saying, "the young lady you are offering me is very pretty, but rather a coquette. I will think about it." He thought about it for all of two days. He was a month short of his sixtieth birthday, but in sturdy health. (He would die at age eighty-eight.) His diplomatic experience in the United States,

73 DIS, No. 64, February 6, 1861.
74 DIS, No. 56, January 29, 1861.
75 M(S), No. 10,055, March 4, 1861.
76 DIS, No. 84, March 2, 1861.
77 M(S), No. 10,069, March 20, 1861.
78 DIS, No. 85, March 4, 1861.
79 DIS, No. 204, July 23, 1861.
80 Santa María to M. L. Amunátegui, February 8, 1861. Amunátegui Solar, *Archivo*, I, 80.

France, and Argentina, his reputation as a moderate *pelucón* who had stayed (inconspicuously) with Montt after the Conservative defection, his public image of amiability and humor, and (not least) his known sensitivity to the prevailing wind – such qualifications made him the ideal figure to preside over a new beginning.

The opposition instantly assumed that he was. *El Mercurio*'s steamship edition reported that his nomination had been "well received" by everybody, and that politics was now in "a promising condition."[81] *La Discusión*, while emphasizing that Pérez would not be "explicitly accepted" by the opposition, believed that "in the last third of his pure and stainless life" he was unlikely to continue Montt's policies.[82] José Antonio Torres, writing in the new *Revista del Pacífico*, suggested that Pérez was someone able to draw the right moral from the recent "violent upheavals," and who would avoid "the perilous roads that lead to the abyss."[83] The National party did not wish to see Pérez in quite this light, presenting him as someone who would uphold the authoritarian tradition, albeit with "a progressive-conservative policy."[84] A circular from the leadership to provincial Nationals explained that Pérez represented the "same principles and ideas" as Varas,[85] an approach that presented no problems for those Conservatives with a residual attachment to strong government, but that slightly alarmed some Liberals, who were still nervous about a possible disintegration of the Fusion.

Their nervousness was misplaced. The Fusion was rescued (if it needed rescuing) by a *deus ex machina* in the form of Archbishop Valdivieso, who returned from his globe-trotting in March 1861, his mood hardly sweetened by the government's suspension of his salary. His triumphal reception in Valparaiso and Santiago (where between seventy thousand and one hundred thousand turned out) was interpreted by *La Discusión* as "a protest" against the government.[86] There were certainly those who tried to make it so. Prominent Liberals mingled with devout society matrons and the brotherhoods of the faithful poor to acclaim the formidable prelate. "Political and religious passions are mixing," editorialized *El Mercurio*, suggesting that the Liberals saw Valdivieso as "a battering ram they can use to overthrow the government."[87] There could have been no sterner portent. Valdivieso's presence on its own reminded politicians of the religious issue, and made it unthinkable for his friends the Conservatives to join hands with his persecutors the Nationals. The Liberals, for their part, hastened to cultivate the

81 English Part, M(V), No. 161, April 17, 1861.
82 DIS, No. 114, April 8, 1861.
83 "Crónica de la semana," April 30, 1861. *Revista del Pacífico*, Tomo IV (1861), p. 586.
84 FE, No. 1637, April 6, 1861.
85 FE, No. 1645, April 16, 1861.
86 DIS, No. 86, March 5, 1861.
87 M(S), No. 10,058, March 7, 1861.

archbishop as assiduously as they could. They did the same with Pérez. In July 1861, seventeen prominent Liberals publicly declared their support for him.[88] *El Ferrocarril* chided the opposition press for its illogicality in trying to "appropriate the Pérez candidacy for itself"[89] while also condemning the electoral process as "illegal."[90] The Fusion saw no contradiction between welcoming Pérez and keeping up its attacks on Montt and Varas. *La Discusión* described Montt's address to Congress on June 1 as a pack of lies, and continued to mock Varas (although more gently than before) as "the last of the Romans, the Napoleon of the Pacific, the Justinian of the West."[91] Its welcome to Pérez, however, was sincere. In *La Discusión*'s view, there was every reason to suppose that he would embrace a policy of "union, peace, concord," and in that sense (*La Discusión*'s logic was somewhat tortuous) the opposition, too, could be said to have "proclaimed" him.[92]

Pérez's election in June 1861 was a foregone conclusion. The Fusion abstained from voting. Pérez won all but two of the votes in the electoral colleges; the two absent *electores* made known their preference for him.[93] Both before and after his inauguration on September 18, the politicians gave themselves over to an orgy of banqueting, which may be briefly evoked as a good illustration of the political style of the time. At the National party's banquet for Pérez, held in the Teatro Municipal at the end of August, a few glasses were raised to the election of Antonio Varas in 1866,[94] although this was not to be. Manuel José Balmaceda expressed the hope that the party, "marching behind its most worthy chief, Don Manuel Montt," would play an important part in the new government. "The church asks for peace between Christian princes . . . ," said Pérez. "We should ask for peace between all types of prince, whether they be Moors or Jews." As for Montt and Varas, he claimed, "history . . . will be more just and impartial toward these two statesmen than their contemporaries."[95] On balance, history has been.

The Liberal banquet, held two weeks later in "the spacious and magnificent dining room" of the old *pipiolo* Melchor de Santiago Concha, was smaller but equally effusive. The Liberals, said Domingo Santa María, did not want reform at the cost of bloodshed, but "without reform, the country cannot move on . . . in its magnificent flight to the future." Pérez was confident that "Reforms that are judged daring today will be accomplished. All

88 DIS, No. 202, July 20, 1861.
89 FE, No. 1650, April 22, 1861.
90 FE, No. 1670, May 15, 1861.
91 DIS, No. 161, June 3, 1861, and No. 236, August 29, 1861.
92 DIS, No. 198, July 16, 1861.
93 FE, No. 1759, August 27, 1861.
94 DIS, No. 252, September 24, 1861.
95 FE, No. 1764, September 2, 1861. DIS, No. 239, August 29, 1861, printed Pérez's remarks but nobody else's.

that is needed is patience and perseverance." Pressed to speak a second time, he added: "Gentlemen, believe me. My intentions are straight and pure." He placed his hand on his heart. "We believe you!" cried the Liberals. The banquet (which had begun at 6:30 P.M.) was followed by a ball, at which the president-elect stayed until six in the morning.[96]

The euphoria produced by Pérez's election seems almost palpable. "The horizon is clearing," declared *El Mercurio*. Pérez's "character, moderate politics and background" presaged "bounteous times for the country."[97] The Fusion, it is true, remained suspicious of the outgoing government. Rumors spread that the troops brought in to attend Pérez's proclamation as president-elect were really there to stage a *coup d'état*.[98] *La Discusión* mocked Montt's farewell to the palace guard in the Moneda patio as a "ridiculous parody" of Napoleon's farewell to his soldiers at Fontainebleau.[99] The Nationals, for their part, were unrepentant. Their banquet for Montt and Varas (September 23), also held in the Teatro Municipal, was decorated with a huge statue of Liberty over the inscription "Liberty in order." Gas lights spelled out CHILE! MONTT! VARAS! Among the many congratulatory speeches and toasts, there was one from the young Ramón Barros Luco, himself to be president half a century later. "From today onward," he said, "it will not be difficult to govern in Chile, for power has raised itself above everything else."[100] Barros Luco probably had a point.

The Triumph of the Fusion

President Pérez's inauguration on September 18, 1861, was acclaimed by cheering crowds. A polka, "The Hope of Chile," was written to honor the day.[101] "Welcome, Sr. Pérez...," editorialized *El Mercurio*. "If the past has been sad and baneful, the future now appears to be smiling and promising."[102] *El Mercurio* even allowed its eccentric American "poet," James Jones, to contribute some of his deplorable verse to its main edition:

> Welcome! Welcome! Welcome! Pérez,
> Through every lane and every crevice...
> As Chile's grand star he now shines!!
> Round flowery and immortal designs!![103]

96 MV, Nos.10,221 and 10,222, September 16 and 17, 1861.
97 M(S), No. 10,210, September 3, 1861.
98 M(S), No. 10,215, September 9, 1861.
99 DIS, No. 252, September 24, 1861.
100 FE, No. 1780, September 24, 1861.
101 DIS, No. 250, September 14, 1861. Pérez also had a march in his honor composed by John White, an English violinist who lived in Brazil.
102 MV, No. 10,223, September 18, 1861.
103 MV, No. 10,226, September 25, 1861.

Poetry of a higher order was offered by Mercedes Marín del Solar, who foretold an era of joy,

> *Porque huyó el tiempo infausto*
> *En que discordia fiera*
> *Encendió impía hoguera,*
> *Y al vértigo fatal de un odio insano*
> *Se derramó la sangre del hermano.*

> For the unhappy time has fled
> When ferocious discord
> Inflamed the impious fire,
> And in the fatal vertigo of insane ire
> The blood of brothers was shed.

Pérez, said the now elderly poetess, was *"el digno ciudadano,"* "the worthy citizen" who would cure Chile's *"dolores,"* "sorrows."[104]

Two days after Pérez's inauguration, a small group of radical Liberals gathered at the statue of General Freire on the Alameda. Among them was the musician José Zapiola, who praised Freire as the only president of Chile (so far) who had never persecuted the press.[105] The first "event" of the Pérez presidency was the publication of a book. For the past few weeks, four prominent Liberals (José Victorino Lastarria, Diego Barros Arana, Domingo Santa María, and Marcial González) had been working feverishly to produce an "instant history" of the Montt presidency, a small-format book nearly six hundred pages long, and furtively printed on the presses of *El Mercurio*. The *Cuadro histórico de la administración Montt* ("Historical Picture of the Montt Administration") was dedicated to Pérez and appeared on the day of his inauguration. It combines a vivid narrative (by Barros Arana), with inevitable emphasis on the repression of the decade, and detailed criticisms of the work of specific ministries, some of which come close to nit-picking. The nits loomed much larger for the book's authors than they do in hindsight. The book was an immediate sensation, and infuriated the supporters of Montt and Varas. *El Ferrocarril* roundly denounced it as an unparalleled "outpouring . . . of malevolence."[106]

The fact that the book's appearance had no discernible consequences for its authors or publisher marked a clear break with the immediate past. Pérez himself would prove a strong champion of the freedom of the press, even when (as happened frequently as his presidency proceeded) the press criticized or satirized (or caricatured) him. By April 1862, Manuel Blanco

---

104 "Oda a S. E. el Presidente de la República de Chile, señor don José Joaquín Pérez," *Revista del Pacífico*, Tomo V (1861), p. 443.

105 MV, No. 10,225, September 24, 1861.

106 DIS, No. 255, September 27, 1861; FE, No. 1779, September 23, 1861.

Cuartín could write that the freedom of the press had never before been so well exercised in Chile.[107] This did not mean a sudden explosion of stable new newspapers. *La Discusión*, the Fusion's main organ since the end of 1860, closed down a few days into the new era. The classic duo of *El Mercurio* and *El Ferrocarril* underwent a strange reversal of roles, *El Mercurio* supporting the Pérez administration and being wryly described by *El Ferrocarril* as a "semiofficial newspaper."[108] *La Voz de Chile*, founded and edited by Manuel Antonio Matta and reflecting a strong Liberal (often radical Liberal) viewpoint, appeared in March 1862 and lasted just over two years. Another Liberal daily, *La Patria* (August 1863), edited largely by Isidoro Errázuriz, continued to appear in Valparaiso until the 1890s. (Like *El Mercurio*, it had a steamship edition.) Not until March 1864 did the Conservatives establish a newspaper of their own, *El Independiente*, which ran until 1891. Its first editors (nobody else could be found) were the decidedly Liberal (and anticlerical) brothers Miguel Luis and Gregorio Amunátegui, but the Conservatives Abdón Cifuentes and Zorobabel Rodríguez were regular contributors and kept an eye on them, fostering the clericalist line developing in the Conservative party.[109]

On September 22, 1861, the new president received a couple of respectful delegations, one consisting of "one hundred young men from the principal families of Santiago," the other consisting of around two thousand artisans.[110] Another group of artisans had visited him a week before his inauguration, expressing the hope that he would immediately raise duties on imported manufactures to 70 percent.[111] He did not, but in other ways he smiled on their renewed efforts at organization. In October 1861, nearly three hundred artisans met and agreed to establish a mutualist society with the name of *La Unión*. It took definite shape and form early in 1862, and in July that year opened its first night school, with President Pérez and the cabinet on hand to celebrate. Times had truly changed. In the prospectus for an abortive artisan news-sheet, journalist Manuel Blanco Cuartín suggested that the artisanate had been "a class which up till now has not been able to have a fixed character or definite tendencies," and that all it wanted was "to be introduced at the banquet of the republic with an invitation and not . . . through abuses and violence," as in the past.[112] Other mutualist societies followed *La Unión*, modestly flourishing in the new political climate. And not only mutualist societies. Other new forms of

107 *Porvenir del Artesano*, Prospecto, April 5, 1862.
108 FE, 1862, *passim*.
109 See Cifuentes, I, 90–91, 96–97.
110 DIS, No. 252, September 24, 1861.
111 DIS, No. 247, September 11, 1861.
112 *Porvenir del Artesano*, Prospecto, April 5, 1862. For *La Unión*, see Grez Toso, *De la "Regeneración,"* pp. 427–28.

civic organization – fire companies (social as well as functional units), new political (and Catholic) associations, masonic lodges – strengthened both "civil society" and the foundations of liberalization.[113]

The language used by Pérez at the time of his inauguration was vague – no doubt deliberately so. He spoke of national reconciliation and his desire for "a government of all for all," whatever that meant. One thing it did mean. On October 4, 1861, he sent a comprehensive amnesty bill to Congress, covering the entire ten years from 1851 to 1861; its phrasing exempted the beneficiaries from liability under the Civil Responsibility Law. Another polka was written to honor the amnesty.[114] The rapid acceptance of the bill by both the National-dominated chambers (the Chamber of Deputies did not even debate it) was symbolic, in its way, of the spirit of reconciliation accepted by Pérez's first cabinet. Of Montt's last ministers, only General Manuel García stayed on as War and Navy minister. The new Interior minister was Manuel Alcalde, a former National deputy. Finance was entrusted to Manuel Rengifo, the son of the minister of the 1830s and 1840s, though not his equal in economic insight. The bishop of La Serena, Justo Donoso, a respectable ecclesiastic, was named Justice minister. It was not the most brilliant cabinet in Chilean history.

"In Chile we are not doing badly," reported Diego Barros Arana to his Argentine friend Juan María Gutiérrez on New Year's Day 1862. "Pérez is starting his government well, dodging the demands of the parties and governing in accordance with the law and with honesty. Everyone is very happy with him, except the most fanatical sectarians of the previous government."[115] *El Ferrocarril* reported (next day) that "the Government continues to enjoy the unanimous sympathy of opinion," and noted "unequivocal signs of a powerful enlivening of the public spirit."[116] Despite its conciliatory style, however, it was unlikely that the Alcalde cabinet would last very long. The Fusion would not be satisfied until it had won control of the government. While the Nationals continued to pressure the new president, the Fusion was in the stronger position. The victory of Chilean liberty, we might say, was achieved not on the battlefield but in the salons and dining rooms of Santiago. The Fusion leaders flattered Pérez without mercy, subjecting him, as *El Ferrocarril* put it, "to a real siege,"[117] and making sure, for instance, that there were enthusiastic crowds and triumphal arches when he paid his first official visit to Valparaiso during the summer recess of 1861–2.

113 For a path-breaking survey of the new organizational forms, see Gazmuri, *El "48" chileno*, pp. 117–265.
114 MV, No. 10,236, October 7, 1861. For the 1861 amnesty, see Loveman and Lira, pp. 186–87.
115 To Gutiérrez, January 1, 1862. RCHG, No. 94 (1939), p. 42.
116 FE, Nos.1866 and 1872, January 2 and 9, 1862.
117 FE, No. 1864, December 31, 1861.

Flattery as a tactic is more often successful than not. At the end of January 1862, *El Ferrocarril*, expressing doubts about the performance of the Alcalde cabinet, speculated for the first time about a possible change of ministers.[118] It was not long in coming. On April 24, 1862, Alcalde, Rengifo, and General García all resigned, as did Bishop Donoso three days later. President Pérez asked them to carry on "for a bit longer," a request that pleased neither the Nationals nor the Fusion, but the ministers (except Bishop Donoso) agreed. There was the usual speculation in the press, the newly founded *La Voz de Chile* suggesting that the "crisis" could well be "the Gordian knot" of the Pérez presidency.[119] Pérez was good at sniffing the prevailing wind, but refused to be hurried. Politicians were already discovering that he was never in a hurry about anything. "Pérez is an excellent man, simple, wise, enlightened, and with more energy than had been thought," wrote Barros Arana in February 1862, "but by the same token he is also lazy, working with excessive slowness, waiting for events to push him."[120] Only in early July 1862, when he felt sufficiently pushed, did Pérez cut the Gordian knot, by inviting the Fusion into a new cabinet: Manuel Antonio Tocornal (Interior), José Victorino Lastarria (Finance), the Conservative Manuel María Güemes (Justice), and General Marcos Maturana (War and Navy). Of these, only General Maturana, a veteran of the wars of independence, had a residual National allegiance. The appointment of the Liberal ideologue Lastarria was a particularly eloquent symbol of Pérez's break with the past. No cabinet had ever begun "under better auspices," declared *El Ferrocarril*.[121] The turn-around was thus complete – or almost. Lastarria's tenure of the Finance ministry proved contentious. His request for tax increases (to cover the deficit brought about by the recession) ran into immediate trouble in Congress. His vanity had not lessened with the years, and he was offended by a harsh *interpelación* from former Finance minister Jovino Novoa. In January 1863, Pérez replaced him with Domingo Santa María, whose skin was thicker than Lastarria's.

The formation of the first Fusion cabinet was greeted by scenes of delirious enthusiasm. Crowds thronged the streets. "Through the patriotism and noble heart of the President of the Republic," commented a Liberal news-sheet, "we are witnessing in these moments the resurrection of the people."[122] "Santiago was like a party," reported Guillermo Matta. "Its inhabitants roamed the streets in their thousands, led by musical bands, and their shouts of jubilation, the echo of the gratitude of an entire people,

118 FE, No. 1890, January 30, 1862.
119 *Voz de Chile*, No. 49, May 9, 1862.
120 To Juan María Gutiérrez, February 28, 1862. RCHG, No. 94 (1939), p. 45.
121 No. 2026, July 10, 1862.
122 *Unión Liberal*, No. 7, July 14, 1862.

reached the Man of Law and his newly organized cabinet."[123] Not all of the enthusiasm was exactly positive. As Domingo Arteaga Alemparte would remember it eight years later, "There was more rancor and vengefulness in their hosannas than love and pleasure."[124] The passions aroused by the Montt decade would last through the 1860s, though not much beyond.

Yet, there *was* something drastically new in the Chilean air in the early 1860s. The new president's style was very different from that of his predecessor. His manner was extremely affable. He chose not to live in the Moneda, preferring the comfort of his home. Either alone or with his wife Tránsito, he was happy to stroll along the Alameda, sometimes resting on its benches, sometimes cracking jokes with (and buying from) its vendors of fruit and *dulces*. These qualities were precisely those needed to induce a mood of calm after the previous decade's excitements. His example did much to reinforce the new consensus, showing his fellow citizens that political passion, even when intense (as it was again at the end of the 1860s, and in the early 1870s with the breakup of the Fusion), did not automatically lead to catastrophe. One measure of the shift is that in 1871 the defeated presidential candidate, José Tomás Urmeneta, seriously contemplated an insurrection but was talked out of it by some of his own supporters, and in 1876 another bitterly disappointed candidate, Benjamín Vicuña Mackenna, rejected the idea with the utmost firmness.[125] Pérez probably deserves more credit than any other nineteenth-century Chilean president for consolidating the national "idiosyncrasy" of (generally) civilized politics. Abdón Cifuentes, whose political career began during Pérez's time, came to think of him in later years as "one of the cleverest rulers Chile has had," and Barros Arana, writing Pérez's obituary in 1889, noted that after his inauguration "no one in Chile talked again of imprisonments and banishments."[126] Barros Arana, alas, spoke too soon. But nearly three decades without the use of emergency powers were an eloquent tribute to what Pérez achieved. For all his indolence and skepticism, he deserves to be remembered as one of Chile's great presidents. Admirers of strong government have not usually seen him in that light.

Previous presidents had tried to govern *above* party, at least in theory, though not always in practice. President Prieto, as we saw, had been able to override the *tocornalista* section of the Conservative party in naming Bulnes as his successor. Bulnes had to accept the Conservatives' choice of Montt in 1850–1. Montt found it impossible to impose Varas, and to a large

---

123 *Voz de Chile*, No. 110, July 19, 1862.
124 Arteaga Alemparte, *Constituyentes*, p. 44.
125 See Ag. Edwards, *Cuatro presidentes*, II, 118; Orrego Vicuña, pp. 331–32.
126 Cifuentes, I, 66; Barros Arana, *Obras*, XII, 321.

extent left the decision to the National party. Pérez accepted from the start that he would govern *in association* with a ruling party or coalition. Once again he was aware of the prevailing wind. There is little doubt that party identities strengthened in the early 1860s, having been more amorphous earlier, greater definition having been forced by the realignment of 1857–8. The displaced Nationals – or *monttvaristas*, as they were often nicknamed after 1861[127] – remained sentimentally attached to the legacy of Montt and Varas. (Varas stayed in Congress and remained an important political figure to the end of his days.) The Fusion succeeded in maintaining itself without too many strains as a governing alliance, although both Liberal and Conservative identities remained perfectly distinguishable, not least because of the growing religious issue. By the end of the 1860s, a number of independent Liberals were distancing themselves from the Fusion, largely over the issue of electoral intervention. Nor were the Liberals able to retain their radical faction, whose divergence from the mainstream had been symbolized in Gallo's Constituent Revolution. These "reformist Liberals," as they at first called themselves, or "red" or "radical" Liberals, as others called them, soon became known simply as Radicals. When the Liberal-Conservative alliance was formally renewed in November 1863, they went their own way. Pedro León Gallo had by then returned to Chile – acclaimed in Santiago and Copiapó. And it was in Copiapó (December 1863) that the Radicals created their first local branch or *asamblea*, with further *asambleas* formed in Santiago and Valparaiso the following year. The Radicals proclaimed uncompromisingly liberal-democratic views, tinged later on by a tone of fervent anticlericalism. This stemmed in part from their close connection with freemasonry. In April 1862, Chilean freemasons formed their own Grand Lodge, independent of the Grand Orient of France, with which they had formerly been affiliated.[128] They would play a significant (though not always traceable) part in Chilean politics for the next hundred years. The Radicals' strong laicizing tendencies enabled them to find common ground with anticlerical Nationals, and to join them in opposition to the Fusion both before and after the congressional elections of 1864. At an earlier point, Chile might possibly have consolidated a permanent two-party division. The diversification implicit in the realignment of 1857–8 meant that the country, or anyway the "political nation," came to feel most at home with a multiparty system. So it has been ever since.

127 Manuel Antonio Matta uses the terms *monttvarismo* and *monttvarista* in an article (written in exile) savaging Montt's June 1, 1861 address to Congress. DIS, No. 196, July 13, 1861. See also MV, No. 10,218, September 12, 1861.

128 See Oviedo, *Masonería*, pp. 100–52. The first two Chilean lodges dated from the mid-1850s, and two more were created in 1862. The first attack on masonry in the ever-vigilant *Revista Católica* seems to be in No. 566, October 16, 1858.

"The Future is Ours!"

To complete its triumph, the Fusion needed control of Congress as well as the cabinet. The loyally National majority elected in March 1861 went in for the systematic obstructionism the Fusion itself had used against Montt, with regular use of the *interpelación* – Interior minister Tocornal, who had introduced the *interpelación* into congressional procedures, was thus hoist with his own petard. His cabinet could counter parliamentary hostility by actively mobilizing "opinion" in loyal deputations to President Pérez, or in rowdier public demonstrations, as in July 1863, when a crowd invaded the Senate to express its solidarity with the cabinet. Matters came to a head a few days later in a particularly violent altercation between Finance minister Santa María and the president of the Senate, after which the cabinet and Congress were completely at loggerheads and legislation was largely paralyzed. It hardly mattered. The parliamentary storms of 1862–3 strike the historian as somehow less real, certainly less serious, than those of 1849–50 or 1858. They were a pointer to the future, not the past. In 1862–3, the outcome was no longer in doubt. Even the most fervent *monttvarista* could tell that the tide had changed. At the very height of the storms, Tocornal himself wrote to his friend Sotomayor Valdés, then in Mexico: "Our future appears serene; we cannot discern the slightest sign that would make us fear future disturbances. We enjoy the most complete internal tranquillity, and everything makes us presume that we shall go on enjoying it for many years, and hopefully for ever."[129]

All the Tocornal cabinet needed to do, in fact, was to wait for the congressional elections of March 1864. Whatever its propaganda may have asserted previously, the Fusion had no intention of abandoning electoral intervention. It was simply too useful. The battle to end it would be won only in 1891. Pérez himself played little part. He was happy to leave such things to his ministers. When the elections came, there were incidents of the usual kind in Aconcagua and Colchagua, but in Santiago the president himself toured the voting tables and persuaded the parties not to assemble intimidatory groups – an episode later evoked by Miguel Luis Amunátegui.[130] The elections yielded a handsome government majority: forty-nine seats in the Chamber for the Fusion (thirty-seven Liberals, twelve Conservatives), the *monttvaristas* reduced to eighteen, and five Radicals winning seats.

The way was now open to constitutional reform – the old Liberal dream, and no longer quite the Conservative nightmare it had once been. It took longer to achieve than many Liberals might have wished. This was partly because of the little war with Spain that broke out in 1865 and overshadowed

---

129 Tocornal to Sotomayor Valdés, September 17, 1863. Sotomayor Valdés, *Noticias*, p. 146.
130 CN/D, June 23, 1870.

politics for the next year or so, and partly also because of the lack of encouragement from President Pérez. But not even Pérez's inertia could hold back the tide. In 1868–9, to look ahead a bit, Radicals and independent Liberals joined with many younger *monttvaristas* to form a network of Reform Clubs in Santiago and the provinces, holding a national convention in September 1869. The strong presence of *monttvaristas* in this movement was especially significant, for it meant the effective withering away of the old authoritarian *pelucón* tendency that had played so large a part in Chilean history up to that point, something foreseen in an interesting article in *El Ferrocarril* as early as 1862. "Where are the pure Conservatives in Chile today?" asked the newspaper. "They have disappeared, or have merged into a moderate liberalism."[131] The *reformista* program of 1868–9 was in fact the purest liberalism: electoral freedom, an expanded franchise, "the principle of industrial liberty," a general reduction of presidential power. It set the agenda for the next phase of Chilean history. Yet, despite public debate of this sort, constitutional reform began only seven years after the Fusion's 1864 triumph, with a prohibition (itself significant) on the immediate reelection of the president, the first amendment (after thirty-eight years) of the hitherto inviolate 1833 Constitution. Pérez was thus to be the last of the four "decennial" presidents.

The triumph of the Liberal-Conservative Fusion, in the cabinet change of July 1862 and the elections of 1864, marks the end of the phase of Chilean history examined in this book. It seems appropriate to end with a question, although a question that is almost certainly unanswerable. We can reasonably ask whether the pattern of peaceful, tolerant, and often vigorous politics into which Chile settled under President Pérez would have been as durable as it proved without the effort of the earlier Conservative regimes to maintain and uphold a tradition of public order and administrative regularity. In the Conservative period, after all, memories of the colonial era and its authoritarian practices still remained strong, too strong for the fragile political experiments that preceded the Conservative regime. The Conservatives surely created the framework within which a more liberal (and Liberal) Chile could develop its active and civilized political life. By upholding that framework against armed challenge, they may have ensured that opposition activism was channeled into constitutional paths, that future oppositions would be loyal oppositions – Portales's old dream.[132] What would a victory by General Cruz in 1851 or by Pedro León Gallo in 1859 have meant for Chile? Had the Fusion triumphed by force of arms in 1859, would the victors' camp (as Martín Palma once speculated)[133] have dissolved in a welter

131 FE, No. 1957, April 21, 1862.
132 Portales to Antonio Garfias, March 16, 1832. EDP, I, 471–72.
133 Palma, *Reseña*, p. 52.

of conflict? We cannot stray too far into the counterfactual realm. At the very least, such victories might have set precedents for further upheavals and given Chile a record similar to that of the other Spanish American republics.

By the same token, it is perfectly fair to ask whether the withdrawal of Montt's candidacy in 1851 would have made the process easier, whether in fact Montt merely *delayed* the outcome. What if the *pelucones* had accepted Ramón Luis Irarrázaval as their candidate? It is highly likely that the Liberals would have viewed him with tolerance, and most unlikely that General Cruz would have risen in rebellion. Who can really say? The publisher Santos Tornero may well have been close to the truth when he speculated, in his memoirs, that Manuel Montt's "character" was the basic problem.[134] It is easy to accept that individual character plays its part in history. But it would not be unreasonable to give the *pelucones*, with their numerous sins of commission and omission, the benefit of the doubt. There is a real sense in which they can be said to have made the republic. It is useful to remember here the remarkable letter of Portales (March 1822) in which he foresees a period of "strong, centralizing government" as the necessary prelude to a "completely liberal government, free and full of ideals, where all the citizens take part."[135] The "omnipotent minister" was far-sighted. But the Liberals, too, helped to create the national tradition, by challenging the Conservatives to live up to the political ideals both parties constantly proclaimed. In the end, most Conservatives came to agree, and helped to move Chile into a new phase of her history. That the Liberals and Conservatives combined out of detestation of a common foe is neither here nor there; such is the stuff of politics. The example they gave was to be emulated by later coalitions, not least the grand alliance that revived Chile's democracy after the terrible storms of the 1970s and 1980s.

By the mid-1860s, to leave the story there, the tide of liberalism (and Liberalism) was becoming irresistible. In the contest between order and liberty, liberty had finally won, and with no sacrifice of order. In the calms and the tempests of the years between Portales and Pérez, a proud republic had been consolidated and the foundations of a great tradition laid – the *Chilean* tradition. Predominantly oligarchic at first, and unavoidably so, the tradition would be (because it *could* be) both widened and deepened in many different ways, with a multitude of new actors taking the stage. It was also not without its upsets and interruptions. The liberal thrust overreached itself at times. In the short term, it was embodied in the congressional demand for supremacy over the executive, a demand satisfied after the civil war of 1891, the outcome of which benefited liberalization at the expense

134 Tornero, pp. 128–29.
135 To J. M. Cea, March 1822. EDP, I, 177.

of effective government. Some kind of balance between the two things was reached after the alarms and excursions of 1924–32. Under the new 1925 Constitution, liberalization eventually assumed a fully democratic form, a form at least as genuine as in any other country in the world. The long dictatorship of the 1970s and 1980s was never able (and did not even try very seriously) to instil in Chileans a set of principles stronger or more persuasive than those of liberal democracy. It is hard not to see the tradition forged in the 1860s as the essential line of Chilean political history, the precious legacy of the Conservatives and Liberals.

For the *dieciocho* of 1862, a few weeks after the Fusion's entry into the cabinet, *El Mercurio* published an especially effusive editorial. "The great civic virtues," it said, "are the only ones that win great triumphs in nations; and those virtues have always blossomed in the hearts of Chileans. The future is ours!"[136] It was, much of the time.

136 MV, No. 10,530, September 18, 1862.

Sources

Contemporary Printed Materials

Contemporary Newspapers, News-Sheets and Periodicals:

All published in Santiago de Chile unless stated otherwise

El Aconcagüino, San Felipe. *La Actualidad*. *El Album*. *El Amigo del Pueblo*. *La Antorcha*. *El Araucano*. *El Artesano* (1841). *El Artesano* (1858). *El Artesano del Orden*. *Los Avisos*. *Balas a los traidores*. *El Barómetro de Chile*. *La Barra*. *Boletín del Ejército Restaurador* (Chilean army in Peru). *Boletín del Sur*, Concepción. *Boletín de Noticias*, La Serena. *Boletín Oficial*. *Cartas de un Polaco*. *Cartas Patriotas*. *El Censor Imparcial*, Valparaiso. *El Ciudadano*, Valparaiso. *La Civilización*. *El Comercio de Valparaiso*, Valparaiso [from No. 787, June 1, 1850, *El Comercio*]. *El Cóndor*, Copiapó. *El Consejero del Pueblo*. *El Conservador* (1840). *El Conservador*, Concepción (1851). *El Conservador* (1857). *El Copiapino*, Copiapó. *El Correo Literario*. *Courrier des Mers du Sud*, Valparaiso. *El Crepúsculo*. *La Crónica*. *El Demócrata*. *El Desmascarado*. *El Diablo Politico*. *El Diario de Santiago*. *El Doce de Febrero* (1838). *El Doce de Febrero* (1858). *Eclipse en Paucarpata*. *El Eco Militar*. *El Eco Nacional*. *El Emisario*, Talca. *El Entreacto*. *La Época* (1839). *La Época* (1851). *La Estrella del Norte*, La Serena. *El Farol*. *El Independiente* (1849). *El Juguetillo*. *La Justicia*. *La Gaceta del Comercio*, Valparaiso. *La Gazette des Mers du Sud*, Valparaiso. *El Guardia Nacional*. *La Libertad*. *El Mensajero*. *El Mensajero de la Agricultura*. *El Mercurio de Valparaiso*, Valparaiso [from No. 4314, January 1, 1843, *El Mercurio*]. *El Mercurio*, Valparaiso, edition for Santiago (numbered as for Valparaiso). *El Mercurio del Vapor*, Valparaiso (*El Mercurio*'s steamship edition). *El Miliciano*. *El Mosaico*. *El Mundo*. *El Museo*. *El Museo de Ambas Américas*, Valparaiso. *El Nacional*. *El Nuevo Maquiavelo*. *El Norte*, Copiapó. *El Nuevo Maquiavelo*. *El Observador Político*. *El País*. *Paz perpetua á los chilenos*. *El Periodiquito de la Plaza*, La Serena. *El Perrero*. *El Pescador*. *El Philopolita*. *El Penquisto*, Concepción. *El Picaflor*. *El Porvenir*. *El Porvenir del Artesano*. *El Progreso*. *El Pueblo* (clandestine, 1859). *La Razón* (clandestine, 1859). *Recuerdos de Colocolo*. *La Reforma*, Valparaiso (and later Concepción). *El Republicano* (1835). *El Republicano* (1846). *La Revista Católica*. *Revista del Pacífico*. *Revista de Santiago*. *Revista Ilustrada*. *La Semana*. *El Siglo*. *Sud-América*. *El Talquino*, Talca. *El Telégrafo de Concepción*, Concepción. *El Tren*, Copiapó. *El Tribuno*. *La Tribuna*. *La Unión Liberal*. *The Valparaiso Echo*, Valparaiso. *Valparaiso English Mercury*, Valparaiso. *El Verdadero Chileno*. *El Voto Liberal*. *El Voto Libre*. *La Voz de Chile*.

Printed or Reprinted Contemporary Writings and Documents

All published in Santiago de Chile unless stated otherwise. In titles, the aberrant Chilean orthography of the period has been modernized.

A la Nación [December 30, 1857] (1857).

A los artesanos (1851).

A los cívicos de Santiago (1841).

Al pueblo (1851).

Alberdi, Juan Bautista. *Legislación de la prensa en Chile, o sea Manual del Escritor, del impresor y del jurado* (Valparaiso, 1846).

Almanak Chileno, útil y curioso, para el año de 1843, XXXIV de nuestra libertad (n.d. ?1842).

Almanaque chileno para el año de 1849 *(n.d. ?1848).

Almanaque chileno para 1854 *(n.d. ?1853).

Almanaque enciclopédico pintoresco para 1860 (n.d. ?1859).

Almanaque para el año bisiesto de 1856 (1856).

Almanaque pintoresco e instructivo para el año de 1851 (1850).

Almanaque popular e instructivo para el año de 1857 (1857).

Amunátegui, Miguel Luis. *La dictadura de O'Higgins* (1853).

Amunátegui Reyes, Miguel Luis, ed. *Don Antonio García Reyes y algunos de sus antepasados a la luz de documentos inéditos.* 6 vols. (1929–36).

Amunátegui Solar, Domingo, ed. *Archivo epistolar de don Miguel Luis Amunátegui.* 2 vols. (1942).

Anuario estadístico de la República de Chile. 15 vols. (1860–84).

Arcos, Santiago. *Carta a Francisco Bilbao* (1852).

Arteaga Alemparte, Justo. *El desquite de un prelado* (1868).

Arteaga Alemparte, Justo. *Los tres candidatos* (1866).

Arteaga Alemparte, Justo and Domingo. *Los constituyentes de 1870* (1910).

Barra, Miguel de la. *Compendio de la historia del coloniaje e independencia de América* (1858).

Barra, Miguel de la. *Reseña histórica de la campaña del Perú de 1838 a 1839 y XI aniversario de la batalla de Yungay* (1851).

Barros Arana, Diego. *Don Miguel Luis Amunátegui, candidato a la presidencia de la República* (1875).

[Barros Arana, Diego, Marcial González, José Victorino Lastarria, and Domingo Santa María]. *Cuadro histórico de la administración Montt* (Valparaiso, 1861).

Bello, Andrés. *Obras completas.* 24 vols. (Caracas 1952–81).

Bilbao, Francisco. *Iniciativa de la América. Idea de un Congreso Federal de las Repúblicas* (Paris, 1856).

Bilbao, Francisco. *Los boletines del espíritu* (1850).

Breve de S.S. el Papa Pío IX y documentos importantes sobre una ruidosa cuestión eclesiástica de Chile (Paris, 1860).

Briseño, Ramón. *Memoria histórico-crítica del derecho público chileno desde 1810 hasta nuestros días* (1849).

Briseño, Ramón. *Estadística bibliográfica de la literatura chilena, 1812–1876*, ed. Guillermo Feliú Cruz. 3 vols. (1965–6) [1st ed. Vol. 1, 1812–59 (1862), Vol. 2, 1860–76 (1879)].

Capilla protestante en Valparaíso (1858).

Carmona, Manuel Antonio. *Manifiesto de Aconcagua* (1845).

Carmona, Manuel Antonio. *Manifiesto de Aconcagua, Cuaderno 20* (1846).

Carmona, Manuel Antonio, *Manifiesto de Aconcagua, Cuaderno 30* (1849).

Carrasco Albano, Juan Manuel. *Comentarios sobre la Constitución Política de 1833* (Valparaiso, 1858).

Carrasco Albano, Juan Manuel. "Memoria presentada a la Facultad de Leyes de la Universidad de Chile . . . sobre la necesidad y objetos de un congreso sud-americano" [1856], in *Colección de ensayos y documentos relativos a la unión y confederación de los pueblos hispanoamericanos.* 2 vols. (1862–7), 1, 257–74.

Catálogo alfabético y por materias de las obras que contiene la Biblioteca Nacional Egaña de Santiago de Chile (1860).

Catálogo general de la Librería de Cueto Hermanos (1849).

Catálogo por orden numerado de los objetos presentados a la Exposición Nacional de 1854 (1854).

¡Católicos! (1858).

Causten, Mary Elizabeth. "Santiago hace cien años," BACH, No. 34 (1946), pp. 43–51.

Censo general de la República de Chile levantado en abril de 1854 (1858).

Chacón, Jacinto. *Discurso redactado con motivo de la oposición a las Cátedras de Historia y Literatura del Instituto Nacional* (1846).

Chilenos! Viva la República – Viva Montt (1851).

Cornwallis, Kinahan. *A Panorama of the New World.* 2 vols. (London, 1859).

Cruz, Ernesto de la and Guillermo Feliú Cruz, eds., *Epistolario de don Diego Portales.* 3 vols. (1937).

Cruz, General José María de la. *Compatriotas!* (Concepción, 1851).

Cruz, General José María de la. *Soldados del Ejército y de la Guardia Nacional* (Concepción, 1851).

Cuestión administrativa-legal suscitada entre el Ministerio de Junio y la Municipalidad con motivo de la destitución del procurador de la ciudad (1849).

Desmadryl, Narciso. *Galería nacional, o colección de biografías de hombres célebres de Chile.* 2 vols. (1854–6).

A Diary of the Wreck of His Majesty's Ship Challenger on the Western Coast of South America in May 1835 (London, 1836).

Díaz Prado, José A. *De la instrucción primaria en Chile* (1856).

Documentos parlamentarios. Discursos de apertura en las sesiones del Congreso y memorias ministeriales. 9 vols. (1858–61).

Domeyko, Ignacio. *Araucanía y sus habitantes.* 2nd ed. (Buenos Aires, 1971) [1st ed. 1845].

Domeyko, Ignacio. *Mis viajes. Memorias de un exiliado*, translated from Polish by Mariano Rawicz. 2 vols. (1978).

Donoso, Armando, ed. *El pensamiento vivo de Francisco Bilbao* (1940).

Errázuriz, Federico. *Chile bajo el imperio de la constitución de 1828* (1861).

Errázuriz, Isidoro. *La emigración chilena y el gobierno de Montt ante el Congreso Argentino* (1860).

Errázuriz, Isidoro. *Historia de la administración Errázuriz, precedida de una introducción que contiene la reseña del movimiento y la lucha de los partidos desde 1823 hasta 1871* (Valparaiso, 1877).

Fernández Concha, Rafael. *Memoria leída . . . en el acto de su incorporación la la Facultad de Leyes y Ciencias Políticas de la Universidad de Chile* (1857).

Gay, Claudio. *La agricultura chilena.* 2 vols. (1973) [1st ed., Paris, 1862–5].

Gazmuri, Cristián, ed., *Santiago Arcos: Carta a Francisco Bilbao y otros escritos* (1989).

Gilliss, J. M. *The United States Naval Astronomical Expedition to the Southern Hemisphere during the years 1849–'50–'51–'52.* Volume 1. *Chile* (Washington. D.C., 1855).

Godoy, Hernán and Alfredo Lastra, eds., *Ignacio Domeyko. Un testimonio de su tiempo. Memorias y correspondencia* (1994).

González, Marcial. *La Europa y la América, o la emigración europea en sus relaciones con el engrandecimiento de las repúblicas americanas* (1848).

Gran Reunión Patriótica (1858).

Grez Toso, Sergio, ed., *La "Cuestión Social" en Chile. Ideas y debates precursores, 1804–1902* (1995).

Guía de forasteros en Chile (Valparaiso, 1841).

Guía general de la República de Chile correspondiente al año de 1847 (Valparaiso, 1847).

Guzmán, Fr. José Javier de. *El chileno instruido en la historia topográfica, civil y política de su país.* 2 vols. (1834–6).

Irisarri, Antonio José de. *Defensa de los tratados de paz de Paucarpata* (Arequipa, 1838).

Lastarria, José Victorino. *Diario político, 1849–1852,* ed. Raúl Silva Castro (1968).

Lastarria, José Victorino. *Don Diego Portales. Juicio histórico* (1861).

Lastarria, José Victorino. *Elementos de derecho público, constitucional, teórico, positivo y político* (1847).

Lastarria, José Victorino. *La Constitución política de la República de Chile comentada* (Valparaiso, 1856).

Lastarria, José Victorino. *Recuerdos literarios* (1878).

Lastarria, José Victorino and Federico Errázuriz. *Las bases de la reforma* (1850).

León L., Marco Antonio, and Horacio Aránguiz D., eds., *Cartas a Manuel Montt: Un registro para la historia social de Chile, 1836–1869* (2001).

Letelier, Valentín, ed., *Sesiones de los cuerpos legislativos de la República de Chile, 1811–1845.* 37 vols. (1887–1908).

Los cívicos de Santiago a sus compañeros a sus compañeros de armas de la Provincia de Colchagua (1851).

Manifestación que los vecinos de Santiago que subscriben han hecho a S.E. el Presidente de la República [June 10, 1851] (1851).

Manifiesto de la oposición de Santiago a la República (1858).

Manifiesto del Partido Conservador a la Nación (1851).

Manifiesto del partido de oposición a los pueblos de la República sobre la nulidad de que adolecen las elecciones hechas en los días 25 y 26 de junio último (1851).

"Manifiesto del partido de oposición a los pueblos de la República sobre la nulidad de que adolecen las elecciones hechas en los días 25 y 26 de junio último" (1851).

Manning, William R., ed., *Diplomatic Correspondence of the United States. Inter-American Affairs 1831–1860.* Vol. V. *Chile and Colombia* (Washington, D.C., 1935).

Manterola, Horacio. "La revolución de Valparaíso del 28 de febrero de 1859," BACH, No. 32 (1945), pp. 57–68.

Matta, Guillermo, *Poesías.* 2 vols. (Madrid, 1858).

Memoria sobre instrucción primaria presentada a la Universidad de Chile (1856).

[Merwin, Mrs. G. B.] *Three Years in Chile* (New York, 1863).

Miquel, Manuel. *Estudios económicos y administrativos sobre Chile entre 1858 y 1863* (1863).

Moerenhout, Jacques. "Visión de Valparaíso en 1828," RCHG (1951), pp. 22–31.

Montt, Ambrosio. *Ensayo sobre el gobierno en Europa* (Paris, 1859).

Montt, Ambrosio. *El Gobierno y la Revolución* (1859).

Montt, Manuel. *Discursos, papeles de Gobierno y Correspondencia de don Manuel Montt, reunidos y anotados por Luis Montt.* 2 vols. (1905).

Noboa, Fr. Tomás H. *Discurso pronunciado por el presbítero Tomás H. Noboa en el XLIV aniversario de la independencia de Chile, el día 18 de Setiembre de 1854* (Valparaiso, 1854).

Noticia de una reunión de ciudadanos habida en esta capital . . . con el objeto de acordarse acerca de los candidatos para las próximas elecciones (1840).

Orrego, Presb. José Manuel. *Memoria sobre la civilización de los araucanos leída el once del corriente ante el consejo de la Sociedad Evangélica* (1854).

Ovalle Castillo, Dario, ed., *El almirante don Manuel Blanco Encalada. Su correspondencia y datos históricos, biográficos y genealógicos de sus contemporáneos, importantes personajes de Europa y América* (1934).

Palavisino, Fray Victorino. *Memoria sobre la Araucanía por un misionero del Colegio de Chillán* (1860).

Palma, Martín. *El cristianismo político, o reflexiones sobre el hombre y las sociedades* (1858).

Palma, Martín. *Los oradores del cincuenta y ocho* (Valparaiso, 1860).

Palma, Martín. *Reseña histórico-filosófica del gobierno de D. Manuel Montt* (1862).

Pérez Rosales, Vicente. *Diario de un viaje a California* (1949).

Pérez Rosales, Vicente. *Essai sur le Chili* (Hamburg, 1857).

Pérez Rosales, Vicente. *Memoria sobre emigración, inmigración y colonización* (1854).

Pérez Rosales, Vicente. *Recuerdos del pasado, 1814–1860.* 4th ed. (1929) [1st ed. 1882].

Pradel, Nicolás. *Don Manuel Montt, candidato a la presidencia de la República, propuesto por el ministerio de abril* (1851).

Proyectos de ley sobre facultades extraordinarias y responsabilidad civil, presentados al Congreso por el Ejecutivo, y discursos de los diputados que han hecho oposición a ellos en la Cámara de Diputados (Valparaiso, 1860).

Ramírez, Francisco Antonio. *Breves ideas acerca del ejército* (1845).

Recollections of a Ramble from Sydney to Southampton (London, 1851).

Registro de la marina de la República de Chile, 1 Julio 1848 (Valparaiso, 1848).

Relación documentada de la expulsión de un sacristán de la Iglesia metropolitana de Santiago de Chile y del recurso de fuerza entablado por el Arcediano y Doctoral de la misma (1857).

Rengifo, Ramón. *Memoria biográfica del Ministro de Hacienda, Consejero del Estado y Senador, don Manuel Rengifo* (1846).

Repertorio Chileno. Año de 1835 (1835).

Rivera Jofré, Ramón. *Reseña histórica del ferrocarril entre Santiago y Valparaíso.* 2nd ed. (1963) [1st ed. 1863].

Roudié, Paul and Philippe, eds. *Un Français au Chili (1841–1853). Correspondance et notes de voyage de Joseph Miran* (Paris, 1987).

Rosales, Francisco Javier. *Apuntes sobre Chile dedicados a sus conciudadanos* (Paris, 1849).

La salvación del país está en el General Pinto (1850).

Santa María, Domingo. *Memoria histórica sobre los sucesos ocurridos desde la caída de D. Bernardo O'Higgins en 1823 hasta la promulgación de la constitución dictada en el mismo año* (1858).

Sarmiento, Domingo Faustino. *¿A quién rechazan y temen? ¿A quién sostienen y desean? A Montt. ¿Quién es entonces el candidato? Montt* (1850).

Sarmiento, Domingo Faustino. *Manuel Montt, su época y sus adversarios políticos* (1851).

Sarmiento, Domingo Faustino. *Motín de San Felipe. Estado de sitio* (1850).

Sarmiento, Domingo Faustino. *Motín de Santiago* (1851).

Sarmiento, Domingo Faustino. *Recuerdos de provincia.* 9th ed. (Buenos Aires, 1961).

Serrano, Sol, ed., *Vírgenes viajeras. Diarios de religiosas francesas en su ruta a Chile 1837–1874* (2000).

Smith, Edward Reuel. *The Araucanians* (New York, 1855).

Sotomayor Valdés, Ramón. *Noticias autobiográficas y epistolario* [*Noticias* written 1876] (1954).

Tocornal, Joaquín. *Discurso pronunciado por don Joaquín Tocornal, Ministro de Estado en los Departamentos del Interior y encargado accidentalmente de los demás ramos del despacho, al recibir el cadáver del señor don Diego Portales* (1837).

Tornero, Santos. *Reminiscencias de un viejo editor* (Valparaiso, 1889).

Torres, Andrés. *Canto a la campaña del Ejército chileno en el Perú* (1839).

Torres, José Antonio. *Oradores chilenos. Retratos parlamentarios* (1860).

Treutler, Paul. *Andanzas de un alemán en Chile, 1851–1863*, trans. Carlos Keller (1958).

Treutler, Paul. *La provincia de Valdivia y los araucanos, tomo 1* (1861) [No second volume published].

Valdivieso, Rafael Valentín. *Obras científicas y literarias*, ed. José Ramón Astorga. 3 vols. (1899–1904).

Valdivieso, Rafael Valentín. *Oración fúnebre pronunciada por el Presbítero R.V.V. en las exequias que se celebraron en la Santa Iglesia Catedral por el alma del finado Señor Ministro de la Guerra D. Diego Portales* (1837).
Valdivieso, Rafael Valentín. *Sermón predicado por el Illmo. y Rmo. Señor Arzobispo de esta arquidiócesis Doctor Don Rafael Valentín Valdivieso en la solemne función que el 8 de diciembre de 1855 se celebró en la Iglesia Metropolitana de Santiago de Chile en honor de la declaración de la inmaculada concepción de María Santísima* (1855).
Vallejo, José Joaquín. *Obras de don José Joaquín Vallejo (Jotabeche)*, ed. Alberto Edwards (1911).
Varas, Antonio. *Correspondencia de don Antonio Varas*. 5 vols. (1918–29).
Varas, Antonio. *Discurso pronunciado por don Antonio Varas a su incorporación solemne en la Universidad de Chile, como miembro de la Facultad de Leyes y Ciencias Políticas el 1 de abril de 1857* (1857).
Varas, Antonio. *Informe presentado a la Cámara de Diputados por el Visitador General de la República en cumplimiento del acuerdo celebrado en la sesión de 20 de diciembre del año anterior* (1849).
El verdadero miliciano a sus valientes y virtuosos camaradas (1841).
Vicuña, Pedro Félix. *El porvenir del hombre, o relación íntima entre la justa apreciación del trabajo y la democracia* (Valparaiso, 1858).
Vicuña, Pedro Félix. *Cartas sobre el Perú. Ocho meses de destierro* (Valparaiso, 1847).
[Vicuña, Pedro Félix]. *Recuerdos biográficos del señor don Francisco Ramón Vicuña* (1849).
Vicuña, Pedro Félix. *Único asilo de las repúblicas hispanoamericanas* (1837).
Vicuña, Pedro Félix. *Vindicación de los principios e ideas que han servido en Chile de apoyo a la oposición en las elecciones populares de 1846* (Lima, 1846).
Vicuña Mackenna, Benjamín. *Le Chili considéré sous le rapport de son agriculture et de l'émigration européenne* (Paris, 1855).
Vicuña Mackenna, Benjamín. *Los girondinos chilenos*, ed. Cristián Gazmuri (1989) [Article first published 1876].
Vicuña Mackenna, Benjamín. *Historia de la jornada del 20 de abril de 1851. Una batalla en las calles de Santiago* (1878).
Vicuña Mackenna, Benjamín. *Historia de los diez años de la administración de don Manuel Montt*. 5 vols. (1862–3).
Vicuña Mackenna, Benjamín. *Introducción a la historia de los diez años de la administración Montt. D. Diego Portales*. 3rd ed. (1974) [1st ed., Valparaiso, 1863, 2nd ed. 1937].
Vicuña Mackenna, Benjamín. *Páginas de mi diario durante tres años de viaje, 1853–1854–1855*. 2nd ed., 2 vols. (1936) [1st ed. 1856].
Vicuña Mackenna, Benjamín, ed., *Historia general de la República de Chile desde su independencia hasta nuestros días*. 5 vols. (1866–82).
Vicuña Mackenna, Benjamín, et al. *Montt presidente de la República de Chile y sus agentes ante los tribunales y la opinión pública de Inglaterra* (Paris, 1859).
Villalobos R., Sergio and Rafael Sagredo B., eds., *Ensayistas proteccionistas del siglo XIX* (1993).
Zapiola, José. *Recuerdos de treinta años, 1810–1840*. 9th ed. (Buenos Aires, 1974) [1st ed., 2 vols. 1874].
[Zapiola, José.] *La Sociedad de la Igualdad y sus enemigos* (1851).

Archival Materials

Archivo Nacional de Chile
Ministry of the Interior archives, Vols. 211, 263.
Intendancy archives (Atacama Province), Vols. 86, 181.
Intendancy archives (Valparaiso Province), Vols. 42, 101.

Biblioteca Nacional de Chile
José Toribio Medina MSS, Vol. 369 .

Books and Articles (Since 1880)

All published in Santiago de Chile unless stated otherwise

Amunátegui, Miguel Luis. *Ensayos biográficos.* 4 vols. (1893–6).

Amunátegui Solar, Domingo. *La democracia en Chile. Teatro político* (1946).

Amunátegui Solar, Domingo. *El Instituto Nacional bajo los rectorados de don Manuel Montt, don Francisco Puente y don Antonio Varas, 1835–45* (1891).

Balbontín, Manuel G. *El príncipe rojo, Patricio Lynch.* 2nd ed. (1967).

Barbance, Marthe. *Vie commerciale de la route du Cap Horn au XIXème siècle. L'armement A.-D. Bordes et fils* (Paris, 1969).

Barros, Mario. *Historia diplomática de Chile, 1541–1938* (Barcelona, 1970).

Barros Arana, Diego. *Historia general de Chile.* 16 vols. (1884–1902).

Barros Arana, Diego. *Un decenio de la historia de Chile, 1841–1851.* 2 vols. (1905–6).

Barros Arana, Diego. *Obras completas.* 16 vols. (1908–14).

Barros Borgoño, Luis. *Proemio al "Gobierno de don Manuel Montt" por Alberto Edwards* (1933).

Bauer, Arnold J. *Chilean Rural Society from the Spanish Conquest to 1930* (Cambridge, 1975).

Bengoa, José. *Historia del pueblo mapuche. Siglos XIX y XX* (1985).

Blancpain, Jean-Pierre. *Francia y los franceses en Chile* (1987).

Brahm García, Enrique. *Tendencias críticas en el conservantismo después de Portales* (1992).

Bravo Lira, Bernardino. *El absolutismo ilustrado en Hispanoamérica, Chile (1760–1860), de Carlos III a Portales y Montt* (1994).

Bravo Lira, Bernardino. "Una nueva forma de sociabilidad en Chile a mediados del siglo XIX: los primeros partidos políticos," in *Formas de sociabilidad en Chile, 1840–1940* (1992), pp. 11–34.

Bravo Lira, Bernardino, ed. *Portales. El hombre y su obra. La consolidación del gobierno civil* (1989).

Bulnes, Alfonso. "Alberdi y Chile," BACH, No. 65 (1961), pp. 5–30.

Bulnes, Alfonso. *Bulnes, 1799–1866* (Buenos Aires, 1946).

Bulnes, Alfonso. *Errázuriz Zañartu. Su vida* (1950).

Cavieres F., Eduardo. "Anverso y reverso del liberalismo en Chile, 1840–1930," *Historia,* No. 34 (2001), pp. 39–66.

Cavieres F., Eduardo. *Comercio chileno y comerciantes ingleses 1820–1880, un ciclo de historia económica* (Valparaiso 1988).

Cifuentes, Abdón. *Memorias.* 2 vols. (1936).

Collier, Simon. "Conservatismo chileno, 1830–1860. Temas e imágenes," translated by Luis Ortega. *Nueva Historia,* Año 2, No. 7 (London, 1982), pp. 143–63.

Collier, Simon. *Ideas and Politics of Chilean Independence, 1808–1833* (Cambridge, 1967).

Collier, Simon. "Religious Freedom, Clericalism and Anticlericalism in Chile, 1820–1920," in Richard Helmstadter, ed., *Freedom and Religion in the Nineteenth Century* (Stanford, Calif., 1997).

Collier, Simon and William F. Sater. *A History of Chile, 1808–1994* (Cambridge, 1996).

Cruz de Amenábar, Isabel. "Diosas atribuladas: alegorias cívicas, caricatura y política en Chile durante el siglo XIX," *Historia,* No. 30 (1997), pp. 127–71.

Daitsman, Andrew L. "The People Shall be All. Liberal Rebellion and Popular Mobilization in Chile, 1820–1860" (Ph.D. dissertation, University of Wisconsin–Madison, 1995).

del Pozo, José. *Historia del vino chileno.* 2nd ed. (1999).

Donoso, Ricardo. *Don Benjamín Vicuña Mackenna. Su vida, sus escritos y su tiempo* (1925).

260 Sources

Donoso, Ricardo. *La sátira política en Chile* (1950).

Donoso Vergara, Guillermo. "Perfiles de 'El Mercurio' escritos por don Santos Tornero," RCHG, No. 155 (1987), pp. 9–36.

Donoso Vergara, Guillermo. "Revolución de 1851 en Talca," RCHG, No. 141 (1973), pp. 88–115; No. 142 (1974), pp. 54–94; No. 143 (1975), pp. 5–45; No. 144 (1976), pp. 21–61; No. 145 (1977), pp. 5–62.

Edwards, Agustín. *Cuatro presidentes de Chile*. 2 vols. (Valparaiso, 1932).

Edwards, Alberto. *La fronda aristocrática*. 7th ed. (1972).

Edwards, Alberto. *El gobierno de don Manuel Montt, 1851–1861* (1932).

Edwards, Alberto. *Páginas históricas* (1972).

Edwards, Jorge. "El Decenio de Bulnes a través de los archivos del Quai d'Orsay," BACH, No. 74 (1966), pp. 7–25.

Encina, Francisco Antonio. *Historia de Chile desde la prehistoria hasta 1891*. 20 vols. (1942–52).

Encina, Francisco Antonio. *Portales: introducción a la historia de la época de Diego Portales*. 2 vols. (1934).

Espinosa, Januario. *Don Manuel Montt* (1944).

Figueroa, Pedro Pablo. *Historia de la revolución constituyente (1858–1859) escrita sobre documentos completamente inéditos* (1889).

Figueroa, Virgilio. *Diccionario histórico y biográfico de Chile 1800–1925*. 5 vols. (1925–31).

Galdames, Luis. *Historia de Chile*. 14th ed. (1974).

Gazmuri, Cristián. *El "48" chileno. Igualitarios, reformistas, radicales, masones y bomberos* (1992).

Gazmuri, Cristián. "El pensamiento político y social de Santiago Arcos," *Historia*, No. 13 (1986), pp. 249–74.

Góngora, Mario. *Ensayo histórico sobre la noción de Estado en Chile en los siglos XIX y XX* (1982).

González Echenique, Javier and Julio Retamal Favereau, "El gobierno chileno y el concepto misionero del estado, 1832–1861, *Historia*, No. 5 (1966), pp. 197–214.

Grez Toso, Sergio. *De la "regeneración del pueblo" a la huelga general. Genesis y evolución histórica del movimiento popular en Chile (1810–1890)* (1997).

Guarda Geywitz, Gabriel. "Un intendente de la era portaliana," BACH, No. 85 (1971), pp. 207–46.

Guerrero Yoacham, Cristián. "Chile y la Guerra de Secesión de los Estados Unidos," BACH, No. 89 (1975–6), pp. 97–267.

Hamuy, Eduardo. *El Problema educacional del pueblo chileno* (1961).

Hernández, Roberto. *Juan Godoy, o el descubrimiento de Chañarcillo*. 2 vols. (Valparaiso, 1932).

Hernández P., Roberto. *Diego Portales* (1974).

Hernández P., Roberto. "La Guardia Nacional de Chile. Apuntes sobre su orígen y organizaciones, 1808–1848," *Historia*, 19 (1984), pp. 53–113.

Ibáñez Santa María, Adolfo. "Los bomberos de Valparaíso. El caso de la Tercera Compañía," in *Formas de sociabilidad en Chile, 1840–1940* (1992), pp. 153–76.

Illanes, María Angélica. "Disciplinamiento de la mano de obra minera en una forma social en transición," *Nueva Historia*, Año 3, No. 11 (London, 1984), pp. 197–224.

Izquierdo, Gonzalo. *Historia de Chile*. 3 vols. (1989–90).

Jaksić, Iván. *Academic Rebels in Chile. The Role of Philosophy in Higher Education and Politics* (Albany, N.Y., 1989).

Jaksić, Iván. *Andrés Bello: Scholarship and Nation Building in Nineteenth Century Latin America* (Cambridge, 2001).

Jaksić, Iván. *Andrés Bello: La pasión por el orden* (2001).

Jaksić, Iván. "Sarmiento and the Chilean Press, 1841–1851," in Tulio Halperín, Iván Jaksić, Gwen Kirkpatrick, and Francine Masiello, eds., *Sarmiento: Author of a Nation* (Berkeley, Calif., 1994).

Jobet, Julio César. *Santiago Arcos Arlegui y la Sociedad de la Igualdad* (1942).

Kinsbruner, Jay. *Diego Portales. Interpretative Essays on the Man and Times* (The Hague, 1967).

Krebs, Ricardo and Cristián Gazmuri, eds., *La Revolución Francesa y Chile* (1990).

Loveman, Brian and Elizabeth Lira. *Las suaves cenizas del olvido. Vía chilena de reconciliación política, 1814–1932* (1999).

Martínez Baeza, Sergio. "Una elección de diputado en 1840," RCHG, No. 151 (1983), pp. 307–13.

Mayo, John. *British Merchants and Chilean Development, 1851–1886* (Boulder, Col., 1987).

Montt, Luis. *Recuerdos de familia* (1943).

Orrego Vicuña, Eugenio. *Vicuña Mackenna. Vida y trabajos.* 3rd ed. (1951).

Ortega, Luis. "Economic Policy and Growth in Chile from Independence to the War of the Pacific," in Christopher Abel and Colin Lewis, eds., *Latin America: Economic Imperialism and the State* (London, 1985), pp. 147–71.

Oviedo, Benjamín. *La masonería en Chile. Bosquejo histórico. La colonia, la independencia, la república* (1929).

Pereira Salas, Eugenio. *Biobibliografía musical de Chile desde los orígenes a 1886* (1978).

Pereira Salas, Eugenio. *Historia de la música en Chile, 1850–1900* (1957).

Pereira Salas, Eugenio. *Historia del teatro en Chile desde sus orígenes hasta la muerte de Juan Casacuberta 1849* (1974).

Ramírez N., Hernán. "El gobierno británico y la guerra contra la Confederación Peru-Boliviana," RCHG, No. 129 (1961), pp. 122–39.

Rengifo, Osvaldo. *Don Manuel Rengifo. Su vida y su obra* (1983).

Romero, Luis Alberto. *¿Qué hacer con los pobres? Elite y sectores populares en Santiago de Chile* (Buenos Aires, 1997).

Ruz T., Fernando. *Rafael Sotomayor Baeza, el organizador de la victoria* (1980).

Sacks, Norman P. "José Victorino Lastarria, un intelectual comprometido en la América Latina," RCHG, No. 140 (1972), pp. 153–93.

Sagredo B., Rafael. "Elites chilenas del siglo XIX. Historiografía," *Cuadernos de Historia*, No. 16 (1996), pp. 103–32.

Sagredo B., Rafael, "Las visitas gubernamentales en Chile, 1788–1861," *Historia*, 31 (1998), pp. 311–47.

Salazar, Gabriel. *Labradores, peones y proletarios* (1985).

Salvat Monguillot, Manuel. "Santiago por los años 1856 y 1857 según Vicente Reyes," BACH, No. 104 (1994), pp. 13–33.

Sanhueza, Gabriel. *Santiago Arcos, comunista, millonario y calavera* (1956).

Santa Cruz, Joaquín. "Recuerdos de la Picantería," RCHG, No. 60 (1928), pp. 40–92.

Sater, William F. *Chile and the United States: Empires in Conflict* (Athens, Ga., 1990).

Serrano, Sol. *Universidad y nación. Chile en el siglo XIX* (1994).

Serrano, Sol and Iván Jaksić, "El poder de las palabras: la Iglesia y el Estado liberal ante la difusión de la escritura en el Chile del siglo XIX," *Historia*, No. 33 (2000), pp. 435–60.

Silva Castro, Raúl. *Eusebio Lillo, 1826–1910* (1964).

Silva Castro, Raúl. *Prensa y periodismo en Chile* (1958).

Silva Castro, Raúl. *Ramón Rengifo 1795–1861* (1957).

Silva Cotapos, Carlos. *Historia eclesiástica de Chile* (1925).

"La Sociedad Literaria de 1842," *Revista Chilena*, Año III, Tomo IX, No. 9 (1920), pp. 425–30.

Sotomayor Valdés, Ramon. *Historia de Chile bajo el gobierno del general Joaquín Prieto*, 3rd ed., 4 vols. (1962–80) [1st ed. 1875–6, 2nd ed. 1900–3].

Stuven, Ana María. *La seducción de un orden. Las elites y la construcción de Chile en las polémicas culturales y políticas del siglo XIX* (2000).

Subercaseaux, Ramón. *Memorias de ochenta años.* 2nd ed. 2 vols. (1936).

Valencia Avaria, Luis, ed., *Anales de la República*. 2 vols. in 1 (1986).

Valencia Avaria, Luis. *Símbolos patrios* (1974).

Valenzuela, J. Samuel. *Democratización via reforma: la expansión del sufragio en Chile* (Buenos Aires, 1985).

Valenzuela, J. Samuel. "Building Aspects of Democracy before Democracy: Electoral Practices in Nineteenth Century Chile," in Eduardo Posada-Carbó, ed., *Elections Before Democracy: the History of Elections in Europe and Latin America* (New York, 1996), pp. 223–57.

Varona, Alberto J. *Francisco Bilbao. Revolucionario de América* (Panama, 1973).

Véliz, Claudio. *Historia de la marina mercante chilena* (1961).

Vergara Antúñez, Pbro. Rodolfo. *Vida y obras del Ilustrísimo y Reverendísimo Señor Doctor Don Rafael Valentín Valdivieso, segundo Arzobispo de Santiago*. 2 vols. (1886–1906).

Villalobos R., Sergio. *Orígen y ascenso de la burguesía chilena* (1987).

Villalobos R., Sergio. *Portales. Una falsificación histórica* (1990).

Villalobos R., Sergio. "Sugerencias para un enfoque del siglo XIX," *Colección Estudos CIEPLAN*, No. 12 (1984), pp. 9–36.

Villalobos R., Sergio, ed. *Historia de la ingeniería en Chile* (1990).

Villalobos R., Sergio and Rafael Sagredo B., *El proteccionismo económico en Chile: Siglo XIX* (1987).

Urzúa Valenzuela, Germán. *Historia política de Chile y su evolución electoral, desde 1810 a 1992* (1992).

Woll, Allen. *A Functional Past. The Uses of History in Nineteenth-Century Chile* (Baton Rouge, La., 1982).

Wood, James Alderfer. "Building a Society of Equals: the Popular Republican Movement in Santiago de Chile, 1818–1851" (Ph.D. dissertation, University of North Carolina at Chapel Hill, 2000).

Zamudio, José. *La novela histórica en Chile* (Buenos Aires, 1973).

Index